THE INTERNATIONAL POLITICS OF EURASIA

Volume 4

THE
MAKING
OF
FOREIGN
POLICY
IN
RUSSIA
AND THE
NEW STATES
OF EURASIA

Editors:
Adeed Dawisha
and Karen Dawisha

M.E. Sharpe
Armonk, New York
London, England

Library of Congress Cataloging-in-Publication Data

The making of foreign policy in Russia and the new
states of Eurasia / editors, Adeed Dawisha and Karen Dawisha.
p.   cm.   —   (The international politics of Eurasia ; v. 4)
Includes bibliographical references and index.
ISBN 1-56324-358-X (cloth : alk. paper).
ISBN 1-56324-359-8 (paper : alk. paper).
1. Russia—Foreign relations—Eurasia. 2. Eurasia—Foreign
relations—Russia. I. Dawisha, A. I. II. Dawisha, Karen.
III. Series.
JX1555.Z7E93   1995
327.4705—dc20   94-49384
CIP

Printed in the United States of America

The paper used in this publication meets the minimum requirements of
American National Standard for Information Sciences—
Permanence of Paper for Printed Library Materials,
ANSI Z 39.48-1984.

∞

BM (c)   10   9   8   7   6   5   4   3   2   1
BM (p)   10   9   8   7   6   5   4   3   2   1

Contents

THE
MAKING
OF
FOREIGN
POLICY
IN
RUSSIA
AND THE
NEW STATES
OF EURASIA

THE INTERNATIONAL POLITICS OF EURASIA

Editors:
Karen Dawisha and Bruce Parrott

This ambitious ten-volume series develops a comprehensive analysis of the evolving world role of the post-Soviet successor states. Each volume considers a different factor influencing the relationship between internal politics and international relations in Russia and in the western and southern tiers of newly independent states. The contributors were chosen not only for their recognized expertise but also to ensure a stimulating diversity of perspectives and a dynamic mix of approaches.

About the Editors and Contributors

Adeed Dawisha is currently a professor of government and politics in the Department of Public and International Affairs at George Mason University in Virginia, and was formerly the deputy director of studies at the Royal Institute of International Affairs in London, England. He received his Ph.D. in international relations in 1974 from the London School of Economics and Political Science. Among his books are *Beyond Coercion: The Durability of the Arab State* (1992), *The Arab Radicals* (1986), *Islam and Foreign Policy* (1983), *The Soviet Union in the Middle East* (1981), *Syria and the Lebanese Crisis* (1979), and *Egypt in the Arab World: The Elements of Foreign Policy* (1976).

Karen Dawisha is professor of government at the University of Maryland, College Park. She graduated with degrees in Russian and politics from the University of Lancaster in England and received her Ph.D. from the London School of Economics. She has served as an advisor to the British House of Commons Foreign Affairs Committee and was a member of the policy planning staff of the U.S. State Department. She has received fellowships from the Rockefeller Foundation, the Council on Foreign Relations, and the MacArthur Foundation. She is a member of the Royal Institute of International Affairs and the Council on Foreign Relations. Her publications include *Russia and the New States of Eurasia: The Politics of Upheaval* (coauthored with Bruce Parrott, 1994), *Eastern Europe, Gorbachev, and Reform: The Great Challenge* (1989, 2d ed. 1990), *The Kremlin and the Prague Spring* (1984), *The Soviet Union in the Middle East: Politics and Perspectives* (1982), *Soviet-East European Dilemmas: Coercion, Competition, and Consent* (1981), and *Soviet Foreign Policy Toward Egypt* (1979).

Bruce Parrott is professor and director of Russian Area and East European Studies at the Johns Hopkins University School of Advanced International Studies, where he has taught for twenty years. He received his B.A. in religious studies from Pomona College in 1966, and his Ph.D. in political science in 1976 from Columbia University, where he was assistant director of the Russian Institute. His publications include *Russia and the New States of Eurasia: The*

Politics of Upheaval (coauthored with Karen Dawisha, 1994), *The Dynamics of Soviet Defense Policy* (1990), *The Soviet Union and Ballistic Missile Defense* (1987), *Trade Technology and Soviet-American Relations* (1985), and *Politics and Technology in the Soviet Union* (1983).

Rouben Paul Adalian is director of the Office of Research and Analysis at the Armenian Assembly of America. He is also adjunct professor at George Washington University and Georgetown University, where he teaches on the Caucasus. He has a Ph.D. from the University of California at Los Angeles. Dr. Adalian's research interests and publications cover topics in Armenian intellectual and political history and the Armenian diaspora.

Leila Alieva is vice president of the Center for Strategic and International Studies in Baku, Azerbaijan. She has taught at Baku State University and was recently a visiting fellow to the Center for Middle Eastern Studies at Harvard University. She has written extensively on regional conflicts, particularly the Nagorno-Karabagh conflict, and on conflict resolution.

Andrew A. Bouchkin is senior researcher in the Japanese and Pacific Studies Center of the Institute of World Economy and International Relations (IMEMO) in Moscow. Dr. Bouchkin received his degree in political science at the Institute of Oriental Studies in Moscow. His research has focused on the international relations of the Asia-Pacific region, and he has published approximately forty articles, conference papers, and books on this topic in Russia, Korea, Japan, and the United States.

Jeffrey Checkel is assistant professor at the University of Pittsburgh, where he holds a joint appointment in the Department of Political Science and the Graduate School of Public and International Affairs. He is the author of *Ideas and International Politics: Foreign Policy Change and the End of the Cold War* (1995) and is currently at work on a cross-national study exploring the diffusion of international norms on citizenship and minority rights in post–Cold War Europe.

Kemal H. Karpat is distinguished professor of history and professor of Middle East studies in the Department of History at the University of Wisconsin. He is the editor of the *International Journal of Turkish Studies* and president of the Association of Central Asian Studies, founded in 1985. Dr. Karpat is the author of numerous books and articles on Turkey and Central Asia. He was most recently the editor of and a contributor to the 1994 volume of *Central Asian Survey*.

Oumirseric Kasenov is director of the Kazakhstan Institute for Strategic Studies in Almaty. He was previously advisor to the vice president of Kazakhstan. Dr.

Kasenov received his Ph.D. from the Academy of Social Sciences, Central Committee of the CPSU, Moscow. He has written widely on the issue of nuclear weapons and Kazakhstan and on regional security issues.

Mark N. Katz is associate professor of government and politics at George Mason University. He is also a senior staff member at the George Mason University International Institute. Dr. Katz received his Ph.D. in political science from the Massachusetts Institute of Technology. He has authored several books on Soviet foreign and military policy. He has also written numerous articles on the international relations of the former Soviet Union and of the Middle East.

Nikolai A. Kulinich is deputy director of the Ukrainian Institute of International Relations at Kiev Taras Shevchenko University and head of the Department of International Organizations and Diplomatic Services within the Institute. Dr. Kulinich received his Ph.D. in international relations from Kiev Taras Shevchenko University. He has published more than forty articles, chapters, and books, including *The Victory That Changed the World* (1990), "The Paradox of Ukrainian Neutrality" (1992), and "Ukraine in the Context of European Security" (1992).

Mohiaddin Mesbahi is associate professor of international relations at Florida International University in Miami. He is the author of several studies on Soviet-Iranian relations and Central Asian security. His most recent works include *Russia and the Third World in the Post-Soviet Era* (1994) and *Central Asia and the Caucasus after the Soviet Union* (1994). He spent 1992–93 as a senior fellow at St. Antony's College, Oxford University, where he concluded research and writing for his forthcoming book, *Moscow and Iran: From the Islamic Revolution to the Collapse of Communism*.

Vyacheslau E. Paznyak is director of international programs at the Minsk Center for Nonproliferation and Export Control and assistant professor at the Department of Sociology and Political Science, National Institute for the Humanities, Minsk. Dr. Paznyak received his Ph.D. in philosophy from the Belarusian State University in 1988. He is the author of numerous articles, chapters, and books, including "Belarus' Foreign Policy in 1993" (1994), "Security Aspects of Belarus' Policies Towards the CIS and Western Europe" (1993), and *Problems and Guidelines of Belarus' Foreign Policy* (1993).

Nodari A. Simonia is director of the Center for Comparative Analysis of Russia and the Third World at the Institute of World Economy and International Relations (IMEMO) in Russia. His published work includes sixteen books and more than one hundred articles and chapters on political and economic development in both Russia and the Third World, including two recent books, *The Synthesis of*

Traditional and Modern in the Evolution of Third World Societies (1992) and *Socialism in Russia: Theory and Practice* (1994). He is currently involved with three research and writing projects: Russia and the CIS (integration-disintegration), the Russian model of statehood, and Russia and the Asia-Pacific region. He lives in Moscow.

Jonathan Valdez received his Ph.D. from the University of Maryland in 1990 and has since taught at the University of California at Los Angeles and the University of Kansas. He is the author of *Internationalism and the Ideology of Soviet Influence in Eastern Europe* (1993) and several articles on ideology and Soviet foreign policy. Dr. Valdez's most recent work is on the influence of nationalism and national identity on Russian foreign policy since the collapse of the Soviet Union.

Peeter Vares studied from 1957 to 1962 at the Moscow Institute of Foreign Languages. From 1963 to 1969, he was affiliated with the Ministry of Culture of the USSR. He worked for the Presidium of the Academy of Sciences in Moscow from 1969 to 1988. In 1973 he received his Ph.D. from IMEMO in international relations at the Institute of General History (Italian-U.S. relations, 1943–1980). In 1980 Dr. Vares transferred to Estonia, becoming deputy director of the Institute of Philosophy, Sociology, and Law at the Academy of Sciences of Estonia. The academy was renamed the Institute of International and Social Studies in May 1994. He specializes in research on Baltic foreign and security policies. He has authored two major books and several publications on international politics.

Preface

This book is the fourth in a projected series of ten volumes produced by the Russian Littoral Project, sponsored jointly by the University of Maryland at College Park and the Paul H. Nitze School of Advanced International Studies of the Johns Hopkins University. As directors of the project, we share the conviction that the transformation of the former Soviet republics into independent states demands systematic analysis of the determinants of the domestic and foreign policies of the new countries. This series is intended to provide a basis for comprehensive scholarly study of these issues.

This volume analyzes the foreign policy institutions and priorities of the new states. The collapse of the Soviet Union and the discrediting of Marxism-Leninism as a source of political legitimacy have prompted a search for fresh principles to guide the foreign policies in all the post-Soviet countries. In this search, one of the strongest potential sources of guidance is in the felt need for a defined national interest. The quest for a national interest, however, can have various political consequences, depending on the specific form of interest that becomes prevalent. This book examines which patterns of national interest formation have begun to emerge within the new states, along with the roles of various leaders and fragile institutions in the formulation of policy toward the outside world.

We would like to thank the contributors to this volume for their help in making the Russian Littoral Project a success and for revising their papers in a timely fashion. We are especially grateful to Adeed Dawisha for supporting the Russian Littoral Project since its inception, for contributing insights that were pivotal in structuring the project's treatment of foreign policy, and for coediting this book. In addition, we are grateful to Janine Ludlam, the executive director of the Russian Littoral Project, for organizing the conferences and undertaking the complex logistics involved in managing such a large project. Florence Rotz also deserves our thanks for assistance with the conferences and for editing the manuscripts of the NIS scholars.

Russian Littoral Project

The objective of the Russian Littoral Project is to foster an exchange of research and information in fields of study pertaining to the international politics of Eurasia. The interaction between the internal affairs and foreign policies of the new states is being studied in a series of workshops taking place in Washington, DC, London, Central Asia, and other locations between 1993 and 1995. Scholars from the new states, North America, and Europe are invited to present papers at the workshops.

Focusing on the interaction between the internal affairs and the foreign relations of the new states, the project workshops examine the impact of the following factors: history, national identity and ethnicity, religion, political culture and civil society, economics, foreign policy priorities and decision making, military issues, and the nuclear question. Each of these topics is examined in a set of three workshops focusing in turn on Russia, the western belt of new states extending from Estonia to Ukraine, and the southern tier of new states extending from Georgia to Kyrgyzstan.

The Russian Littoral Project could not have been launched without the generous and timely contributions of the project's Coordinating Committee. We wish to thank the committee members for providing invaluable advice and expertise concerning the organization and intellectual substance of the project. The members of the Coordinating Committee are Dr. Adeed Dawisha (George Mason University); Dr. Bartek Kaminski (University of Maryland and The World Bank); Dr. Catherine Kelleher (The Brookings Institution); Ms. Judith Kipper (The Brookings Institution); Dr. Nancy Lubin (Carnegie Mellon University); Dr. Michael Mandelbaum (The School of Advanced International Studies); Dr. James Millar (George Washington University); Dr. Peter Murrell (University of Maryland); Dr. Martha Brill Olcott (Colgate University); Dr. Ilya Prizel (The School of Advanced International Studies); Dr. George Quester (University of Maryland); Dr. Alvin Z. Rubinstein (University of Pennsylvania); Dr. Blair Ruble (The Kennan Institute); Dr. S. Frederick Starr (Oberlin College); Dr. Roman Szporluk (Harvard University); and Dr. Vladimir Tismaneanu (University of Maryland).

We are grateful to the National Endowment for the Humanities, and to David Coder and Martha Chomiak at NEH, for funding the workshops from which this book is derived. Other workshops within the project have been funded by the John D. and Catherine T. MacArthur Foundation; the Friedrich Ebert Stiftung; the Pew Charitable Trusts; and the Ford Foundation. We have benefited enormously from the support and advice we have received from program officers in the course of organizing these sessions.

We also wish to thank President William Kirwan of the University of Maryland at College Park and President William C. Richardson of the Johns Hopkins University, who have given indispensable support to the project. Thanks are also due to Dean Irwin Goldstein, Associate Dean Stewart Edelstein, Director of the Office of International Affairs Marcus Franda, and Department of Government and Politics Chair Jonathan Wilkenfeld at the University of Maryland at College Park; to Provost Joseph Cooper and Vice-Provost for Academic Planning and Budget Stephen M. McClain at the Johns Hopkins University; to Professor George Packard, who helped launch the project during his final year as dean of the School of Advanced International Studies, to SAIS Dean Paul D. Wolfowitz, and to SAIS Associate Dean Stephen Szabo.

Finally, we are grateful for the guidance and encouragement given by Patricia Kolb at M.E. Sharpe, Inc. Her confidence in the success of the project and the volumes is deeply appreciated.

Karen Dawisha
University of Maryland
at College Park

Bruce Parrott
The Johns Hopkins University
School of Advanced International Studies

THE
MAKING
OF
FOREIGN
POLICY
IN
RUSSIA
AND THE
NEW STATES
OF EURASIA

1

Introduction

Foreign Policy Priorities and Institutions: Perspectives and Issues

Adeed Dawisha

Foreign policy is usually defined as "the actions of a state toward the external environment and the conditions under which these actions are formulated."[1] There is thus a clear linkage between the state's domestic situation, where policy is formulated, and its external environment, in which policy is implemented. However, while a linkage exists, the measure of authoritative control exercised by the political authority over the two environments varies considerably.

Within the state, a government is accorded the authority to initiate legislation and pass laws that become binding on individuals. The essence of a government's role in domestic politics is to provide order and protection for citizens. While this protection of course is not absolute, "a domestic political system nearly approaches the absolute because of the monopoly of power and authority which governments claim and hold."[2] Beyond the borders of a state, however, there are no binding rules and laws. There exists a system of international law, which in theory is supposed to regulate the activities of states and national governments; in reality, the conduct of states in the international arena is constrained "by the decisions of the states themselves, not by any authority external to them."[3] In other words, the basic feature of international society is its "anarchical nature."[4] Consequently, in dealing with foreign states and other international entities, lack of control means that governmental decisions are apt to be frustrated, or at least compromised, unless the government in question leads a state that is powerful enough to be able to ensure foreign compliance with its decisions.

These foreign policy vulnerabilities are compounded when, as in the case of the successor countries to the Soviet Union, states are operating in conditions of enormous structural fluidity and change. Domestically, excessive pressure is placed on decision makers "in minimizing conflict among competing actors in the decision process, maintaining fragile coalitions, and reorganizing bureaucratic procedures"[5] when new approaches are desperately needed to cope with an unpredictable international environment. This is especially true today in the new states of the former Soviet Union. "Even in a country such as Russia," Karen Dawisha and Bruce Parrott write, "where the new Ministry of Foreign Affairs has established a strong institutional basis and has the confidence of its president, it has come under intense attack from other powerful institutions. New parliaments, opposition political parties and movements, and military industrial establishments are just some of the institutional actors that have been promoting quite different foreign policies."[6] Dawisha and Parrott conclude that in most of these countries, there simply is no consensus on what the national interest is.[7]

Nevertheless, the state ultimately has to adapt to its environment.[8] According to K.J. Holsti, governments need to balance domestic institutional tensions with external demands and priorities or risk failure, which in such fragile countries could lead to political and socioeconomic collapse. Within this context, Holsti maintains that unlike large developed states, which tend to be "satisfied" with their external relations, smaller, less developed countries, because of their lack of power to influence events, tend to feel more acutely the need to restructure their foreign policies.[9]

This argument is borne out by the way the states of the former Soviet Union have behaved in the international environment. It has been especially the smaller republics that have scrambled to restructure the old patterns of their external relations. They have entered into new alliances, indulged in new conflicts, endeavored to broaden the scope of their international relations, and wherever possible sought help and protection from global and regional actors that earlier had been inaccessible to them.

Indeed, Russia too behaved according to the tenets of Holsti's argument. Within its own regional environment, vis-à-vis the weaker republics, Russia acted as the quintessentially "satisfied" status quo power, insisting on preserving the balance of the old power relationships (which of course was heavily skewed in its favor) and doing everything possible to sabotage the efforts by the smaller republics to break out of Russia's influence. Yet vis-à-vis the politically more stable and economically more powerful Western states, Russia behaved like a developing country in the way it undertook a massive restructuring of its political, economic, and foreign policy orientations.

One thing that the above discussion tells us is that "a state's situation conditions its policy and the outcome of its policy may affect its situation."[10] To say that foreign policy is situational helps us understand the pattern of interstate relations in the regional system that encompasses the countries of the former Soviet Union. The most abiding feature of that regional system is the existence of an all-pervasive hegemon in the form of Russia, a situational imperative that has to be taken into consideration every time any republic makes a foreign policy decision. So while a web of interdependence gradually emerges among the republics, the fact remains that at the center lies Russia, which "is in the best geopolitical position to offer leadership to the other new states." [11] And if there is one theme that runs through every chapter of this book, it is this overpowering presence of Russia in the region, not only in a geopolitical sense, but more crucially in the calculations and perceptions of the leaders and policy makers of the other republics.

The chapters that follow examine the foreign policies of Russia and other selected states of the former Soviet Union. Each chapter analyzes the conduct of foreign policy within the context of each state's unique situation. The authors were provided with a number of suggestions about the kind of questions they were expected to ask and attempt to answer. Beyond these general guidelines, the authors were not asked to adhere to a rigid theoretical framework, or "model," not least because of the absence of sophisticated theoretical formulations in the study of foreign policy change and restructuring.[12] Nevertheless, after the papers were presented and discussed during three days of workshops, the editors, with an eye toward comparison, provided another set of detailed suggestions to each author to incorporate into his or her chapter. One of the papers presented at the workshop was not revised for this volume. And the chapters by Mark N. Katz, Vyacheslau E. Paznyak, and Peeter Vares were commissioned separately for this volume. In all cases, the editors decided to leave the authors to research and write their various contributions in their own individual ways.

The chapters by Nodari A. Simonia and Jeffrey Checkel deal with general aspects of Russia's foreign policy. In his "Priorities of Russia's Foreign Policy and the Way It Works," Nodari Simonia starts from the premise that while a new economic elite (the economic nomenklatura) has replaced the old ideological elite, and while this new elite depicts its foreign policy as novel, in fact it is not that much different from past policies. From 1945 to 1990, Soviet policy had always promoted national security as the main foreign policy goal to which other goals and concerns (e.g., economic and political reform, rule of law) were sacrificed. Simonia maintains that after the collapse of the Soviet Union, the Russian government, whatever its declared and anticipated priorities, has found itself immersed in the security issue area, necessitated by the new and chaotic geostrategic situation. Simonia adds that this geostrategic imperative has been augmented by institutional developments in Russia's domestic politics, particularly the power struggle between the president and parliament, which have promoted the military at the expense of the Foreign Ministry and other civilian institutions. This imbalance, according to Simonia, can hardly be redressed by the huge expansion in the number of civilian foreign policy bureaucrats, most of whom seem to care more about "gainful employment" and their connections to the emerging economic elites than foreign policy. In short, while he concedes that differences do exist, Nodari Simonia believes that present Russian foreign policy, emphasizing the security issue area, and increasingly dominated by the interests of the military and the economic nomenklatura, is beginning to more and more resemble the old Soviet foreign policy.

Much, if not all, of Simonia's analysis is reflected in Jeffrey Checkel's "Structure, Institutions, and Process: Russia's Changing Foreign Policy." Checkel relates that the West has noted how the liberal buzzwords of the Gorbachev era have been replaced "with dark forebodings of a new 'muscular,' 'neoimperial,' and 'nationalist' Russian foreign policy." Moreover, the emergence of direct executive oversight over foreign policy conjures images of the tsarist and Soviet eras. Checkel argues that these changes were ushered in by Russia's increasingly troubled relations with the former Soviet republics, which allowed organizations and institutions that held a zero-sum view of international politics, such as the military, the Duma, and nationalist political groupings, to demand a redefinition of state interests that paid greater attention to traditional geopolitics. Thus the Russian Ministry of Defense, for example, paints the external environment as hostile, necessitating a ready and strong military. In Checkel's view, this vision is increasingly supplanting the more liberal perception, advanced by the Foreign Ministry, of a condominium of great powers united by common values centered on market economies and political pluralism. Here again, the geostrategic situation seems to lead to, as well as be influenced by, institutional developments at the domestic level. Checkel, however, is hopeful that Russia's clear preference for integration into the global political economy, augmented by growing transnational ties and networks, may in the future influence Russian policy making and constrain the more extreme aspects of its behavior.

The chapters by Andrew A. Bouchkin and Jonathan Valdez examine the various determinants and conduct of Russian foreign policy toward important world regions, such as the near abroad, the West, and the Far East. The conflict among Russia's political elite is the starting point of Andrew Bouchkin's chapter, "Russia's Far Eastern Policy in the 1990s: Priorities and Prospects." He argues that in the foreign policy arena, this conflict has produced two political factions: the "Atlanticists" and the "Eurasianists." The former promotes the concept of a new world order based on a partnership with the West in combating threats from the "South" (e.g., terrorism, Islamic fundamentalism, armed aggression). The Eurasianists, pointing to Russia's long border with countries of the "South," argue that it is the non-Western world (presenting both threats and opportunities) that should demand Russia's primary attention. Bouchkin argues that "the most important factor among those that will determine Russia's place in the world is its relationship with its neighbors in the East." And of these countries he places China at the forefront. Particularly important in this relationship is the issue area of military cooperation, where "with Russia's help the Chinese military is making an important changeover from ground-based defense forces to a capability that can be used throughout the Far East and beyond." Turning to South Korea, Bouchkin argues that for Russia, the essence of the relationship has been economic gain. But this has been hampered by Russia's corrupt bureaucracy, unclear legislation concerning the rights of foreign investors in the Russian Federation, a messy taxation system, and the sometime nebulous line of authority that Moscow exercises with regard to some of Russia's autonomous regions. Japanese businessmen, according to Bouchkin, have similar misgivings about Russia's business environment. But the situation with Japan is complicated by the unresolved territorial dispute over the South Kurils. And Japan can hardly be comforted by Russia's military presence in the region, a concern to be heightened by the strong showing of nationalists, communists, and conservatives in Russia's December 1993 elections.

In his "Near Abroad, the West, and National Identity in Russian Foreign Policy," Jonathan Valdez endeavors to explain the vacillation in Russian foreign policy that culminated in the 1993 shift to a more assertive, nationalist stance by reference to the difficulties the Russians have encountered in defining their national identity after the collapse of the Soviet Union. He argues that "from the earliest moments of the existence of the Commonwealth of Independent States, Russians have had to come to grips with the fact that the former Soviet republics were truly independent countries." The question remained as to what constituted the parameters of Russia as a civilization. Initially, this was defined in terms of Western values: Russia was to become an active member of the democratic Western world, integrated in its global, free market economy, fully adherent to its moral norms. But by 1993, a reorientation toward the near abroad (involving a more assertive stance) had occurred, facilitated at least partly by a redefinition of Russian national identity following the Soviet collapse. Echoing the earlier chapters, Valdez sees in this change an ascendancy of the views of the nationalists and the military over those of the Foreign Ministry. Even so, he argues that the reality is much more complex. Apart from the consensus that the near abroad must be a priority of Russian foreign policy, the various groups in Russia's political elite vary widely in their motivations for involvement in the area. In particular, Valdez introduces the idea that a "Russophone" foreign policy that eschews imperial aims and means may yet emerge in Moscow.

Turning to the Western states, the chapters by Nikolai A. Kulinich, Vyacheslau E. Paznyak, and Peetr Vares see the regional and international behavior of the state as a function of domestic factors. Foreign policy as the hostage of social and economic maladies is the theme of Nikolai Kulinich's chapter, "Ukraine in the New Geopolitical Environment: Issues of Regional and Subregional Security." He reminds us that economic and social concerns claim such a large part of the psychological landscape of the Ukrainian population, that a 1994 opinion poll placed foreign policy only in seventeenth place among people's main concerns. Even so, Kulinich endeavors to analyze Ukraine's foreign policy priorities within the context of economic, military-political, and geopolitical issue areas. Foreign investment is an essential foreign policy priority if Ukraine's economic woes are to be alleviated. However, so far, a number of structural problems (which are being slowly dealt with) have hampered the growth and rate of foreign investment. In the military-political issue area, Kulinich argues that Ukraine's military doctrine is purely defensive in nature, concerned with thwarting threats to the country. This is evidenced by Ukraine's efforts in the conversion of defense industries and by its nuclear disarmament stance. In the case of the latter, Kulinich contends that Ukraine initially procrastinated only because it was asked to relinquish its nuclear capacity without meaningful security guarantees and with little reciprocal socioeconomic benefits. As for the geopolitical issue area, Kulinich argues for a new concept of neutrality that allows Ukraine to "return" to Europe, even join NATO, without neglecting its interests in the East. Indeed, "normal interaction with Russia and the CIS states is one of the preconditions of Ukrainian integration into Europe."

In his "Belarus's Foreign Policy Priorities and the Decision-Making Process," Vyacheslau E. Paznyak begins the chapter by reminding the reader that political forces were taken by surprise by the rapid collapse of the Soviet Union. Consequently, "no elaborate scenarios of independence had existed by the time the Declaration of Sovereignty was adopted." However, certain basic goals were agreed upon and achieved. Foremost among these has been the consistent search for diplomatic recognition. By 1994, Belarus's independence had been recognized by 123 countries. The republic also joined a number of international organizations, as well as acceding to the Nuclear Nonproliferation Treaty and ratifying the START I Treaty and the Lisbon Protocol. But the pursuit of more general foreign policy goals has been hampered by institutional competitions, derived from personal ambitions and rivalries among political parties. For instance, the Council of Ministers of Belarus has been dealing with issues of national security at the expense of the Security Council of the Republic of Belarus (SCRB), which had been created to deal with national security and was presided over by the chairman of the Supreme Soviet. The result has been a number of confrontations between the chairman of the Supreme Soviet, on the one hand, and the prime minister and foreign minister, on the other hand. This competition reflected a more general rivalry among the various political parties to which the main political players belonged. This, among other reasons (one of which is the paucity of foreign policy specialists), has led to several inconsistencies in the country's foreign policy. Beyond the confines of the domestic arena, the internal political debate has centered on Belarus's position in its region. The debate has ranged from full-fledged commitment to the CIS, to leaving the CIS and entering a new Baltic–Black Sea Association, to an intermediate proposal whereby Belarus remains within the CIS, but joins another association that includes the Baltic states as well as some former COMECON countries. But in all this, Belarus has to adjust to the reality of its geostrategic situation: the country is squeezed between two power centers of European politics, and of these Russia remains the most formidable.

As to the Baltic states of Lithuania, Estonia, and Latvia, Peeter Vares in his chapter, "Dimensions and Orientations in the Foreign and Security Policies of the Baltic States," reminds us that after the collapse of the Soviet Union, these states achieved immediate independence, gaining diplomatic recognition from fifty states in three weeks. However, they were not prepared for independence or for purposeful foreign policy. All three of the Baltic states had little knowledge of foreign affairs, knew little of international law, and had not been involved in strategic and security studies. Thus, the institutions they developed to deal with foreign affairs were highly deficient, drawing on personnel who were completely lacking in diplomatic knowledge and skill and whose appointments contingent on political affiliations rather than expertise. These problems were compounded by the struggling economies of these states and the presence in these countries of Russian troops. Notwithstanding these constraints, the Baltic states pursued a variety of foreign policy directions: with the Nordic countries, with whom they share common political, security, and environmental interests; with each other, as a natural consequence of the Soviet collapse; with Russia, which continues to constitute a massive geopolitical presence; with the United States, which was seen as an advocate for the independence and advancement of the Baltic states; and with the European community, which the Baltic states have tried hard to join. In the case of security policy, Russia is considered the main, even "only," source of threat to the Baltic states. Lacking the military capability to counter the Russian threat, the Baltic states have tried their hand at military cooperation and have sought associated partnership with NATO and the West European Union.

Turning to the states of Central Asia, general sociopolitical and geostrategic aspects of these countries' international relations are dealt with in the chapters by Kemal H. Karpat, Mohiaddin Mesbahi and Mark N. Katz. In "The Sociopolitical Environment Conditioning the Foreign Policy of the Central Asian States," Kemal Karpat begins by placing Central Asia in its historical setting, especially as part of the Soviet empire, which tried to create a nation out of diverse ethnic groups, and asks whether Russia wants to become a true nation with a unique identity and culture or to continue to view other ethnic and national groups as part of its Russianness. The Turkic states, however, have no problems with self-identity, which is based "on concrete and genuine ethnolinguistic bases, and on a historical background suitable to the formulation of a national history." Their problem has been with their geostrategic situation, which is dominated by Russia. This is why, Karpat argues, these states focused their foreign relations first and foremost on securing international recognition, which they hoped would not only bring to an end their global isolation but also bring them international protection. They were hampered, however, by their inexperience in foreign relations. They did not possess the bureaucratic organization and professional staff capable of efficiently executing foreign policy. Unlike Russia, "the Central Asian states had to recruit anew their foreign ministry staffs from whatever source was available." Nevertheless, it is the presidents of these countries who generally are in charge of foreign affairs. And these leaders on the whole seem relatively popular because of their use of Islam (a primary source of national culture) as an avenue to court the support of the masses. Decision makers, therefore, have to cope with "a domestic audience increasingly influenced by nationalist-populist Islam while at the same time maintaining a facade of neutrality toward Islam often disguised as 'secularism' in order to soothe the apprehensions of the Russians and Westerners."

Mohiaddin Mesbahi, in the chapter titled "Regional and Global Powers and the International Relations of Central Asia," considers first the role of Turkey. Marginalized in the European and Middle Eastern regions, Turkey saw in Central Asia "an unprecedented historical opportunity to explore a completely new horizon in its foreign policy." Turkey pursued a multidimensional strategy toward Central Asia that included numerous diplomatic initiatives, wide-ranging economic transactions, a number of infrastructural projects, and many cultural and educational agreements. But, according to Mesbahi, Turkey's record thus far has been at best spotty. The country is not an economic giant and it has to work against the still enduring Soviet/Russian legacy in the area. And it is further constrained by its geographical distance from Central Asia. Iran, on the other hand, encounters no such constraint. It is geographically contiguous to Central Asia and presents the area with a potential for developing an outlet to the sea through the Persian Gulf. Thus, like Turkey, Iran has followed an activist policy toward the area, that has been pursued on various levels, but mostly in the economic domain. However, the "Islamic factor" supposedly inherent in Iran's foreign policy has been a major constraint on the country's relations with Central Asia. But contrary to conventional wisdom, Mesbahi argues, the Islamic factor has been grossly exaggerated by Central Asian leaders for political purposes. Other states and powers, like Afghanistan, the United States, and China, have also been active in Central Asia, but none can equal Russia's depth of involvement. Russia has been able to preserve its central position in the area primarily because of the enduring military, economic, and political legacies of the Soviet Union. While internal changes may occur in the future in Russia and/or in Central Asia that might affect the current relationship, at present Russia remains the dominant power in the area.

Mark N. Katz, in his chapter "Emerging Patterns in the International Relations of Central Asia," investigates the domestic sources of the countries' foreign policies, as well as their international relations with outside powers. He sees three possible paths for Central Asia's political evolution: preservation of the status quo (old communists maintaining power), a move toward pluralist democracy, or the emergence of radicalized, anticommunist, and anti-Western Islamic regimes. The three tendencies are examined through an analysis of the foreign policies of the ruling and nonruling parties in Central Asia. The ruling parties, seeking to maintain the status quo, have made close military relations with

Russia their priority. The reason is clear: Moscow can help them stay in power. Moreover, to attain legitimacy through international recognition, they have joined the CSCE and other international groupings, and have pursued cordial relations with the West and with geographically and culturally proximate states. Katz maintains that similar motivations inform the foreign policies of nonruling parties. They all seek broad international support, at least in their pronouncements, in their efforts to bring about political change in their favor. That is why the Islamic parties tend not to be implacably hostile to the United States and the West, nor are the democratic parties especially antagonistic to Iran. In the case of external powers, Russia continues to be the primary actor. Here, both democrats and nationalists endeavor to maintain close ties with Central Asian regimes primarily for domestic reasons. Of the other external actors, Iran and Turkey, the most influential of the proximate states, have tended to follow pragmatic policies that generally avoided the infusion of ideology and/or religion. The result of all this, according to Katz, is that in the short term the status quo regimes are able to maintain themselves in power, but their long-term prospects are poor because of the increasing demands for democratization.

With specific reference to Kazakhstan, Oumirseric Kasenov, in his chapter "The Institutions and Conduct of Foreign Policy of Postcommunist Kazakhstan," places good neighborly relations, especially with Russia, as Kazakhstan's predominant foreign policy goal. This is due to Russia's immense power and to the existence of a substantial Russian community in Kazakhstan. He further argues that this is also a reason (among other reasons) why, while taking into consideration the "Islamic factor," Kazakhstan cannot become a "Muslim state." As to the making of foreign policy, no institution has the power that the chief executive wields. Constitutionally, the president has "supreme responsibility" in foreign and defense matters, with parliament having only a limited role. This imbalance is exacerbated by the fact that few parliamentarians are interested in, or especially knowledgeable about, foreign affairs. And this lack of expertise pervades the Foreign Ministry, the media, the political parties, and public opinion. As for Kazakhstan's foreign policy orientations, it is clear from Kasenov's analysis that as a new, relatively weak state, bordering on a major nuclear power that sometimes exhibits hegemonic tendencies, Kazakhstan is concerned first and foremost with securing recognition (and protection) from the international community. This explains the many accords and treaties (detailed by Kasenov) with other countries and international organizations, including the United States, that the country has entered into since its independence. For example, Article 3 of the accord with the United States stipulates that "the United States of America recognizes the security, independence, sovereignty, territorial integrity, and democratic development of the Republic of Kazakhstan as the highest values."

Russia and the issue of security figure prominently as primary foreign policy concerns in the case of the Caucasian states of Azerbaijan and Armenia. Leila Alieva makes clear in her chapter, "The Institutions, Orientations, and Conduct of Foreign Policy in Post-Soviet Azerbaijan," that the main threat Azerbaijan has had to deal with since independence has been Armenia's territorial claims on Azerbaijan. Alieva argues further that Russian involvement in the Azeri-Armenian struggle essentially has been on the Armenian side. While there were a number of reasons for this, one primary motivation was to coerce Azerbaijan into joining the CIS, and thus keep it in Russia's sphere of influence. The fall of the liberal, and clearly Western-oriented, Elchibey government in Azerbaijan is attributed by Alieva at least partially to Azeri territorial losses in its conflict with Armenia. Having learned its lesson, the present government of Gaidar Aliev has pursued close relations with Moscow, hoping that Russia would use its influence with Armenia to resolve the Nagorno-Karabagh problem. If no satisfactory solution is arrived at, Gaidar Aliev, according to Alieva, might turn his attention to Turkey. In this he could count on the support of the Azeri population, the majority of whom support the Turkish method of political development. In reality, however, Turkey has done little in the past to affect Armenian-Azeri relations, thus leaving Turkey with little influence and indirectly weakening the West's strategic position in Azerbaijan. But in any case, Alieva argues, Azerbaijan's relations with Western countries are determined independently of other factors by the existence or otherwise of Armenian communities (operating as political lobbies) in the various Western countries. Consequently, little or no movement has occurred in the Nagorno-Karabagh issue area, a situation that could lead to the radicalization not only of Azerbaijan but also of neighboring countries such as Turkey. An eventuality such as this would be clearly anti-Western and antidemocratic.

Similar concerns, but from a different, completely opposite perspective, define the chapter by Rouben Paul Adalian titled "Armenia's Foreign Policy: Defining Priorities and Coping with Conflict." Adalian echoes the theme that runs throughout this book by placing geography at the center of Armenia's foreign policy concerns: a small, landlocked country bounded by a hostile Azerbaijan, an unfriendly Turkey, an anarchic Georgia, and an international outcast in the form of the Islamic Republic of Iran. Other determinants of Armenia's foreign policy have been ethnicity and religion, both of which have tended to isolate the country from its politically and geostrategically more natural environs. Partly due to this, and partly because of Armenia's economic dependence on Russia for the last hundred years, Russia continues to be a major player in the country's domestic and foreign policies. Yet initially, according to Adalian, Armenia's primary foreign policy objective was to become politically and economically integrated into the world community. This goal, however, was hindered by the conflict with Azerbaijan over Nagorno-Karabagh. As long as the Armenians of Nagorno-Karabagh continued to insist on transferring sovereignty over the district from the Azeris to the Armenians, Armenian foreign policy was bound to remain captive to powerful nationalist sentiments. In fact, on this issue, the opposition parties have been more militant than the government. The result of all this was a greater reliance on Russia, to the detriment of Armenia's broader international aspirations and priorities. Adalian argues that at present there is a real convergence of interests between Russia and Armenia: "Russia wants a presence in the Caucasus. Armenia needs that presence in the Caucasus." And beyond the Russian-Armenian nexus, Nagorno-Karabagh also has developed into the overriding factor that has governed Armenia's relations with an international community that has "essentially regarded the right of a people to self-determination as secondary to the right of state sovereignty" over its borders, regardless of how these borders came to be drawn.

It is immediately apparent from this short overview of the substantive chapters that will follow that our authors consider the geostrategic factor to be the most crucial element in the international relations of the region under investigation.

This is not to imply that other factors have been absent. The need for economic aid, whether manifested in requests for financial credits or infrastructural projects, has been an important determinant of foreign policy. Culture too has played a significant role in determining the direction of foreign policy. For example, it is superfluous to analyze the international relations of the Central Asian republics without examining the linguistic, historical, and religious ties the region has with countries such as Turkey, Iran, Afghanistan, and China.

But the argument is that, while these and other factors have had an impact on the region's international relations, it has been the geostrategic factor that has constituted the key element in the perceptions and politico-strategic calculations of decision makers.

And there can be little doubt that within the geostrategic domain, it is Russia that is the dominant player. As has been pointed out earlier, the most prominent feature of the regional system that encompasses the countries of the former Soviet Union is the existence of a seeming hegemon in the form of Russia. While our authors look at different countries and subregions, and analyze various policy factors and imperatives, they all tend to agree that at present no other power has more direct and substantial impact on the foreign policies and international relations of the region than Russia.

Notes

1. K.J. Holsti, *International Politics: A Framework for Analysis* (Englewood Cliffs, NJ: Prentice Hall, 1972), p. 21.

2. Howard H. Lentner, *Foreign Policy Analysis: A Comparative and Conceptual Approach* (Columbus, OH: Charles E. Merrill, 1974), p. 2.

3. P.A. Reynolds, *An Introduction to International Relations* (London: Longman, 1971), pp. 9–10.

4. The term is coined by the late Hedley Bull in his classic study, *The Anarchical Society: A Study of Order in World Politics* (London: Macmillan, 1977).

5. Jerel A. Rosati, Joe D. Hagan, and Martin W. Sampson III, eds., *Foreign Policy*

Restructuring: How Governments Respond to Global Change (Columbia, SC: University of South Carolina Press, 1994), p. 28.

6. Karen Dawisha and Bruce Parrott, *Russia and the New States of Eurasia: The Politics of Upheaval* (New York: Cambridge University Press, 1994), pp. 195–96.

7. Ibid., p. 196.

8. James N. Rosenau calls this "adaptive behavior," where the political organism is always in motion, adjusting to internal developments and external circumstances. See James N. Rosenau, *The Study of Political Adaptation: Essays on the Analysis of World Politics* (New York: Nichols, 1981).

9. K.J. Holsti, ed., *Why Nations Realign: Foreign Policy Restructuring in the Postwar World* (London: Allen and Unwin, 1982), p. 7, quoted in Rosati et al., *Foreign Policy Restructuring*, p. 10.

10. David O. Wilkinson, *Comparative Foreign Relations: Framework and Methods* (Belmont, CA: Dickinson, 1969), p. 4.

11. Dawisha and Parrott, *Russia and the New States of Eurasia*, p. 198.

12. Rosati et al., *Foreign Policy Restructuring*, pp. 4–14; see also Robert Gilpin, *War and Change in World Politics* (New York: Cambridge University Press, 1981).

I

Russia

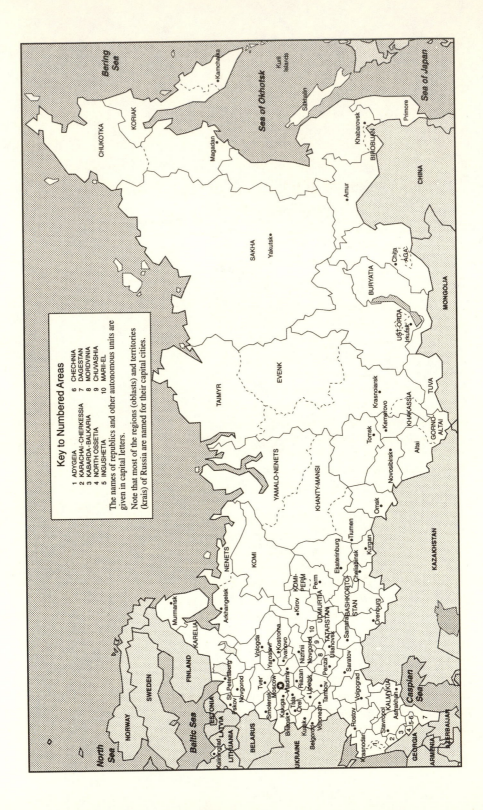

Key to Numbered Areas

1 ADYGEIA	6 CHECHNIA
2 KARACHAI-CHERKESSIA	7 DAGESTAN
3 KABARDA-BALKARIA	8 MORDVINIA
4 NORTH OSSETIA	9 CHUVASHIA
5 INGUSHETIA	10 MARI-EL

The names of republics and other autonomous units are given in capital letters.

Note that most of the regions (oblasts) and territories (krais) of Russia are named for their capital cities.

2

Priorities of Russia's Foreign Policy and the Way It Works

Nodari A. Simonia

During 1992–93 Russia was working hard through what is bound to be a long process of changeover to a new type of statehood. The scramble for political power going on in this context and the confrontation of the old and the new forces (those in the making, to be exact) were still far from their final and logical conclusion. Hence the strategic instability of Russia's foreign policy, frequent zigzagging and discordance, and conflicting statements and moves during that period. In the long run, foreign policy always depends on domestic policy. It may deviate from it one way or another, but over a longer stretch of the evolution of society the balance and concordance between them will be redressed just the same. This is a point that has to be taken into account in any serious assessment of foreign policy. But this implies, in turn, the importance of the proper appreciation of the character of internal change within society, that is, the correct interpretation of the events of August 1991 in the Soviet Union. With skeptical and sensible comments few and far between, both Russia and the West (especially the United States) were swamped with euphoria over the "victory of democracy," the course of economic and political reform, and so on. This euphoria was felt in Russia's official foreign policy, too. From the very beginning its Ministry of Foreign Affairs (MFA) was committed to bringing the country into the club of Western democratic nations right away, losing no time in securing, for example, Russia's full-scale partnership with the Group of Seven (G–7).

It has since become obvious to many that this euphoria has been premature, that events require some backtracking and readjustment in thinking. Hard as it may be for some individuals to accept, the defeat of the attempted coup in August 1991 was no victory for democracy. Political democracy was the dominant tendency, but there was neither the social nor the economic base necessary for the establishment of democracy. A civil society had not yet been created.

Properly speaking, it was not its own goals that Russia's political democracy fought for; rather, it was clearing the way to power not for itself but for an entirely different social force—the top level of the party and state managerial establishment, which we call the economic nomenklatura. Until then, the dominant force was the ideological nomenklatura (its leaders best known in the West were Mikhail Suslov and Egor Ligachev). It ruled the whole of society, including the party and state managerial establishment. Yet in August 1991 it was removed from power once and for all. But while the remnants of the ideological nomenklatura waged rearguard battles against Russian democracy, an economic nomenklatura moved into position to attain political power. At this point, therefore, Russia's foreign policy reflects the interests of this economic nomenklatura and will do so to an even greater extent in the future. Its political and ideological exponents today are the so-called statists.[1]

Furthermore, Russia's foreign policy was not being made from scratch, although its official spokespersons tried (in the best Soviet traditions) to present it as something fundamentally new and different from past policy. That is not true, of course. Along with a certain novelty, there also was a certain continuity. For this reason, it would be worthwhile to glance back, to see how far the foreign policy strategies of the Stalinist, Gorbachev, and Yeltsin periods have met the interests of ensuring national security in the full sense of the term, encompassing, at least, five major aspects: preservation of national integrity and survival within the given frontiers; military-political security; economic security; legal protection of the population; and ecological security.

The Stalinist Period

It is the military-political aspect of security that predominated from the end of World War II right up to 1985. The arms buildup was carried on at the expense of nearly all the other aspects of national security. Moreover, under Stalin expansionism was viewed (quite in tune with the tsarist policy of the nineteenth century) as a major expedient for strengthening Russia's own security (gaining control of Eastern Europe; annexing some territories in the north, west, and south of European Russia; supporting the armed struggle in Greece and the popular fronts in France and Italy; slicing off some territories in the Far East; dominating North Korea and China; supporting the armed uprisings and guerrilla warfare of the communist parties of Southeast Asia; etc.). The national integrity of a multiethnic state was maintained through a unitarian policy by force of arms and police rule. The economy was based, essentially, on the expansion of industrial productive forces. The issues of ecology and law were simply ignored.

The consequences of such a system of priorities in assuring national security were potentially disastrous (beginning as early as the 1970s, and culminating in the late 1980s and early 1990s). The methods of military-administrative coercion did not resolve any domestic contradictions but swept them under the carpet and turned them into time bombs that have now begun to explode. The inadequacy of legal protection of the population has now developed into a total contempt for the rule of law and today also threatens Russia's integrity and security. The "outer circle" of security, made up of satellite countries, created problems and drew off tremendous resources even in the early stages. And there was less and less ground as time went on for it to be seen as a "defense belt" for Russia's own frontiers. In the context of a global confrontation of the two systems, Moscow had to resort from time to time to armed methods of assuring the loyalty of its allies (the German Democratic Republic, Poland, Hungary, Czechoslovakia, China). By the 1960s it had lost control over China, the Democratic People's Republic of Korea, and most of the communist movement in the East. An attempt to make it up by shifting the accent to the so-called socialist orientation in the countries of Asia, Africa, and Latin America brought no military-political advantages to speak of but drained the country of more of its financial and material resources.

Legal nihilism in the context of undivided control by the command administration system and the diversion of immense resources for an expansionist foreign policy blocked social and economic progress and a breakthrough to the postindustrial level and in that way created a real threat to the national security of the USSR. Total neglect of safety engineering and the military-industrial complex's criminal mismanagement of nuclear, chemical, and bacteriological experimentation brought the nation to the brink of ecological catastrophe.

The Gorbachev Period

Mikhail Gorbachev's perestroika, in its dynamics and evolution, was an attempt (though never followed through in many ways) at resolving the problem of national security on a fundamentally new basis. By its methods this policy was intended not for a landslide destruction of the old order but for an evolutionary-reformist way of development, and by its end results would have meant a revolutionary kind of change in domestic social and international relations. The trend that got under way in domestic policy was one toward democracy, if still rather uncertain and inconsistent. The union state, which was federative only nominally, while remaining essentially unitarian, was to have obtained more of a "federative" substance as a result of the Novo-Ogarevo process.[2]

Yet another trend that slowly got under way, just as inconsistently and controversially, was the transition to commercial relations in the economy. That new orientation in the internal evolution of society was matched by changes in its foreign policy course, which came to be called the "new thinking." It was a historic breakthrough expressed, first of all, in the repudiation of global confrontation on ideological grounds, which was expected to create a favorable external environment to ensure the country's economic security. Important steps were taken toward starting partnership relations with the nations of the West and promoting broader economic cooperation. The policy with respect to the Third World countries was one of progressively reshaping relations with them (rather than breaking them off in one fell swoop), notably, by ending the support for pseudorevolutionary or warlike regimes and by revamping economic relations to suit commercial principles. A start was made toward promoting normal relations and mutually advantageous cooperation with such important Asian countries as China, South Korea, Thailand, and Singapore.

The Yeltsin Period

The failure of the coup in August 1991 inspired hopes for a sweeping acceleration and substantial extension of the positive changes already ongoing in society and in foreign policy. Unfortunately, what has happened since has given no reason for such optimism. This is primarily because of the uncontrolled, landslide disintegration of the USSR that followed the announcement by the leaders of Russia, Ukraine, and Belarus that they had agreed (at Belavezh, near Brest) to form a Commonwealth of Independent States (CIS). None of the positive expectations promoted by the founders of the CIS have ever come true. On the contrary, their decisions generated a whole series of vexing problems and exacerbated some existing domestic and foreign policy problems. In fact, many doubt, from a historical perspective, that the timing and the manner of the disappearance of the imperial union was hardly a foregone conclusion.

The essential aspect of the problem here is that the overwhelming destruction of the territorial integrity of the Soviet Union was a result of the exclusively subjective ambitions of a group of political leaders and their scramble for political power rather than a consensus of all or the majority of the members of the union. It is for just this reason that Russia found itself immediately faced with the problems of, for example, maintaining the security of its new frontiers; making policy in respect to the new states; overcoming (or making up for) the consequences of the sudden disruption of economic, transport, communication, and other connections; interceding for the Russian-speaking population in the independent republics; and dealing with new regional conflicts and conflict situations.

Russia and the Former Soviet Republics

So Yeltsin found himself in a totally different setting, confronted by principally new priorities. For an accurate assessment of the importance of these new priorities, the specific character of the relationship between Russia and the former Soviet Union needs to be taken into account.

The fact is that Soviet imperialism was a rather unusual phenomenon. After the revolution of 1917 there was not only a quick reintegration of the empire but an essential transformation. Lenin's idealistic concept of the equality of various nations was put into effect by Stalin, but in a jesuitically perverted way: all did actually turn out to be equal, or equally without rights, in the face of the totalitarian regime he had created. The new, rather specific "metropolitan country" finally took shape as a central bureaucratic party and state machinery (establishment), with the military-industrial complex (MIC) as its mainstay. All the republics, including the Russian Republic, found themselves in the position of one big colony exploited by this metropolitan country. All ethnic communities were under the sway of the same political system, which led, for example, with equal indifference, to the destruction of Russia's villages; millions of deaths from starvation in Ukraine; ecological disaster in Russia's Volga country and Kazakhstan; and ruthless colonial exploitation of the natural resources of Russia's Siberia and Uzbekistan.

The metropolitan country fulfilled its function of exploitation within the framework of the "integrated national economic complex" it claimed to have created. The establishment, however, could discharge its exploitative function only because this role was closely intertwined with another, useful function—running and regulating the economy within the framework of a union state. It discharged this function by methods of command and injunction. That is why the establishment actually bungled it. Many economic links were set up exclusively in the interest of the military-industrial complex and were based on geopolitical and purely military considerations. But those links were real and crucial, indeed, to the lives of millions.

It is precisely on account of this dual function of the establishment that the tasks of structurally reforming production and scrapping artificial and economically ineffective relations cannot be accomplished through the abolition of the "metropolitan country" or the breakup of the "common economic space," since that might lead to severance of useful and vital economic links, too. Because the economies of the former Soviet republics had never been national, the radical rupture of links between them in 1992 ended with not so much a structural reshaping as a sweeping destruction of the entire system of production. It is not a coincidence that even the Ukrainian president, Leonid Kravchuk, should admit in April 1993, "We were in a hurry then to sever artificially the links that are so needed today and will be needed tomorrow. The Belavezh documents contained no framework for intelligent economic integration."[3] As a result, in July 1993, Ukraine signed the Treaty on Economic Union with the other countries of the Commonwealth of Independent States.

So what kind of policy toward the former Soviet Union should the democratic Russian government have adopted?

An appropriate strategy for such a government would have been to adopt a purposeful and clear-cut policy of eliminating the remnants of the old colonial division of labor. Such a policy would provide the basis on which equitable and mutually beneficial cooperation could develop, no matter whether this cooperation would be effected within the framework of a new federation or a kind of confederation. Instead, Russia has spent some two or three years making general declarations about the necessity of goodwill and cooperation, mixed with periodic attempts to exert different kinds of pressure (economic, political, military). From the very beginning, the Burbulis-Gaidar government adhered to the slogan "Russia first!" and to the idea that Russia is the "milch cow" for the other republics (this expression, with reference to the relationship of Russia to some of the republics of Central Asia, was used by Vice Premier A. Nechaev in August 1992).[4] Some of the responsibility lay, evidently, on the American advisor to Yeltsin's team, Jeffrey Sachs, who early in April 1993 was insisting on the need for Russia to totally refrain from subsidizing trade in energy resources and ruble credits to the republics. If the republics needed external aid, it had to come from the West, not from Russia, Sachs held.[5]

Another distinctive feature of Soviet colonialism was the status of the Russian population in the other republics, which was entirely different from the role and behavior of "the white man" in classical Asian and African colonies. In the former Soviet republics, the Russian population as a whole did not have any particular privileges, unlike representatives of the metropolitan nomenklatura, who today seem content in the independent republics, some of them holding high-ranking posts in local governments (right up to prime minister or minister of defense). The rank-and-file Russians and Russian-speaking people, on the other hand, like indigenous residents, have always been an object of exploitation by the nomenklatura, both central and local. Their living conditions were not much better, and sometimes were even worse, than those of the indigenous population. With the exception of Kazakhstan and Kyrgyzstan, where compact rural settlements of Russians and Ukrainians existed, in the main the Russian-speaking population massed in the cities, thus supplying MIC enterprises and mining and local industries with labor and administrative and engineering personnel.

The historical experience of other countries (for example, overseas Chinese in the Southeast) shows us that the most appropriate policy would have been for the Russian government to allow the Russian-speaking former Soviet citizens to freely choose their new citizenship. Thus, if they chose the local citizenship, they would have to obey the local laws. But if they preferred Russian (Ukrainian, etc.) citizenship, they would be considered foreigners and have to face the consequences. Instead, in early 1994 the Russian government, and the Ministry of Foreign Affairs in particular, proposed a kind of imperial solution to this problem: dual citizenship for the Russian-speaking population in the former Soviet Union.[6] Among other things, the program stipulated that 20 to 30 percent of Russian assistance to the former Soviet Union be specially allocated to the Russian population. Critics of the program liken it to the creation of a Russian "fifth column." No wonder many former Soviet republics were unhappy with it.

The Domestic Origins of Russian Foreign Policy

The destruction of the USSR has posed a real threat to the security of the Russian state itself. In fact, the seeds had been planted in the early half of 1991 in a bid to create an image of greater democracy and greater liberalism through ill-considered declarations of the sovereignty of autonomies and just as ill-considered laws regarding the rehabilitation of once-repressed peoples.

What emerged in Russia right after the breakup of the USSR was some loose, unconsolidated political power. The community had no social, let alone political, consensus, not only in the context of the interparty struggle but also within the structures of supreme power. The result was overall political destabilization and inconsistency in the conduct of domestic and foreign policies, which both directly and indirectly tended to sap national security.

Social and legal security in the community had deteriorated rapidly during the 1970s and 1980s. It is not just today that corruption and criminality have arisen, but by 1992–93 they had assumed unprecedented strength and, together with the government's economic reform, brought the social protection of the population down to an incredibly low level. Unprofessionalism, bureaucratization, and rampant corruption have led to a situation that the press has rightfully called *bespredel* (without limits).

None of the basic objectives formulated by the government within the framework of its monetarist policy have been achieved. There has been no structural reorganization of social production or, for that matter, any stabilization of the economic situation and, consequently, the ruble. The disruption of the relationship between privatization and price liberalization in 1992–93 brought on an overall curtailment of production. Nor has the issue of foreign investment been properly resolved. In short, the move toward economic security has been negligible.

The unresolved issue of power has had a deplorable impact on Russia's present foreign policy. Russia's foreign policy has been so inconsistent and variable as to give the impression that the nation is conducting several foreign policies at the same time. For example, during 1992–93, foreign policy virtually became hostage to the politicking and confrontation of various social forces and power structures and even factions within the same structures (as on the issues of the Kurils, the Russian-speaking populations in the former republics, the attitude toward regional conflicts, and Western aid). Russia's foreign policy now aims to prove that it is far more democratic, liberal, and progressive than it was under Gorbachev. Hence its oft-noted lopsidedness. There are fewer restrictions and more devotion to Western (American) ideals. Economic partnership with the West has been pursued to an absurd extent.[7]

Promised Western credits and loans have only been trickling in (and so have direct investments). This is happening at a time when cooperation and trade with traditional partners in Eastern Europe and the Third World have hit bottom. Russia's foreign policy, as a result of the mistakes and illusions of the leadership, has hardly coped with one of its basic tasks, ensuring favorable conditions for the development of the national economy and the achievement of economic security.

Russia needs to orient its foreign policy to suit its national interests, for it is these interests that will determine on what issues and in what areas it will look to the West, or to the East.

Russia is in the midst of transition from one social system to another. The main national interest lies in the sphere of economic reforms, in overcoming the existing technological gap and catching up with the developed Western countries. To concentrate on the economy, Russia must avoid a one-sided dominance by the military-political aspects of national security and refrain from an expansionist foreign policy permeated by ideological considerations. At the same time, Russia is a big power deeply involved in the process of nation-state building, which definitely conflicts with tendencies toward globalization. Today a more balanced foreign policy based on the concept of multipolarity is preferable for Russia. Herein lie the roots of the partial incompatibility of Russian and Western (especially American) interests. While the final aim of Russia is to be integrated into the world community, it is not yet prepared for this, either economically or politically. Economic and social stability is more essential for Russia today than formal adherence to principles of human rights. Political democracy in Russia, however much desired, should not be imposed from the top, or from abroad. It should appear only as a result of socioeconomic and political development and as an outcome of a long sociopolitical struggle bringing about a fully shaped civil society.

The main priority and most urgent interest at the given moment, from the standpoint of preserving Russia's national-political integrity and ensuring its survivability, is the problem of developing normal military-political and mutually advantageous economic relations with the former republics of the Soviet Union. The solution to this problem is crucial to shaping Russia's relations with both the West and the East. The way this problem will be tackled will prove or disprove the validity and sincerity of the commitment to rejuvenating Russia, and making it a civilized member of the world community. Also, resolving this problem will be essential to the security of Russia's borders, and to the elimination of a possible hostile encirclement. Regrettably, the leadership of Russia has taken too long to realize this order of priorities. In fact, the initiative in resolving this problem has been surrendered by the Ministry of Foreign Affairs to the spokespersons for military and civilian statists.

The relationship with the West remains a major priority from the standpoint of military, political, and, eventually, economic security. Backing up efforts toward a well-balanced disarmament by promoting close military-political cooperation with the leading developed nations (above all, the United States) is Russia's best guarantee of domestic stability and security. Yet it has been typical of Russia's leadership until recently to delude itself into believing it possible to have economic security assured with massive Western financial support. However, plagued by problems of their own, Western countries are able to give only so much, thus putting the onus on Russia to reform its own economy. It is high time for Russia to understand that by now it has received nearly the maximum that the West is willing to give. Moreover, the West does not want a powerful rival of its own making to emerge within such a historically short space of time. Therefore, while it is necessary to maintain and expand economic cooperation with the West wherever possible, it is also necessary to understand that there will be no breakthrough in the near future. And in any case, since the buildup of authoritarian trends in Russia is inevitable (today even most of the former democrats desire it), so, too, will be the disenchantment of Western democracies, especially the United States.

From the standpoint of assuring Russia's economic security, an indisputable priority is a radical turn toward the Asia-Pacific region, not only because it is one of the world's most important economic regions, but also because for Russia it holds inestimable opportunities for joint cooperation. The tapping of the resources of Siberia and the Far East is, in fact, fundamental to revitalizing Russia in the long run. But the only way to do that is through large-scale cooperation with the East. The main obstacle, however, is the underestimation of such cooperation by the leadership and the absence of strong political will capable of normalizing relations with the nations of the East. Unless Russia improves relations toward that end, it will hardly rise beyond the status of a second-rate economic power.

The Mechanism of Decision Making

One major obstacle in the way of devising and implementing a consistent course in foreign policy has been the absence of a well-ordered mechanism of decision making. In earlier times, the supreme agency that endorsed the strategy of foreign policy, as well as some of the most important moves by the Soviet state in the area of foreign political and economic relations, was the Politburo under the general secretary. The Supreme Soviet (parliament) played no part at all beyond rubber-stamping the decisions it had no hand in framing. The Politburo relied on the Secretariat of the Central Committee in its decision making. The staff of the Secretariat resolved all major issues by using back channels coming from appropriate ministries or agencies (especially the Ministry of Foreign Affairs, the KGB, the Central Intelligence Board of the Ministry of Defense, the Ministry of Foreign Economic Relations, the State Committee for Economic Cooperation, and the Academy of Sciences). The key role in the Secretariat was played by the International Department and the unnamed "Department of the Central Committee," which dealt with socialist countries. They all constituted something like a "superministry" of foreign affairs, that amassed information and drafted would-be resolutions. In the closing stages of decision making certain corrections could be made by the staff of the general secretary's aides. (Under Gorbachev, especially after the office of the presidency was introduced, this staff actually began to play a more important part than the Politburo.)

The Ministry of Foreign Affairs could introduce various proposals on the country's foreign policy but, as a rule, its major function was to implement the decisions made by the top party bodies. True, depending on the minister's own status, the ministry could play a somewhat greater (or lesser) role in shaping the course of foreign policy (for instance, the ministry's influence was strengthened substantially after Andrei Gromyko was elected Politburo member in 1973, and then under Shevardnadze, owing to his close personal relationship with Gorbachev).

Invariably the KGB was involved in foreign policy decision making, albeit discreetly. Its influence worked in two ways: directly, through appropriate proposals and information sent to the Central Committee, and indirectly, through a network of KGB officials on the staff of all other departments, including the Central Committee. The secret of the KGB's uncommon effect in influencing foreign policy lay exactly in the integrated character of this organization's activities, namely, the combination and intertwining of its foreign and domestic functions. This is what distinguished it from the Central Intelligence Board, which did its part toward shaping and implementing foreign policy within the restricted professional limits of its military interests, and almost never took any initiative in general policy making.

A certain part in framing a particular foreign policy concept or adopting a decision that was intended for immediate application was played by the Academy of Sciences of the USSR, a group of academy-controlled institutes concerned with foreign affairs. They either prepared background briefs or offered expert assessments on the documents drafted by the Ministry of Foreign Affairs, the Ministry of Foreign Economic Relations, or other departments. They also were invited by these departments as experts or consultants to work abroad.[8]

So every major foreign policy decision had to pass through this entire "high rise" structure in the drafting stage, being worked up (and often worsened and simplified) as it went through until formalized as resolutions by the Central Committee of the CPSU and the Council of Ministers of the USSR. But thereafter all departments and organizations had to follow the spirit and the letter of the decision unfailingly. Little by little this mechanism began to fall to bits while still under Gorbachev (especially during the latter half of his rule). True, changes involved only the topmost components of the former system: it was now the president and his staff who were the final decision makers instead of the Politburo. Moreover, Gorbachev used in parallel the old party structures and the presidential ones that were still in the making, so that a certain discipline, consistency, and continuity in foreign policy implementation were preserved. The involvement of scientists and scholars in the formulation, and even implementation, of foreign policy was appreciably increased in the Gorbachev period. A number of important decisions (such as those on the unequivocal and strong condemnation of Saddam Hussein's aggression or the establishment of diplomatic relations with South Korea) were made by Gorbachev as a result of the close cooperation of his staff with a number of scholars of the Academy of

Sciences, including those of the Institute of World Economy and International Relations.[9]

In his turn, Foreign Minister Eduard Shevardnadze, trying to "relate" his department to science, organized an unprecedented three-day scientific conference at the Ministry of Foreign Affairs in July 1990, inviting a large group of scientists and scholars in various fields of knowledge; he also required all embassies to organize seminars attended by scientists on business visits to the countries concerned.

Starting in December 1991 the former mechanism of foreign policy making was abandoned, while the new process took more than two years to form (and was still forming as of late May 1994). In the course of these years, the glasnost and political pluralism brought in by Gorbachev effectively surpassed all reasonable limits and at times turned into total anarchy. In this period the new presidential staff proved incapable of coordinating the actions of various departments involved in foreign policy. Of course, one of the major reasons behind this lack of coordination was the continuing scramble for power, as well as the fact that most departments were overstaffed with representatives of the old nomenklatura opposed to President Yeltsin, or with people who were just doing nothing and biding their time to see how the scramble for power would end. Yet another point was the quality of the new staff Yeltsin was creating for himself. The size was all right. There were, in fact, more than enough aspirants to "gainful employment" on the new executive level (especially when it involved the chances of foreign travel). Therefore, Gorbachev's titanic efforts to trim the staff were soon reduced to naught. The staff of the president of the Soviet Union comprised a little over two hundred people, and his federal Security Council ten at most, while the number of "responsible officials" of the Central Committee of the CPSU appointed by Gorbachev rose to nine hundred. In contrast, the staff of the president of Russia at this juncture is upwards of thirty-five hundred, and the staff of the Security Council numbers in the hundreds and is still expanding.[10] It is not surprising that the new presidential staff found it difficult to get on with Chernomyrdin's government staff in the huge set of buildings that once belonged to the Central Committee of the CPSU. The consequence of such a massive and rapid expansion of staff and its recurrent reshuffling "on the go" was to impair the quality and boost unprofessionalism. Compounding the situation was the fact that throughout this period the "new men" on the staff cared about nothing, as a matter of fact, beyond their own welfare (apartments, cars, country cottages, privileged health care, etc.) and, of course, still more gainful employment.

Such a situation, made worse by a president who had no clear foreign policy strategy of his own, led to practically all departments pursuing independent courses of action.[11] And they did act, often in discord, following their own particular departmental interests without so much as trying to coordinate their actions. So a new kind of situation arose: while in earlier times the general secretary and the Politburo strictly controlled the situation, confident of their position and of the prospect ahead and acting within the framework of an established system, now the president, constantly preoccupied with strengthening and preserving his power, has found himself compelled to steer a middle course between various departments, particularly those we call power wielding, that is, the ministries of Defense, Interior, and National Security.

One trend that has made itself quite clear in the context of weak presidential authority has been for some individuals in the president's immediate entourage, the top level of his staff, to build up their influence in domestic and foreign policies. There was a kind of regeneration, in a peculiar form, of a phenomenon that occurred in prerevolutionary Russia, especially in the reign of Nicholas II, namely, the court cabal, or "shadow cabinet," more powerful than the official government. (The opposition press has called this phenomenon the "collective Rasputin.") Just as in those times, the makeup of this shadow cabinet has changed from time to time, with some figures pushed into the background and others brought to the forefront (Burbulis, Petrov, Iliushin, Poltoranin, Malei, Kotenkov, Makarov, and Korzhakov, to name just a few).[12] Owing to their close association with the president, some of these men acquired a significance in society in general and foreign affairs in particular that was incommensurate with their human dimensions. Without any coordination and sometimes in defiance of the policies of the Ministry of Foreign Affairs and even of the president himself, these men made important statements on foreign affairs, confused Russia's partners, and made Russia's foreign policy unpredictable. (Suffice it to recall the mess that arose over the problem of Russo-Japanese relations, with conflicting pronouncements by Gennadii Burbulis, Mikhail Poltoranin, and Boris Fedorov, to name just a few.) The president's decision to set up the Security Council has not resolved the problem, for it has yet to become a viable coordinating agency. Under Iurii Skokov, this council has turned out to be sufficiently effective to thwart Yeltsin's visit to Tokyo, one that was already agreed on and arranged for by the Ministry of Foreign Affairs, but still not influential enough to end departmental discord within the realm of domestic and foreign policies. Even after the removal of Skokov and the appointment of Oleg Lobov to replace him, the Security Council has not yet found its proper place in Russia's power structure.

On the whole, however, most of the overall destabilization of the political situation in the country and the inconsistency of its foreign policy before October 1993 arose from the contradictions and conflicts between the executive and legislative authorities. Foreign policy had become, in point of fact, hostage to this confrontation. Decisions and resolutions were adopted more often than not just in defiance of the opposing side rather than out of considerations of expediency and the interests of the state. In the larger sense, the principal responsibility for the confrontation of the two branches of power lies with the president himself. Instead of reconciling radical and moderate reformers, contributing toward the consolidation and enlargement of the centrist forces in parliament, and so facilitating the country's peaceful evolution, he sided with radical reformers and backed up their uncompromising course. In that way he made a head-on collision inevitable and brought the nation to the brink of a military coup. The army turned out to be unprepared when his decree of 21 September disbanding the Supreme Soviet provoked an armed clash with the defenders of parliament. In consequence, parliament was excluded from the array of the nation's political forces as a more or less essential factor of domestic and foreign policy. The new constitution, approved by a minority of the electorate, substantially strengthened the authoritarian nature of the executive authority and just as substantially weakened legislative authority.

It should be noted that it was not only the contradiction between the executive and legislative authorities that had its effect on Russia's foreign policy making leading up to the events of 3–4 October 1993. Executive authority itself was far from homogeneous. That was made particularly clear in the growing estrangement, notably, of Vice President Aleksandr Rutskoi from the presidential team and the Ministry of Foreign Affairs. His military-statist patriotism kept on growing. He began to lend direct assistance to the action of the "intractable" generals in the conflict-ridden areas of the newly independent states and, in the end, jointed the cause of the Supreme Soviet and its speaker, Ruslan Khasbulatov, in their defiance of President Yeltsin.

The Russian Military and Foreign Policy

It is worth noting, in particular, the uncommonly enhanced role of the military as a subject of Russia's foreign policy. In all fairness it should be pointed out that it was not on the army's initiative that this happened, but in consequence of the general destabilization of the situation in the country, the landslide breakup of the USSR, the mounting criticism both of the army structure and of the order within it by radical democrats, and the persistent attempts by politicians of all stripes at regional and federal levels to draw the army into the whirlpool of a political struggle for power. In short, one objective circumstance that made for the army's involvement in politics was that many of the new problems of foreign policy had important military undertones right from the outset.

Until October 1993, the noisy bickering between the Supreme Soviet and the executive authorities diverted attention from the more essential contradiction between the military and the Ministry of Foreign Affairs, which was, incidentally, part of a larger contradiction between the statists and the "radical democrats." By its very nature, the army is today the most organized and centripetal force. It is objectively interested in a strong central government, the maximum preservation of its infrastructure within the bounds of the territory of the former Soviet Union, and the extension of the CIS bounds so that the commonwealth takes on as many features of statehood as possible (at least on the federal level). The army is just as vitally interested in preserving the major nucleus of the military-industrial complex as the backbone of its modernization. It is not surprising, therefore, that the army command presented stiff opposition to the policy of Russian radical democracy, which was directed toward a faster cutback of military spending (budget appropriations for defense orders were slashed by 70 percent in 1992), conversion of the MIC and the opening of some of its structures to the West, and the accelerated pullout of troops from Eastern Europe and the former republics of the USSR. The timidity typical of the army command in the honeymoon of Russia's democracy with the West after the breakup of the USSR was on the wane. The army's courage mounted with the evaporation of the euphoria over the creation of the CIS, and it became increasingly obvious that the political leadership of the newly independent states, including Russia, was unable to resolve numerous problems through a peaceful negotiating process. So the area of foreign affairs as applied to the states became the first battlefield on which the army command would flex its muscles. It became obvious to many before long that the army pursued a line of its own with respect to the newly independent states, parallel, yet far from always coincident, with the position of the president and, more particularly, the Ministry of Foreign Affairs. The military's line aimed at "pressurizing" the governments of the respective states with a view to bringing them into the system of a collective security system under Russia's aegis, preserving the old military bases and getting new ones, and keeping up military-political control along the perimeter of all or most of the territory of the former Soviet Union.

One may say that 1993 was the year of the army's comeback. It had become certain by the beginning of that year that the CIS was on the brink of total breakup and that the politicians in power were utterly helpless and incapable of coping with numerous problems. Taking advantage of this situation, the Russian military leadership virtually took the initiative into its own hands, especially after the Supreme CIS Strategic Command had been unilaterally abolished by the Russian leadership. From then on the action of the army leadership was increasingly in undisguised conflict with the peacemaking political efforts of the president and the Ministry of Foreign Affairs. There is, furthermore, the supposition that there was a kind of deliberate tactic of a "division of labor," which cast the president in the role of a peacemaking politician seeking appropriate accords through reasonable compromise arrangements, while the "evil and disobedient" military leadership (supposedly, by the way, only at the regional or local level) scuttled those accords. Even if there is such a division of labor today, it has not emerged overnight but has resulted from a series of concessions from a president increasingly disappointed in what is now commonly described as "romantic democratism," which has turned out to be incapable of resolving any of the regional conflicts and has even put the integrity of Russia itself at stake.

Examples of the army going it alone in the newly independent states are known too well to analyze them in this context in detail, but a cursory account of some of them should suffice.

Tajikistan

Radical democracy attempted (and managed for a short while) to force the president into supporting the so-called democratic and Islamic opposition. But what prevailed, in the long run, was the line of the statists who believed Russia's national interests required, above all, the stability of Central Asia. In consequence the Russian army supported the representatives of the old nomenklatura. Russia's Ministry of Foreign Affairs (Kozyrev) tried to save its "democratic face" by insisting on negotiations and compromise arrangements, at least with part of the opposition. Most likely nothing good will ever come out of it.

Ukraine

There is a strong faction in the Russian government that supports a separate, close economic alliance of the three Slavic republics. But in contrast with Belarus, which appears ready for the closest possible relationship with Russia, Ukraine has been distancing itself from Moscow right from the start. In point of fact, its negative position was the main reason behind the less than modest success in the effort on behalf of integration within the CIS. For its part, the action of Russia's generals has already more than once had the effect of dramatically exacerbating Russian-Ukrainian relations. Presidents Yeltsin and Kravchuk have more than once come to terms on a compromise solution on the issues of the Black Sea fleet and the military base at Sevastopol, but each time the army has expressed its dissent (notably through the resolutions of officer assemblies) with yet another compromise arrangement, while the president has had to stomach the army's insubordination to the nation's top leadership and to the supreme commander of the armed forces.

Georgia

President Yeltsin and the Russian Ministry of Foreign Affairs have more than once acted as peacemakers in the Georgian-Abkhazian conflict. Quite concrete accords were achieved, but the Russian generals behind the scenes kept on lending whatever assistance they could to the Abkhazian side, thwarting the accords achieved. The same plot was followed by the events in the fall of 1993, until at last Georgia was compelled to join the CIS and to agree to four more Russian military bases being set up in its territory.[13]

The Baltics

During his visit to Finland in October 1993, Pavel Grachev made a statement in which he linked the withdrawal of Russia's forces from Latvia and Estonia to the human rights issue involving the Russian-speaking population in these countries.[14] Such a statement amounted to the defense minister's interference in the handling of political questions that do not, of course, fall within his department's competence. This statement by the military, however, has not been rescinded in any way. On the contrary, it was the position of the Ministry of Foreign Affairs that was readjusted later to favor that of the military.

Indirect yet quite unambiguous evidence of the enhanced role of the military in the resolution of foreign policy issues between Russia and the newly independent states has been provided by the following: President Yeltsin's message to the North Atlantic Treaty Organization (NATO) nations asking for a revision of the 1990 Conventional Forces in Europe Treaty concerning the dislocation of military hardware in the North Caucasus and permission for Russia to overstep its seven-hundred-tank limit; and the active efforts by the minister of foreign affairs, Andrei Kozyrev, to seek UN recognition of Russia's priority role in the settlement of conflicts in the territory of the former Soviet Union.

Although conflicts in the newly independent states have been the major bridgehead for the rising role of the military in Russia's foreign policy, this is not all there was to it. A certain backtracking from the positions of democratic romanticism in 1993 was observable also in Russia's political relations with foreign nations outside the former Soviet Union. The active role of the top military leadership in this process has been particularly manifest in arms traffic and defense cooperation on a commercial basis. With the course of foreign policy changed, Russia drastically cut its arms exports. While in the 1980s the USSR's share of world arms exports was close to 40 percent, in 1991 it was less than 20 percent,[15] and it continued declining in 1992. However, recurrent commentaries by military as well as civilian MIC spokespersons in the press during 1993 (one of them, particularly active, was Mikhail Malei, Yeltsin's conversion advisor and presently chairman of the Security Council's Interdepartmental Commission on Conversion) rejected the one-way denigrating position on the MIC and argued the usefulness and necessity of arms exports as an important source of hard currency. The propaganda of the "new" approach to the MIC and arms trade went on throughout 1993, yet the actual breakthrough in this respect was made after the events of 3–4 October, when the "Basic Provisions of the Military Doctrine of the Russian Federation" (approved by the Russian Federation Security Council and adopted by presidential decree on 2 November 1993) and a number of presidential decrees were hurriedly adopted. On 6 November, for example, Boris Yeltsin signed the Decree on the Stabilization of the Economic Position of Enterprises and Organizations of Defense Industry and Measures to Ensure State Defense Orders, which required the government to ensure, among other things, the uninterrupted financing of the conversion programs (until the year 2000) and a doubling of the pay rates for the MIC staff.[16] (That decree alone made Egor Gaidar's subsequent resignation a foregone conclusion.) On 18 November, Yeltsin signed another secret decree establishing a public arms export-import company to be known as Rosvooruzhenie. The new company was called upon to make investments within the MIC framework, "above all, for the development and promotion of competitive types of armaments and military equipment to bring into the world market" and to export and import all types of armaments, military equipment, dual-use technology, and so forth. The decree charged the Ministry of Foreign Affairs with the task of aiding the new public corporation.[17]

Attempts to come to prominence at arms fairs in the Middle East and Southeast Asia were made in the course of 1993, in keeping with the new trends now in evidence. Defense Minister Pavel Grachev and other top-ranking military men made a number of foreign visits as part of this effort. However, they achieved next to nothing, mainly because of stiff opposition from Western rivals. Yet Russia's military did quite well in some other traditional areas, notably relations with certain countries that were committed to a socialist orientation and had once been important consumers of Soviet arms and military technology. The first in this group of nations is China, of course. Military contacts with it have been more intensive than diplomatic ones over the last eighteen months. Close defense links were established in 1992 through an exchange of visits by China's defense minister to Moscow (in August) and Vice Premier Aleksandr Shokhin (who was then responsible for Russia's arms trade) to Beijing (in November). The first major military technology agreement, a $1.8 billion deal, was signed later that year.[18] There was a succession of exchange visits by defense officials in 1993, culminating, in November, in the visit by Defense Minister Grachev to Beijing, where he signed a five-year accord (with secret clauses) on rather broad cooperation with China's Department of Defense. It was reported to provide, notably, for coproduction of some new items of military hardware. Further contacts were planned for 1994.[19]

One point discussed during the Vietnamese foreign minister's visit in October 1993 was the extension of the agreement allowing Russia to use the Cam Ranh Bay naval base beyond the year 2000, when it is due to expire.[20] There were also confidential Russian-Cuban talks in Moscow in November 1993, reportedly concerned with retaining the Russian radio-electronics center on the island and the submarine base at Cienfuegos and discussing Pavel Grachev's projected visit in 1994.[21] Parallel to this, the government of Russia decided to grant a $350 million credit to Cuba and to resume a direct sugar-to-oil swap, while Vice Premier Oleg Soskovets declared that Russia "regards Cuba as its next-door neighbor."[22] The conclusion one can make is that during the period under review the military has been active (along with the Ministry of Foreign Economic Relations) in pushing Russian arms (and, indirectly, influence) into external markets.

The Role of the Ministry of Foreign Affairs

As far as the Ministry of Foreign Affairs is concerned, it is not difficult to infer from all the foregoing that the ministry's position within the framework of the mechanism for formulating and implementing Russia's foreign policy has been rather unenviable. Originally, the ministry's top executives were still attempting to work out an independent foreign policy line. In doing so, they strove to draw on, among other things, the positive experience of the ministry's predecessor, notably in the practice of building up contacts through science. In February 1992 the ministry held a scientific conference on "A Remade Russia in a Remade World" that discussed the topical problems of Russia's revised foreign policy. It was then announced that the ministry was setting up a Foreign Relations Council, comprising sixty-one representatives of the scientific world and educational establishments, the press, members of parliament, the clergy, and the business community. The council, however, never developed into a scholarly laboratory capable of drafting anything like serious recommendations on foreign policy. Instead, it turned out to be a mixture of Brezhnevism and Khasbulatovism: the council's deliberations boiled down to hearing the "distinguished opinion" of the minister or his deputies, the bandying of words between the opposition-minded politicians and representatives and partisans of the pro-Yeltsin executive establishment, as happened at the sessions of the Supreme Soviet. As late as 27 November 1992, the council discussed the draft foreign policy concept (later formalized in April 1993 in the "Basic Provisions of the Concept of the Foreign Policy of the Russian Federation) that was to have been subsequently endorsed in the top echelons of power but which got lost in the jungle of the presidential headquarters. This document was of a rather formal and eclectic character, having collected everything there was to collect, including many comments from the opponents. In the end it remained unclear what this council's strategic foreign policy line was. It was quite obvious that it had been formulated by the ministry just to fend off the unending charges (in parliament and the press) that the ministry had no concept to speak of.

On balance, the general decrease in the level of professionalism in the Russian establishment afflicted the ministry as well. The contacts of the Russian Foreign Ministry with the scientific community that began to develop and gain ground in the Gorbachev-Shevardnadze era fell into decay. So did the system of preparation of experts' background briefs by the scientists and scholars of the Academy of Sciences, as well as the serious direct exchange of ideas in general. Either the ministry staff no longer needs scientific advice, or they are so eager to partake of the "public pie" as to have no time or desire left to care about science. Yet they readily attend international (especially overseas) scientific activities sponsored by foreign and Russian scientists and scholars.

Great damage to professionalism in politics has been done by the Yeltsin-Gorbachev duel. A large proportion of the highly skilled and competent intellectuals who worked in the Gorbachev period have actually found themselves out of business and elbowed aside by the pushy young parvenus who had made their way into the forefront under the slogans of "democratization" and "liberalization" (for all their glorious Komsomol and party record). Even if any official budding scientists or scholars do come to the ministry and other government institutions, their participation does little to foster professionalism, since they are quickly bureaucratized and lose contact with the institutions of the Academy of Sciences, thus being deprived of their "nutritional medium." The former system of "foreign policy-science" was advantageous because science was autonomous and could propagate fairly independent judgments. At this juncture, science is free to state absolutely independent judgments, but there is no more demand for them, a point of no mean importance, considering that early in 1994 scientists hit bottom in terms of pay rates among all of Russia's social groups.

By and large, the Ministry of Foreign Affairs has failed to thrash out a new independent foreign policy line. From the very outset it found itself constrained to tread in the old rut that had been made in the Gorbachev period. But, naturally, to demonstrate in any way possible the novelty and distinction of Russian foreign policy from the former federal policy of the Soviet Union, Kozyrev has set about more forcefully peddling old approaches, taking them occasionally beyond the limits of rationality and conformity with Russia's national interests as a body politic. It is not surprising, therefore, that the ministry soon came under scathing criticism from the Supreme Soviet and the vice president. Yet even the elimination of these two opponents from the scene did not greatly ease the ministry's lot. By this juncture, its contradictions with the army generals had already assumed a rather distinct character. There was an increasingly frequent divorce from other departments, and not only those we call power wielding. For instance, there was some friction with the neighboring Ministry of Foreign Economic Relations, which held to more statist positions. Nor did the situation change upon Sergei Glaz'ev's resignation. The new minister, Oleg Davydov, actually kept up and even intensified the former line.[23]

In the resulting situation, Foreign Minister Kozyrev had to defend himself by arguing that the Ministry of Foreign Affairs had no independent foreign policy and that it simply implements the policies of the president. What made this argument open to criticism was that the president himself had long since embraced, if unannounced, a policy of concessions to, and compromise arrangements with, the military and also with some civilian statists. Therefore, the ministry's leadership soon found itself facing a dilemma: either to go on obediently following the president's evolutionary line or to confront it openly, which would mean Kozyrev's unavoidable resignation, because it is the president who today is his only pillar of support in all power structures. The minister chose the former option and is now covering up his own gravitation toward statism by pressing for the banner of patriotism and nationalism to be recaptured from the "war party."

The Subsequent Evolution of Russia's Foreign Policy

The record of the past years has conclusively demonstrated the unpredictability of quick change in the domestic political situation and, accordingly, in Russia's foreign policy. In the turbulent periods of the dismantling of old social relations in so large and manifold a country, all possible zigzagging, sudden leaps, and abrupt rollbacks are inevitable. Nevertheless, on closer examination, one can trace certain trends and try to single out the main ones, at least, for the near future.

The major trend of domestic and foreign policy development, which had already made itself quite clear during 1993 (especially in its latter half) and, apparently, will be gaining ground (Yeltsin or no Yeltsin), is for the position of the statists to be strengthened and for authoritarianism to be enhanced. The weak and loose authoritarian rule of 1992–93 is being succeeded by a more consolidated and more homogeneous presidential rule, although this process is not yet quite over, mostly because of the president's own subjective qualities.

The enhancement of presidential rule has been going on in two ways. First, formally, thanks to the approval by a minority of the registered electorate, the new constitution has greatly enlarged the president's powers at the expense of parliament's, which, incidentally, had already been as good as hamstrung owing to predictable election returns. Divided into factions, none in actual leadership, intent on material welfare and privileges, engrossed in disabling infighting, the parliament has just no way of balancing out the president, thus leaving him free to rule by decree (and so making him capable, in fact, of turning this parliament, too, into a breeding ground of antipresidential forces).

Second, through a government reshuffle, the president brought under his direct control all the power-wielding ministries as well as national broadcasting and television. By the president's Decree on the Membership of the Security Council of the Russian Federation, in early February 1994, this body was rid of Egor Gaidar, Viktor Danilov-Danilian, Eduard Nechaev, and Boris Fedorov. It is mostly the power-wielding ministers who remained, along with the minister of foreign affairs.[24] That made it a more homogeneous and more "consolidated" agency. Besides, the president has at his disposal his "private guard" (the Kremlin regiment), an autonomous presidential security service and a special airborne regiment made up of the units brought in early October 1993 to break up the parliament, with a communications unit in Moscow's Skol'niki district used as its staging camp.[25]

In short, the events of early October 1993 brought out what a careful observer saw perfectly well even before: Yeltsin increasingly had to fall back on the military and his staff, not on legitimate electoral support. This recourse contributed toward building up the army's influence in domestic and foreign affairs as well as strengthening its alliance with the ruling segment of the economic nomenklatura. The latter circumstance has become particularly noticeable since November 1993 and has gone far toward reducing the chances of an armed coup. Significantly enough, Defense Minister Grachev, replying to a suggestion that the new parliament might want to amend the military doctrine, said, "We'll amend the parliament." And later on, while briefing the press on this doctrine, he specified that it would not be brought before the Federal Assembly at all.[26] The monopoly-like public corporation, Rosvooruzhenie, provides a clear case of enhanced cooperation of the military leadership with the economic nomenklatura. This organization was set up in conjunction with the Ministry of Defense (Lieutenant General Viktor Samoilov) on the initiative of two vice premiers, Vladimir Shumeiko and Oleg Soskovets, while its control was left, pursuant to the president's decree, to his security service under Aleksandr Korzhakov.[27]

What keeps the military and the economic nomenklatura united, apart from their common material interest, is the fundamental affinity of their geopolitical approaches and their joint interest in building up the framework of a common military and economic space involving the greatest possible number of newly independent states (neoimperial ambitions). Gaidar and Burbulis, however, had all along professed the idea of "Russia first!" which, as it took effect, led not only to the breakup of the Soviet Union in December 1991 but to the actual disintegration of the CIS, which progressed throughout the whole of 1992. This contradiction does not divide the military and the government dominated by the economic nomenklatura. Accordingly, there are mounting integration trends within the CIS (Belarus was the first big swallow), while the very makeup of the CIS is expanding by admitting new members (Azerbaijan, Georgia, Moldova, and perhaps others before long).

Premier Viktor Chernomyrdin's increased independence and political activity have become an important factor in the growing authoritarianism of the regime and change of accents in foreign policy. On the one hand, the government reshuffling seemed to have limited the scope of his competence to purely economic matters. On the other hand, the resulting consolidation of the government and the strengthening of Chernomyrdin's control of it have made him politically strong, too. He has, as a matter of fact, already begun to express the interests of both civilian and military statists, and not only those of Russia but also those of some other newly independent states where the nomenklatura is firmly in power. Now the policy he carries on in support of major emergent industrial corporations assures bureaucratic state capitalism the role of the leading sector in Russia's mixed economy in the making.[28] It is difficult to judge today whether Chernomyrdin will make a Russian "Iron Chancellor." As some scholars and politicians note, there is not complete unanimity between Chernomyrdin and Yeltsin. There is, besides, the problem of a "court cabal," which destroyed Petr A. Stolypin at the turn of the century. The modern-day cabal, however, has no roots reaching as deep into the bedrock of Russian life as it did under Nicholas II. The times, too, are different. There are indeed some contradictions between Yeltsin and Chernomyrdin, but are they that deep? When accepting Gaidar's resignation, Yeltsin declared, "The policy of reform will be continued, proceeding from the democratic principles lying at the root of the new Russian Constitution and considering, above all, Russia's strategic interests."[29] This statement is quite in accord with Chernomyrdin's position and numerous comments of recent times.

As stated earlier, the new internal political trends led to a major shift in foreign policy and the ending of the honeymoon in the Russia–West (including the Russia–United States) relationship. What is setting in is a period of the "family daily round," which will have—indeed, already has—sorrows and quarrels, not just joys in it. The latter-day rulers in Moscow are of no mind to seek any impairment of this relationship either now or in the future. But the main accent will still be made, after all, not on a far-fetched equal partnership with the seven leading economic powers (Gaidar), nor on a natural alliance with them (Kozyrev), but on the championship, above all, of Russia's own national interests, which do not in every single case coincide with the interests of the other powers, whether great or not so great.

These new accents have already appeared in the statements and acts of Russia's top leaders. In the area of foreign economic relations there is, in fact, first, a departure from the former Gaidarian approach, which was characterized by excessive reliance on financial support from the G–7 and international financial institutions; second, repudiation of liberal romanticism and illusions about Russia's economic interface with the West; and third, renunciation of the course that to secure the IMF-recommended financial stabilization meant undoing the potential of a postindustrial technology that had taken decades to build up. New accents have appeared, notably, in Chernomyrdin's capture of the initiative in foreign contacts and in his more frequent foreign visits (to the United States, Italy, Switzerland, etc.), all keynoted by the argument that Russia needs no help. Russia is a great power seeking economic cooperation on equal terms. Finally, the new accents have also shown themselves in enhanced protectionism in favor of the system of bureaucratic state capitalism (which is still in the making) against the excessive openness of the economy[30] and in the increased aggressiveness of the government's export policy.[31]

The change of approach in the area of foreign affairs and diplomacy has been so substantial as to allow one today to speak of a new, different Kozyrev, Kozyrev the statist, or, at least, half-statist (granting that we do witness a bifurcation of personality or a divorce between one's inner ambitions and enforced official stance). Suffice it to recall his statements about the necessity of upholding Russia's interests in the newly independent states, even by force of arms, and the possible delay in pulling troops out of the Baltics (considering the violations of the rights of the Russian-speaking population there); the desire (to his chagrin) of the countries of Eastern Europe to join NATO; and the threat by the Ministry of Foreign Affairs to use the right of veto in the UN Security Council over sanctions against Libya. All these problems may provoke or have already provoked certain annoyance in relations between the United States and Russia.

In fact, there have been some elements of ambiguity and insincerity in the personal relationship between the presidents of the two countries. President Clinton had taken at face value Yeltsin's assurances about presidential elections in the summer of 1994, but then Yeltsin lightly went back on his promise as early as October 1993 during his visit to Tokyo (and later on did so again). In his turn, Clinton, in every way demonstrating his friendship and support for Yeltsin, nevertheless failed to invite him to the Seattle summit of the Asia-Pacific Economic Cooperation.[32] Yeltsin repaid in the same coin. During Clinton's visit to Moscow there was a spectacular show of keeping radical liberals in the government, which, once the U.S. president was gone, was followed up by just as spectacular a show of ejecting Gaidar and those like him out of the government. In short, there are further tests for Russian-American relations to undergo, and only time will tell how well these two great powers will pass them.

Thus, all the attempts of Russian liberals and radical democrats to hold power, undertake liberal reforms by means of "shock therapy," and thereby turn Russia into a Western-type democracy have actually failed. Starting with the second half of 1993, and especially after January 1994, statists, representing the interests of the economic nomenklatura and "great power" national-patriotic forces, have been gradually but steadily gaining control over the state. This has led to a certain shift in the country's foreign policy. The period of "liberal romanticism" is over. Principally new trends in Russia's relations with former union republics, as well as with the countries of the so-called far abroad, have emerged.

Along with the resignation of Gaidar and his adherents, the "Russia above all" idea, being interpreted in the spirit of Russia's deliverance from the "colonial burden" of the former union republics, has faded. Instead, the president, the premier, and the minister of foreign affairs have been more and more firmly expressing the ideas of Russia's special interests on the territory of the former USSR. Russia's role as a nucleus of integration processes has substantially increased. These processes have been advanced through military-political means (agreements on Russian military bases in the former union republics, for example), but also with economic levers (particularly, energy resources and the Russian ruble).

As far as relations with the "far abroad" are concerned, Russia has started to demonstrate its unwillingness to unconditionally support the decisions and actions of the West. Unrealizable hopes for large-scale Western aid, as well as the illusions of a "natural alliance" and equal partnership within the G–7 and NATO, have been substituted by statements about Russia's capability of carrying out its reforms with its own energy and taking into account its national qualities, as well as emphasizing its independent foreign policy and determination to maintain national interests as a great power. Russia's role in settling regional conflicts (Bosnia, the Middle East) has become more active, its foreign economic policy has become more "aggressive" (including arms trade), and economic cooperation with a number of the former major partners of the USSR (though mainly on a commercial basis) has started to resume.

These new trends are most likely to dominate in the coming period. The only question is, will Russia's leadership be able to keep the country's policy within the range of "common," peaceful, and positive "great powerness" and avoid relapses into the confrontational atmosphere of the Cold War era? This to a great extent will depend on the reactions of the West, primarily the United States.

Notes

1. In the history of emerging capitalism, the state always defended the interests of the new entrepreneurial class with all kinds of protectionist measures. Russia is no exception. Of course, the economic nomenklatura is not entirely homogeneous and coherent. A numerically insignificant part of it consists of new financial groupings preoccupied predominantly with nonproductive speculative activities (as we say in Russia, making money from nothing or from air). Contradictions between the financial and industrial nomenklaturas are of strategic importance: the dominance of the financial group would mean substantial destruction of Russia's scientific-technological potential and inevitable dependence on more advanced countries. With the defeat of the Gaidar-Fedorov group, the influence of the financial nomenklatura is doomed to decline.

2. That is, the process of the negotiations between Mikhail Gorbachev and the other leaders of the former Soviet republics on an updated union. The process is named after the place near Moscow where the negotiations proceeded.

3. *Moskovskie novosti*, 4 April 1993.

4. See *Kommersant*, no. 32 (8–10 August 1992). In August 1991 Yeltsin told Kuzbass workers, "Maybe there was a time when it was necessary to help Central Asia and other republics get on their feet, but now we see that they are more steady on their feet than Russia." See *Journal of Soviet Nationalities*, vol. 1, no. 2 (1990), p. 67.

5. See *New York Times* (Russian ed.), 30 March–12 April 1993. But the point was precisely that adequate Western aid to the former Soviet Union was not coming and Russia was, for all practical purposes, the major source of assistance. According to International Monetary Fund data, the former Soviet Union in 1992 received $17 billion from Russia (technical credits and subsidies). *Segodnia*, 25 May 1993.

6. *Izvestiia*, 17 February 1994.

7. See A. Kozyrev, interview, *Moskovskie novosti*, 25 October 1992.

8. Starting in 1963 the author was frequently invited by the International Department of the Central Committee to carry out such assignments. In addition, at the request of the Ministry of Foreign Affairs of the USSR, he participated as an expert in the work of the twenty-seven-nation UN group on the 1980–81 Disarmament and Development Project and accompanied various official delegations to international conferences as a consultant.

9. It was rather uncommon in the light of preceding practice, for example, for the Gorbachev staff to decide in October 1989 to send this author to Angola to make President José Eduardo dos Santos and his Politburo see the futility of the socialist orientation.

10. *Moskovskie novosti*, 8 December 1993. Along with the principal members of the Security Council, this body embraces several interdepartmental commissions (on foreign policy, conversion, etc.) and the Scientific Council.

11. Here is only one of many proofs of this statement: From the very beginning of 1992 Yeltsin relied heavily on the Foreign Ministry's pro-Western policy. But after strong criticism from many different quarters of society, he responded in October 1992 with his similarly critical speech in the ministry, the result of which was a few high-level visits to Asian countries.

12. Gennadii Burbulis, former deputy prime minister, now coordinator of the party Russia's Choice; Iurii Petrov, former Yeltsin chief of staff, now head of the State Investment Corporation; Viktor Iliushin, head of the presidential administration; Mikhail Poltoranin, former information center chief, now head of the Information Policy and

Communications Committee; Mikhail Malei, resigned October 1993 as Yeltsin'a advisor on defense industry affairs, now chairman of the Interdepartmental Commission on Conversion, Security Council; Aleksandr Kotenkov, former head of the president's State Legal Affairs Administration; Andrei Makarov, former head of the Administration for Securing the Activities of the Joint Commission for Combating Crime and Corruption; Major General Aleksandr Korzhakov, Yeltsin's bodyguard, now head of the Presidential Security Service.

13. *U.S. News and World Report*, 4 October 1993, p. 33.

14. *Izvestiia*, 22 October 1994.

15. "World Armaments and Disarmaments," *SIPRI Yearbook 1992* (New York: Oxford University Press, 1992), p. 271.

16. *MN Business* (Moscow), 14 November 1993.

17. *Moskovskie novosti*, 19 December 1993.

18. *Izvestiia*, 6 November 1993.

19. *Izvestiia*, 9, 11, 12 November 1993.

20. *Kommersant Daily*, 30 October 1993.

21. *Izvestiia*, 30 November 1993.

22. *Izvestiia*, 23, 24 December 1993.

23. While Kozyrev supported the Western resolution on a Libyan embargo at the UN Security Council, Oleg Davydov, soon after his appointment in October 1993, led an official delegation to Libya to discuss, among other things, prospective economic cooperation, the establishment of Libyan companies to make investments in Russia, and further joint venturing. *Izvestiia*, 17 November 1993.

24. *Izvestiia*, 2 February 1994.

25. *Moskovskie novosti*, 21 November 1993.

26. Ibid.

27. *Moskovskie novosti*, 19 December 1993; *Komsomol'skaia pravda*, 23 December 1993.

28. In November 1993 Oleg Soskovets brought off a reorganization of the Council on Industrial Policy, enlarging its makeup 4.5 times by admitting top executives of ministries and departments, industry-crediting banks, and enterprise chiefs. The chairman of the council, V. Kadannikov, known to have supported Gaidar, has been replaced by M. Yuriev, a young force of the "managerial corps." *Izvestiia*, 9 November 1993.

29. *Izvestiia*, 18 January 1994.

30. In November 1993, for example, a presidential decree limited the activities of a number of foreign banks in Russia. *Izvestiia*, 20 November 1993.

31. One case in point is Gasprom's recent confrontation with its German partners, which ended in a revision of prices in Russia's favor. *Izvestiia*, 21 January 1994. Another one is the agreement signed by Gasprom on the construction of a gas pipeline in Serbia. *Izvestiia*, 23 December 1993.

32. The refusal to admit Russia to this organization was motivated essentially by the argument that Russia was not a significant economic power in the Asia-Pacific region. Yet they did admit, in Seattle, so "significant" a country as Papua-New Guinea and voted to suspend the admission of new members for three years or more.

3

Structure, Institutions, and Process

Russia's Changing Foreign Policy

Jeffrey Checkel

> *I tell Yeltsin and I tell you, a prime minister must have*
> *elementary power, not just ideas.*
> —Arkadii Vol'skii
>
> *I voted for [Russian Prime Minister] Chernomyrdin*
> *with both hands. . . . I'm sure Gaidar is clever, but theory*
> *must be correlated with practice.*
> —A local industrial manager in Russia[1]

These sentiments, while addressing the domestic political scene in post-Soviet Russia, find striking parallels in the foreign policy arena, where many also feel that "ideas" and "theory" have gotten ahead of "practice" and "power" considerations. Indeed, "new political thinking," the set of liberal ideas that informed Soviet foreign policy under Gorbachev, has come under withering attack from a number of quarters. This chapter sets the current developments in a broader perspective. I begin by establishing a baseline for measuring the recent changes and argue on institutional grounds that Western expectations for a continuing liberal foreign policy in post-Soviet Russia were unrealistic.

Next, I turn to the period since late 1991, arguing that Russian foreign policy formulation has been profoundly influenced by a series of international structural and domestic institutional changes. The result, in the near term, has been a "turn to the right" in Russian policy. Over the longer term, however, a continuation of this trend is not a foregone conclusion. Much will depend on events outside Russia, especially in the Soviet successor states. A less noticed determinant of future Russian behavior is the degree to which its domestic polity becomes further entangled in the institutions and actors of the contemporary global political economy.

My approach, which is broadly comparative, has two dimensions. One is longitudinal: I consider Soviet/Russian policy over time. A second is more cross-national in nature: I utilize concepts first developed in the comparative politics and international relations literatures to examine more systematically "the sources of Russian conduct" in the post-Soviet era.

Soviet Russia

Where has the new thinking gone? The buzzwords of the Gorbachev era—"interdependence," "mutual security," and the like—have been replaced, at least in Western analyses, with dark forebodings of a new "muscular," "neoimperial," and "nationalist" Russian foreign policy.[2] Implicit in many of these reports is a belief that the foreign policy changes of the Gorbachev era were destined to continue, albeit in modified form, in the new Russia. In other words, the baseline for evaluating the present is the Gorbachev years. This is indeed the correct baseline, but it can be used properly only if one understands the structure of foreign policy making in the former USSR, and how this influenced the process of change.

The nature of Soviet political institutions was such that decision-making elites were insulated and access to the process was highly restricted. The Soviet state, in other words, was autonomous and "strong"; organizations within it were not terribly permeable to broader societal influences. In addition, foreign policy formulation was centralized in the "executive branch," primarily the apparatus of the Communist Party Central Committee (Secretariat and departments) and Politburo.[3]

This particular set of institutional parameters structured foreign policy formulation in important ways and deeply affected the manner in which change could occur. Certain beliefs about international politics, for example, had taken root in influential and insulated agencies.[4] This was particularly true of the Ministry of Defense and the Central Committee's International Department. The ministry, which had a very important role in the formation of national security policy, saw international politics primarily as a zero-sum affair and emphasized a narrow definition of national security, giving primacy to military instruments. It had, in other words, a pessimistic, Hobbesian vision of the world.[5]

The International Department, which oversaw key aspects of Soviet Third World policy, also viewed politics in starkly zero-sum terms and, in addition, placed extraordinary emphasis on the class-based nature of the international system. Two true believers in Soviet ideology—Mikhail Suslov and Boris Ponomarev—had overseen this unit since the early 1960s and deeply influenced its development.[6]

The point to emphasize is that key avenues for bringing change to Soviet politics were blocked by these dominant ideologies. Soviet state interests, as articulated by top political leaders, seemed heavily influenced by this balance-of-power, Soviet Marxist vision of the international arena.[7]

If the Soviet state was so strong and these ideas were so powerfully entrenched, then an obvious question needs to be answered: How did change ever come about? After all, both in the late 1960s and, especially, in the mid-1980s, elite beliefs and foreign policy behavior did change in important ways. The answer is that political leaders reached out and around these strong state organizations for new ideas and expertise.[8]

This "end-around" strategy, as it might be called, was successful precisely because of the extraordinarily centralized nature of foreign policy decision making. While this made it difficult for new ideas to reach the top and influence the direction of change, their consolidation, once there, was easier because elites controlled key instruments for disseminating them. The likelihood of foreign policy change was mediated, in other words, by institutional context.[9]

The last point is worth addressing in greater detail, especially for the Gorbachev period. Foreign policy decision making under Gorbachev remained highly centralized until 1989–90, first in the Politburo and Central Committee apparatus and later in the presidential staff. The continuing strength of the Soviet state, at least in this area, created certain incentives for elites as they attempted to consolidate a radically new approach in foreign policy.

Indeed, in executing their end-around strategy, Gorbachev and his allies utilized a number of tried-and-true mechanisms of Soviet politics. These included centrally supported press campaigns to promote the new thinking in its formative years (1986–87), a very clear effort to mobilize the Soviet academic community in support of it, and the use of appointment powers to place supporters of the new approach in key party/state positions (Dobrynin as International Department head, Shevardnadze as foreign minister, Yakovlev and Primakov as key foreign policy advisors, to name just a few).

During the early Gorbachev years (1985–88), this strategy worked. The new political thinking had a very far-reaching impact on Soviet international behavior and did much to insure that the Cold War came to an unexpected and peaceful end. By 1990–91, and especially in the post-Soviet period, however, such a strategy became increasingly problematic as the institutional logic behind it began to change. In the centralized Soviet state, with numerous resources and controls at their disposal, Gorbachev and his allies had few incentives to institutionalize this new approach to foreign affairs. Yet institutionalization is necessary if policy change is to endure and remain influential after its initial sponsor(s) leaves office.

The process of institutionalization takes place in two ways. In the near term, it often occurs through organizations, as new ones are created or existing agencies are revamped. While the latter is difficult (due to the well-known problem of organizational inertia), it is possible and occurs through a combination of enlightened leadership, changes in hiring and promotion practices, and the inculcation of a new organizational ethos or ideology (through training procedures and publications). Over the longer term, institutionalization denotes a process whereby earlier changes influence the very terms of societal discourse/debate, the interests of relevant political actors, and the normative/legal context of policy formulation.[10]

In Gorbachev's USSR, the Foreign Ministry under Shevardnadze was the most likely target for a near-term strategy of institutionalization. Yet there is little evidence that Gorbachev or Shevardnadze attempted to translate the latter's personal authority as an advocate of the new thinking into an enduring institutional ethos. Shevardnadze did not carry out the sort of personnel and structural reforms at the ministry that would have been necessary to make it a forceful advocate of the new approach in foreign policy. This lack of a bureaucratic home within the state meant the new thinking fared poorly as time progressed.[11]

Not surprisingly, then, once the centralized institutions of the Soviet state and the personal advocates of radical change in foreign policy were both swept aside in December 1991, the new thinking would become only one of several competing foreign policy strategies for the "new" Russian state. As I argue below, this shift away from a liberal foreign policy demonstrates how institutional change can radically alter the context of policy formulation in transition states such as post-Soviet Russia.

Foreign Policy Formulation in Post-Soviet Russia

My analysis proceeds in four stages. I begin with an overview of the changes in Russian policy making and actions during 1992–94. The next three sections place these changes in context. First, I examine the new international structures within which Russia finds itself. My purpose is both to consider their likely influence on any state in Russia's position and to explore the constraints, incentives, and opportunities this setting creates for domestic political actors engaged in Russian foreign policy. This new environment, I argue, would have produced a hardening of Russian policy no matter who had succeeded the Soviet/Gorbachev leadership.

Second, I consider the changing institutional context, arguing that decentralization, along with the inability of the Yeltsin government to exercise leadership and build state capacity, has contributed to the politicizing of foreign policy decision making. As a result, foreign policy has become hostage to domestic politics in ways inconceivable during the Soviet era. With the rise of conservative and nationalist opposition to the Yeltsin reforms, this new domestic political context has further promoted a conservative turn in Russian foreign behavior.

Finally, I return to the international level and explore how a different set of factors may affect Russian policy formulation and constrain its behavior in future years. Here, I examine the degree to which its domestic polity is becoming entangled in the institutions and actors of the contemporary global political economy and argue that this transnational context will play an increasingly important role in shaping Russia's behavior if it manages to continue along the dual roads of market and democratic reforms.

Overview

The early post-Soviet years have seen a considerable weakening of political institutions in Russia. This should have three important effects on foreign policy formulation. First, in this newly decentralized environment, it will be easier for foreign policy ideas (liberal or conservative) to reach key elites; however, their eventual implementation and consolidation will be less likely. Second, individual proponents of change ("policy entrepreneurs") will find their comparative advantage diminishing relative to their position in a stronger state. Finally, politics will matter more in the making of foreign policy, as top elites are less insulated from various societal pressures and other parts of the state apparatus.

Evidence from post-Soviet Russia provides backing for these predictions. For one, it is quite clear that a rather broad array of foreign policy ideas has been reaching key elites, especially President Yeltsin. Indeed, Yeltsin's own thinking on international politics has come to resemble an unusual (and, it would seem, incompatible) mixture of neoliberal institutionalism and realism. The former, with its stress on a rather benign international environment and the use of international institutions to mitigate the effects of anarchy, clearly informs Yeltsin's policies on relations with the industrialized West.

The latter, with its focus on a threatening security environment and (potential) use of military instruments, has increasingly come to dominate policy and elite commentary regarding the former Soviet republics. While such a combination of liberal and realist foreign policies may be of interest to theorists, it is highly questionable that it can form the basis for a coherent Russian policy.[12]

In addition, there is clear evidence that individual agents of foreign policy change, or policy entrepreneurs, are presently less influential than they were in the authoritarian Soviet state, where elites were relatively insulated from broader societal and bureaucratic forces. The problem for such entrepreneurs in post-Soviet Russia is that they find themselves competing with a growing number of organizations and forces for the attention of key decision makers.[13]

The behavior of Russian Foreign Minister Andrei Kozyrev is a case in point. In 1991–93, he was clearly a man with a "solution looking for a problem," that is, a policy entrepreneur. The solution that he forcefully advanced was that post-Soviet Russia could best protect its state interests by closely aligning itself with the institutions and policies of the industrialized democracies. His "problem" was the breakup of the USSR in December 1991. Seizing this opportunity, Kozyrev aggressively promoted his neoliberal vision during the first half of 1992 and clearly had some influence on Yeltsin's thinking.

Beginning in the summer of 1992, however, other entrepreneurs and organizations began a quite open competition with Kozyrev over defining Russia's new state interests. Their "problem" was created primarily by the Russian Federation's increasingly troubled relations with the former Soviet republics. Pointing to this threatening environment, they argued for a definition of state interests that paid much greater attention to traditional geopolitics.

Both Yeltsin's more recent commentary as well as the official statement of Russian state interests—the revised "Basic Provisions of the Concept of the Foreign Policy of the Russian Federation" released in early 1993—reflect the influence of ideas from these various sources. Thus, in post-Soviet Russia the difficulty faced by promoters of foreign policy change is not getting access to the top (as it was in the USSR); rather, it is to insure that their proposals, once they reach elites, have some lasting influence on policy. From an institutional perspective, this is precisely what one would expect.[14]

Finally, the importance of politics and coalition building has increased as the strength of the Soviet/Russian state has declined. Indeed, it is not simply a competition among different ideas that explains the mixture of liberal and realist principles in more recent elite commentary and Russian foreign policy behavior. It is also that Yeltsin is engaged in a very complicated coalition-building process as he seeks support for his government and its policies.

This process has mandated that he make concessions to the views of other influential actors, such as the Supreme Soviet/Duma, Russian military, and, more recently, nationalist political groupings—all of which have expressed much more conservative opinions on a range of foreign policy issues. As one former government minister put it, "Political realities force Yeltsin to do some things that are not always explainable or easily accepted."[15]

With this overview in hand, I turn to the details of the Russian case, exploring the international contexts and institutional dynamics affecting its process and policies.

International Environment

Structural or neorealist theories argue that state interests and behavior can be inferred from a country's position in the international system. Such approaches have rightly been criticized in recent years on a number of grounds, including their inability to explain change in international politics and lack of specificity.[16]

Yet if used with care, structural approaches may offer important insights on the foreign behavior of a state situated such as the Russian Federation. Structuralists emphasize the impact of anarchy on state behavior, how it leads states to build up their military forces and act assertively in a "self-help" international system.

Of course, as many have noted, anarchy does not seem to be an accurate depiction of the present international system. Where states are tied together by shared values, economic ties, and international institutions, the effects of anarchy are mitigated and the structural logic does not obtain. Such a situation currently holds among the industrialized democracies. At the same time, where countries do not share common values and norms, economic linkages are poorly developed, and international organizations are ineffective, the structural logic may be much more relevant.[17]

It is precisely the latter situation that describes a critically important aspect of Russia's new international environment: the successor states to the USSR or, as Russians prefer, the "near abroad." Do the countries of the Commonwealth of Independent States (CIS) share a common commitment to market economics and pluralist democracy? Are they tied together by the sorts of economic relationships typical among the industrial democracies? Is the CIS an effective international institution, one with a strong bureaucratic infrastructure, clear rules, and agreed-upon sanction mechanisms? In all cases, the answer is "no."

This structural context creates powerful incentives for Russia to act more forcefully and fill any incipient power vacuums. Indeed, given the presence of a militarily strong neighbor (Ukraine) and the anarchy and conflict evident elsewhere in the CIS (the Transcaucasus and Tajikistan), it would have been surprising not to see Russia reassert a more dominant role in the former Soviet area. Put more bluntly, great powers often carve out spheres of influence. One need not know anything about Russia's leaders, changing political institutions, or the differing ideas in play to have predicted such an outcome.

In both Russia and the West, the preferences of even liberally oriented politicians seem partly shaped by this structural dynamic. President Yeltsin, for example, has argued on more than one occasion that "geopolitics" force Russia to maintain a strong presence in Eurasia. Foreign Minister Kozyrev has noted the "power vacuum" surrounding Russia and the incentives this creates for states to intervene in the former Soviet area. During a January 1994 visit to Moscow, U.S. President Bill Clinton employed similar logic, noting that "you [Russia] will be more likely to be involved in some of these areas near you, just like the United States has been involved in the last several years in Panama and Grenada and other places near our area."[18]

Up to this point, I have "black boxed" the state in the structural/neorealist tradition, assuming it to be a unitary actor responding to international stimuli. If one rejects this assumption, it becomes necessary to explore how the international environment creates incentives and opportunities for specific groups and actors involved in policy making. Proponents of this approach ("second image reversed," as it is often called) typically argue that over the longer term a country's position in the global political and economic order directly influences the institutions and domestic interests that evolve within it. At particular critical junctures, however, these international influences can decisively reshape current politics as domestic actors seize upon external events to promote their preferred policy options.[19]

This dynamic is especially relevant for explaining some part of the conservative turn in Russian foreign policy over the course of 1993. Organizations (the Ministry of Defense), political groupings (Zhirinovsky's Liberal Democratic Party), and influential individuals (Sergei Karaganov of the Institute of Europe; Evgenii Ambartsumov of the now-disbanded Supreme Soviet) all have pointed to one particular aspect of Russia's new international environment—the near abroad—to promote a more assertive foreign policy.

Two comments are in order at this point. First, my analysis should not be read as an apology for Russian behavior. Rather, its purpose has been to explore the international context shaping the conduct of Russia's policy. This radically changed international environment, and the weakly institutionalized basis of new thinking in Gorbachev's USSR have combined to "stack the deck" against the continuation of a liberal foreign policy.

Second, while this structural level predicts general patterns of behavior (a reassertion of Russian influence in the former Soviet region), it leaves important questions unanswered. How will this influence be reasserted? Through what mechanisms? To address such questions, it is necessary to explore the domestic level in much greater detail—a task to which I now turn.

Institutional Change

My analysis has two parts. I begin by examining institutional change in post-Soviet Russia and its effect on foreign policy formulation, as well as particular organizations involved in the process. These changes are illuminated by exploring the debate over Russia's "new" state interests that took place over much of 1991–93. Next, I consider how a failure of political leadership by the Yeltsin government has further politicized the foreign policy process and weakened the capacity of the Russian state in this critical issue area.

Beginning with the institutional context, the striking thing is the significant degree of change in a relatively short time. First, access to decision makers is increasing. Indeed, a complaint one hears in the Moscow policy community is that too many people have access to policy makers such as Yeltsin and Kozyrev (and their respective staffs). Personal ties, then, are still key; however, there are many more of them.

This state of affairs has angered some of those privileged by their access under the Soviet system. Georgii Arbatov, one of those with direct ties to top decision makers under Brezhnev as well as Gorbachev, has complained of the confusion resulting from this enhanced access. However, younger researchers at Moscow think tanks, who were not privileged under the old system, marvel at the contact they have with policy makers today. Of course, access does not automatically translate into influence. Indeed, while the former has increased, the direct influence of individual academics on policy may well have decreased as their proposals compete with many others in a more decentralized environment.[20]

Second, the foreign policy process is becoming less centralized. This is seen most dramatically in the significant role the Supreme Soviet created for itself during 1992–93. It regularly demanded that Kozyrev report to it on various issues, sent fact-finding missions to Serbia (among other places), and attempted to subject the defense and foreign ministers to parliamentary confirmation. Of course, this assertiveness by the Supreme Soviet on questions of foreign policy was just one manifestation of a much larger debate over the division of powers between the executive and legislative branches.[21]

These broader institutional changes have made the coordination of foreign policy making much more difficult. Yeltsin and Kozyrev have bemoaned this fact, and the Russian press has carried a number of articles on the topic. Russian policy making, it would appear, is becoming more like that found in the United States, where there are multiple access points to the process and power/authority is dispersed.[22]

Such a comparison may have been valid as of late 1992, but events since then paint a somewhat different picture. Indeed, a clear trend toward recentralization was evident throughout 1993. In the first months after the collapse of the USSR, Yeltsin, Gennadii Burbulis (Yeltsin's closest advisor at that point), and Kozyrev had argued in favor of decentralization—with the Foreign Ministry playing a much greater role than before in the formulation and implementation of Russian policy. Given the Soviet historical context, where virtually all foreign policy decision making was centralized in the Central Committee and, later, the presidential apparatus, such a move would indeed have signaled an important change.[23]

Over the course of late 1992 and 1993, however, this trend was moderated if not reversed. The first change came in November 1992, when Yeltsin decreed that the Foreign Ministry coordinate the work of all governmental ministries in the sphere of foreign policy. This was less a victory for the Foreign Ministry in its battle to play a more prominent role in policy making than a recognition on Yeltsin's part that his government was speaking with too many voices on key foreign policy issues.[24]

Throughout 1993, there were further signs of recentralization. In particular, Yeltsin sought more direct, personal control over foreign policy by vesting the newly created Russian Security Council with the coordinating role previously accorded to the Foreign Ministry. The Security Council, which has grown in size to include a number of "interdepartmental committees" coordinating various aspects of foreign (and domestic) policy, is part of the presidential apparatus and under Yeltsin's direct supervision.[25]

Events in the fall of 1993 furthered this move toward recentralization. The violent dissolution of the Supreme Soviet, its replacement by a considerably weakened legislature, and the promulgation and adoption of a new, executive-centered constitution all point to a clear desire for a more centralized policy process. While these changes will have their greatest effect on domestic policy formulation, they could also lead to a more coherent Russian foreign policy than was the case throughout most of 1992–93.[26]

The pattern of decentralization/recentralization over the course of 1991–93 suggests the "stickiness" of historically constructed institutions. Recent months have in fact seen a partial restoration of the direct executive oversight of foreign policy that was a hallmark of both the tsarist and Soviet eras.[27]

These broader institutional changes have deeply affected the bureaucratic politics of Russian foreign policy making. While such processes were at work throughout the Soviet era (and especially in the post-Stalin period), their influence on policy was limited by the central control exercised by key decision-making elites. This has now changed in a dramatic way.[28]

Of special importance is the death of one particular organization: the CPSU and its associated apparatus. Its deeply embedded ideology, which emphasized class conflict and a zero-sum view of international politics, has lost the bureaucratic platform that so greatly enhanced its influence on policy. Indeed, former CPSU officials, current policy makers, and scholars are unanimous in stressing the pivotal importance of this fact; they all feel that a broad ideational constraint on policy making has been lifted.[29]

The removal of this constraint, along with the weakening of central control, has clearly motivated the surviving bureaucratic players to seek an enhanced role in foreign policy formulation. As was the case in the Soviet era, two of the key players are the Ministry of Foreign Affairs and the Ministry of Defense. In important ways, both organizations are continuations of their Soviet counterparts; thus, to understand their current behavior a brief look back is necessary.

Historically, the Foreign Ministry was a less insulated organization than the military. This difference arose in part because the ministry's role dictated that it have a greater amount of international contact (in various negotiating forums and embassies) than the Defense Ministry. These contacts increased, slowly but steadily, over the past twenty-five years as the USSR sought greater interaction with its international political, security, and economic environments. The degree of insulation had an important bearing on the extent to which ideologies had become embedded in each organization.

During the Soviet era, a particular ideology of international affairs had taken root at the Defense Ministry. This organizational ethos appears to have survived the Soviet–Russian transition more or less intact. The Russian Defense Ministry's organizational structure is similar to its Soviet counterpart, and includes the all-important General Staff system that did so much to instill a sense of corporate identity in the military during the Soviet era. In terms of worldview, the Russian Ministry of Defense continues to stress a threatening external security environment and the importance of military instruments (for example, in ensuring the safety of Russian minority populations in the former Soviet republics). It is also developing a military doctrine that overlaps significantly with doctrine of the Soviet era.[30]

The situation at the Foreign Ministry is different. Here, the lower degree of insulation seems to have left a less ideologically determined legacy. This in turn left greater room for leadership, with Foreign Minister Kozyrev introducing, in the early post-Soviet years, a number of changes designed to give his ministry the resources, information, and expertise to be a full-fledged participant in policy making. Most important, the ministry acted to increase its access to new ideas. In a break with past practice, several of Kozyrev's early appointees as deputy foreign ministers had academic backgrounds. In addition, the ministry created a Foreign Policy Council. Both the new appointees and the council were purposely designed to bring new blood into the ministry.[31]

Beyond these domestic sources, the ministry also sought expertise and advice from abroad. A special unit modeled on the U.S. State Department's Policy Planning Department was established with precisely such a purpose. It held workshops with several German research institutes and at least three American universities (George Washington, Harvard's Kennedy School, and the National Defense University).[32]

In addition, Foreign Minister Kozyrev invested a great personal stake in articulating for the ministry and Russia a new, liberal ideology of international politics. He sees the present international system as fundamentally different from that which existed in either the tsarist or Soviet periods. It is a system where the majority of great powers are united by a common system of values centered on market economics and political pluralism, and where status is defined most importantly by levels of scientific-technical progress and a country's position in world markets.

Moreover, growing ties of economic interdependence have led to a situation where interstate relations are no longer a zero-sum game. As the foreign minister likes to say, "the better off my neighbor is, the better off I am." Indeed, Kozyrev's bottom line is that "no developed, democratic, civil society . . . can threaten us."[33]

The foreign minister also sees international institutions as playing an important role in world politics. This should come as no surprise, since Kozyrev worked for sixteen years (1974–90) in the Directorate of International Organizations at the Soviet Foreign Ministry.[34] Such institutions, he suggests, can have their greatest effect in those regions where countries are not joined together by shared norms and values. Kozyrev thus stresses the role they can play in resolving conflicts within and between the former Soviet republics.[35]

The effect of these various institutional/organizational changes on policy making is clearly seen in the debate over Russia's state interests that took place over much of 1991–93. In the immediate wake of the USSR's collapse, Foreign Minister Kozyrev's liberal model seemed set to play a dominant role in shaping Russia's interests. Inspired by the beliefs embodied in new thinking, these ideas would have provided a radically different road map for interpreting Russia's new international realities.[36]

As of early 1992, the Foreign Ministry (and Kozyrev) had been accorded a new and more important role in the policy process. Key elites had made it clear through their pronouncements and a government-mandated search for a foreign policy concept that they were looking for fresh insights to make sense of Russia's new international environment. Moreover, Yeltsin, in his statements on foreign policy, echoed many of the same themes as Kozyrev. Perhaps the high point for the influence of this model came in June 1992, when Yeltsin forcefully articulated many of its central elements in a speech to the U.S. Congress.[37]

In addition, throughout 1992, the Foreign Ministry was at work on a draft of the foreign policy concept that was heavily influenced by Kozyrev's liberal international vision. The draft, officially titled "Basic Provisions of the Concept of the Foreign Policy of the Russian Federation," took as its "holy book" the documents and charter of the Conference on Security and Cooperation in Europe (CSCE) and other international institutions. It favored the promotion of Russian "interests in the first place through participation in different international organizations."[38]

The above suggests that a new set of beliefs for defining Russian interests was on the verge of being adopted. Unfortunately for Yeltsin, the Foreign Ministry, and Kozyrev, they were about three years too late. That is, the changing nature of political institutions in post-Soviet Russia and the consequent partial decentralization of decision making drastically reduced the likelihood that this particular set of beliefs would have any lasting policy impact.

In fact, beginning in June 1992, the draft foreign policy concept became a political football, something unthinkable in the former USSR, as other, competing proposals for defining Russian state interests were advanced and publicly debated by a broad array of individuals, groups, and organizations. The International Affairs Committee of the Supreme Soviet played an important role here. Under the leadership of its strong-willed chair, Evgenii Ambartsumov, the committee rejected the ministry's draft concept, sending it back for reworking.[39]

Ambartsumov, in particular, was highly critical of Kozyrev's radical vision and definition of Russian interests. Among other things, he attacked the Foreign Ministry's belief that the rights of Russian minority populations in the former Soviet republics could best be served by reliance on norms and procedures of international institutions. In closed hearings, Ambartsumov advocated a Russian Monroe Doctrine declaring the "entire geopolitical space of the former union a sphere of [Russia's] vital interests." Furthermore, he added, Russia should be given the legal right to defend its ethnic kin throughout this region.[40]

Utilizing his bureaucratic base to block the Foreign Ministry's foreign policy concept and with access to top decision makers, Ambartsumov was successful in advancing this set of beliefs. Yeltsin seems to have been partially swayed by such thinking. Indeed, by early 1993 he had incorporated elements of both the Ambartsumov and Kozyrev models into his pronouncements. He spoke much more forcefully about protecting Russian minorities in the near abroad, for example, and came increasingly to employ geopolitical frameworks in his discussions of Russian policy.[41]

The revised version of the Foreign Ministry's foreign policy concept, completed in November 1992, also reflected this mixed set of beliefs. A concern for utilizing "the technical resources as well as expert advice" of international institutions to define and advance Russian interests was still present, but now coexisted with a more traditional stress on interests as given by geopolitical imperatives. However, on the all-important issue of protecting Russian minorities in the former Soviet republics, the revised concept maintained the earlier commitment to politico-diplomatic methods and the "mechanisms of international organizations."[42]

This brief review suggests the importance of the changing institutional context for understanding contemporary Russian foreign policy formulation. Its partial decentralization has introduced new access points for those wishing to influence policy. As students of public policy might predict, this enhanced access has led to more "static" in the process and less coherence in policy goals. Put another way, the politics of policy making have come to play a much greater role as the Russian state has weakened.[43]

In this sort of fluid institutional environment, elites are susceptible to greater political pressures. Responding to and managing such pressures require leadership, a skill notably lacking in the Yeltsin government. In post-Soviet Russia, political leadership in the foreign policy sphere requires bureaucratic skills (to engage in the give-and-take necessary in a more decentralized environment); a commitment to building state capacity (so the government has the instruments to pursue an effective policy); and articulation of a coherent foreign policy vision by top elites (to mobilize political support). On all three accounts, Yeltsin and his allies have failed miserably.

Foreign Minister Kozyrev clearly exemplifies the bureaucratic problem. In Russia's decentralized decision-making arena, bureaucratic leadership means the ability to engage in political give-and-take with other influential competitors (the legislature or Ministry of Defense, for example). On this point, Kozyrev's record during the early post-Soviet years was nothing short of abysmal.

Interviewees at the Foreign Ministry praise his vision while simultaneously criticizing his lack of political acuity. He is not a political animal by nature and all too often has let his emotions get the better of him. In a speech given at the Foreign Ministry in late 1992, Yeltsin hinted at this problem, strongly urging Kozyrev to improve relations with various parts of the government and keep his emotions in check.[44]

The second element of political leadership, a commitment to building state capacity in foreign policy, has also been notably lacking. Capacity refers to the administrative and coercive abilities of the state apparatus to implement official goals. Such abilities are increased by the existence of career officials who are relatively insulated from ties to dominant socioeconomic interests; a promotion and tenure system based on some sort of merit review; and a large and coherent bureaucratic machine.[45]

Clearly, the development of state capacity is a long-term, historical process, and one cannot fault the Yeltsin government for failing to create capacity in its brief time in power. However, the Yeltsin team can be criticized for not articulating any coherent plan in this area.[46] Observing the actions of the government, one can only conclude that there is no long-term plan; rather, there have been a series of seemingly ad hoc measures. During 1992, the emphasis was on building bureaucratic infrastructure around a reinvigorated and professionalized Foreign Ministry.[47]

Since late 1992, however, a different plan seems to have been at work. Yeltsin and his close advisors decided that the best strategy for building state capacity was to recentralize foreign policy decision making and strengthen the bureaucratic structures associated with the office of the president. Hence, one had the creation of the Security Council and, more recently, a significant increase in the size of that part of the presidential apparatus devoted to foreign affairs.[48] This lack of direction has clearly hampered the ability of the Russian government to build a cadre of professional foreign policy experts, a critically important goal given the highly politicized apparatus bequeathed to it by the USSR. Moreover, this confusion has alienated parts of the Moscow foreign policy establishment who should, given their views, be allies of the Yeltsin–Kozyrev team.[49]

The lack of political leadership along these first two dimensions is overshadowed (and perhaps caused) by the inability of the Yeltsin government to articulate a coherent foreign policy vision for Russia in the post-Soviet, post–Cold War world. Here, the blame must be laid directly at Yeltsin's doorstep. There are both empirical and theoretical reasons for arguing that his role is central. Empirically, there is the tsarist-Soviet context. Tsars and, more recently, CPSU general secretaries have played the central role in foreign policy formulation. Their visions and beliefs have mattered, a point dramatically demonstrated during the Gorbachev years.[50]

A second reason for according a central role in foreign policy to somebody in Yeltsin's position is more theoretically grounded. In Russia today, there is a missing link in its evolving set of institutions, something comparativists call "intermediate associations." These are the political parties and interest groups that link government and society. When such links are weakly developed, elite decision makers, as well as their beliefs and ideologies, can play an enhanced role in shaping outcomes.[51]

Some might dispute my assertion, arguing, for example, that Russia has a growing number of political parties. This is true; however, one must not mistake form for substance. With very few exceptions, these "parties" are in reality loose groupings with little discipline and poorly articulated foreign policy platforms.[52]

Thus, Yeltsin and his foreign policy views should play an important role in policy making. Does he have a vision? Does he know what sort of international role Russia should play in the post-Soviet world? Early signs to the contrary (the first half of 1992; see above), all the evidence indicates the answer is "no." Whether one is interviewing policy makers and specialists in Moscow or reviewing Yeltsin's own commentary, the conclusion is inescapable: he is uncertain. His foreign policy vision is defined only by negatives: Yeltsin does not want a return to Soviet-era diplomacy, nor will he countenance the forceful, militarized foreign policy of the radical nationalists. Beyond this, however, things are very unclear.[53]

This lack of vision has two important political ramifications. For one, it has made it difficult for the government to mobilize political support for the moderate foreign policy it seemingly wants. Equally important, Yeltsin's lack of conviction has made him more susceptible to the political pressures that are a central feature of politics in post-Soviet Russia.[54]

In late 1993, these pressures increased with the election of a sizable right-wing faction to the new State Duma. Many of these "national patriots" define Russian interests in stark balance-of-power terms and hold a zero-sum view of international politics; they also demand the forcible protection of Russian minorities in the near abroad and the reestablishment of the "union." For example, Vladimir Zhirinovsky, leader of the misleadingly named Liberal Democratic Party, has argued that the Russian Federation should pursue a foreign policy similar to that of imperial, tsarist Russia, seeking, among other goals, the restoration of Russian sovereignty over the territory of the former USSR.[55]

Do the views of the extremists have any influence on foreign policy? They do indeed, but not by shaping the beliefs of elites in the Yeltsin government. Rather, it is Yeltsin's own uncertainty, along with the growing importance of politics and coalition building, that has accorded these extremist beliefs some role. Throughout 1993, and most clearly after the defeat of reformist parties in the Duma elections in December, politicians in the Yeltsin camp were compelled to pay greater attention to the views of the nationalist right, especially on the question of Russian minorities in the former Soviet republics. Indeed, even such a committed liberal as Foreign Minister Kozyrev felt it necessary to moderate his ideology by mixing it with elements of Realpolitik. Asked in the spring of 1994 to explain this "shift" in his views, Kozyrev noted that "as a democrat he felt constrained to take into account public opinion on foreign policy matters."[56]

It is important to ask whether these politicians could become prisoners of their own rhetoric. That is, could a form of "ideological blowback" occur as successor elite generations came to believe in the nationalist ideology earlier articulated for the instrumental reason of building a viable political coalition? The answer, unfortunately, is that it all depends, in this case, on the nature of political institutions that emerge in post-Soviet Russia. If Russia continues a slow transition to a more pluralist political system, the likelihood of such "blowback" will be lessened because of the institutional checks and balances and free exchange of information present in such settings.[57]

International Institutions and Transnational Relations

To this point, my analysis has focused on the past and present, examining the structural, institutional, and leadership variables affecting foreign policy formulation in Russia today. Here, my task is a different one. I look to the future and consider how a different set of international variables may influence Russian policy making and constrain its behavior.

Students of international relations have long studied how interdependence, international institutions, and transnational relations affect state behavior. In recent years, however, they have examined more closely how such factors directly shape policy making and politics within states. Among other issues, this research has explored the effects of economic interdependence on the interests of firms and sectors, and how international institutions and nongovernmental organizations (NGOs) can reshape state policy making by diffusing knowledge and providing resources.[58]

Until very recently, it was assumed that transnationalism could play little role in shaping the policies of authoritarian states. Careful research has now shown this assumption to be false. For example, transnational ties were an important factor influencing policy on arms control and nuclear weapons testing in the former USSR.[59]

This work suggests several ways in which future Russian foreign policy may be constrained. One is long term in nature. To the extent that Russia continues to seek integration with the global political economy, various industries and domestic interests should acquire a self-interest in maintaining such open ties. Clearly, this will be an evolutionary process, but one with definite implications for the foreign policy of any future Russian government. If that government is even semidemocratic, it will have to respond to such (reshaped) interests; this will mandate maintaining good relations with its economic partners.[60]

Do Russians want such integration? With the exception of the radical nationalists, the answer pretty much across the political spectrum is "yes." Moreover, such integration is a clear priority of the Yeltsin government, as evidenced by its membership or application for membership in the G–7 grouping of industrial democracies, the International Monetary Fund (IMF), the World Bank, the General Agreement on Tariffs and Trade (GATT), and the Council of Europe. Also indicative of this priority is the accord signed by Russia and the European Union in December 1993.[61]

A second way in which this transnational context may affect Russian policy is more direct. Post-Soviet Russia has seen an explosion in the number of NGOs seeking to influence an array of foreign policy issues. These include think tanks such as the Foreign Policy Association, as well as a number of organizations concerned with strategic, environmental, and human rights issues. A growing number of these associations are part of larger transnational networks. Responding to these new realities, the Russian Foreign Ministry has created a unit one of whose duties is to maintain contact with the various NGOs.[62]

One example suggests the possible influence of such transnational ties on Russian policy making. In the wake of the violent dissolution of the Russian Supreme Soviet in October 1993, a state of emergency was decreed in Moscow.

Seizing upon this opportunity, officials in the mayor's office sought to restrict the rights of nonresidents living in Moscow.

Domestic human rights NGOs with ties to both the Council of Europe and the Conference on Security and Cooperation in Europe vigorously protested this action, declaring that it discriminated against non-Russians and violated norms embodied in United Nations and Council-sponsored conventions on human rights. Clearly responding to this pressure, President Yeltsin refused to endorse the measures of the city government; they were subsequently partially rescinded.[63]

The point here is not that such dynamics will dictate future Russian policy. Rather, it is to argue that if the Russian Federation continues its slow transition to a market-based economy and pluralist polity, then such factors could exert an increasingly strong and, from a Western perspective, beneficial influence on its policy formulation and behavior. For students of Russian foreign policy, the lesson is that the traditional focus on the "power ministries" and high government offices and agencies should be supplemented by an exploration of the influence of the growing nonstate sector, be it privatized firms, domestic NGOs, or transnational alliances.[64]

Conclusions

To sum up, the weakly institutionalized basis of Gorbachev-era new thinking and fundamental changes in the international and domestic environments of post-Soviet Russian policy making have stacked the deck against a continuation of a liberal foreign policy. While political leadership, domestic politics, and bureaucratic maneuvering clearly matter as well, their changing role and influence cannot be understood in isolation from these broader structural and institutional contexts.

The perceptive reader will have noted a problem in the preceding paragraph (and the chapter as a whole): My outcome, the conservative turn in Russian policy, is overdetermined. That is, any of the main causal variables—international structure and domestic institutional context—could independently explain this rightward shift. I have two responses to such a query, the first of which is that overdetermination is inevitable when one has more variables than cases, as I do here.

My second response is that the international and domestic variables are in fact interacting, and it is thus quite difficult (and perhaps not very useful) to discern their independent effect. As I argued earlier, Russia's new international environment has provided important opportunities for domestic actors wishing to steer foreign policy in a more conservative direction.

This dynamic has been most evident in the case of the large Russian ethnic minority populations (totaling over 25 million) in the states of the former USSR. Nationalist political groupings, centrist-conservative foreign policy elites (Karaganov, Stankevich, and Migranian, for example), and, most importantly, elements in the Russian Defense Ministry have seized on this "problem" to promote a more assertive foreign policy in the former Soviet region and vis-à-vis the West more generally.

If my analysis is correct, how can the West influence the course of Russian policy? Two possibilities suggest themselves. First, the West must play a more active role in stabilizing the situation in the non-Russian Soviet successor states; stability in those countries means fewer opportunities for Russian conservatives to steer policy in a confrontational direction.[65] The very helpful American mediation of the bilateral Ukrainian-Russian nuclear dispute is an encouraging sign that policy makers in Washington have finally come to realize that states aside from Russia do indeed exist in the former Soviet area.

The next step is to recognize that there are *nonnuclear* states in the region also deserving of Western concern. Some Russian policy makers will not appreciate this Western "interference"; however, such actions can be made much more palatable if they are coupled with increased attention to the rights of Russian (and other) minority populations in the successor states. Clearly, such a Western policy will have to walk a thin line, recognizing as legitimate those cases where, by the standard of international norms, the rights of Russian minorities have been infringed and condemning instances where the ethnic issue has been blatantly manipulated and distorted by Russian policy makers (the Trans-Dniester region of Moldova, for example).

Second, the West should rethink the role it sees for international institutions in Russia. Most importantly, it should disabuse itself of the notion that institutions such as the IMF or the CSCE have their greatest and only influence on policy in the very near term. It is almost laughable how every time an IMF mission or CSCE observer team arrives in Russia, there is an expectation of immediate policy impact.

As I suggested earlier, however, such institutions may play an equally important and more subtle role. By providing resources and expertise to domestic political groupings and acting as clearinghouses for policy networks composed of domestic and international NGOs, they can slowly help reshape the political process in Russia. For this policy to be effective, the West must continue to strengthen the financial base and bureaucratic infrastructure of the CSCE, the Council of Europe, the European Bank for Reconstruction and Development, and the several European Union programs specifically targeted on Eastern Europe and the former Soviet region, among many others. The potential payoff may be slow, but well worth the wait.[66]

Notes

Thanks to Jennifer Barney and Aaron Hoffman for their research assistance. For their comments on an earlier draft, I would especially like to thank Hannes Adomeit, Karen Dawisha, and Bruce Parrott.

1. See Leyla Boulton and John Lloyd, "Industrial Czar Puts Russia's Leader on Spot," *Financial Times*, 29 October 1992; and Steven Erlanger, "From This Boss's Seat, Yeltsin Appears Small," *New York Times*, 8 January 1993.

2. Among many others, see Suzanne Crow, "Russia Asserts Its Strategic Agenda," *RFE/RL Research Report*, vol. 2, no. 50 (17 December 1993); Celestine Bohlen, "Nationalist Vote Toughens Russian Foreign Policy," *New York Times*, 25 January 1994; and "A Hero of Our Time," *Economist*, 12 February 1994. For a more sober and balanced view, see Dmitri Simes, "The Return of History," *Foreign Affairs*, vol. 73, no. 1 (January/February 1994).

3. On the autonomy of the Soviet state, also see Matthew Evangelista, *Innovation and the Arms Race: How the U.S. and the Soviet Union Develop New Military Technologies* (Ithaca, NY: Cornell University Press, 1988). On state "strength" more generally, see Stephen Krasner, *Defending the National Interest: Raw Materials Investment and U.S. Foreign Policy* (Princeton, NJ: Princeton University Press, 1978). Thomas Wolfe, in *The Salt Experience* (Cambridge, MA: Ballinger Press, 1979), discusses the centralized nature of the Soviet policy process.

4. This point is explicit in Jack Snyder, "The Gorbachev Revolution: A Waning of Soviet Expansionism?" *International Security*, vol. 12, no. 3 (winter 1987–88); it is implicit in James Richter, "Perpetuating the Cold War: Domestic Sources of International Patterns of Behavior," *Political Science Quarterly*, vol. 107, no. 2 (summer 1992).

5. On the ministry's role, see Condoleezza Rice, "The Party, the Military and Decision Authority in the Soviet Union," *World Politics*, vol. 40, no. 1 (October 1987). My depiction of the military's ideology of international politics derives from a reading of numerous ministry publications of the early and mid-1980s, as well as published interviews with top ministry and General Staff officers. Military organizations in general tend toward the realist worldview described here. See John Lepingwell, "Soviet Civil-Military Relations and the August Coup," *World Politics*, vol. 44, no. 4 (July 1992), pp. 547–48.

6. On the International Department's role in policy formulation, see Mark Kramer, "The Role of the CPSU International Department in Soviet Foreign Relations and National Security," *Soviet Studies*, vol. 42, no. 3 (July 1990). My characterization of Suslov, Ponomarev, and the department's ideology draws on Kramer; interviews with two former high-ranking officials in the department and with Aleksandr Yakovlev; and Roy Medvedev and Dmitrii Ermakov, *"Seryi kardinal": M.A. Suslov: Politicheskii portret* (Moscow: Respublika, 1992).

7. See William Wohlforth, *The Elusive Balance: Power and Perceptions During the Cold War* (Ithaca, NY: Cornell University Press, 1993), chaps. 6–7.

8. On the Gorbachev era, see Jeffrey Checkel, "Ideas, Institutions and the Gorbachev Foreign Policy Revolution," *World Politics*, vol. 45, no. 2 (January 1993); and Matthew Evangelista, "The Paradox of State Strength: Domestic Structures, Transnational Relations and Security Policy in the USSR and Russia" (paper presented at the 1993 annual meeting of the International Studies Association, Acapulco, Mexico). On the Brezhnev period, see Jeffrey Checkel, *Ideas and International Politics: Foreign Policy Change and the End of the Cold War* (New Haven, CT: Yale University Press, forthcoming), chap. 3.

9. That historically constructed institutions affect the direction and nature of policy change is a central insight of the domestic structures literature in international political economy and the historical institutionalism in comparative politics. For recent applications, see Peter Katzenstein and Nobuo Okawara, "Japan's National Security: Structures, Norms and Policies," *International Security*, vol. 17, no. 4 (spring 1993); and Frank Longstreth et al., eds., *Structuring Politics: Historical Institutionalism in Comparative Perspective* (New York: Cambridge University Press, 1992).

10. On institutionalization more generally and its importance for consolidating policy

change, see Judith Goldstein, *Ideas, Interests and American Trade Policy* (Ithaca, NY: Cornell University Press, 1993); and Margaret Weir, *Politics and Jobs: The Boundaries of Employment Policy in the United States* (Princeton, NJ: Princeton University Press, 1992).

11. Shevardnadze did introduce several innovations—establishing, for example, a "Scientific Coordination Center" to allow the academic community a greater say in ministry policy formulation. These changes, however, were pursued in an ad hoc manner and were quite limited in their personnel and bureaucratic reach, strongly suggesting that Shevardnadze had no strategic plan for institutionalizing a liberal foreign policy at the ministry. For details, see Checkel, *Ideas and International Politics*, chap. 5.

12. See James Goldgeier and Michael McFaul, "A Tale of Two Worlds: Core and Periphery in the Post-Cold War World," *International Organization*, vol. 46, no. 2 (spring 1992).

13. Also see Evangelista, "Paradox of State Strength."

14. This is, of course, an argument familiar to students of American politics, where the challenge is not so much to get a hearing for one's proposal (this is usually quite easy) but to insure that, once adopted, it has some enduring impact on policy. For the theoretical rationale behind such arguments, see Margaret Weir, "Ideas and Politics: The Acceptance of Keynesianism in Britain and the United States," in *The Political Power of Economic Ideas: Keynesianism Across Nations*, ed. Peter Hall (Princeton, NJ: Princeton University Press, 1989).

15. See Steven Erlanger, "Russian Finance Chief Tells of Enemies Within," *New York Times*, 4 June 1993.

16. On the neorealist logic, see Christopher Layne, "The Unipolar Illusion: Why New Great Powers Will Rise," *International Security*, vol. 17, no. 4 (spring 1993), for example. Two excellent critiques are Stephan Haggard, "Structuralism and Its Critics: Recent Progress in International Relations Theory," in *Progress in Postwar International Relations*, eds. Emanuel Adler and Beverly Crawford (New York: Columbia University Press, 1991); and Richard Ned Lebow, "The Long Peace, the End of the Cold War and the Failure of Realism," *International Organization*, vol. 48, no. 2 (spring 1994).

17. See Goldgeier and McFaul, "Tale of Two Worlds."

18. See *RFE/RL Daily Report*, 1 February 1993, 19 January 1994; and Elaine Sciolino, "Contain Your Joy: Russia's Back on the World Stage," *New York Times*, 20 February 1994.

19. On the "second image reversed," see Peter Gourevitch, *Politics in Hard Times: Comparative Responses to International Economic Crises* (Ithaca, NY: Cornell University Press, 1986). For a partial application to the former USSR, see Jack Snyder, *Myths of Empire: Domestic Politics and International Ambition* (Ithaca, NY: Cornell University Press, 1991), chaps. 2, 6.

20. Interviews with Arbatov, Vladimir Benevolenskii, scientific secretary at the Institute of the USA and Canada (ISKAN), and Sergei Blagovolin, senior researcher and department head at the Institute of World Economy and International Relations (IMEMO). ISKAN and IMEMO are the two leading international affairs research institutes supported by the Russian Academy of Sciences. For evidence that academic influence on policy may be declining at present (in comparison to the Gorbachev era and early Yeltsin years), see the chapter in this volume by Nodari Simonia.

21. See ITAR-TASS (in Russian), 26, 27 June 1992—a speech by Foreign Minister Kozyrev to the Supreme Soviet concerning policy toward Serbia; Vladimir Volzhskii, "V etoi bor'be pobeditelei ne budet," *Nezavisimaia gazeta*, 25 July 1992; Robert Hubert and Vladimir Savelyev, "Russian Parliament and Foreign Policy," *International Affairs* (Moscow), no. 3 (March 1993); and "Parliament Votes to Check on Foreign Ministry Work," *Foreign Broadcast Information Service Central Eurasia Daily Report*, 12 August 1993 (hereafter *FBIS Daily Report: Central Eurasia*.)

22. See A. Sychev, "Avtor Rossiiskikh initsiativ ostaetsia inkognito," *Izvestiia*, 8 February 1992; "Doklad Prezidenta Rossiiskoi Federatsii B.N. El′tsina," *Rossiiskaia gazeta*, 8 April 1992; Andrei Kozyrev, "Voina i MID," *Komsomol′skaia pravda*, 9 June 1992; and Mikhail Karpov, "Velikoi i samobytnoi Rossii," *Nezavisimaia gazeta*, 28 October 1992. On the weak American state, see Krasner, *Defending the National Interest*, chap. 3.

23. The information on Yeltsin and Burbulis comes from interviews at the Foreign Ministry. For Kozyrev, see "Vystuplenie A.V. Kozyreva," *Rossiiskaia gazeta*, 21 April 1992.

24. See Viacheslav Elagin, "Povod dlia bespokoistva," *Nezavisimaia gazeta*, 26 November 1992.

25. See Aleksandr Rahr, "Liberal-Centrist Coalition Takes Over in Russia," *RFE/RL Research Report*, vol. 1, no. 29 (17 July 1992); Aleksandr Shal′nev, "Andrei Kozyrev: 'Prezident El′tsin i ia otvechaem za vneshniuiu politiku Rossii,' " *Izvestiia*, 5 January 1993; "Foreign Policy Tasks of Security Council Commission Outlined," *FBIS Daily Report: Central Eurasia*, 9 February 1993; and *RFE/RL Daily Report*, 18 December 1992, 14 and 18 January, and 22 October 1993. The presidential apparatus as a whole also grew considerably over the course of 1993 (to over 3,500 personnel) and now includes at least one department overseeing foreign affairs. See "Russia: Darkness in June?" *Economist*, 29 January 1994; and *RFE/RL Daily Report*, 16 February 1994.

26. One analyst already claims to see a new "consensus" in Russian foreign policy. See Crow, "Russia Asserts Its Strategic Agenda."

27. On the tsarist era, see Robert Slusser, "The Role of the Foreign Ministry," in *Russian Foreign Policy: Essays in Historical Perspective*, ed. Ivo Lederer (New Haven, CT: Yale University Press, 1962).

28. The argument here—that the importance of bureaucratic politics was shaped by the broader institutional context—is consistent with the conclusions Evangelista reached in his comparative study of the US/USSR weapons innovation process. See Evangelista, *Innovation and the Arms Race*.

29. Interviews with personnel at the Russian Foreign Ministry, a former sector head at the CPSU Central Committee's International Department, Aleksandr Iakovlev's former chief aide, and Iakovlev himself.

30. See Stephen Foye, "Post-Soviet Russia: Politics and the New Russian Army," *RFE/RL Research Report*, vol. 1, no. 33 (21 August 1992); Scott McMichael, "Russia's New Military Doctrine," *RFE/RL Research Report*, vol. 1, no. 40 (9 October 1992); and Stephen Foye, "Updating Russian Civil-Military Relations," *RFE/RL Research Report*, vol. 2, no. 46 (19 November 1993). For a sampling of the new ministry's old worldview, see "Geostrategiia nas obiazyvaet," *Krasnaia zvezda*, 4 December 1992.

31. Interviews with Foreign Ministry personnel. On the council, see Andrei Kozyrev, "Raspakhivaia dver′ vo vneshnii mir," *Rossiiskaia gazeta*, 27 December 1991; Mikhail Karpov, "Demokraticheskie sily mobilizuiutsia," *Nezavisimaia gazeta*, 28 November 1992; and "Foreign Policy Council Discusses Eastern Europe Policy," *FBIS Daily Report: Central Eurasia*, 3 November 1993.

32. Interviews with personnel in this new unit. Its establishment marked a much more systematic effort than undertaken by Shevardnadze to give the ministry access to a broad range of policy-relevant expertise and advice.

33. See Andrei Kozyrev, "Dumat′ o svoikh interesakh," *Izvestiia*, 2 October 1991; idem, "Preobrazhennaia Rossiia v novom mire," *Izvestiia*, 2 January 1992; and "Kozyrev Writes on Country's National Interests," *FBIS Daily Report: Central Eurasia*, 21 October 1993.

34. Beginning in 1979, this directorate was headed by Vladimir Petrovskii, a scholar and pragmatist who would later become an early and outspoken advocate of Gorbachev's new thinking.

35. See Andrei Kozyrev, "Preobrazhenie ili kafkanskaia metamorfoza," *Nezavisimaia gazeta*, 20 August 1992; idem, "K slovu 'patriotizm' prilagatel'nye ne nuzhny," *Krasnaia zvezda*, 26 November 1992; idem, *Nezavisimaia gazeta*, 24 November 1993; and Douglas Hurd and Andrei Kozyrev, "Challenge of Peacekeeping," *Financial Times*, 14 December 1993.

36. For full details on the debate, see Jeffrey Checkel, "Russian Foreign Policy: Back to the Future?" *RFE/RL Research Report*, vol. 1, no. 41 (16 October 1992); Aleksandr Rahr, " 'Atlanticists' versus 'Eurasians' in Russian Foreign Policy," *RFE/RL Research Report*, vol. 1, no. 29 (29 May 1992); and Suzanne Crow, "Competing Blueprints for Russian Foreign Policy," *RFE/RL Research Report*, vol. 1, no. 50 (18 December 1992).

37. ITAR-TASS (in Russian), 18 June 1992. Also see Aleksei Arbatov, "Russia's Foreign Policy Alternatives," *International Security*, vol. 18, no. 2 (fall 1993), pp. 9–10.

38. Interviews at the Foreign Ministry; Iurii Leonov, "Khorosha kontseptsiia, no vriad li osushchestvima," *Nezavisimaia gazeta*, 20 February 1992; and Interfax, 21 February 1992.

39. Interviews at the Foreign Ministry. Policy debates certainly did occur in the former USSR. However, they were restricted to a narrow set of actors and much less in the public domain than such debates in post-Soviet Russia.

40. See Konstantin Eggert, "Rossiia v roli 'Evraziiskogo zhandarma'?" *Izvestiia*, 7 August 1992; and Andranik Migranian, "Podlinnye i mnimye orientiry vo vneshnei politike," *Rossiiskaia gazeta*, 4 August 1992. Migranian was at this point an advisor to Ambartsumov. For a sampling of Ambartsumov's views, see Evgenii Ambartsumov, "Sami sebia zagnali v ugol, samim iz ego i vykhodit'," *Rossiiskaia gazeta*, 13 April 1992.

41. See *RFE/RL Daily Report*, 1 February 1993—a Yeltsin speech before the Indian parliament. Also see Leyla Boulton, "Yeltsin Pledges Tough Foreign Policy to Please Right Wing," *Financial Times*, 4 January 1994.

42. See Mikhail Zinin, "MID nakonets-to nameren zaiavit' o svoem ponimanii vneshnei politiki," *Nezavisimaia gazeta*, 21 October 1992; Mikhail Karpov, "Rossiia ne rassmatrivaet ni odno gosudarstvo kak vrazhdebnoe," *Nezavisimaia gazeta*, 27 November 1992; and "Kozyrev Offers Draft Foreign-Policy Guidelines," *Current Digest of the Post-Soviet Press*, vol. 44, no. 48 (30 December 1992), pp. 14–16.

43. On access points more generally, see Desmond King, "The Establishment of Work-Welfare Programs in the United States and Britain: Politics, Ideas and Institutions," in Longstreth et al., *Structuring Politics*, pp. 219–20.

44. Kozyrev's lack of political savvy is especially evident in "Partiia voiny nastupaet: i v Moldove, i v Gruzii, i v Rossii," *Izvestiia*, 30 June 1992—an article that earned the foreign minister a public reprimand from Yeltsin. Also see Aleksandr Gol'ts, "Seans 'shokovoi diplomatii,' " *Krasnaia zvezda*, 16 December 1992. On Yeltsin's speech, see Gennadii Charodeev, "El'tsin gotov otbit' ocherednuiu ataku," *Izvestiia*, 27 October 1992.

45. See Kathryn Sikkink, *Ideas and Institutions: Developmentalism in Brazil and Argentina* (Ithaca, NY: Cornell University Press, 1991), chap. 5.

46. By "coherent," I refer to a well-articulated and stable set of organizational-bureaucratic and educational-training initiatives designed to augment state capacity.

47. Interviews at the Foreign Ministry. Also see Checkel, "Russian Foreign Policy."

48. See note 25 above.

49. See, for example, the scathing criticism in Arbatov, "Russia's Foreign Policy Alternatives." On the unprofessional and politicized foreign policy apparatus of the Soviet era, see the remarks by Andrei Kozyrev on Russian television, 28 December 1991.

50. See Checkel, *Ideas and International Politics*, chap. 5.

51. See Gourevitch, *Politics in Hard Times*, pp. 81–83; and Stephan Haggard, *Pathways from the Periphery: The Politics of Growth in Newly Industrializing Countries* (Ithaca, NY: Cornell University Press, 1990), chap. 2.

52. On the last point, see Fedor Shelov-Kovediaev, "Nam nuzhna sil'naia, no ne imperskaia Rossiia," *Literaturnaia gazeta*, 8 December 1993. For useful overviews of the chaotic, weakly developed nature of political parties, see Leyla Boulton, "Reformers in Russia Seek New Identity," *Financial Times*, 23 June 1993; and "Can They Make a Democracy?" *Economist*, 2 October 1993.

53. For an example of Yeltsin's lack of clarity on foreign policy, see his address to the first session of the Federation Council. "Vystuplenie Prezidenta RF na otkrytii zasedaniia verkhnei palaty parlamenta," *Rossiiskie vesti*, 12 January 1994. Western observers have also noted Yeltsin's uncertainty over Russia's new international role. See John Lloyd, "Mr. Absent Without Leave," *Financial Times*, 20 February 1994; and "Russia: The Road to Ruin," *Economist*, 29 January 1994.

54. For the theoretical rationale behind such an argument, see Haggard, *Pathways from the Periphery*, pp. 47–48. Commentators in the West have likewise noted how current American foreign policy is particularly susceptible to public opinion and political pressures due to President Clinton's lack of a well-defined "worldview." See "Why America Doesn't Lead," *Economist*, 30 April 1994.

55. See Vladimir Zhirinovsky, "Milliard dollarov—i ia u vlasti," *Rossiia*, 1992, no. 27; and Igor Torbakov, "The 'Statists' and the Ideology of Russian National Imperialism," *RFE/RL Research Report*, vol. 1, no. 49 (11 December 1992).

56. See *RFE/RL Daily Report*, 19, 20, January 1994—reporting on a speech Kozyrev gave to Russian ambassadors gathered in Moscow; and Andrei Kozyrev, interview, *Segodnia*, 30 April 1994, as summarized in *RFE/RL Daily Report*, 2 May 1994. Also see Leyla Boulton, "Moscow Less in Love with West: But Foreign Policy Has No Truck with Extreme Nationalism," *Financial Times*, 3 February 1994.

57. See Snyder, *Myths of Empire*, chap. 2.

58. For example, see Helen Milner, *Resisting Protectionism: Global Industries and the Politics of International Trade* (Princeton, NJ: Princeton University Press, 1988); Peter Haas, *Saving the Mediterranean: The Politics of International Environmental Cooperation* (New York: Columbia University Press, 1990); Kathryn Sikkink, "Human Rights, Principled Issue-Networks and Sovereignty in Latin America," *International Organization*, vol. 47, no. 3 (summer 1993); and Robert Keohane, "Contested Commitments in American Foreign Policy" (unpublished paper, February 1994)—especially the section on "institutional enmeshment."

59. See Evangelista, "Paradox of State Strength." Evangelista's paper is part of a larger book-length study examining the role of transnational networks in Soviet security policy of the post-Khrushchev era. Several doctoral dissertations at Berkeley, Columbia, and Cornell are also exploring this transnational context of Soviet/Russian policy. On its importance in the Soviet era, also see Arbatov, "Russia's Foreign Policy Alternatives," p. 24.

60. Also see Kim Zisk, "The Foreign Policy Preferences of Russian Defense Industrialists: Integration or Isolation?" (paper presented at the 1994 annual meeting of the International Studies Association, Washington, DC).

61. See "Joint Russia-EU Policy Declaration," *FBIS Daily Report: Central Eurasia*, 10 December 1993. Russia also recently renewed its application for membership in GATT. See *RFE/RL Daily Report*, 22 February 1994. The stress on integration with the global political economy is also found in the revised foreign policy concept. See "Russia's Foreign Policy Concept," *International Affairs* (Moscow), no. 1 (January 1993).

62. See Checkel, "Russian Foreign Policy"; and Crow, "Competing Blueprints for Russian Foreign Policy." Interview with ministry personnel.

63. On the decree and reaction to it, see *RFE/RL Daily Report*, 9 and 23 November 1993; and Judith Ingram, "Refugees Find No Haven in Moscow," *New York Times*, 24 December 1993. For the views of the human rights NGOs, see "Zaiavlenie prav-

ozashchitnykh organizatsii," *Literaturnaia gazeta*, 13 October 1993. More recently, Foreign Minister Kozyrev has called for a strengthening of the CSCE's human rights activities throughout the former USSR. See *RFE/RL Daily Report*, 1 December 1993. Evangelista, "Paradox of State Strength," provides other examples of how transnational ties are shaping current Russian foreign policy.

64. Recall that the revised foreign policy concept explicitly recognizes the possible role of international institutions in providing "technical resources as well as expert advice" to Russia. See "Kozyrev Offers Draft Foreign-Policy Guidelines."

65. Also see Ted Hopf, "Managing Soviet Disintegration: A Demand for Behavioral Regimes," *International Security*, vol. 17, no. 1 (summer 1992).

66. My proposal here is similar to what some call "soft mediation" by international institutions. See Jenonne Walker, "International Mediation of Ethnic Conflicts," in *Ethnic Conflict and International Security*, ed. Michael Brown (Princeton, NJ: Princeton University Press, 1993).

4

Russia's Far Eastern Policy in the 1990s

Priorities and Prospects

Andrew A. Bouchkin

The domestic situation as it has taken shape in Russia since the abortive communist coup of August 1991 is one of sharp contrasts. The totalitarian system has crumbled and yet lingers on as its ruling establishment stays in power, having changed the flag and the vocabulary. The Soviet empire has fallen apart, but an imperial mentality still often determines the behavior of the new Russian leadership. The economic reform, carried on exclusively by ruling forces from above and in the interest of the bureaucratic elite, has not affected the foundations of the state-controlled property relations under the Soviet system. Production is in a tailspin, while the military-industrial complex (MIC) retains its advantage. There is galloping inflation, a rapidly growing threat of impending mass unemployment, and unprecedented impoverishment and corruption. One indication of the all-pervading and deepening crisis in which Russia now flounders is the buildup of the forces of a communist backlash, though today they are not so persistent in advocating orthodox ideology. Instead they are flaunting their ultrachauvinistic and Nazi-like slogans and trading on pseudopatriotic sentiment. This is, in broad outline, the social and political situation—an unfavorable one to say the least—in which Russia is trying to find its place in world politics.

Lord Palmerston's maxim about Britain having neither permanent friends nor permanent enemies but only permanent interests remains relevant and certainly applicable to Russia's present need to define its standing interest in the international arena and to find ways to safeguard it. It is extremely important not only to define this interest correctly but also to achieve a social consensus about it. Only then will Russia's long-term foreign policy be safe from unexpected twists and turns and survive the change of governments and presidents as do the world's leading nations. But it has turned out to be very difficult, if not altogether impossible, to achieve a consensus in Russia's setting.

The absence of a single agreed-upon position by various state agencies on the issues of domestic and foreign policies seriously compounds the situation. Quite often the disagreement is not so much a matter of fundamental divergence of approaches as a contest of departmental and personal ambitions. One outstanding feature of recent times has been the rise of all kinds of casual and incompetent individuals, even from among the lowest strata of society, to positions of government in a country that has for decades been rigidly structured under the rule of a nomenklatura hierarchy. This massive grassroots coming-to-power induced a quick coalescence of rival political elites realizing their interests only through the struggle for spheres of influence. The view of power as an end in itself rather than a means to achieve the long-term objectives of politically organized forces devalues national strategy. This is what is happening in Russia today, although perhaps it is not so evident in the field of foreign affairs as it is in, say, economic reform.

Foreign Policy Decision Making:
In Search of Natural Allies

By and large, foreign policy remains outside the political mainstream. This leaves the Ministry of Foreign Affairs (MFA) relatively free (for the time being, at least) to bring off Minister Andrei Kozyrev's liberal reformist initiatives. But it was clear that such a situation could not last forever. Kozyrev has all along sought and gained President Boris Yeltsin's support. It is this tandem of politicians in Russia's present leadership that we should regard as the architects of the declared foreign policy course committed to an alliance with the West, the United States in particular. They wanted Russia to be integral to the general future of developed nations of the North. This course, however, soon came under fire from those in Russia who believe that the country has never particularly identified itself with Western political and cultural traditions. They argue that today Russia has to face some problems similar to those of many developing countries and, therefore, must not break off links with the Third World but rather find for itself the specific role of mediator or bridge between the rich industrialized societies and developing nations.

This circumstance, naturally, has attracted the attention of researchers who have christened the opposing political factions "Atlanticists" and "Eurasianists."[1] The Eurasian lobby was thought to depend on parliament, which challenged the Ministry of Foreign Affairs for primacy in conceptualizing foreign policy. Indeed, many members of parliament, including ex-speaker Ruslan Khasbulatov, missed no chance of finding fault with the ministry and Kozyrev for whatever reasons (suffice it to recall their showdown over the issues of the South Kurils and Serbia in 1992). But in point of fact such scuffles were again over the ambitions, not the positions, of individual politicians, and they rather self-righteously used whatever episode (or problem) they could to attack their political opponents.

If we try to look at the problem in the light of this dichotomy, we will get something like the following picture: after the idea of a Slav community, which had risen from the ruins of the USSR, actually fell flat and the Commonwealth of Independent States (CIS) was established, an Atlantic lobby came into play in Russia. The concept it stands for is based on the suggestion that the confrontation between East and West develops into one of North and South. The West is seen not as an opponent but as a partner in establishing the new world order. In the opinion of that lobby, the West and Russia have common values—democracy, market-based economies—and before too long may find themselves facing the threat of migration, terrorism, Islamic fundamentalism, and even armed aggression coming from the developing countries of the South. Yeltsin's proposal for creating a united political system of northern industrialized countries and his plea for the formation of a joint American-Russian nuclear defense system spring from the same position. The Atlanticist lobby rejects the view of the Eurasianists about Russia's certain specific role or mission in world politics.

Kozyrev, as the main spokesperson for the Atlantic lobby, believes that one major achievement of Russian foreign policy consists in the fact that the West has recognized the Russian Federation as a legal successor to the USSR in world affairs and that Russia has taken over from the USSR its membership in the United Nations Security Council. The Atlanticists count on Russia's eventually joining the Group of Seven (G–7), thus making it G–8, or at least G–7.5, and therefore, bank on the federation's enhanced role in the United Nations, the Commission on Security and Cooperation in Europe (CSCE), and the International Monetary Fund; a subsequent drive for membership in NATO is also planned. They deny that Russia must have some specific interest in Asia beyond that related to the issues of national security.

The Yeltsin-Kozyrev foreign policy, however, became the subject of sharp criticism from the Eurasian lobby, whose members hold that the Atlanticists do not pay proper attention to the South. They believe that Russia's traditional and natural interest lies precisely in the South rather than in the West, though for completely or partly different reasons. Some of them do not consider the South to be a zone of friendship and warn that in the face of a conflict arising between the North and the South, it is Russia, not the West European countries, that would be the first to be involved and become the main target for attack, since its frontiers lie close to the potential aggressor nations. Others, on the contrary, want to see Russia locked in embrace with Saddam Hussein. But the main, and most serious, point many Eurasianists are making is that the Russian Federation at this stage cannot enter into or compete with the G–7. Therefore, they reason, Russia cannot fail to take into account the possibility of worsening relations with China or the Muslim world when it is on the brink of economic collapse itself. In any case, the Eurasian bloc does not seem to be a monolith at all. What is more, one should always keep in mind that statements of that kind are frequently being made in Russia for the purpose of saying something different or contradictory to what has been heard from the opposing political camp.

Such a head-on contradistinction is not only excessively speculative and schematic but also inconsistent, in essence, with actual foreign policy practice. Moreover, there is no sense in trying to find through this kind of approach which lobby's stance is more in line with Russia's interest. This contradistinction, in fact, appears to have been suggested by attempts at perceiving the process of Russia's foreign policy framing and the mechanism of decision making in this field in the transitional postcommunist period. In actuality, there is no such polarization, nor has there ever been any; nor is there any clear boundary between the supporters of these different views on foreign policy, and hardly will anybody be in a position to determine the makeup of these lobbies (the Atlanticists, for example, have always been found in parliament, while in the Ministry of Foreign Affairs are found those who would insist that China must come first in Russia's set of priorities). And it is quite obvious that there must be a "golden mean," that is, a well-balanced approach that will be optimal for Russia's interest.

Beyond dispute, there has been a certain overdependence on "romantic infantile pro-Americanism," as the Russian Federation ex-ambassador to the United States, Vladimir Lukin, now chief of the parliamentary International Affairs Committee, has called it.[2] It is likewise clear that this emphasis has been a way of making up for the prodigious overworking of the confrontational approach of Cold War times, and the present pro-Americanism has already gathered a certain momentum of its own that now has to be restrained. It is worth noting Kozyrev's persistence in pushing his argument about "our natural allies," referring above all—or even exclusively, he seems to suggest—to the nations of the West, especially the G–7.[3] This argument is rather disputable and, indeed, lame, even in the theoretical respect, if only because it is unreasonable, to say the least, to offer oneself obtrusively to be anybody's ally, thereby narrowing the room for political maneuvering. This has been evident throughout the history of world diplomacy. But can Russia enter an alliance with the United States, for example, in relation to Iran? According to the Iranian leadership, the United States is still Satan, and the Americans' response is no less hostile. For Russia it is important to have Iran as one of the good neighbors all along its borders (or CIS borders, which are transparent in Central Asia).

What, in general, is the meaning of the concept of natural allies? What standards must make nations eligible for such a title? That the nations of the West are Russia's natural allies is, according to some critics, an assertion without foundation. There are many arguments to bear this out, most notably that the Russian Federation and the Western nations have no common ground for such an alliance, which must arise primarily from the identity (or, at least, similarity) of sociopolitical and economic systems, common ideologies, philosophies of life, and cultures. There is nothing of the sort, nor will there be in the foreseeable future. Russia will maintain its distinctive identity for a long time to come owing to roots reaching deep in its history. From the global point of view, this is a positive, rather than negative, feature. And in this sense the line of reasoning the Eurasianists stand by looks quite convincing.

By this juncture, the contest between the Atlanticist and Eurasianist lobby factions, even if one assumes that such a contest has taken place, has abated. It is hoped that Russia will commit itself in earnest to a multivector-balanced foreign policy, removed from a pro-Western slant. (Given Russia's political priorities, however, its current foreign policy is far from balanced.) But this does not at all mean that the Eurasianists have got the upper hand over the Atlanticists or vice versa. It is noteworthy that Kozyrev, for all the cabinet reshuffling, has kept his job, and one must admit that he has worked wonders in the art of diplomacy. His pet maxim of late has been "Russia's foreign policy is the president's foreign policy." At the same time, he has been quite emphatic in dismissing the current claim that the role of the military in shaping Russia's policies, particularly in foreign affairs, will considerably rise in the aftermath of the breakup of parliament in October 1993. The source of the president's authority, in the minister's view, is not in the military power structures but in the people's mandate, which is something that the generals at the top realize very well, to judge by their loyalty during the attempted coup.[4]

Though it may be inaccurate to claim that the military and the Ministry of Foreign Affairs are in competition, it is perfectly right to say that the initiatives and statements coming from the MFA mean next to nothing to the generals and the military-industrial complex. They just do not care about what is going on in the sphere of diplomatic relations between Russia and other countries; they pursue a foreign policy of their own. The MIC has its own problems of survival in the ruined Russian economy and sees no reason why it should subordinate its interests to those of the Foreign Ministry. For the same reasons, the generals are apt to make pronouncements about such "purely theoretical" issues as foreign policy doctrine or the national interests of Russia. What the Foreign Ministry, on the one hand, and the Defense Ministry, the MIC, and what is left of the KGB, on the other hand, really compete for is a quota in the Russian embassies and missions abroad especially, in such key countries as the United States, Japan, and the People's Republic of China (PRC) and the European countries. Their main aim is to keep their seats in the embassies, since a new wave of military and bureaucratic personnel wait their turn to be paid in hard currency. Now, as far as the newly elected Duma is concerned, its members, like those of the defunct Supreme Soviet, spend more time in political infighting than on foreign policy. It is noteworthy that there was no foreign policy debate at all in the recent election campaign, as is discernible from the platforms of the parties and blocs, a circumstance totally inconceivable anywhere in Europe or the United States (discounting, of course, the irresponsible utterances of Vladimir Zhirinovsky). In addition to Lukin's abovementioned committee, three more have been established recently, and they seem intent on interfering in foreign policy issues. These committees are headed by Zhirinovsky's parliamentary faction members and by former communist leaders. Anyhow, one can expect rivalry and contradictions between these committees, and eventual attempts by the Ministry of Foreign Affairs to play on these contradictions.

At one point Kozyrev, responding to allegations of a pro-Western slant in Russia's foreign policy, made visits to Beijing, Seoul, and Tokyo in March 1992, introducing a new East Asian dimension into Russian diplomacy. Even in that case, however, the Western card was still being played: Moscow clearly saw his trip as principally concerned with Seoul and Tokyo, which politically and economically fall within the group of countries normally viewed as the West in Russia. Though not of this group, Beijing deserves, of course, to be something more than a staging base in the foreign travels of Russian politicians.

China: Do-No-Harm Principle in Action

There have been quite a few commentaries in the Russian press of late making a well-argued case that "the loss of initiative in the development of relations with the Eastern neighbor [the People's Republic of China] is a historical mistake."[5] It is beyond dispute that the most important factor among those that will determine Russia's place in the world is its relationship with its neighbors in the East, more particularly with the one that shares the longest common border—China.

Today it is obvious that China's weight and influence, which for a long time have been determined by balancing its position in the bipolar system of international relations, have diminished, though its material weight, if measured economically, has certainly increased. Moreover, while still professing its commitment to the notorious socialist option, the present Chinese leadership has found itself just about one-on-one with the whole Western world.

But this world of ours is ever in a state of flux. Indeed, it is, after all, perfectly clear that the championing of socialist values by this leadership has more to do with preserving the present political structure of Chinese society than with defending the essential characteristics of the sociopolitical system, and that these values might be quickly and gently reduced to naught, the Chinese way (quite painlessly, incidentally, in contrast with how it happened in the former Soviet Union), and replaced with other values.

Russia needs to be made aware of all the various options if it expects to play a starring role in world leadership. China's changing role in international affairs, in fact, springs from Russia's inability to claim the role of a global power and the apparent weariness of the United States in carrying the burden of world leadership. China, on the other hand, has enough grounds for aspiring to the role of regional and eventually global leader (considering its large population, the Chinese diaspora all over the world, and its growth rate in the gross national product in recent years).

Certain steps attesting to an appreciation of this trend have already been taken by the Russian leadership. The Beijing summit in December 1992, with a package of accords signed, marked a new level of relations between the Russian Federation and the People's Republic of China. Moscow is extremely cautious in its official comments on the most sensitive issues for Beijing: the human rights situation, Tibetan separatism, and the Taiwan problem.[6] That is, the do-no-harm principle appears to be fundamental in framing Russia's policy with respect to China, now and in the foreseeable future. The Chinese leadership, for its part, is pursuing the same policy, standing by the principle of noninterference on such issues as Russians in the "near abroad," ethnic conflicts in Russia, and rivalry in political leadership.

Military cooperation has become the major area of the China–Russia interface. In fact, Beijing is clearly trying to make Moscow and Washington vie for the colossal Chinese arms market. Only in this context could one understand the visit by Russian Federation Defense Minister Pavel Grachev to Beijing in November 1993, following the visit by U.S. Assistant Secretary of Defense Charles Freeman. The latter arrived, as a matter of fact, just to report Washington's readiness to resume military cooperation with the PRC, which was interrupted after the Tiananmen Square massacre in 1989. General Grachev's trip had been organized in keeping with all the "honeymoon" rules; he was even invited to visit an air force base accommodating SU–27 combat aircraft purchased from Russia. An important bilateral cooperation agreement providing, notably, for an exchange of officers and military technologies was signed.

By some estimates, Moscow sold at least a billion dollars' worth of arms of all kinds to Beijing in 1992. In addition to the SU–27s, these included MiG–29 fighters, Iliushin transport aircraft, and air defense systems delivered at rock-bottom prices. Around a thousand Russian nuclear and missile technology specialists are working in the PRC today. Within an incredibly short span of time they helped Beijing substantially improve the performance of China's military equipment. Taking advantage of the present situation in Russia, where many of the best arms production specialists simply draw no salary at all and the government can no longer keep them from going abroad, China has stepped up its efforts to enlist the services of Russian staff working at what once had been classified establishments. The Chinese visit defense factories and institutes, offering workers a high salary (up to $2,000 a month, which is at least twenty times more than the average pay in Russia) and excellent conditions. In fact, there is no need for many to leave Russia at all—they can just as well send their blueprints and designs by electronic mail.

This policy of China, directed toward the development of nuclear weapons and ballistic missiles, seriously worries the Clinton administration, which fears that the efforts made by Beijing may eventually enable it to create strategic nuclear forces capable of striking out at the United States. The reaction of Japan to all this is self-evident. The Chinese, however, for all the obvious advantages they stand to gain, are not particularly pleased with the latest trend toward one-sided buildup of military links with Moscow (and, consequently, increased technological dependence), a position they are forced into by Western sanctions. Chinese emissaries have more than once voiced their discontent on this score to members of the U.S. administration. Nevertheless, it is evident that with Russia's help the Chinese military is making an important changeover from ground-based defense forces to a capability that can be used throughout the Far East and beyond. Considering the current state of Russian Federation defenses, it is not clear how this development can be changed.

That Russia is now consciously helping to build up the strategic and conventional military power of this large neighboring country should not be regarded as state policy or the design of the Russian government, however, as if it does not understand possible (and obvious) drawbacks to large-scale arms sales and military technology transfer to China. But this understanding cannot help change the situation, since the arms sales in postcommunist Russia have been turned into a certain kind of MIC foreign policy, that is actually beyond the control of the parliament, the Ministry of Foreign Affairs, and even the Ministry of Defense. In reality any military plant can easily avoid bans or restrictions imposed by the government in selling weaponry to another country, if not directly, then through intermediary commercial companies, which tend to disappear the day after the deal is done. (Also, the seller can easily bribe customs officials, who will register a MiG fighter, for example, as scrap metal.)

The latest official meeting between representatives of the two countries was between Kozyrev and his Chinese counterpart, Qian Qichen, in late January 1994. The Russian foreign minister arrived in Beijing after visiting Heihe, a border town in Heilongjiang Province. The talks centered on frontier checkpoints and border trade. The normalization of relations led to actual decontrol of the transportation of goods from China to Russia and other countries of the CIS via the so-called shuttle business, which has become widespread. In 1993 alone transboundary trade amounted to $2.5 billion, with a total of 2.5 million people crossing the border. There has been a sharp rise in the number of PRC nationals illegally residing in the territory of Russia, especially in the cities of Siberia and the Far East: Chita, Irkutsk, Khabarovsk, and Vladivostok. Mounting crime, including organized mafia gangs, is in evidence. Local authorities are seriously concerned lest such a state of affairs precipitates an outburst of anti-Chinese sentiment. Routine though they might seem, these circumstances are in fact escalating into just about the most complex series of problems in bilateral relations, with no solution in sight. There are some territorial issues in dispute, too. Although back in the late 1980s China dropped most of its territorial claims against the USSR and, later on, against Russia, both sides still dispute some territories, above all, a couple of islands on the Amur River constituting only about 40 to 45 kilometers of the 4,300-kilometer-long common border.

During his visit Kozyrev announced Russia's intention of setting up more border checkpoints and limiting the entry of Chinese. As far as economic cooperation is concerned, he called for the transition from spontaneous forms of trade to coproduction and joint investments. The talks ended in the signing of an agreement on border ports and a protocol on consultations between the foreign ministries of the two countries.

There is no longer any ground for charging Russia with underrating, let alone ignoring, China, as was the case only a couple of years ago in the opening stages of Russia's foreign policy making. Relations have been on a normal, pragmatic basis, with China standing to gain more, in practical terms, from this interface. Yet there is still a certain coolness in Moscow's attitude toward Beijing, which responds by rather carefully observing Moscow's policy. Beijing is worried by Moscow's commitment to an alliance with the West and active political rapprochement with the United States. The Chinese leadership fears Moscow might follow in Washington's tracks on the human rights issue. Finally, China is uneasy over the prospect that Russia's development of links with Taiwan might transcend the framework of trading and economic relations.

Korea: Finding a Balance Between Seoul and Pyongyang

While the Russian Federation's relations with the PRC, for all its unavoidable complexities, are still on the upgrade, those between Moscow and Seoul appear somewhat different. On the one hand, beyond dispute, there is the greatest possible measure of mutual understanding and amicability between the states, which were outspokenly hostile toward each other just a few years ago. On the other hand, the situation is uncertain because of the problems that have arisen in bringing substance to these amicable relations. The start made in reshaping Russia's foreign policy coincided with the end of the honeymoon between Moscow and Seoul, which culminated in the establishment of diplomatic relations in September 1990. This breakthrough will forever go down in history as an achievement of what was still Soviet diplomacy. The former president of the Republic of Korea, Roh Tae Woo, for his part, having superbly played the Soviet card in his game with Gorbachev, brought off a master stroke to consummate his Northern policy. Yeltsin and his South Korean counterpart, Kim Young Sam (and the foreign ministries of the two countries), had a far less rewarding job to do—actually arranging the interface of the two nations to have it pay off, that is, to have the relationship rise high enough to benefit both sides.

The starting point of Russia's policy with respect to South Korea would have to be Kozyrev's visit in March 1992, when Russia, figuratively speaking, "showed the flag" in the Far East. In Seoul the Ministry of Foreign Affairs chief succeeded in securing the unblocking of the remaining $1.2 billion out of the $3 billion credit that had been granted in Gorbachev's time. And that was done, incidentally, at the top political level by President Roh, for the Korean financiers themselves, being unaware of who would be paying back the $1.8 billion already provided, were in no mind to do so. The president's generous move came about after the Russian minister had promised Russia's adamant support to Seoul, notably at the UN, in its efforts to get Pyongyang's nuclear program placed under international control, and assured him that Russia did not intend to sell offensive arms to the North. The South Koreans were favorably impressed, moreover, by Kozyrev's statement that the 1961 treaty with the Democratic People's Republic of Korea (DPRK), which Russia had inherited from the USSR and still virtually bound it to intervene militarily in the event of a conflict on the Korean peninsula, was excessively ideologized and altogether out of date.

The man to follow in Kozyrev's tracks was President Yeltsin, who went to Seoul in November 1992. The effect of the summit was to sign the Basic Treaty between the Russian Federation and Republic of Korea (ROK), and about a dozen other important agreements and documents.

Nevertheless, some critics remain pessimistic about the outcome of these bilateral relations. Moscow, it seems, was motivated by economic considerations in seeking a closer relationship, whereas Seoul was motivated by politics. And Russia's economy, which has by no means ceased to be Soviet in many respects, is ill-prepared for an interface with such partners as the major South Korean corporations.

There are problems galore: in particular, the inefficiency and incompetence, which have still not disappeared after the breakup of the communist empire, of officials operating between Russian and Korean business partners; and the omnipotence of official bureaucracy and its widespread corruption, which had nothing to match it in the USSR (it would be no exaggeration at all to say that Russia's government structures, bound together by economic and, more particularly, foreign economic relations, are criminal in their essence). But the main obstacles are the extremely slow reshaping of property relations, the weak and confused legislation concerning the rights of foreign investors in the Russian Federation, and the taxation system, which is in a real mess. The commodity exchange (both civilized and shuttle) has been growing from year to year, but the Russian export mix, predominantly made up of raw materials and semimanufactures, has little promise and benefit even for Russia. As far as direct capital investment is concerned, which Russia is so keen on and which has figured prominently in its far-reaching plans intended, above all, for the Far Eastern region, it has nothing of real value to speak of.

Another aspect of the Russian Federation's troubling economic interface with the nations of the Far East is related to the full-scale drive for sovereignty in some of Russia's republics and autonomous regions, which occasionally go so far as to declare their own independence. Korean, Chinese, and Japanese businessmen are hard-pressed to discern the boundaries between the rights and powers of the federal government, the "appanage princes" who are now all "presidents," and the local bureaucracy, which is in a hurry to get its share of the benefits. From time to time, politicians, or, to be exact, politickers, in the Far East of Russia (the so-called Far Eastern Republican Party), depending on the intensity of political confrontation, resume speculation about the prospect of reviving something like the Far Eastern Republic, which existed in the territory of the Soviet Far East in 1920–22 and then vanished into thin air within Soviet Russia (separatists in the region treat this process as nothing short of forcible annexation).[7] Now, as far as Korea is concerned, there is yet another pressing issue: the possibility of a Korean autonomy being created in the south of the Maritime Territory. For the time being, local authorities resolutely reject the idea, which has been put forward by the Association of Ethnic Koreans in the CIS, but the situation may well change one day.[8] South Korean businessmen are all too eager to employ Koreans residing in various parts of Russia, Kazakhstan, and Uzbekistan.

There is some uncertainty in the area of political relations between the Russian Federation and the ROK. On the one hand, there are no global or regional problems on which the positions of the two countries differ substantially. This situation applies, incidentally, to the issue of U.S. military presence in Korea. There are no official statements coming from Moscow, naturally, in this regard, just to avoid annoying Pyongyang for no particular reason. In actuality, however, the subject is neither posed nor discussed, and Moscow appears to acquiesce in the motives that prompt Seoul to insist on the continuing U.S. presence.

On the other hand, there is no point to a political interface between the Russian Federation and the ROK. These two countries belong to different security structures, while the idea of creating a collective security system along the lines of the CSCE in East Asia remains no more than a piece of theorizing divorced from reality (with Gorbachev off the stage, there are no more leaders willing to beat the air with their "historic initiatives"). Under these circumstances the political aspect of bilateral relations essentially boils down to the North Korean factor and a discussion of the notorious Kim Il Sung regime. Seoul continues to plea for influence or pressure to be brought to bear on Pyongyang over a particular aspect of the Korean settlement (at this juncture, notably, the debate revolves basically around the issue of International Atomic Energy Agency inspection). Moscow's formal response has been to promise something in an attempt to bolster up the image of a great power and to stimulate Seoul's political interest in the continued pursuit of a closer relationship, but in actuality Moscow has long since lost practically all leverage with Pyongyang. Moreover, Russia's present attempts to interfere in any way whatsoever in the problems of the Korean settlement, even if by mediating (for example, between Pyongyang and Seoul or between Pyongyang and Washington), are bound to be counterproductive.

Any official document of Russia's Ministry of Foreign Affairs on relations with the Democratic People's Republic of Korea claims that these relations are deideologized and governed by the principles of free choice, mutual benefit, and considerations for the interests of both sides. While perhaps true in theory, in actual practice the slogan does not work in every case. Relations between the Russian Federation and the DPRK are the best evidence. In present-day Russia there is a kind of allergic reaction to communism, particularly the bizarre and ugly form seen in North Korea. Russia's rejection of the *Juche* ideological orthodoxy and everything related to it prevents the normalization of bilateral relations. There are no political contacts to speak of at the government level between the two countries; interparliamentary links for that matter have been cut off.

While Gorbachev did not find enough reason to visit Pyongyang, although it was precisely at that time that he and ROK President Roh Tae Woo held three summit meetings in less than a year, Yeltsin has nothing to discuss with the North Korean leaders. Any prospect of organizing a summit between the leaders of North Korea and Russia is hampered by both the essence of the *Juche* state and its policies, and the personality of Kim Il Sung himself.

The North Korean leadership is categorically deprecating current reforms in Russia: the introduction of the principles of political pluralism and a multiparty system, market economics, equal rights in property ownership, freedom of the press, and so forth. The Pyongyang regime has been citing the Russian Federation as a case by which to demonstrate to its own population "the fateful consequences of a capitalization of society," stopping just short of outright public invectives against its neighbor and the Russian leadership.

Moscow's foreign policy is strongly resented by Pyongyang and is now totally bracketed with those of the United States and other Western countries, the regime's traditional enemies. Moreover, in view of Pyongyang's recent increased interest in the normalization of relations with Washington (or, at least, the promotion of regular high-level contacts), Russia has a good chance of succeeding the United States as the republic's chief foe. Russia's disarmament initiatives and proposals for a nuclear test moratorium have been dismissed in Pyongyang with undisguised irritation, and its signing of the SALT II Treaty has been criticized. While Pyongyang newspapers delight in noting the general decline of Russia's role in world affairs, official Pyongyang has made no mention at all of the measures for security and cooperation in the Asia-Pacific region as proposed by Yeltsin and the Ministry of Foreign Affairs.

Pyongyang's particular displeasure rests on Moscow's unequivocally pro-Seoul stand on the problem of the Korean settlement. North Korean leaders have noticed that Moscow has ceased to echo Pyongyang's supposedly constructive initiatives, although Russian authorities have not in fact dissociated themselves from what had been said in support of Pyongyang all through the early years of "fraternal friendship." Russia's position on the Korean settlement and, more particularly, on the relations of the DPRK with the International Atomic Energy Agency and inter-Korean nuclear inspections have become, in principle, almost identical with that of the world community (above all, the United States and South Korea). It is not surprising, therefore, that Pyongyang should have been particularly annoyed by Russia's attempts to bring political pressure to bear precisely on these issues. Pyongyang invariably claims that Russia is incapable of promoting the denuclearization of the peninsula.

The irreconcilable collision of opinions and positions on these matters most seriously vitiated the atmosphere of the latest official contact between Moscow and Pyongyang, namely, the visit of Russian Deputy Minister of Foreign Affairs Georgii Kunadze to North Korea in January 1993. The parties concerned did no more than exchange routine diplomatic courtesies, failing to come to terms on any of the key issues beyond mutual assurances of a desire to resume and promote all-embracing contacts and get a better understanding of each other's positions. It was made perfectly clear, however, that the regime frowned on Russia's attempted involvement in the international resolution of the Korean problem. In fact, the North Korean negotiators hinted that North Korea was not going to join the Convention on the Prohibition of Chemical Weapons. Among the other issues raised in the negotiations was the Russian delegation's warning against any attempts by the DPRK to conclude contracts with Russian munitions factories for the purchase of weapons without strict government control, although there was a reaffirmation of Russia's readiness to supply the DPRK with nonoffensive arms on a commercial basis, provided the DPRK had no intention of selling them to other countries and only as long as the DPRK was not subject to any international sanctions. Pyongyang was also warned against trying to recruit the staff of classified defense establishments in Russia in circumvention of the existing laws (particularly, the Official Secrets Act).

Further tension in relations between the Russian Federation and the DPRK has centered on opposite approaches to human rights. Having qualified the statement of the Russian senior delegate at the forty-eighth session of the United Nations Human Rights Commission as "interference in the internal affairs of North Korea," the Pyongyang regime declared its intention of presenting counterclaims against Russia. Russia's action in granting political asylum to a North Korean postgraduate student in June 1992 and then extraditing him to the ROK was interpreted in Pyongyang as yet another example of impairing relations and contravening the existing legal assistance treaty.

The process in bilateral relations between the Russian Federation and the Democratic People's Republic of Korea, it seems, is based on a buildup of problems and contradictions, mutual claims and displeasures that combine to produce a rather gloomy picture overall. It is duly complemented by the ongoing problematic economic relations between the two.

Technically speaking, Russia is trying to abide by the principle of "equidistance" (in the political sense) from the two Koreas, and it keeps insisting that its foreign policy is deideologized.[9] Whatever the slogans, the plain fact is that North Korea and Russia have fewer and fewer points of contact (not counting the common border) and fewer and fewer issues on which some mutual understanding at least could be possible. At the same time, it is clear that it is necessary to do everything possible to keep the DPRK from slipping into a position of outspoken hostility toward Russia. Seoul is no less interested than Moscow in the preservation of correct, if not friendly, working relations between Moscow and Pyongyang.

At this point, the primacy of relations with the Republic of Korea for the

Russian Federation is expressed quite clearly, particularly with respect to preserving the status quo in the peninsula. This priority, incidentally, is reflected in the Basic Treaty signed in November 1992, a document of the new times, different both in spirit and in letter from similar treaties once concluded by the Soviet Union. And yet, although not conflicting, the treaty is still somewhat out of step and incompatible with those signed in 1961 between North Korea and the USSR and in 1954 between South Korea and the United States.

Japan: Dancing in Circles

Yet another burden Russia has taken over from the USSR is the extremely involved relationship with its other Far Eastern neighbor, Japan. In the last two years, in spite of a rather intensive exchange of visits by diplomats and politicians, including President Yeltsin's visit to Tokyo in October 1993, there has been no way to achieve anything like a breakthrough in this relationship. It cannot be called normal, and what mars it is the problem of a never-signed peace treaty and the additional issue of the South Kurils. In this respect, Russia and Japan resemble waltz partners dancing in circles around a point, unable to either part "the good way" or find a way to resolve the problem.

Numerous studies have been written about the problem of the "Northern territories." There are no secrets here, and the situation as a whole is more or less clear. One point of interest in this context, though, is the political and psychological aspect, for there has been a rather dangerous kind of change in national awareness in Russia, an awareness poisoned by communist propaganda and subservient science, which has created the myth of the "historical fairness" of the return of the Kurils to Russia (which, incidentally, were quite peaceably swapped by Russia for Sakhalin as early as 1875). Today this problem has become an instrument of political struggle. Some opportunists, appealing to patriotic sentiment, are trying to gain political capital by playing it up, while others insist on quick and simple solutions, seeking an economic effect as soon as possible. Few individuals in fact, especially among "nationalists," are actually concerned about Russia's national interest. Russia's approach to the problem should be one of respect for international law and a willingness to resolve the issue on that basis, which means recognizing the Russian Federation's commitments emanating from the joint declaration of 1956, which provided for the transfer of the Habomai and Shikotan islands to Japan upon the signing of a peace treaty between Moscow and Tokyo and for negotiations on other problems.

The territorial issue may be considered in abeyance, as it were, for the time being. In the joint statement issued at the end of the recent summit, both sides confined themselves to reaffirming their intention to continue the negotiations regarding the nationality of the Kurils. Even the prospect of a solution is enough to deem the summit a success.

The summit brought the Russian Federation and Japan nearer the option Moscow had earlier suggested: not to make the economic interface contingent on the solution of the territorial problem but rather to start cooperating, since such cooperation is one of the factors that could contribute toward resolving the issue. Top officials in Tokyo today avoid recalling the cornerstone principle of "inseparable union of politics and economics." In this respect, the new coalition cabinet has turned out to be more tractable than the mono-party Liberal Democratic cabinet, and Russian diplomacy has taken full advantage of its coming to office.

But of the prospect ahead for the bilateral relationship, the problems will persist. On the one hand, it is noteworthy that Tokyo has dropped its invariable demand for a reaffirmation of the 1956 declaration, but on the other, the reference to the four islands of the South Kurils in the concluding document of the summit puts more pressure on Russia. As far as Japanese businessmen are concerned, they care not so much about the territorial problem as about investment security and repayment of Russia's debts. In the context of the economic depression that has been going on for over a year, the Japanese business community pins certain hopes on two major projects: the exploitation of Sakhalin oil and gas fields and the construction of the Hokkaido–Sakhalin underwater tunnel. But in the long run, Japan, unlike Korea and especially China, has no particular economic advantage to gain from cooperation with Russia, since now the dependence of the Japanese economy on imported energy resources is much less than it used to be in, say, the 1970s. For that matter, South Korea, which is also rapidly climbing the technological stairway, is on the same path. Therefore, Russia, by slowly pushing forward economic reforms, is year by year losing the advantage of a complementary economy. What is more, as of today both Japan and Korea find it cheaper to import, say, timber from Australia than from the Khabarovsk Territory.

It is, of course, Japan that has been most critical within the G–7 of the aid programs for Russia. One could presume, however, that in the wake of Yeltsin's visit Japan's involvement in these programs would increase and some of the strings Japan used to attach to it would gradually be dropped. These expectations, however, might prove to be futile because of the recent parliamentary elections in Russia, which have resulted in a stronger representation of nationalists, communists, and other conservative forces.

Another consideration in the relationship between Russia and Japan is the military sphere and arms trade. Russia's military presence in the region keeps unnerving Tokyo. The Japanese defense yearbook for 1991, for example, noted that the armed forces of the USSR "make the military-political situation in the area of Japan extremely tense." Focusing on the Russian troops stationed in the Far East, the authors of the 1992 and 1993 editions of this publication said the troops "are a factor of instability from the standpoint of assuring security in the region."[10] Japanese experts, however, admit that the Far Eastern military contingent is gradually losing its former power and fighting capacity. Compared with 1989, the record year in this sense, the strength of this contingent has dwindled by one hundred thousand, and the number of aircraft and warships by 30 to 40 percent. As Minister Kozyrev declared at the Singapore session of the Association of Southeast Asian Nations in July 1993, Moscow intended to halve its forces in the Far East by 1995. The Japanese view this as evidence of Russia's intention to create a compact modernized contingent in the region.

Modernization is in full swing already. Fourth-generation combat aircraft have appeared in the Far East; by the beginning of this year they made up half the aircraft inventories. The number of T–80 tanks has been brought up to fifteen hundred. The withdrawal of troops from the South Kurils, however, as promised by Yeltsin in Tokyo, came just as the program for overall troop reduction took effect and was thus seen in Japan as only a token gesture. (The pullout of MiG–23 fighters from the islands, for instance, has in no way weakened Russia's air defenses because the islands are covered by the MiG–31s stationed in Sakhalin.)

It is quite obvious that the Joint Russian-Japanese Statement on Nonproliferation of Weapons of Mass Destruction and Delivery Vehicles and Development of Transparency in Regard of Conventional Arms is aimed, in part, also at limiting Russia's possible exports to other countries of the region. The statement imposes no restrictions on the parties concerned but declares "the importance of multilateral regimes in the field of control over the export of material, equipment, and technologies which could be used for the development of weapons of mass destruction." This phrase was purposely written into the text in view of Moscow's numerous references to an intention of joining the missile technology monitoring system.

Some events of recent times lead to the assumption that not everybody in Moscow liked the military aspect of the documents signed in Tokyo. A case in point is the controversial radioactive waste disposal in the Sea of Japan by a Russian Pacific fleet tanker. Another is the intrusion of a Russian fighter plane into Japanese air space on 31 August 1993, which appeared to have "accidentally coincided" with the decisive phase of the preparation for Yeltsin's October visit. Apparently, serious negotiations on the northern territories are being impeded not so much by public opinion (of course, not by the inhabitants of the Kurils) as by top military personnel and industrial "generals" from the Russian MIC.

The Road to Self-Determination and Good Relations

One development bound to have an impact on Russia's present and future relationship with the countries of both the West and the East is the character of Russia's political system, which will be in the making for a long time to come. There is no reason to expect anything like a rapid breakthrough on the road to democracy to account for objective circumstances. There has never been a shortcut to democracy anywhere. The regime that has taken shape in the Russian Federation after the turbulent domestic political developments of recent years cannot fail to be at least half-authoritarian by the methods of reform implementation, but the general trend toward a democratic society is still there, as far as one can see, notably in the area of foreign affairs. Much will depend on the timing, mode, and outcome of presidential elections in Russia.

Relations between the Russian Federation and the United States continue to be of paramount importance. President Clinton gives his unequivocal support to Yeltsin, but he is just as unequivocal in showing that this support will depend on how democracy develops in Russia. There are all kinds of judgments on how long the United States will play the key role in Russia's foreign policy making. So long as strategic issues remain within the field of vision of the Russian Federation and the United States, they will be assured high priority in relations between the two countries. Eventually, however, this primacy will diminish as the issues involving nuclear weapons are gradually resolved, and priorities will arise in other areas.

Russia's long-term strategic interest in the Far East consists, apparently, in maintaining well-balanced relations with all the nations of the region, without encouraging any claims by them to dominate the relations. Yet, above all, it is relations with China that are particularly important, politically as well as economically, and they must ideally be brought in line with American and European dimensions in Russia's set of priorities. In the long term, it is hoped the foreign policy swing will be stopped and the long-sought-for balance achieved. But in today's actual political context it is Russia's relations with Europe that are coming to the fore at the expense of relations with the United States and Russia's Far Eastern neighbors. This reality, incidentally, is reflected in the Russian Federation's official foreign policy doctrine. Of the various factors conducive to such a shift, economic relations with Europe stand out, particularly in regard to the scope of potential trade.

The bid to shift Russia's policy toward greater self-determination is a necessary and natural readjustment that must not be seen as an ill-intentioned departure from the reformist democratic policy of forging a closer relationship with the West. It is important for the West and above all the United States to make clear their own strategy with respect to Russia. Much has been done spontaneously of late and not always after proper consideration because of the pressure of time. Support for the reforms in Russia has by no means lost its relevance for Western policy, but it is important also to establish the proper methods for this support, which must imply not so much the backing up of certain personalities within the power structures as helping to shape up sociopolitical institutions that will subsequently assume these relations. Such support should help bring Russia closer to democracy.

Notes

1. *Nezavisimaia gazeta,* 8 July 1992; Sergei Goncharov and Andrew Kuchins, "Domestic Sources of Russian Foreign Policy," in *Russia and Japan: An Unresolved Di-*

lemma Between Distant Neighbors, ed. Andrew Kuchins, Tsuyoshi Hasegawa, and Jonathan Haslam (Berkeley: International and Area Studies, University of California 1993), pp. 389–92.

2. *Nezavisimaia gazeta*, 20 October 1992.

3. Andrei Kozyrev, "Russia: A Chance for Survival," *Foreign Affairs*, vol. 71, no. 2 (spring 1992).

4. *Segodnia*, 19 October 1993.

5. See, for example, *Nezavisimaia gazeta*, 21 July 1992.

6. See the interview of Deputy Foreign Minister Georgii Kunadze on the eve of President Yeltsin's visit to Beijing under a typical newspaper headline, "A Stable and Prosperous China Is in the Russian Interest," in *Nezavisimaia gazeta*, 10 December 1992.

7. *Moscow News*, no. 41 (1992).

8. *Nezavisimaia gazeta*, 20 October 1992.

9. "Does Russia Have to Choose One of the Two Koreas?" was the headline of an interview by the Korea department chief of the Russian Federation Ministry of Foreign Affairs, with the whole thrust of it being to rule out such a possibility. *Rossiiskaia gazeta*, 28 March 1992.

10. Quoted from *Krasnaia zvezda*, 28 July 1992, and *Segodnia*, 21 October 1993.

5

The Near Abroad, the West, and National Identity in Russian Foreign Policy

Jonathan Valdez

Introduction

With the collapse of the Soviet Union, Russia inherited much of its predecessor's foreign policy apparatus and responsibility for adhering to international agreements. One new facet of Russian foreign policy, however, was an apparently pro-Western tilt that went well beyond former Soviet leader Mikhail Gorbachev's desire to improve relations with the USSR's former Cold War adversaries. Despite the criticism of many communist and nationalist opposition figures, President Boris Yeltsin and Foreign Minister Andrei Kozyrev carried out a foreign policy that in the main coincided with Western perspectives on a number of international issues. By the end of 1993, however, it was possible to discern a marked shift of foreign policy priorities away from the West and toward Russia's more traditional areas of concern—the republics of the former Soviet Union, or what has come to be called the "near abroad" in Russian parlance. Even before Yeltsin's disbanding of the legislature, the subsequent antigovernment violence in Moscow, and the resulting bombardment of the Supreme Soviet in October 1993, Russian foreign policy had begun to exhibit a much more assertive and even nationalist stance. The relative success of extreme nationalists and communists in the December 1993 elections to the new Federal Assembly reinforced the perception among observers that Russia was moving away from its initial pro-Western orientation.

What explains this shift in priorities, and what does it portend for the character of Russian foreign policy in general? This chapter will argue that the Russian Federation's vacillation in foreign policy derived in large part from the difficulties Russians have encountered in defining their national identity after the collapse of the Soviet Union. Russian foreign policy in the last two years can best be seen as a product of, and a response to, the promotion of different concepts of Russia's national identity. One analyst has referred to this as a "psychological reevaluation"[1] on the part of foreign policy makers. What does this psychological reorientation consist of? How has it affected the development of Russian foreign policy since the demise of the Soviet Union?

I will address these questions by focusing on the development of Russian policy toward the near abroad and toward the conflict in the former Yugoslavia, the two areas where Russian foreign policy has been most influenced by debates over national identity. I will devote special attention to the views of Russian foreign policy elites on the issue of peacekeeping and defending Russians and Russian-speakers in the former Soviet republics. For the most part, this chapter will focus on the views of Foreign Minister Andrei Kozyrev, given that he is the personification of the new Russian foreign policy focus and the target of much of the criticism of that policy. The views of major institutional actors in foreign policy making today—the Ministries of Foreign Affairs and Defense, the Foreign Intelligence Service, and the Security Council—will also be discussed where appropriate. Given the apprehension raised in the West by the strong showing of nationalist forces in the recent parliamentary elections, a major portion of the analysis will also concentrate on the foreign policy positions of those parties that gained representation in the State Duma, the lower house of the Federal Assembly. Unfortunately (if understandably), the parties contesting the elections focused predominantly on domestic issues, and statements concerning foreign policy were few and far between, except for those of the most virulent nationalist of them all, Vladimir Zhirinovsky of the Liberal Democratic Party of Russia. Nonetheless, the basic outlines of each party's foreign policy planks can be discerned.

National Identity and Nationalism

In order to study how debates over national identity can influence foreign policy, we must come to some understanding of the term itself. Nationalism and national identity are sometimes used interchangeably; more fundamentally, many studies of the influence of nationalism fail to address the crucial issue of the roles it plays in a society, whether for elites or nonelites.

This study proceeds from the assumption that nationalism and national identity are two distinct phenomena.[2] Scholars commonly view national identity in one of two ways: either as "primordial and fixed," focusing on the supposedly permanent features of the nation such as religion, language, and customs; or as primarily a modern phenomenon that promotes group cohesion in the interests of modernization.

An example of a "primordialist" perspective on Russian national identity can be seen in the following statement made by a Russian observer at the end of 1992, one year after the collapse of the Soviet Union:

> [p]olitical parties are born and die, leaders come and go, but the state, while developing and changing from one form to another, remains. And it is of no importance what the political system in it is today.[3]

According to this writer, Russia had certain permanent interests regardless of its political system; in this case, those interests were held to be fundamentally similar to those of the former Soviet Union. In referring to the permanent interests of the Russian state, he illustrated one of the cardinal features of the primordialist approach, an assumption of historical continuity between the nation and the state. In other words, the nation has certain permanent interests that the state will inevitably reflect.

For Western-oriented Russian reformers, on the other hand, foreign policy tasks were defined first and foremost by the character of the state and the conception of its national identity. Russian Foreign Minister Andrei Kozyrev illustrated this approach perfectly in a comment on foreign policy in the spring of 1993:

> First of all, we have to be aware of what kind of state we have, get our own internal bearings, and then get our bearings in relation to the surrounding world. The concept of the Russian state is now taking shape and is followed, accordingly, by the concept of foreign policy.[4]

In other words, the foreign policy interests of the state are by no means fixed or constant. They change, depending on how the state is defined.

The approach utilized in this study falls somewhere between these "primordialist" and "modernist" understandings of nationalism. Nationalism and national identity are best understood as distinct but related concepts.[5] The former is based on the latter, inasmuch as nationalism must have some cultural basis on which to draw. "National identity" forms the cultural basis of nationalism; nationalism itself can be variously defined, but is generally held to be a principle that elevates the political rights (broadly defined) of one ethnic group above all others, within and often outside the country. Some observers make a distinction between (usually benign) patriotism and (usually aggressive) nationalism, but this really is just a matter of degree. George Schöpflin has similarly defined nationalism as the politicization of a community's culture, where culture is defined as

> the sum total of the subjective perceptions in a community; the rules by which it orders its life, its sense of common past and shared future and its socially constructed picture of the world.[6]

By focusing on nationalism as based on a national identity, and national identity in turn as politicized culture, we come to an understanding of how a national identity develops. It evolves through a process of interpretation of a nation's enduring cultural symbols by various actors in society. A nation's identity is therefore neither fixed nor infinitely malleable, as primordialists or modernists would have us believe. Instead, a nation's identity is constantly subjected to a process of reinterpretation, usually by each succeeding generation.[7] In the case of "new" states, this process is even more easily observable, as commonly accepted aspects of the nation's identity are questioned or discarded in light of institutional and societal change.

In Schöpflin's terms, the former Soviet republics today face a number of tasks intimately related to national identity: the task of deciding on a "socially constructed picture of the world," the need to devise the rules by which to order their political lives, and especially the problem of coming to a proper understanding of their past and future. What are the proper conclusions to be drawn from Russia's past, imperial and Soviet? What is Russia's role in the world? What has been, and what will be, Russia's role in imperial Russia, the Soviet Union, and now the Commonwealth of Independent States (CIS)? The cultural (or symbolic) approach to nationalism used in this study makes it possible to examine the development of a national identity by following both broad trends within society (usually through its mass media) and narrow trends within a political elite (through analysis of their views and public statements).

It is essential to analyze the motivations behind the promotion of various interpretations of a nation's identity, as well as the identity itself. As implied by the term "modernist," many scholars suggest that nationalism arises from "the need to establish an effective state to achieve a group's economic and security goals,"[8] goals that cannot be met by smaller, localized groups due to the growing complexity of modern life. Nationalism is seen primarily as a form of collective action through "conflict groups" whose membership is based primarily on nationality.

Nationalism is therefore conceived of as primarily a means of promoting modernization. Schöpflin, however, stresses that it may also be a response to the pressures and uncertainties created by political and economic change. He suggests that "cultures are threatened by change, particularly economic and technological change," because of the way it forces communities to redefine the rules by which they live.[9] This suggests that nationalism can also be understood as an attempt to frustrate modernization by establishing boundaries (physical and otherwise) that will protect communities from the unpleasant prospect of change.

It is also essential to stress the role that national identity can play for individuals. Donald Horowitz argues that people bond together in ethnic groups out of a "fundamental human need to feel worthy," which "is satisfied in considerable measure by belonging to groups, that are in turn regarded as worthy."[10] While the approach utilized in this study pinpoints additional motivations for the development of a national identity, I nonetheless feel that Horowitz's approach is helpful, especially in determining the intensity of feeling sometimes displayed by the most ardent nationalists.

This need to belong to inherently worthy groups is intensified in the case of "humiliated nations," such as Weimar Germany before World War II and post-Soviet Russia today. To describe this phenomenon, Isaiah Berlin has used the analogy of the "bent twig," suggesting that any nation that has been humiliated but not defeated will inevitably experience a resurgence of nationalism. One possible problem with the "bent twig" analogy is that it tells us only that nationalism *will* be important, not necessarily how. Taking the analogy a bit further, it should be apparent that bent twigs may inevitably snap back, but never to precisely the same shape and attitude. This would suggest that the form of nationalist resurgence is dependent on other factors, such as political culture and the domestic political structure. In other words, it need not necessarily be a violent or aggressive reaction.

In essence, we can identify essentially two motivations for promoting a national identity: in the first place, it may be a response to modernization (either to promote or to frustrate it); and second, it may be one of the means by which individuals discover a sense of personal worth. These two motivations can be related; in bad economic times, I would argue, it is difficult for individuals to develop a sense of worth. This difficulty is compounded in the former Soviet Union and Eastern Europe by the absence of well-developed civil societies in which people can find ways of fulfilling themselves. In healthy economies, it is easier for citizens to develop a sense of worth outside the context of ethnic groups, and within a broader civil society.

I argue that the success of nationalist politicians in the former Soviet Union and Eastern Europe represents more than simply voters' rejection of harsh economic conditions imposed by the transition to a market system. Nationalist politicians enjoy success in postcommunist societies not only because of their pledges to ameliorate the pain of economic transition, but also because they promise to restore glory and greatness to national identities that were previously suppressed. In the process, they offer the restoration of personal worth to individuals in societies that were almost universally robbed of it (both spiritually and materially) under Soviet-style socialism. It is significant also that one of the major concerns of Vladimir Zhirinovsky's supporters in the December 1993 election was crime and the breakdown of order; most were young to middle-aged blue-collar males earning average or higher-than-average wages in state-owned industrial enterprises.[11] Certainly many who voted for Zhirinovsky were among those who have been economically deprived by post-Soviet economic reform, of course, but the point is that for perhaps a majority of his supporters the fact that they had been economically pauperized was not their primary motivation. "Anarchy" and "weak government" in Russia as a whole were said to be among Zhirinovsky supporters' primary concerns. One of the reasons Zhirinovsky supporters want to combat crime is because it is one of the signs of national decay.

National Identity and Russian Foreign Policy

In the view of many observers, 1993 witnessed a shift in Russia's foreign policy from an emphasis on relations with the West to an emphasis on the countries of the "near abroad," understood here to mean the other fourteen former Soviet republics. A number of various explanations have been proposed for such a shift in priorities, ranging from Russia's supposed traditional inclination to dominate its neighbors to an apparent willingness on the part of the West to encourage or at least tolerate such ambitions.[12]

It seems to be the case that in the early stages, Russian policy makers saw both the near abroad and the West as equal priorities. As early as February 1992, for example, Kozyrev stated in an interview that Russian foreign policy would be based on "geopolitics," as opposed to the ideologized foreign policy of the Soviet era.[13] Kozyrev defined geopolitics as "a normal view of natural interests"; accordingly, Russia's first priority of interests was the near abroad. As a way of understanding the second sphere of Russia's interests, the foreign minister suggested the analogy of the Russian two-headed eagle, looking both East and West. In other words, Russian policy would focus on Eastern Europe, Western Europe, and the United States in the West, while looking to Japan and South Korea in the East.

Part of the difficulty in determining Russia's foreign policy priorities is that for much of the first year following the Soviet dissolution, it did not have a well-developed policy toward the countries on its borders. In some ways, Russians were simply having trouble separating domestic and foreign policy; an interesting parallel might be in how Stalin viewed Eastern Europe in the post–World War II period as essentially an extension of Soviet domestic politics, and his to control.[14] From the earliest moments of the existence of the Commonwealth of Independent States, Russians have had to come to grips with the fact that the former Soviet republics were truly independent countries. The difficulties of making such an adjustment were seen in the response by Evgenii Primakov, director of the USSR Central Intelligence Service (now the Russian Federation Foreign Intelligence Service), when asked about the future of the Soviet Union without some of its constituent republics.

> [*Interviewer*]: What kind of a Union will this be . . . without Ukraine, without Georgia?
> *Primakov*: Indeed . . . But I will say to you that Ukraine disturbs me more than Georgia, because without Ukraine . . . it is even difficult to imagine what this will be.[15]

In other words, even for this well-known liberal it was "difficult to imagine" what the Soviet Union, or Russia, would be without Ukraine. One of the cardinal questions of Russian national identity is whether "Russia as a civilization embraces only the Russian Federation or [whether] it also includes Ukraine and Belarus."[16] Allen Lynch and Reneo Lukic put the problem in a slightly different way: "Can a liberal Russian state be built if Russia is to retain imperial responsibilities outside Russia itself, and can an effective Russian state—liberal or not—be constructed in the absence of Russia's historical imperial hinterland?"[17]

Another relevant question concerning the possible options for Russia is whether or not a marketized and democratic society can be created without a Western-oriented foreign policy. In other words, can Russia assert what it has come to call its own "independent interests" in the world while at the same time carrying out reform along Western lines? In some ways, Russian policy makers in the immediate post-Soviet period evinced a desire to have their cake and eat it, too; in other words, they wanted to focus on both the near abroad and the West. In dealing with the near abroad, however, the new Russian state had to grapple with the historical legacies of imperial Russia and the Soviet Union, polities in which Russia had played the leading and oftentimes oppressive role in non-Russian regions.

Kozyrev's statement quoted above suggests that Russian foreign policy was not initially pro-Western in its orientation, yet the overwhelming perception was that in fact it was. How are we to explain this discrepancy? One cardinal distinction between Soviet and Russian policy, of course, were the goals—broad-based democratization and marketization as understood in the West were not the Soviet Union's goals, even if it did aim to enter the world economy. In that sense alone, Russian foreign policy in the initial post-Soviet period was distinctly pro-Western in its orientation. The aim of Egor Gaidar and other ardent "shock therapists" in the leadership was to integrate Russia into the Western-led international community. Both in their vision of Russia's future as a modern, market-oriented society and in their hope that the West would provide much of the funding to carry out such a transformation, radical reformers saw Russia as essentially part of the Western world. In other words, they promoted a Western-oriented national identity for Russia. Those less well disposed to reform (or at least to Gaidar's shock therapy), meanwhile, promoted a more traditional concept of Russian national identity that was often at variance with the one promoted by radical reformers.

Almost nowhere was this more evident than in policy toward the former Yugoslavia. Russian policy on the question of contributing troops for peacekeeping in Croatia and toward the conflict in Bosnia-Herzegovina clearly displayed how debates over national identity served to shape policy and crystallize the differences between leading political figures.

One of the first acts of the new Russian state was to send a battalion of troops to participate in United Nations peacekeeping operations.[18] After some initial resistance by both the Supreme Soviet and the Russian military,[19] the former approved Yeltsin's request for an infantry batallion to be sent to Yugoslavia. In justifying Russian participation, Yeltsin made two basic arguments, both of which support the view that peacekeeping in the region was a means of promoting a Western-oriented national identity at home and abroad. In the first place, Yeltsin suggested that taking part in the UN operations in Yugoslavia "would help strengthen Russia's international prestige."[20] Second, he also indicated that peacekeeping in the former Yugoslavia "would also be valuable from the viewpoint of our internal problems."[21]

In explaining Russia's vote for sanctions against Serbia later that spring in an attempt to stop the fighting in Bosnia-Herzegovina, a Russian government statement echoed the same themes. Russia, the statement claimed, was "discharging its responsibility as a great power for the maintenance of international law and order."[22] The Russian government also urged the Security Council to develop a list of criteria that would form the basis for deciding when to consider sanctions against those guilty of aggression, "in order to put a stop to current fratricidal wars deriving from interethnic conflicts and to avert fresh ones."[23]

These statements were notable for a number of reasons. In the first place, they support the contention that Russian participation in peacekeeping was primarily a means of demonstrating Russia's desire to be seen as a reliable member of the international community. In other words, it was part and parcel of the attempt to establish a Western-oriented identity in terms of becoming a member of what Kozyrev often called the "civilized world." Second, Russia's participation in Yugoslav peacekeeping and its later support for sanctions against Serbia also served a domestic purpose. It demonstrated that Russia would not tolerate or condone the use of force to settle ethnic disputes. In other words, it was a way of demonstrating to those within Russia (and the CIS) that the Russian national identity was indeed changing away from the traditional image of aggressive Russian nationalism that lashed out at its neighbors or against its ethnic minorities. It was therefore just as much a means of setting a good example in the hopes of sparing Russia the fate of Yugoslavia as anything else.

In a move that was symbolic of the importance of the near abroad in Russian foreign policy, Kozyrev was forced to interrupt his weeklong "peace mission" to the former Yugoslavia in May 1992 to return to Moscow to address the Supreme Soviet on the issue of the Crimea. In commenting on his trip, Kozyrev in fact referred to the relevance of Yugoslavia for his own country, urging lawmakers to reach a compromise with Ukraine over the issue of the Crimea.[24] Once again, this illustrates that Russian foreign policy was driven primarily by domestic motivations.

After addressing the Supreme Soviet on the Crimea issue, Kozyrev returned to Yugoslavia, only to leave once more, this time to attend the Lisbon Conference on aid to the former Soviet republics. As with his earlier departure, this is also symbolic of other Russian foreign policy priorities. It was after his return to Yugoslavia a third time that he was able to broker a cease-fire among the warring parties in Bosnia-Herzegovina, a cease-fire that was almost immediately broken, reportedly by Serbian forces that shelled Sarajevo, killing sixteen people in a breadline.[25]

Late May 1992 was a turning point in Russian policy. On 29 May, Russia joined Great Britain, France, and the United States (China abstained) in voting for sanctions against Serbia as the main perpetrator of the violence in Bosnia-Herzegovina. Following this vote, policy toward Yugoslavia became the first major test in what was to be a continuing struggle between the president and the Supreme Soviet for control over Russian foreign policy. At the end of June the

Supreme Soviet issued a resolution that attempted to force the Foreign Ministry to raise the issue of easing sanctions against rump Yugoslavia in the UN Security Council.[26] More broadly, the resolution also instructed the Foreign Ministry to consult with the parliament's leaders and with its Committee for International Affairs and Foreign Economic Relations "on questions that affect Russia's fundamental state interests."

In addition to closed sessions with various parliamentary leaders, the Foreign Ministry was also subjected to public criticism in both opposition and moderate newspapers. For example, the opposition weekly *Den'* published a leaked telegram from the Russian representative to the UN, Iulii Vorontsov, to the Foreign Ministry in Moscow in which he argued against "aggravating" the West on the eve of Yeltsin's visit to the United States, and therefore strongly urged Russia to vote with the West in favor of sanctions against Serbia.[27] *Den'* spoke for many conservative deputies when it published the telegram and accused the government of "betraying" Serbia. The noted political commentator Andranik Migranian, meanwhile, also reflected a general view developing among many opponents of radical reform that "constant concessions [to the West] are not actually producing the concrete and momentous economic infusions and financial aid which were expected" from a pro-Western orientation.[28] In a statement that highlighted the degree to which many Russians were coming to see Western aid as humiliating, Migranian characterized attempts by the West to make aid conditional on Russia's international behavior as "the most blatant blackmail."

Beyond policy toward Yugoslavia, two other events reinforced the perception that Russian foreign policy was being held hostage to Western interests. One observer, for instance, noted that Yeltsin supported sanctions against Serbia only after a meeting with European Community Commission Chairman Jacques Delors on rescheduling the Soviet debt.[29] What is more, all these apparent concessions came on the heels of the significant tension produced in relations with the United States by the latter's pressure on Russia to cancel a planned $250 million sale of rocket booster engines to India. The sale was eventually allowed to proceed with modifications that satisfied U.S. suspicions that it violated the Missile Technology Control Regime; regardless, many Russians (and not just hardliners or conservatives) perceived this as an attempt by the West to relegate Russia to second-rate status and to push it out of lucrative arms markets.[30]

Therefore, throughout the summer of 1992 Kozyrev was forced to justify Russia's foreign policy stance, and was especially at pains to explain why Russia would not find itself a junior partner of the West simply by sharing some of the same policy positions. He rejected the supposed link between Russian support for sanctions and the request for Western debt rescheduling, claiming that "unfortunately, we still do not have in the government the kind of coordination which enables us to link one political step to another."[31] Whether or not that is true does not negate the possibility that different political actors in Russia would promote pro-Western policies in an unspoken quid pro quo.

After his return from Yugoslavia, Kozyrev went to great pains to illustrate how Russia could share the fate of Bosnia-Herzegovina. Condemning the possibility of a Pan-Slavic or Pan-Orthodox tilt in foreign policy, he noted,

> If we allow these concepts to develop, they may, first, cause the deepest schism in the Russian community for the simple reason, at least, that we have millions of Muslims living in our country.[32]

If anything, the debate over Russia's national interests served to crystallize and sharpen the differences between the radical reformers and their opponents, so much so that whereas in February 1992 Kozyrev was willing to characterize the near abroad as equal in priority to the West, by the following August he put a much clearer emphasis on the West. Writing on the anniversary of the August coup, the Russian foreign minister maintained his view that a "normal vision of geopolitical interests" was taking the place of ideology.[33] More important for our purposes, he listed four priorities for Russian foreign policy, the fulfillment of which would create favorable conditions for political and economic transformation. In apparent order of their importance, Kozyrev listed the following as priorities for Russian foreign policy:

> First, there is the entry as a great power into the family of the most advanced democratic states with market economies. . . . The second priority is the formation of good-neighbor relations with all the states along the perimeter of the Russian border. Here, of course, a special place belongs to the CIS countries and the major powers of Asia, such as India and China.[34]

The third priority was said to be attracting foreign investment for the Russian economy, while the fourth priority "was to safeguard human rights, especially for the Russian-speaking populations in neighboring republics." This prioritization of Russian foreign policy interests was almost the exact opposite of what one would expect from the opponents of radical reform; more to the point, it is clear that three of these priorities put great emphasis on becoming a member of the Western world, whether in terms of integrating Russia into the world economy or promoting adherence to commonly accepted norms of human rights (albeit primarily in defense of Russians abroad).

Another strong statement of this position was made by Kozyrev in December 1992, in the lead-up to a crucial session of the Congress of People's Deputies one year after the Soviet collapse. He criticized both "centrists" and "champions of superpowerism" who spoke of Russia's special path; such a belief, he claimed, would lead to a foreign policy of "semiconfrontation with the West and a semi-ingratiating stance toward it, making the country suffer from an inferiority complex."[35] It is worth pointing out that Kozyrev has repeatedly referred to this tendency of those of a great-power orientation to harbor feelings of inferiority vis-à-vis the West.[36] It suggests that Russian national identity was a means of realizing a sense of personal worth for those of a Western orientation as much as for their opponents, albeit in different ways. For Kozyrev and other reformers, promoting Russia's identity as an essentially Western nation was a means of providing a sense of personal worth gained through membership in a group, to use Horowitz's phrase, that is in turn viewed as worthy, in this case the West.

Kozyrev listed one of Russia's fundamental national interests as the need to ensure "favorable conditions for shaping an effective market economy to match the status of a great power."[37] In other words, creating favorable conditions for market reform was one of Russia's foreign policy interests requiring, accordingly, good relations with the West. The goal of relations with the West was said to be "partnership and alliance relations" in order to facilitate Russia's successful economic reform and integration into the world economy and to gain political and financial support for reform.[38] Later that month (December 1992), the Foreign Ministry presented its draft "Basic Provisions of the Concept of the Foreign Policy of the Russian Federation" to the Supreme Soviet. A review of the document quoted it as reflecting Kozyrev's view that Russia must promote relations "first of all with the economically powerful and technologically developed Western nations and newly industrialized countries in different regions."[39]

The importance of the near abroad thus seemed to fall in relation to the growth of the importance of the West. In the December document, the primary goal of policy toward the near abroad was said to be the creation of a "belt of good-neighborliness."[40] In an April 1993 interview, Kozyrev noted the "fundamental [and] qualitative" change in Russian foreign policy by virtue of its emphasis on the West. He went on to note that this foreign policy orientation "began to be supplemented by the less ideological but very important thesis of the belt of good-neighborliness."[41]

At least three factors contributed to this reorientation of Russia's foreign policy. In the first place, Western aid never developed into the large-scale infusion of cash that many reformers expected and felt was necessary for successful reform. Billions of dollars and deutsche marks have been pledged, but the record of implementation is spotty. In addition, there is a public relations element to much Western aid; debt rescheduling and purchases of Western goods destined for Russia are often included in the announced aid package totals. This type of aid helps, of course, but it is not the kind of massive, direct investment that reformers and ordinary Russians had assumed would flow from the West with the collapse of the Soviet Union.

Second, Western aid came to be seen as humiliating in Russia. Conservatives and liberals alike saw Russia as a once-proud country now reduced to begging for aid that came with heavy conditionality. In addition, the fact that Yeltsin's government under Gaidar relied heavily on Western economic advisors such as Jeffrey Sachs or the International Monetary Fund contributed to a public perception that once again Russians were being told what was in their best interests, as the Communist Party had done since 1917.

Finally, increasing emphasis on the near abroad can also be seen as an aspect of the changing Russian national identity following the Soviet collapse. Prior to December 1991, Russian support for the independence of non-Russian republics or autonomy for ethnic regions within Russia was in effect a strategy designed to achieve the goal of weakening the Soviet center. This strategy worked, perhaps too successfully; the outright destruction of the Soviet Union was not one of the Russian leadership's goals.[42] With the Ukrainian vote for independence in December 1991 and the subsequent demise of the Soviet Union, however, promoting independence for the former Soviet republics could be interpreted as working against Russia's national interests. Many of the newly independent states would look first to developing good relations with countries other than Russia, most likely the West. Russia's interest in maintaining some semblance of unity among the former Soviet republics was determined by both the high level of economic interdependence among them inherited from the former Soviet planned economy and the presence of large numbers of Russians in the non-Russian republics.

Foreign Policy Institutions and the Near Abroad

Accordingly, a number of contentious issues have arisen in Russia's relations with its closest neighbors in the last two years. While specifics vary from country to country, the following questions are important for virtually all the former Soviet republics. One is the question of the re-creation of a common economic space and the coordination of economic reform. A second question, no less important from the Russian point of view, is the treatment of Russians and Russified non-Russians in these republics. Third is the issue of managing and resolving regional and local conflicts on the territory of the former Soviet Union. To some degree this is related to the question of Russians abroad, given that they are often either the target of such outbursts of violence or themselves combatants. This section focuses on the last two aspects of Russia's policy toward the near abroad, inasmuch as it is here that the influence of nationalism is most keenly felt and easily observable.[43]

Official focus on the near abroad was enshrined in the first document meant to lay out the principles of Russian foreign policy, adopted by presidential decree in April 1993.[44] The "Basic Provisions of the Concept of the Foreign Policy of the Russian Federation" was composed by the Russian Security Council on the basis of interagency discussions, that included the Foreign Ministry. The Security Council itself was set up on the recommendation of the Second Congress of People's Deputies in May 1992,[45] and later in the year it was given the task of coordinating foreign policy under an Interdepartmental Foreign Policy Commission. According to some observers, the Security Council was the scene of bureaucratic turf battles for control over foreign policy.[46]

If the "Basic Provisions" are any indication, the Foreign Ministry seemed to have lost the first round. Comparing the Foreign Ministry's December 1992 draft document on foreign policy and the April 1993 "Basic Provisions," it is obvious that the latter sets a much less Western-oriented tone for Russian foreign policy. The "Basic Provisions" characterized Russian foreign policy tasks as (1) "guaranteeing processes in the formation of the statehood of Russia"; (2) "defending its territorial integrity"; (3) "creating conditions which ensure the stability and irreversibility of political and economic reforms"; (4) securing "the Russian Federation's active and full participation in building a new system of international relations in which it is assured a fitting place"; and (5) "protection of the interests of Russian citizens abroad."[47]

Oleg Osobenkov, as the council's spokesman on the "Basic Provisions," pointedly stated that "the actions of certain powers bent on securing their hegemony on a global or regional level" contradicted attempts to develop collaborative methods of guaranteeing national security.[48] Armed conflicts in neighboring states were seen as one of the main threats to Russia's security. Significantly, Osobenkov also pointed out another possible threat to Russian security: by opening up its economy to the outside world, the country's industrial potential could be weakened. As a result, Russia could find itself in the position of specializing in the supply of fuel and raw materials to the developed world. This is a favorite theme of those Russians who favor a slower pace of reform and suggests a Soviet-style propensity to see heavy industry as the guarantor of the nation's security. It also betrays a concern with status and prestige; the implication is that a "raw materials appendage" to the developed world cannot be a great power. Of course, maintaining the country's heavy industries can also be economically motivated, inasmuch as arms sales will most likely remain the one area where Russia might remain competitive with the West.

Concerning the near abroad, Osobenkov maintained that "Russia does bear a special responsibility—this is simply a reality—for building a new system of positive relations among the states which previously belonged to the USSR."[49] Use of the term "responsibility" is curious; in some ways, it is reminiscent of Gorbachev's "new thinking" in foreign policy, which held that superpowers had not a right but a responsibility to act in world affairs. If this is indeed a holdover from Soviet ways of thinking about international relations, then it suggests that old habits die hard, and that Russia may be successor to the Soviet legacy psychologically as well as materially.

Between the adoption of the "Basic Provisions" in April and Boris Yeltsin's dissolution of the Supreme Soviet in September, a certain change in emphasis toward the near abroad could be observed. This was seen vividly in an article that Kozyrev published in *Nezavisimaia gazeta* one week before an appearance at the United Nations. Whereas in 1992 and the first half of 1993, he, too, had spoken of a "responsibility" for maintaining stability in the near abroad, in September, Kozyrev characterized Russia's peacekeeping role in the near abroad as a financial "burden" (*bremia*) borne by it alone.[50] A sense of "missionary zeal" has often been said to underlie Russian national identity, and Kozyrev's use of the term suggested a belief that Russia was bearing a similar burden now.

Russia had been asking for UN approval for its peacekeeping operations more or less since February 1993.[51] In doing so, Yeltsin himself expressed the view that Russia had a "special responsibility" to maintain stability in the region, but neither Yeltsin nor his spokesman ever referred to this role as a "burden" that Russia was willing to bear for the good of the international and regional community. It is rarely the case, of course, that states act purely out of humanitarian motivations, and some observers see the Russian desire for a UN stamp of approval for its peacekeeping operations as a means of securing Western and international recognition of Russia's sphere of interest in the region.[52] Just as important, however, is the fact that instability in the near abroad does in fact pose a threat to Russia proper, both in the danger of spillover and by encouraging the growth of chauvinistic nationalist sentiment domestically if Russians are threatened and the government does little or nothing to respond. Those who asserted that, by September 1993, Russia had "[ceased] to hide its great power ambitions behind the rhetorically more palatable guise of humanitarian assistance"[53] were unwilling to recognize the legitimacy of Russia's desire for stable states on its borders. Maintaining stability in the former Soviet Union can prevent the much-feared "Islamization" of the Central Asian republics and stymie Iranian or fundamentalist Muslim influence, which in fact coincides with Western interests. Of course, there is also the very real danger of local conflicts spilling over into Russia itself; maintaining stability in the near abroad can therefore promote stability at home. On the other hand, the financial and human costs of peacekeeping can increase the strains on the Russian economy and, perhaps, the influence of the armed forces. In seeking UN approval for its peacekeeping role in the region, Russia was also seeking UN financial assistance to maintain those forces and limit the impact on its economy.

Much as in foreign policy, Russia was forced to develop a new military doctrine to take into account changing domestic and international conditions. And as with the "Basic Provisions," the Russian military was left without such a programmatic document for all of 1992 and much of 1993. It was only in the aftermath of the disbanding of the Supreme Soviet and the use of the military to dislodge its supporters from the Russian White House that Russia adopted a new military doctrine that had reportedly been under consideration for some time.[54]

A "detailed account" of the new military doctrine (but not the actual document) was released to the public in mid-November 1993.[55] Again, as with the "Basic Provisions" in foreign policy, the new doctrine specifically mentioned cooperation (in this case, military) with the CIS as the priority for the Russian Federation.[56] More significantly, the document characterized "existing and potential local wars and armed conflicts" on Russia's borders as one of the major threats to the country's security;[57] accordingly, one of the major principles of the

Russian Federation's military policy was said to be the "maintenance of stability in regions adjoining the borders of the Russian Federation [and] neighboring countries."[58]

These principles gave Russia a doctrinal and theoretical groundwork for the use of political and military means to guarantee stability in the near abroad. It seems to have been part of a general hardening of the Russian attitude toward its traditional areas of concern, as witnessed by the universally negative reaction generated among Russian policy elites by the prospect of NATO membership for East European countries (Poland, Hungary, the Czech Republic, and Slovakia). Among the most vocal of Russian foreign policy institutions on this issue was the Foreign Intelligence Service (FIS), more or less the inheritor of the Soviet KGB's external intelligence functions.

As part of the general Russian foreign policy offensive geared at preventing East European entry into NATO, the FIS released a position paper, "The Expansion of NATO and Russia's Interests." An account of a section of the paper devoted to Russia's concerns made repeated reference to the effect that NATO expansion might have on the "psychological state" of Russians—notably, on the military.[59] Noting that Russians had long been raised in an anti-NATO spirit, the FIS suggested that including former Soviet allies in NATO

> will be seen by a significant portion of society as "the drawing near of danger to the borders of the motherland." This can give an impulse to anti-Western forces in the [Russian Federation], and supply them with arguments for single-minded attempts to discredit the [Russian] government's course.[60]

The document also frankly suggested that NATO expansion would force the military to rethink its doctrine, force structure, and deployment patterns; given Russia's dire economic straits, this raised the possibility that the government would not be able to keep the military satisfied. This could in turn lead to the discontent of military circles, "which clearly is not in the interests of either the political or military leadership of Russia, or of the country as a whole."[61]

Such views suggested that some Russian policy makers were concerned not so much with extending Russian influence abroad as with preventing external relations from undermining reform at home. That Kozyrev remained committed to this thinking was shown by an October 1993 article, again in the well-known *Nezavisimaia gazeta*, in which he portrayed democracy and peacekeeping as "two sides of the same medal."[62] He argued once more that the UN and the international community should support Russian peacekeeping effort and repeated his September proposal of creating an international fund in order to assist in doing so.

Ultimately, this brings us back to the question of national identity and foreign policy. Only here it is a case of foreign policy being used to promote a certain brand of national identity at home. By seeking international approval for their peacekeeping efforts, Russian reformers attempted to frustrate the growth of nationalist sentiment by defusing the issue of Russians abroad. In his October article, Kozyrev raised the possibility that if Russia did not undertake peacekeeping efforts in "zones of [its] traditional geopolitical interests," the vacuum will be filled by others "not necessarily friendly to us, and in any case competing" with Russia. His September article, however, had made this fear more explicit—"this vacuum will be filled by others, first of all by the forces of political extremism, threatening Russia itself."

Russian Political Parties and the Near Abroad

The success of nationalist politicians in the December 1993 elections takes on a different hue when seen in light of the fact that Russian foreign policy had already swung away from its Western orientation by the end of that year. The success of nationalists and communists did not cause Russian foreign policy to swing to the right so much as it prompted continued moves in this direction by increasing the likelihood that Yeltsin and other reformers would find it necessary to preempt their increasingly powerful opponents. Coming out on behalf of Russians in the near abroad or standing up in defense of Russia's national interests should simply be seen as one element of this preemption.

The new constitution enshrined the powers of the president, and it is unclear to what degree the new Federal Assembly will be able to do anything more than nip at the ankles of the executive branch in its formulation and execution of foreign policy. In the conditions of institutional flux prevailing in Russia today, however, it is nevertheless appropriate to examine the foreign policy positions of those parties represented in the new legislature.

Eight parties exceeded the 5 percent threshold in party list balloting to gain representation in the State Duma, or lower house: Russia's Choice (RC), 70 seats, based on party lists and single-mandate districts; the Liberal Democratic Party of Russia (LDPR), 64; the Communist Party of the Russian Federation (CPRF), 48; the Agrarian Party, 47; the Yavlinskii-Boldyrev-Lukin bloc ("Yabloko"), 23; the Party of Russian Unity and Accord (Russian acronym PRES), 19; the Democratic Party of Russia (DPR), approximately 14; and the Women of Russia (WOR), 23. Independents gained about 130 seats.[63]

In their attempts at categorizing the basic foreign policy orientations in Russia today, many authors have turned to a relatively simple three-tiered schema— "Westernists" (or "Atlanticists"), "Eurasianists," and "Extreme Nationalists."[64]

Such characterizations of foreign policy attitudes miss many of the nuances of the current debate in Russia today. A more satisfactory approach is that used by Dawisha and Parrott in their 1994 study of Russian foreign policy.[65] They list five basic orientations in Russian foreign policy attitudes: (1) Westernist, or Atlanticist; (2) Eurasianist; (3) Great Power (*derzhavniki*); (4) Isolationist or Slavophile; and (5) Extreme Nationalist. These five orientations are listed more or less in order of increasingly negative attitudes toward the West.

Westernists, or Atlanticists, of course, are those such as Kozyrev who promote a Western-oriented foreign policy. Activist but not expansionist, they see Russia as essentially a Western nation. The next two categories, Eurasianists and *derzhavniki*, promote closer ties first of all with Russia's immediate neighbors. The main difference between these two groups is their view of Russian national identity and hence the proper form of statehood; Eurasianists tend to see Russia as essentially multiethnic and democratic, while *derzhavniki* place more emphasis on the development of a strong, often ethnically defined, Russian state. Isolationists, meanwhile, are exactly that—isolationist, and concerned first of all with Russia's "spiritual rebirth."[66] They also tend to have a Slavophile streak, but at the same time are rather anti-Western. While essentially concerned with domestic affairs, they might make common cause with those on the extreme right who would support ties with Serbia or other Slavic nations, based on bonds of blood or Orthodoxy. Extreme Nationalists are those on the far right of the political spectrum who tend to blame all of Russia's problems on foreigners or ethnic minorities within Russia. They commonly define the Russian state in ethnic or religious terms, rather than secular or democratic, and propose xenophobic solutions, both domestically and internationally.

Two of the eight parties with Duma representation, Women of Russia and the Agrarian Party, can best be characterized as Isolationist or Slavophile in their foreign policy orientation. Neither party devoted much (if any) attention to the question of Russia's foreign policy during the election campaign. Both were concerned largely with domestic social issues, although an anti-Western tinge can be detected especially in the Agrarian Party's emphasis on Russia's spiritual rebirth based on its rural traditions.

The reformist parties displayed a similar lack of attention to foreign affairs. The fact that Andrei Kozyrev was a member of the leadership of Russia's Choice, however, suggested that his foreign policy views were to some degree those of his party. More important is the fact that Gaidar, Fedorov, and other ardent reformers are unabashedly pro-Western in their orientation and remain so.

"Yabloko" also had a number of foreign policy specialists within its leadership, including former ambassador to the United States Vladimir Lukin and First Deputy Foreign Minister Anatolii Adamishin. As with most other parties, Yabloko devoted little attention to foreign policy in its campaign. The Russian army newspaper *Krasnaia zvezda*, however, characterized the bloc's foreign policy priority as "the political settlement of armed conflicts around Russia." The paper also noted that the bloc came out in favor of a defense alliance among the CIS countries.[67] Lukin has elsewhere been described as one with a tendency to emphasize Russia's status as a great power and its role in the near abroad, suggesting a Eurasianist streak to his thinking.[68]

Adamishin, meanwhile, displayed a view closer to that of his boss, Kozyrev, in discussing Russian views on East European entry into NATO. Fearing Russian isolation if Poland, Hungary, the Czech Republic, and Slovakia joined

NATO, he explained that the fragility of Russian democracy argued against such a move: "If people see that we are in an isolated position, . . . it will be difficult for a democratic government to say: Do not be afraid, these [i.e., the West] are good people."[69] Therefore, it appears that two of the top figures in the Russian Foreign Ministry were concerned not so much with the opportunity to expand their influence through the use of peacekeeping forces or by keeping the East Europeans out of NATO, but rather with the anticipated effects of these policies on the domestic political scene.

The remaining parties—the DPR, the CPRF, and the LDPR—were all to varying degrees much more assertive vis-à-vis the near abroad. Sergei Glaz'ev, the economic advisor for the DPR, devoted considerable attention to his party's foreign policy platform. Between January and August of 1993, Glaz'ev was the Russian Minister for Foreign Economic Relations; in this position, he argued for a strong regulatory role for the state in order to improve the trade balance and protect domestic industries.[70] In one sense, it may be encouraging that an economic advisor was addressing foreign policy issues, inasmuch as it suggests support for a less militarized policy toward the near abroad. On the other hand, Glaz'ev's unabashed preference for a larger state role in the system of foreign trade also suggests that the DPR would be more than willing to flex Russian economic muscle on behalf of perceived interests in the region.

Indeed, Glaz'ev stated that the main foreign policy goal of the DPR was the restoration of Russia's political and economic influence in the world. He contended that "it is extremely important to us that no further weakening of Russia's position is allowed to occur on the huge territory of the former USSR." He also urged more "political influence" in Eastern and Southeastern Europe and spoke out as well against reliance on the West: "Western loans generate bureaucracy and set a bad example for the population." Instead, he argued for efforts to lift discriminatory Western trade barriers.[71] In essence, these positions suggest that the DPR was concerned with promoting Russia's economic recovery through integration with the near abroad, while at the same time guaranteeing the economic interests of Russians in the region.

The CPRF, meanwhile, was one of two parties (the LDPR was the other) to come out openly in favor of restoring some sort of union on the territory of the former USSR. Bemoaning the loss of superpower status and the redefinition of Russia's identity was a common campaign theme of the CPRF, suggesting that the motivation behind its call for restoration of the union was more political and psychological than economic.[72]

Significantly, the LDPR of Vladimir Zhirinovsky was virtually alone in devoting a considerable amount of attention to questions of foreign policy. He laid out his party's domestic and foreign policy most succinctly in a preelection article in *Rossiiskaia gazeta*.[73] He characterized his party's priorities toward the near abroad as the cessation of aid to countries outside of Russia and use of the funds to improve the lives of Russian citizens instead. He called for a "union of

Slavic states" on the basis of Orthodoxy, in the long term, and declared that in the short term Russia should focus its attention first of all on the "southern salient: Turkey, Iran, Afghanistan, the Caucasus, and Central Asia." He had spoken out elsewhere against the CIS, as well as the Soviet Union, and in favor of a Russian state within the borders of the USSR circa 1977 (the year of the last Soviet Constitution).[74] Notably, he proposed a strictly territorial administrative division of Russia, as opposed to its current ethnic and territorial division. The same was true for the countries of the near abroad, especially Central Asia, which he would bring back into Russia along the lines of their historical provincial status. Finally, as far as his position on the question of Russians abroad, Zhirinovsky declared:

> Naturally, we do not remove from the agenda the slogan of the defense of Russians throughout the territory of Russia and the former USSR and that brings us close to our country's truly patriotic forces.[75]

Zhirinovsky then, by his own admission, shared the position of those on the Russian extreme right in his attitude toward the protection of Russians abroad. If his comments are taken with a grain of salt, he appears to be nothing more than a somewhat extreme *derzhavnik*. Viewed less kindly, his comments betray a xenophobic and extreme Russian nationalism. It is unclear how much of his bravado and hyperbole he really believes; the danger is that such sentiments promote the worst kind of Russian nationalism and may take on a life of their own even if intended only as crass political manipulation.

Conclusion

A number of conclusions concerning the relationship between national identity and foreign policy can be drawn from this overview of Russian attitudes toward the near abroad and Yugoslavia.

In the first place, it is apparent that Russian foreign policy has served a number of purposes in terms of national identity, as outlined in the introductory sections of this study. Russia's foreign policy has been aimed first of all at creating favorable conditions for domestic economic and political transformation. In the case of the former Yugoslavia, this entailed adhering to the positions of the world community in terms of imposing sanctions on Serbia for its role in the fighting in Bosnia-Herzegovina. The intent, for Russian reformers, was to demonstrate that Russia was a responsible member of the world community; in other words, a state that would uphold its international obligations, would adhere to international standards of conduct, and was therefore worthy of participation in international organizations and worthy of investment in its attempts to reform its economy. In a word, promoting a Western identity should here be seen as an attempt to promote modernization. At the same time, it was also a means of developing a sense of individual worth, in this case by being seen as part of a wider community that was in turn seen as worthy.

Opponents of the government's policy, on the other hand, were those who were least likely to see the West as a worthy group—communists and nationalists in particular. Long years of training made them suspicious of the West's good intent. What is more, if we choose to make a value judgment for the moment about whether a Western-oriented market economy and political democracy are inherently more modern, it is possible to see the opponents of radical reform as trying to frustrate modernization, in Schöpflin's terms. Political modernization threatens the political privileges of some, and, more important, it is guaranteed to require a rethinking of what for seventy years were the customary modes of behavior and interaction.

Second, a broad consensus has developed among Russia's foreign policy elite that the near abroad is just as much a priority in Russian foreign policy as are relations with the West, if not more so. This view was codified in the Security Council document on foreign policy adopted in April 1993, and is seen most visibly in Russian attempts to gain international endorsement (if not aid) for its peacekeeping activities in the region.

Despite this consensus, the motivations for such involvement vary immensely. Westernists are most likely to see peacekeeping in the near abroad as a means of protecting Russians and Russian-speakers, thereby preempting criticism from the far right. It is also a means of maintaining stability in Russia itself by preventing the spillover of local conflicts. Foreign policy in the near abroad is thus a function of domestic goals: creating favorable conditions for economic and political reform along Western lines. Part and parcel of successful reform is the promotion of a Western-oriented national identity, which is facilitated by making the issue of Russians abroad less salient. Adherents of this view include the leaders of Russia's Choice, Foreign Minister Kozyrev, and most likely the First Deputy Foreign Minister Adamishin.

Adamishin's colleague in Yabloko, however, Vladimir Lukin, and the majority of parties in the State Duma may be safely characterized as Eurasianist in their foreign policy attitudes. Russian involvement in the near abroad is seen primarily as a means of guaranteeing Russia's economic interests, as laid out, for example, by representatives of the DPR. Alternatively, for the *derzhavniki* policy toward the former Soviet republics can be seen as a means of restoring political influence and imperial and/or Soviet greatness. Meanwhile, for parties such as the CPRF and extremists such as Zhirinovsky, the near abroad is valued mainly as historically Russian territory, whether imperial or Soviet. Large numbers of ethnic Russians make it a natural area for the exercise of Russia's influence.

Russophone Foreign Policy?

In many Western discussions of the issue of Russians in the near abroad, both popular and scholarly, there is a tendency to use shorthand and to refer to the protection of just "Russians," usually meaning ethnic Russians. Many Russian policy makers point to Russia's responsibility to protect not only "Russians" in the near abroad, however, but also "Russian-speakers" (*russkoiazychnye*).[76] (In some Western analyses, this is characterized as a concern for "Russified non-Russians.")[77] In Russian, of course, there are two different terms used to denote what we in the West refer to as "Russians": *russkie*, meaning ethnically Russian (derived from Rus´, the historical term for Russia), and *rossiianin*, usually translated as "Russian citizens." This latter term is used today to denote both Russian and non-Russian citizens of the Russian Federation.

"Russified" non-Russians living abroad, however, pose something of a problem, given that they are neither ethnically Russian nor citizens of the Russian Federation. Nonetheless, they often look to Russia for political protection. This was graphically demonstrated to Yeltsin during a phone-in interview in July 1992. One of the issues most commonly raised by callers from as far away as Riga, Donetsk, and Chişinău was the status of Russians and Russian-speakers. A rough count suggests that five or six of the approximately twenty-five callers expressed concern about protecting minority rights for the Russian and Russian-speaking population in the near abroad.[78]

A number of observations can be made about protection of "Russian-speakers" abroad as a foreign policy priority. First, there seems to be some similarity here to what may be characterized as a "Francophone" foreign policy, in which France puts a high priority on maintaining good relations with its former colonies where French is spoken, many expatriates live, and France still has significant interests. One Russian official, Deputy Defense Minister Andrei Kokoshin, in fact compared Russian policy in the near abroad to French foreign policy in sub-Saharan Africa.[79]

What would be the characteristics of a "Russophone" foreign policy? Based on the French example, we might expect to see an activist foreign policy focused on maintaining influence in former Russian "colonies," in this case the former Soviet republics. This influence would be based on the presence of large numbers of Russians and Russified non-Russians, in other words, those with a cultural affinity for Russia. It would also seek to promote Russian economic interests in the region and most likely would claim a privileged position (a "responsibility," perhaps?) in the region. There is always the possibility, of course, that this type of activist foreign policy on behalf of "Russians" abroad may simply be a cover for what is commonly suspected to be "neoimperialist" ambitions of recreating a sphere of political influence. Whether that is so depends in large part on who is promoting the policy. When Kozyrev promotes protection of Russian-speakers, it is a quite different and most likely more benign activism than one promoted by Zhirinovsky.

Second, this may indicate a change or evolution in the Russian national identity. Speaking out in favor of Russian-speakers in the near abroad may mean that a broader understanding of Russian national identity is taking shape. This expansion of the meaning of Russian national identity suggests that it is evolving in the direction of a civic conception of national identity. Many scholars have pointed to the difference between *ethnic* and *civic* concepts of the nation. The civic (or "Western") conception of the nation stresses territory, "a community of laws and legal institutions," citizenship, and a common culture; the ethnic (or "Eastern") relies much less on formal laws or institutions and instead looks to "genealogy, populism, customs and dialects, and nativism" as the primary means of deciding who does and who does not belong to the nation.[80] Ethnic conceptions are inherently exclusivist, while the hallmark of civic conceptions is that they are inclusive. They may be roughly compared to the "primordialist" and "modernist" understandings of nationalism discussed earlier. Upholding the rights of Russian-speakers can be seen as part of the trend toward a civic conception of the nation, inasmuch as it indicates that those who adopt Russian culture and language can also be considered worthy of membership in the Russian Federation. An ethnically bound conception of the nation, on the other hand, would not focus on the rights of Russian-speakers given that they need not be ethnically Russian.

Third, based on the distinction between *russkii* and *rossiiskii* (similar to the distinction between *russkie* and *rossiianan*), we can make an argument that protection of "Russians" abroad is not necessarily a manifestation of an aggressive Russian nationalism. It depends on the term used and the interpretation of what it means to be Russian—whether it is seen as an inherent quality, and therefore stresses the ethnic nature of Russian identity (*russkii*), or one that can be acquired through adoption of Russian language and culture and participation in Russia's institutions (*rossiiskii*).

Given their multinational populations, most of the former Soviet republics have chosen to promote civic conceptions of the nation.[81] But such Western-oriented conceptions are frequently challenged by extreme nationalists who attempt to promote their own ethnic group at the expense of others within the state. Protecting Russified non-Russians, however, may be a means of promoting exactly the type of inclusive national identity seen as most conducive to stability. Speaking out on behalf of Russified non-Russians therefore may work to promote nonethnic concepts of the nation within Russia itself.[82]

In essence, then, Russian foreign policy seems likely to continue or even increase its emphasis on the "near abroad" for a variety of reasons. A Russophone foreign policy stressing the interests of ethnic Russians and Russified non-Russians in the "near abroad" is likely to be less onerous than many of the more ethnically oriented alternatives. Berlin's analogy of the "bent twig" suggests that Russia will inevitably be concerned for the fate of its compatriots in the "near abroad." The task for the West is therefore not to automatically reject Russian efforts to maintain stability in the "near abroad" on the assumption that they represent a throwback to imperial thinking. Instead, we should assess the motivations behind Russian involvement in the "near abroad" and selectively encourage such activity when it promotes the development of civic conceptions of national identity. This will help promote the development of Russian democracy, which will be one of the main determinants of the character of Russia's foreign policy.

Notes

I would like to thank Greg Miller and A.C. Cutler for research assistance on this chapter.

1. Suzanne Crow, "Russia Asserts Its Strategic Agenda," *RFE/RL Research Report*, (17 December 1993).
2. The discussion in this section is based on Anthony Smith, *The Ethnic Origins of Nations* (Oxford: Blackwell, 1986).
3. Vladimir Petrovskii, "Russia: National Security Priorities," *Rossiiskie vesti*, 29 December 1992, in *U.S. Foreign Broadcast Information Service Daily Report: Central Eurasia Report* (hereafter FBIS-SOV), FBIS-SOV–92–251, pp. 21–23. The author was described as a Lieutenant Colonel and Candidate of Military Sciences.
4. Andrei Kozyrev, interview by Anatolii Pankov, *Kuranty*, 16 April 1993, in FBIS-SOV–93–072, pp. 4–7.
5. Anthony Smith, *National Identity* (New York: Penguin, 1991).
6. George Schöpflin, "Nationalism and National Minorities in East and Central Europe," *Journal of International Affairs*, vol. 45, no. 1 (summer 1991), pp. 51–66.
7. This is a point made by both Smith, in *The Ethnic Origins of Nations*, p. 212, and Eric Hobsbawm, *Nations and Nationalism Since 1870: Program, Myth, Reality* (Cambridge: Cambridge University Press, 1990), p. 11.
8. Jack Snyder, "Nationalism and the Crisis of the Post-Soviet State," *Survival*, vol. 35, no. 1 (spring 1993), pp. 1–26.
9. Schöpflin, "Nationalism and National Minorities," p. 53.
10. Donald Horowitz, *Ethnic Groups in Conflict* (Berkeley: University of California Press, 1986), p. 185.
11. See the analysis by the All-Russian Center for the Study of Public Opinion in *Izvestiia*, 30 December 1993, in *RFE/RL Daily Report*, 3 January 1994. See also *Rossiiskaia gazeta*, 17 December 1993, in FBIS-SOV–93–242, p. 28; and Mikhail Leont'ev, "The Bell Has Tolled. Even Louder Than We Wanted," *Segodnia*, 16 December 1993, in *Current Digest of the Post-Soviet Press*, 12 January 1994, pp. 14–15.
12. Crow, "Russia Asserts Its Strategic Agenda"; also John Lough, "The Place of the 'Near Abroad' in Russian Foreign Policy," *RFE/RL Research Report*, 12 March 1993.
13. Andrei Kozyrev, interview by Elizaveta Leont'eva, *Rossiiskaia gazeta*, 21 January 1992, in FBIS-SOV–92–014, pp. 28–30.
14. See, among others, Karen Dawisha, *Eastern Europe, Gorbachev, and Reform: The Great Challenge*, 2d ed. (Cambridge: Cambridge University Press, 1990), pp. 83–84.
15. Evgenii Primakov, interview by Andrei Karaulov, *Nezavisimaia gazeta*, 21 December 1991, in FBIS-SOV–92–002, pp. 6–10.
16. Konstantin Pleshakov, "The Russian Dilemma," *New Times* (Moscow), no. 7 (February 1992), p. 15, as quoted in Karen Dawisha and Bruce Parrott, *Russia and the New States of Eurasia: The Politics of Upheaval* (Cambridge: Cambridge University Press, 1994), p. 64.
17. Allen Lynch and Reneo Lukic, "Russian Foreign Policy and the Wars in the Former Yugoslavia," *RFE/RL Research Report*, 15 October 1993, p. 28.
18. As an example of how context changes perceptions, in 1992 the West had noticeably fewer qualms about Russian participation in peacekeeping efforts than it was to have

two years later, when Russia moved some of those same troops to Sarajevo to oversee the withdrawal of Serbian heavy weapons in the face of threatened NATO air strikes.

19. See the comment by Foreign Ministry spokesman Urii Deriabin, Interfax (in English), 24 February 1992, in FBIS-SOV–92–036, p. 32.

20. Interfax (in English), 6 March 1992, in FBIS-SOV–92–045, pp. 34–35.

21. Ibid.

22. ITAR-TASS (in Russian), 30 May 1992, in FBIS-SOV–92–105, p. 11.

23. Ibid.

24. Teleradiokompaniia Ostankino Television First Program Network (in Russian), 18 May 1992, in FBIS-SOV–92–097, p. 9.

25. Maksim Iusin, "Storm Clouds Gathering Over Belgrade," *Izvestiia*, 30 May 1992, in FBIS-SOV–92–105, pp. 10–11.

26. Resolution no. 3135–1 of the Russian Supreme Soviet, "On Promoting the Settlement of the Yugoslav Crisis" (dated 26 June 1992), *Rossiiskaia gazeta*, 14 July 1992, p. 1, in FBIS-SOV–92–137, p. 54.

27. See Andranik Migranian, "No Two Concessions Are Alike," *Rossiiskaia gazeta*, 17 June 1992, p. 7, in FBIS-SOV–92–119, pp. 46–48.

28. Ibid., p. 47.

29. "International Panorama," Teleradiokompaniia Ostankino Television First Program Network (in Russian), 14 June 1992, in FBIS-SOV–92–119, 19 June 1992, pp. 48–49.

30. Dawisha and Parrott, *Russia and the New States of Eurasia*, p. 244.

31. O. Dmitriyeva, interview with Andrei Kozyrev, *Diario* (Madrid) (in Spanish), 14 June 1992, in FBIS-SOV–92–122, pp. 23–24.

32. Sergei Gryzunov and Andrei Baturin, "Andrei Kozyrev: I Had No Illusions Coming to Sarajevo, *Literaturnaia gazeta*, 3 June 1992, p. 9, in FBIS-SOV–92–110, pp. 10–11.

33. Andrei Kozyrev, "Transformation or Kafkaesque Metamorphosis: Russia's Democratic Foreign Policy and Its Priorities," *Nezavisimaia gazeta*, 20 August 1992, pp. 1, 4, in FBIS-SOV–92–167, pp. 19–25.

34. Ibid., p. 25.

35. Andrei Kozyrev, "Minister of Foreign Affairs Andrei Kozyrev: In the Republic's National Interests," *Rossiiskie vesti*, 3 December 1992, in FBIS-SOV–92–234, p. 10.

36. For example, see Andrei Kozyrev, "How Will We Live?" interview on Russian Television Network (in Russian), 4 July 1992, in FBIS-SOV–92–129, p. 38.

37. Ibid., p. 12.

38. Ibid., p. 13.

39. "Diplomatic Panorama," Interfax, 1 December 1992, in FBIS-SOV–92–232, pp. 3–5.

40. Kozyrev, "Minister of Foreign Affairs," p. 10.

41. Kozyrev, interview by Pankov.

42. See, for example, Kozyrev, interview by Leont'eva.

43. An excellent example of how national identity can influence foreign economic policy is seen in Belarus. Although ostensibly removed on suspicion of corruption, Supreme Soviet Chairman Stanislau Shushkevich was removed largely because of his unwillingness to tie his country's economy more closely to Russia's. His opponents in the Supreme Soviet and the government have a much more pro-Russian view of Belarusian identity, as opposed to Shushkevich's neutralist (and essentially pro-Western) stance.

44. Oleg Osobenkov, interview by Dmitrii Kosyrev, *Rossiiskaia gazeta*, 29 April 1993, in FBIS-SOV–93–083, pp. 19–21. Osobenkov was described as the deputy chief of the Russian Security Council Strategic Security Administration and chief of the Department for the Analysis and Preparation of Foreign Policy Decisions.

45. Jan Adams, "Legislature Asserts Its Role in Russian Foreign Policy," *RFE/RL Research Report*, 22 January 1993.

46. Dawisha and Parrott, *Russia and the New States of Eurasia*, pp. 203–4.

47. Osobenkov, interview by Kosyrev, p. 20.

48. Ibid., p. 20.

49. Ibid.

50. Andrei Kozyrev, *Nezavisimaia gazeta*, 22 September 1993, p. 1.

51. See Crow, "Russia Asserts Its Strategic Agenda."

52. Ibid.

53. Ibid., p. 5.

54. Andrei Kokoshin (deputy defense minister), interview by Laure Mandeville, *Le Figaro*, 27/28 November 1993, in FBIS-SOV–93–228, pp. 43–45.

55. "Detailed Account of 'The Basic Provisions of the Military Doctrine of the Russian Federation'" *Rossiiskie vesti*, 18 November 1993, in FBIS-SOV–93–222-S, pp. 1–11.

56. Ibid., p. 4.

57. Ibid., p. 2.

58. Ibid., p. 4.

59. "Is the Expansion of NATO Justified? The Particular Opinion of the Foreign Intelligence Service of Russia," *Nezavisimaia gazeta*, 26 November 1993, pp. 1, 3.

60. Ibid., p. 3.

61. Ibid.

62. Andrei Kozyrev, *Nezavisimaia gazeta*, 13 October 1993, pp. 1, 3.

63. *Economist*, 8 January 1994, p. 55.

64. See, for example, S. Neil MacFarlane, "Russia, the West and European Security," *Survival*, vol. 35, no. 3 (autumn 1993), pp. 3–25. Aleksei Arbatov offers a four-tiered breakdown, dividing "moderates" into moderate liberals and moderate conservatives, depending on whether they consider relations with the republics of the former Soviet Union to be top priority, or whether they see Russia's foreign policy priorities in relations with the countries to the South and East, including perhaps China. See Aleksei Arbatov, "Russia's Foreign Policy Alternatives," *International Security*, vol. 18, no. 2 (fall 1993), pp. 5–43.

65. Dawisha and Parrott, *Russia and the New States of Eurasia*, pp. 199–201.

66. Ibid., pp. 201–2.

67. Vladimir Ermolin, "Army Card of Blocs and Parties," *Krasnaia zvezda*, 2 December 1993, in FBIS-SOV–93–230, pp. 25–26.

68. See Dawisha and Parrott, *Russia and the New States of Eurasia*, pp. 200–201; also see Konstantin Eggert, *Izvestiia*, 7 December 1993, in FBIS-SOV–93–234.

69. Anatolii Adamishin, p. 8.

70. Mikhail Berger, "We Should Not Expect Any New Surprises from the New Minister of Foreign Economic Relations," *Izvestiia*, 3 April 1993, in FBIS-SOV–93–064, p. 51.

71. Maiak Radio Network (in Russian), 2 December 1993, in FBIS-SOV–93–231, p. 30.

72. Russian Television Network (in Russian), 29 November 1993, in FBIS-SOV–93–228, pp. 28–29.

73. Vladimir Zhirinovsky, *Rossiiskaia gazeta*, 3 December 1993, in FBIS-SOV–93–231, pp. 29–30.

74. Maiak Radio Network (in Russian), 25 November 1993, in FBIS-SOV–93–226, pp. 34–35; see also the "Voter's Hour," Ostankino Television First Channel Network (in Russian), 25 November 1993, in FBIS-SOV–93–228, pp. 30–32.

75. Zhirinovsky, *Rossiiskaia gazeta*, FBIS-SOV–93–231, p. 30.

76. One of the earlier references was in Andrei Kozyrev's article on the first anniversary of the August 1991 coup; *Nezavisimaia gazeta*, 20 August 1992, in *FBIS Daily Report: Central Eurasia*, 27 August 1992.

77. See Lough, "Place of the Near Abroad."

78. Account of phone-in interviews with President Boris Yeltsin by R. Zaripov et al., *Komsomol'skaia pravda*, 3 July 1992, pp. 1, 2, in FBIS-SOV–92–129, pp. 29–35, 6 July 1992

79. Kokoshin, interview by Mandeville.

80. Smith, *Ethnic Origins of Nations*, pp. 135–38; see also Smith, *National Identity*, pp. 9–13.

81. The Baltic republics are a notable exception, to some extent.

82. An example of this dynamic at work was seen in comments made by the chairman of the Russian Supreme Soviet Council of Nationalities in June 1992. Ramazan Abdulatipov urged a "policy of protecting all the people of the Russian Federation," in regard to the conflict in South Ossetia. (Postfactum, [in English], 10 June 1992, FBIS-SOV–92–114, p. 58.) Such a comment suggested that a broader understanding of what it meant to be "Russian" might be promoted by protecting the rights of non-Russians abroad. Much depends on the successful development of Russian democracy, however; only in an open political system will ethnic minorities be able to hold the state accountable and force it to live up to its constitutional promises of equal treatment for Russians and non-Russians alike.

A possible criticism of this argument, of course, is the implication of a cultural superiority for Russia, or that Russification is innately good. To the degree to which Russification can foster a civic form of identity (within Russia, at least), it may well be positive. I think it is important to point out that I am neither condoning nor condemning Russification; I am simply making an observation of the process and some conclusions that can be drawn from that. Second, it also suggests that, as in Western countries, there is a dominant culture that assimilates other peoples in the process of creating a civic national identity. If nothing else, this is similar to the creation of an American culture—commonly, immigrant ethnic groups shed their specific identities (to a degree) in attempting to assimilate to the dominant American culture. Russification may have been forced in the Soviet Union and the Russian empire; what has changed now is that Russification has ceased to be a conscious state policy. If it occurs as a "natural" or organic process, it may in fact be a positive development. This in turn suggests that if Russia does develop along these lines, ethnic identities within the Russian (civic) identity may eventually reassert themselves sometime in the future (again, as in the West).

II

**The Western
Newly Independent States**

6

Ukraine in the New Geopolitical Environment

Issues of Regional and Subregional Security

Nikolai A. Kulinich

At the brink of the twenty-first century our world is undergoing great changes. Geopolitical unions and concepts are disintegrating: new states and new social and political structures are being formed. An independent and revived Ukraine is emerging from the froth of this complex historic tumult and is determined to occupy its due place in the world community.

The radical sociopolitical changes in Central and Eastern Europe at the end of the 1980s and the beginning of the 1990s have signified the termination of the Cold War and have led to structural changes in the geopolitical environment in this region with far-reaching consequences for the existing world order. In essence, a new system of international relations is now being formed at global, regional, and subregional levels, and Ukraine is a part of this new order.

It is of vital necessity for the future of the country and its national security that Ukraine define itself in the new geopolitical encirclement, establish appropriate relations with its nearest neighbors as seen on the world political map, and earmark strategic foreign policy interests.

Formation of the New Geopolitical Environment of Ukraine

The political fate of Ukraine for the past few centuries was largely determined by historic cataclysms resulting from the constant recarving of the geopolitical environment of Central and Eastern Europe. Located in a borderland between agrarian and nomadic cultures and faced with the main burden of thwarting Tatar-Mongol aggressions in the thirteenth century, the Ukrainian "post-state" became an object of division in the scramble among stronger neighbors to the west, east, and south. These circumstances over the long term determined the fate of the geopolitical environment of Eastern Europe, complicated the process of Ukraine's state formation within its ethnic frontiers, and shaped the behavioral patterns of its neighbors.

The completion of the formation of the Russian Empire and Russia's entry into the forefront of European politics in the early and mid-seventeenth century, the division of Poland, the creation of the coalition against Napoleon (late eighteenth and early nineteenth centuries), the Vienna Congress of 1815, the birth of a unified German state, the Balkan wars, the onset of the fall of the Ottoman Empire—these are landmarks of European geopolitics, exemplifying what Carl von Clausewitz called the use of war as the continuation of policy. World War I was a historic cataclysm radically changing the European and world geopolitical environment. The breakaway parts of the Russian, Austro-Hungarian, and Ottoman empires became the basis for the formation of new states in Central and Eastern Europe and played an important role in structuring international relations in the region. It was under those historic conditions that attempts to found an independent Ukrainian state were made, and these attempts once again turned out to be unsuccessful. The consequences of World War I, World War II, and the Cold War proved to be decisive in forming the geopolitical environment of twentieth-century Europe. The main lesson that should be drawn from this history is that any division of the European continent on the basis of confrontational military-political groupings (the Triple Entente and the Tripartite Alliance, the Axis states and the anti-Hitlerite coalition, NATO and the Warsaw Pact states) leads to sociopolitical upheaval, the results of which are radical geopolitical changes. Moreover, it is difficult to consider the latter as a victory for one of the military-political groupings.

At present, acute scholarly debates are taking place on the character, driving forces, and factors in the formation of the new geopolitical environment of the European continent, especially in its central and eastern parts. Economic, geographical, sociopolitical, ethnic, and even civilizational dimensions are used as the bases of different approaches.[1] All these factors are systemic and must be considered as a whole in analyzing relations among the various European nations.

The formation of the new geopolitical environment of Ukraine is taking place under the influence of two opposing tendencies. First, there is the process of disintegration and decentralization of the totalitarian system that existed eastward from the Berlin Wall. Second, there is the creation of new Central and East European countries and their entry into the existing but changing regional institutions. The process of disintegration has dominated events in Central and Eastern Europe for the past four years, commencing with the collapse of military-political and economic groupings (Warsaw Pact, Council for Mutual Economic Assistance) and leading to the breakup of certain states (the Soviet Union, Yugoslavia, Czechoslovakia) and to the further disintegration of their constituent parts (Moldova, Georgia, Bosnia-Herzegovina).

The crises that have gripped the majority of the East European states and the territory of the former Soviet Union are in urgent need of resolution. Only through the united efforts of the postcommunist states can that come about. First of all, it is necessary to stop the process of disintegration and enter a new level of subregional cooperation. If adequate democratic solutions are not found today toward economic and political closeness at both regional and continental levels, then the role of integrator will be taken up by totalitarian, antidemocratic forces that look forward to the re-creation of the geopolitical imperial structure that existed in the vast territory stretching from the Berlin Wall to the Kuril Islands. There is no place for independent, democratic states within the framework of such a structure, and the same holds true for independent Ukraine.

The postwar history of Europe bears testimony to the fact that the process of forming military-political blocs, economic groupings, and integration systems is complex and contradictory. In some cases it took place constructively and successfully (e.g., Western Europe), and in other cases (the Warsaw Pact and the Council for Mutual Economic Assistance) it failed. These are lessons that Ukraine as a European state should draw on. Today, three spheres of integration are clearly noticeable on the continent: in Western Europe, where the Maastricht process is successfully uniting this part of the continent into one geopolitical area; in Central Europe and the Baltic states, where states are, with different degrees of success, overcoming crises in their development and making their first attempts at regional cooperation; and in Eastern Europe, where the former republics of the Soviet Union are uniting in a specific interstate union, the Commonwealth of Independent States (CIS). Each state entering the CIS has its own aims and interests in contributing to the content of this union, although it is evident that Russia plays a dominant role in this regard, declaring neighboring states to be the zone of its vital interests. Each of these spheres differs in its level of internal integrative capacity, economic potential, and sociopolitical stability.

The salient feature is that each of the East and Central European states is eager to be involved in the integration process of the West European model. That the West European "common home" is not in a hurry to open its doors to its East European neighbors is completely understandable. The countries of Central and Eastern Europe, including Ukraine, must first undergo certain stages of adaptation aimed at demonstrating their capability to function as viable economic and political bodies emergent from the demise of totalitarianism.

In order to determine Ukraine's role in the world community, and in the European geopolitical environment in particular, it is necessary to define the relevance of Ukraine's foreign policy priorities to its national interests since these interests guarantee national security. Considering the intricate and dramatic road toward independence traveled by Ukraine, it may be stated with assurance that true independence can exist only if the people of Ukraine are provided with reliable guarantees of its national security. Such security is not an end in itself but a means to achieve the fundamental interests of the Ukrainian people.

The highest national interest of Ukraine lies in the formation of a truly democratic civil society, where the rule of law prevails and the political, social, and spiritual interests and rights of all its members are guaranteed.

The national security of Ukraine implies a condition wherein the vital interests of the individual, social groups, the society, and the state as a whole are safeguarded from external and internal threats and the Ukrainian state has the wherewithal to ensure its continuation. Such a condition can be sustained by the creation of an overall system of guarantees for the protection and development of the people of Ukraine in a healthy democratic environment. The formation and realization of this policy should be based on the rule of law and should evolve from the priorities of vital national interests, such as adopting timely political measures rather than using force to resolve conflicts.

It is pertinent to note that in the three-year period of an independent Ukraine, the issue of how to prioritize the national interests has been the topic of sharp political and scholarly debate. The controversy centers on the fact that Ukrainian society today is divided into a large number of social and political groups and parties, each of which possesses its own order of priorities of national interests.

In connection with this, research conducted by the National Institute for Strategic Studies under the president of Ukraine is undoubtedly of special interest. The scientific research was based on sociological opinion polls of various social groups within the population and the ruling elite. Its purpose was to prioritize the national interests of Ukraine. Out of a total of thirty-seven indicated priorities, the six highest (absolute priorities) were interests connected with reforms and stabilization of the social and economic life of the Ukrainian state. Creation of an effective system of power (without which functioning of the state is impossible) placed eighth among the national interest priorities; active foreign policy, seventeenth; entry into the system of European and international security, twenty-fourth; and creation of a regional system of collective security, thirty-fourth.[2]

As is evident from the data, issues of foreign policy and international aspects of national security are at the peripheral areas of public awareness in Ukraine. Considering the fact that in the public's perception, the term "foreign policy" is commonly understood to mean the "far alien states" (and not the republics of the former USSR), it may be concluded that today a large part of the population does not relate the solutions of Ukraine's most acute problems (in the economic and social spheres) to the activation of the state's foreign policy.

Notwithstanding the low priority of foreign policy concerns among the Ukrainian population, Ukrainian foreign policy must possess a set of goals that would enhance the country's national interests. These goals include (1) a general increase in Ukraine's direct participation in the economic and political activities of international institutions and organizations at the global and regional levels, particularly European economic and political bodies; (2) the unconditional fulfillment by Ukraine of all international treaties and obligations in the areas of disarmament (primarily nuclear) and security as well as in the areas of human rights and freedom; (3) formulation of a flexible and balanced policy in the field of international relations and the establishment of ties with the countries of the CIS, particularly Russia; (4) development of economic and cultural contacts with the Ukrainian diaspora, and with countries that have a considerable number of ethnic Ukrainians (the United States, Canada, Australia, Argentina, Israel, and others), as well as support for the Ukrainian minorities in the CIS; and (5) development of transport communications (maritime, land, and air), information, and telecommunications systems necessary for the normal development of the economy and the safeguarding of the interests of the Ukrainian state.

Ukraine is also aware of other global and regional factors that, in certain circumstances, may hinder the realization of these foreign policy goals and pose threats to Ukraine's national security.

The main forms of threat are quite multifarious in their structures, and they impinge upon various spheres of Ukraine's social life. Threats from abroad are of natural interest to this study. Such threats to the national security of Ukraine, according to the National Security Council, are as follows: interference in the internal matters of Ukraine by other states; territorial claims on Ukraine; incomplete solution of issues related to the strategic nuclear arsenal of the former USSR, as well as the presence of foreign troops on the territory of Ukraine; instability of state power structures in neighboring countries, particularly Russia; and the spread of separatist movements in certain regions of Ukraine, supported covertly or overtly by certain outside forces.

It is difficult to identify and analyze the whole system of priorities of the national interests of Ukraine, as well as the system of internal and external threats to these interests. This discussion will be limited to certain key issues that reflect vital national interests and determine Ukraine's main foreign policy priorities. The issues are economic, military-political, and geopolitical in scope.

Economic Issues

The Ukrainian economy at the start of 1994 reflects a deep structural crisis (see Tables 1 through 7 on pages 133–138). In fact, the question is not merely economic independence but survival of the Ukrainian state. As previously mentioned, the majority of Ukrainians see economic interests and threats to these interests to be of the highest priority.

What follows is an attempt to analyze the main parameters of Ukraine's economic situation based on Ministry of Statistics and the Economic Revival Fund of Ukraine data as of 1 October 1993.[3]

During 1993 the financial situation was grave: production continued to fall, prices continued to rise, and the people's standard of living dropped dramatically. The net national product, in comparison with the corresponding period of 1992, decreased by 11 percent. National income in the material sphere declined by 12 percent, productivity of labor by 8 percent. According to data provided by

Volodymyr Lanovyi, the former deputy prime minister of Ukraine and current president of the Economic Revival Fund of Ukraine, the situation is in fact much worse. According to his evaluation, the decline in production of raw materials, metallurgy, chemicals, and agriculture reached 20 percent, and in other branches of industry production fell by 35 to 38 percent in comparison with the same period the previous year. The state budget deficit constituted 5,280.7 billion Ukrainian karbovantsi (the exchange rate for the Ukrainian karbovanets in relation to the U.S. dollar as of 1 October 1993 was approximately 20,000 karbovantsi to the dollar). To a considerable extent, this was caused by state subsidy of certain branches of industry, support to people in low-income brackets, a continuing slump in production, and an unfettered rise in prices. A 100 percent monthly price increase had occurred as early as September 1993 (per official data of the Ministry of Statistics, the monthly price rise of raw materials was 80 percent and in finished goods, 35 percent).

Ukrainian foreign trade for the first nine months of 1993 constituted $4.1 billion: $2.5 billion in exports and $1.6 billion in imports. The apparent prevalence of exports in foreign trade, however, does not signify the export-oriented industrial production of the country. The positive balance of foreign trade is explained by a significant reduction in the import of energy resources, crude oil by-products, timber, paper, and ferrous metals.

The percentages of crude oil, gas, and crude oil by-products in the total volume of imports constitute 13.6 percent, 51.5 percent, and 4 percent, respectively. Timber and paper, equipment for processing agricultural products, garments, footwear, household electronics, and office equipment make up the bulk of remaining imports.

Ukraine's export trade is largely dependent on shipments of raw materials, automobile tires, mineral fertilizers, and means of transport. The export of agricultural products such as sugar ($24.9 million), meat, and vegetable oil has also increased.

The East European countries are the main recipients of Ukrainian raw materials and finished goods. Their economies are dependent to some extent on such goods as electricity, the export of which constituted 5.8 billion kilowatt-hours, or 2.5 percent of Ukraine's internal needs.

Among the West European states, the chief recipients of Ukrainian exports are Italy ($98.3 million) and Germany ($52.4 million). The most active exporters are Germany ($210 million) and France ($75.7 million). The negative balance of trade with Germany is compensated by German credits.

Wider development of ties with Asian business was noticeable during 1993, with China ($347.9 million) and Turkey ($134.4 million) as the main exporters and Japan ($47.9 million) and China ($42 million) as the main importers. Japanese electronic goods and cheap wholesale consumer goods head the list of import items.

Import ($94.5 million) prevail over export ($70.2 million) in Ukraine's trade with the United States.

The relative stability in the balance of payments ($444.6 million) with the larger CIS states (32 percent of total imports and 37 percent of exports) is due to the reduction in the supply of natural gas from Russia. The percentage of energy resources imported from the beginning of 1993 increased by 20 percent, equal to one-third of the previous year's supply. The supply of crude oil by-products, ferrous metals, timber, and paper has decreased by almost one-half.

The most promising area of foreign trade is the export of services, amounting to 23 percent of the total volume of trade, the chief service spheres being transportation and tourism. Convenience of transit from Russia to Southern Europe makes port and road infrastructures alluring and evokes interest among Western investors in building consignment storage facilities in the republic.

The level of foreign investment in Ukraine is an indication of the development of market relations. This issue is both an economic and a political one in Ukraine, where more than 90 percent of the economy is state-controlled. Foreign investments in Ukraine mean growth and development of industry, creation of employment, access to new technology and know-how, and introduction to a new system of management. The investors in their turn are attracted by high-skilled and relatively cheap labor, a favorable geographic location, the low exchange rate of the national currency, and legal enactments fostering investment (the law on foreign investments adopted by the Supreme Rada encompasses safeguarding of investments, repatriation and reinvestment of profits, a compensation system for losses, tax abatements, etc.). The inflow of foreign investments into Ukraine, however, is restricted by a number of factors, such as the attachment of the Ukrainian economy to the countries of the former USSR. These countries are also undergoing crises and problems, such as disruptions in economic links; a dearth of energy supplies; lopsided economies that heavily favor the defense sectors; underdeveloped infrastructures; backward banking and finance systems; nonconvertible national monetary units; inflexibile taxation systems; and organizational and management forms that do not meet international standards.

This has added to the apprehensions of foreign investors who already harbored fears about Ukraine's political and economic instability. So far as Ukraine is concerned, the repercussions could undermine efforts at improving relations with certain countries.

Therefore, the vital task of the national economy is to create the necessary legal, financial, and organizational infrastructures to attract foreign investment to Ukraine. This especially means consolidating a favorable investment climate (for example, equal rights for national and foreign firms and companies and wider tax abatements for investments in the most promising branches of the economy); assisting investment in the most promising branches of the economy; developing insurance systems for foreign firms (the experience of Kazakhstan may be applied); soliciting wider international cooperation in assisting and guaranteeing capital investment; ensuring a more active state role in redressing possible negative social consequences of certain investment projects in Ukraine; and creating conditions for the development of business, both small and large, and widening the scope for investment.

Speaking at the congress of the League of Enterprises with Foreign Capital, its chairman, Valery Evdokimov, cited the following data. Since 1991 the number of enterprises with foreign capital in Ukraine tripled, to forty-five hundred. The number in Kiev alone is about nine hundred. Of the $1 billion invested, about 30 percent is distributed among those enterprises with investments of less than of $1,000; 45 percent among those with investments of $10,000 to $100,000; and only 5 percent among those with investments of up to $1 million.[4] All of them, by law, were exempt from taxes for a year.

One of the apparent indicators of the difficult process of economic reforms in Ukraine is the issue of privatization. In fact, the growth rate and volume of privatization in Ukraine lag far behind those of Russia. Until 1994, it was small-scale privatization that was spoken of (privatization of municipal housing and small shops and enterprises). Then Ukraine's Cabinet of Ministers decided to embark upon large-scale privatization (large enterprises, unfinished construction sites, and others). Out of ten thousand large enterprises, only thirteen hundred have been earmarked for privatization. Russia's experience demonstrates that the success of market reforms, as well as the survival of the postsocialist economy, depends on a successful privatization process. It was a good sign for the privatization process when President Leonid Kravchuk stated in his interview with the American press, during his visit to Washington in March 1994, that thirty thousand businesses of varying size would eventually be converted to private ownership.[5]

The energy crisis is one of the major issues hindering Ukraine on its road to economic and, ultimately, political independence. The sordid state of affairs unfortunately reflects the development of heavy industry based on the uneconomic and inefficient use of energy by the Soviet Union in the territory of Ukraine. Within the framework of the USSR, energy was imported from Russia, Turkmenistan, and Azerbaijan, leading also to a decline in the productive use of local petroleum and gas resources.

These facts and figures bear testimony to the present dependence of the Ukrainian economy on imported energy resources, primarily petrol and gas. Ukraine's yearly need for petrol constitutes forty-four million tons. Ukraine receives about 90 percent of its petrol and 70 percent of its gas from Russia.[6] During 1993, with the supply of petrol and gas from Russia cut back, Ukraine's debt to Russia for these resources became a serious problem. By the end of 1993 Ukraine owed Russia $900 million for gas supplies alone.

A complex situation emerged in Ukraine's atomic power industry. Since 1988 electricity generated from atomic power stations has declined steadily. Ukraine has five atomic power stations, with a total capacity of 12.8 million kilowatts, which in 1990 supplied about 30 percent of the total electricity generated in Ukraine. Today the stations bear a load of 40 percent (owing to the decline in fossil fuels). There is a lack of nuclear fuel, which is supplied from Russia. Servicing of the stations is also an acute problem. Personnel from Ukrainian atomic power stations, who typically spend three to five years in training, are migrating to Russia, where the pay is ten times higher.[7]

Consequently, Ukraine was facing a paralytic economic collapse in the area of energy resources by the end of 1993. As a result of successful negotiations at the Ashkhabad summit of the CIS (December 1993), however, and with the signing of the Tripartite Agreement on the Elimination of Nuclear Weapons in Moscow (14 January 1994), Ukraine received assurances regarding the supply of gas and petrol. At the Ashkhabad summit, agreements were reached between Russian Prime Minister Viktor Chernomyrdin and Ukrainian Prime Minister Efim Zviahils'kyon the supply of sixty billion cubic meters of gas at $50 per cubic meter and twenty-five million tons of petrol at $75 to $80 per ton for 1994, far below world prices. In early 1994, in Kiev, an agreement with Turkmenistan on the supply of gas (twenty-eight billion cubic meters) was reached. These measures give hope that Ukraine will gradually overcome its energy crisis.

In conclusion, the social and economic crises that have plagued Ukraine have undoubtedly had a decisive impact on Ukraine's national interests and the determination of its foreign policy priorities.

In making predictions about socioeconomic development in the near future, it seems reasonable to assume that the crisis in Ukraine has not reached its peak. Taking into consideration positive trends set earlier in 1994, when relations between Ukraine, Russia, and the other countries of the CIS improved slightly, there is a possibility that tendencies to overcome the socioeconomic crisis are likely to emerge.

Military-Political Issues

Ukraine's military-political interests are for the most part regional (Europe and its neighboring countries). Military-political activity by Ukraine on a global level, however, may occur in the context of international peacekeeping missions. Ukraine has already acquired experience, to a certain extent, in peacekeeping operations in the territory of the former Yugoslavia, under the mandate of the United Nations. On 19 November 1993 the Supreme Rada of Ukraine, in response to a request by UN Secretary General Boutros-Ghali, decided to increase the already existing number of Ukrainian armed forces in Yugoslavia from 400 to 1,220, with three infantry battalions to protect the safe defense zone in Bosnia. It was the first time that Ukrainian representatives participated in the group of military observers and civil police of the United Nations.

Since the collapse of the Warsaw Treaty Organization and the USSR, stability in Europe has, to a great extent, declined. This trend is the result, in part, of the weakening of security in the region and the general tendencies toward disintegration. Consequently, there are heightened fears of spontaneous, uncontrollable developments that could alter the strategic situation in the East European region as a whole from peaceful relations to armed conflicts and abuses of human rights and freedoms. At the same time, however, factors having a positive influence on European stability and security are also emerging, such as the termination of the highly tense East-West military posture and the absence of ideological antagonisms that served as stimuli for this posture.

The adoption of the military doctrine of Ukraine by the Supreme Rada on 19 October 1993 was important for the determination of Ukraine's defense policy. Three main aims may be ascertained from this document: first, creating military and political conditions of strategic balance with those states whose interests may conflict with those of Ukraine, thus raising the possibility of military confrontation; second, creating preconditions for regional and global systems of collective security that facilitate stable development and social progress without the presence of conflicts; and third, establishing relations of cooperation and goodwill with neighboring states in the sphere of defense, as a way of ensuring long-term and reliable peaceful development.

The military doctrine of Ukraine is purely defensive in nature and aimed at thwarting possible military threats, such as attempts to disrupt the nation's territorial integrity, annex a part of it, or infringe on its sovereignty. There also remains the possibility that armed clashes may erupt in neighboring states and spill over into Ukraine.

During the drafting and adoption of the military doctrine, the issue of a "potential military enemy" was debated. A potential enemy may be considered either an established state, or coalition of states, with definite defense capacity, or a hypothetical enemy. A hypothetical military rival may be assumed by considering the salient features of the armed forces and their potential military capacities, as circumscribed by the defense policy of Ukraine.[8]

The conversion of Ukraine's defense industry complex and the presence of nuclear arms on the territory of Ukraine are the two most critical military issues related to the national interests of Ukraine today.

In the case of the former, Ukraine inherited from the former USSR an economy excessively oriented toward the defense sector. According to data furnished by the minister of machine building, defense industry complex and conversion, V. Antonov, at the international symposium "New Prospects of Ukraine's Security" (May 1992, Kiev), 1,870 enterprises, scientific research institutes, and construction bureaus, with a total of three million employees, were involved in the defense industry. Of these, about seven hundred were factories and construction bureaus with one million employees, two hundred thousand of which were working under contracts with the armed forces. In total, approximately 60 percent of Ukrainian industries worked in defense.

One of the peculiarities of Ukraine's defense industry complex is that the production cycle of the most important defense items is not a "closed circuit." Despite an agreement between Russia and Ukraine on the mutual supply of component parts for military equipment, for example, not all obligations are fulfilled, and for this reason Ukraine is unable to provide its armed forces with every needed accessory. Russia, on the other hand, has a closed-circuit technology cycle and thus is able to solve all problems independently. Another peculiarity is the industry's dependence on the supply of strategic raw materials from abroad, giving the defense industry a precarious existence.

The situation in the defense industry complex, furthermore, has been greatly aggravated by the general economic crisis and the decline in production. The absence of raw materials, disguised unemployment, and the high cost of conversion technology complicate the process of conversion. Thus, according to certain data, the cost of destroying one tank is equal to the cost of its production—enough grounds for some politicians and managers of production to speak in favor of restricting conversion and producing and selling modern weapons to "traditional" clients of the Soviets. These clients are well known to the world community. Such restrictions of the conversion process might lead to escalating tension in the world's arms market and have a negative impact on the international scene as a whole.

It follows that one of the priorities of Ukraine's foreign policy should be to attract foreign investments in the sphere of conversion. Effective conversion is not possible otherwise. This is not an easy option, however, since great amounts of money and high technology are needed. In sum, successful implementation of conversion programs and diversification of the defense industry would have a decisive impact on the framing of Ukraine's market. A cut in the excess defense production would go far in stabilizing the economy and elevating the level of national security.

The issue of nuclear weapons on the territory of Ukraine since the collapse of the USSR is today the most acute military-political problem. For a true understanding of the "nuclear factor" in Ukraine, and for a worthy evaluation of the consequences of the signing of the Tripartite Agreement on the Elimination of Nuclear Weapons, it is necessary to review the origins of the issue, including the approaches and stands of interested parties.

Until the signing of the Tripartite Agreement in Moscow on 14 January 1994, the nuclear defense potential located on the territory of Ukraine ranked third in strength after Russia and the United States. It included 1,512 nuclear warheads, delivered by 212 strategic carriers, of which 176 were intercontinental ballistic missiles (of these, 130 were liquid-fuel RS–18s and 46 were solid-fuel RS–22s), and 36 heavy bombers equipped with long-distance, air-based rockets. This nuclear capacity exceeds the total quantitative nuclear arsenal of such countries as France, Great Britain, and China.

In the Declaration on State Sovereignty of Ukraine (16 July 1990) and the Proclamation of Nonnuclear Status (24 October 1991), the Supreme Rada identified the intention of Ukraine to be a nonnuclear state as one of its chief strategic priorities. It was virtually a unilateral declaration of future nuclear disarmament that would be carried out gradually and without jeopardizing national security and stability.

Initially, Ukraine's position on nuclear disarmament was influenced by the idealistic perceptions of the nonnuclear world, the moral-psychological factor of the Chernobyl tragedy, strong pressure from the West and Russia, and the expectation of favorable international conditions for achieving Ukraine's independence and international recognition. These factors were reflected in the Supreme Rada's Proclamation of Nonnuclear Status, which oriented the legislative and executive bodies of power toward unilateral nuclear disarmament, but without actual clauses, conditions, and guarantees. Under intense pressure, however, Ukraine was asked to relinquish its nuclear capacity without any meaningful security guarantees and without the benefits of a nonnuclear policy. The results of an opinion poll conducted by the research center Democratic Initiatives and the Institute of Sociology of the Academy of Sciences of Ukraine on the future nuclear status of Ukraine—and conducted before the ratification of the START I Treaty (October 1993)—are interesting: 6 percent were in favor of an open, unconditional nuclear state status for Ukraine; 27 percent were in favor of keeping nuclear weapons until receiving international guarantees of security; 33 percent favored a simultaneous declaration of nonnuclear status and initiation of complete destruction of nuclear weapons on the planet; 6 percent were indifferent; and only 22 percent were categorically against the presence of nuclear weapons in Ukraine.[9] Public opinion, it seems, largely defined the Supreme Rada's stand on the ratification issue of the START I Treaty and its protocol, signed in Lisbon on 23 May 1992.

The Strategic Arms Reduction Treaty signed on 31 July 1991 in Moscow not only stipulates restriction of arms escalation, which was the aim of earlier negotiations in this area, but for the first time determines the concrete levels of such reductions, which can be achieved only by physical destruction of a major part of the nuclear potential of the United States and the former USSR. This treaty creates the basis for a drastic reduction in strategic nuclear arms of both the United States and Russia and conforms with the vital interests of Ukraine. Although the ratification of the START I Treaty and the Lisbon Protocol by the Supreme Rada of Ukraine took place in November 1993, it was marked by internal political strife, between those in favor of and those against the nuclear status of Ukraine not only within the parliament, but between the legislative and the executive bodies of power (the president spoke openly in favor of the treaty). Public opinion in Ukraine also played a role. One of the major reasons for the consternation and concern of Ukrainians was and still remains the tough, imperial-like pressure by Moscow. Suffice it to recall here the decision of the previous Supreme Soviet of the Russian Federation on the Russian status of the city of Sevastopol (July 1993) and the adamant stand taken by President Boris Yeltsin in his Massandra negotiations in the Crimea with President Leonid Kravchuk (September 1993). As a result, on 18 November 1993, the Supreme Rada of Ukraine voted in favor of the ratification of the START I Treaty and the Lisbon Protocol, but with thirteen stipulations that, by and large, complicated the process of fulfillment of the treaty.

The ratification of the START I Treaty with these stipulations evoked highly negative reactions in the international community. The stipulations, though in general fair and justified in character and reflective of the national interests of Ukraine, were at the same time difficult to understand. Furthermore, world public opinion on these stipulations was unduly influenced by information supplied solely from Moscow. Nevertheless, the situation after the ratification of the START I Treaty by the Supreme Rada of Ukraine proved to be critical. There emerged the urgent need to search for some way out of this no-win situation and settle on some compromise. The meeting of the presidents of the United States, Russia, and Ukraine on 14 January 1994 in Moscow and the signing of the Tripartite documents regulating the transfer and removal of nuclear arms from the territory of Ukraine were a breakthrough in this direction, marking a genuine success for American, Russian, and Ukrainian diplomacy.

It was emphasized in the documents that the three presidents would cooperate with one another as full-fledged equal partners and that relations between countries would be based on respect for independence, sovereignty, and territorial integrity. President Kravchuk confirmed that Ukraine would enter the Nuclear Nonproliferation Treaty as a state not possessing nuclear weapons. President Clinton and President Yeltsin expressed their readiness to guarantee Ukraine's security as soon as the START I Treaty becomes effective and Ukraine enters into the Nuclear Nonproliferation Treaty.

The importance of compensating Ukraine, Kazakhstan, and Belarus, for the highly enriched uranium in the warheads located on the territories of these states was recognized. Agreements were reached regarding the delivery of fair and timely compensation, and the transportation of nuclear warheads to Russia for dismantling. It was decided that, to start with, Russia would supply Ukraine with fuel containing one hundred tons of low, enriched uranium for a period of ten months as compensation. During this time two hundred nuclear warhead SS–19 and SS–24 missiles would be transported to Russia for dismantling. Ukrainian representatives would be present to oversee the dismantling process.

It is important to note that the majority of the stipulations made by the Supreme Rada of Ukraine concerning the START I Treaty were taken into account in the Tripartite documents. Finally, in February 1994, the Supreme Rada ratified the START I Treaty in its final form.

Overcoming socioeconomic crises and stabilizing the economic and political life of Ukraine are evidently the primary issues facing the country. Because of Ukraine's close links with and economic dependence on the former Soviet republics, especially Russia, these crucial socioeconomic reforms must be carried out in close cooperation with these states, particularly Russia. But an analysis of real and potential threats to the national interests of Ukraine reveals that Russia is either the chief source of such threats, or in some way related to them. Herein lies the paradox of Ukraine's national security.

Ukraine's Strategic Choice: Europe or Eurasia?

Ever since the attainment of independence by Ukraine, the state's political leadership and representatives of research circles have tried to find a solution to the paradox of Ukraine's national security and define the directions of strategic moves in the geopolitical environment. These attempts have been guided by the formula "movement in all directions," which is a far cry from the "neither East nor West" of the Iranian fundamentalist leadership or the Chinese formula of "equidistance" from global power centers.

This was to be expected, given that the people of Ukraine have had to solve the issue of their security under conditions that have no parallel in world practice. The question of geostrategic choice was very clear: either enter the civilized area of geopolitically integrated Europe, confirming and installing Ukraine's historic place in it, or be reintegrated into the Eurasian geopolitical environment constituted by the post-Soviet states, with Russia as the natural nucleus of integration.

The idea that Ukraine has to choose between a "civilized" West and a "Eurasian" East corresponds to the notion that there is a "civilizational clash," as proposed by Samuel Huntington of Harvard University and William Wallace of Oxford University.[10] The essence of the concept as put forward by Huntington takes the following line. Future conflicts will occur that will divide the world into civilization formations based on cultural-historical, ethnic, inter- and intrafaith, and other factors. One of the civilization frontiers between Western Christian and Orthodox Christian civilizations runs through the territory of Ukraine, dividing western Ukraine, which would gravitate toward the West European civilization center, from eastern and southern Ukraine, which would gravitate toward the Moscow Orthodox civilization center. This frontier not only is conditioned by history but also corresponds to socioeconomic and political differences in modern Ukraine as well. This differentiation is noted by many leading Western researchers and political scientists.[11]

Further preservation of the status quo in Ukraine's economic and political crises would only aggravate current disintegrative tendencies, along the lines of "civilization" gaps and along the lines of intra-ethnic confrontation.

Perhaps, therefore, the best way for Ukraine to go is with the Declaration of State Sovereignty of Ukraine, dated 16 July 1990, which emphasized that Ukraine "will strive for permanent neutrality."[12] This obliges Ukraine not to participate in armed conflicts emerging between other states, join any military unions or blocs, or allow its territory to be used by foreign armed forces and for military bases.

According to international law, a neutral state has the right to resort to armed force when its neutral status comes under threat. The presence of armed forces in large numbers in Ukraine and its status of neutrality are not mutually exclusive, but mutually inclusive.

Up to this time, three states in the world have enjoyed the status of permanent neutrality: Switzerland, according to the decisions of the Vienna Congress of 1814–15 and guaranteed by the Paris Act of 1815; Austria, according to the State Treaty of 1955 and the Federal Constitutional Law on Neutrality of 1955 (four large states stand as guarantors against any *Anschluss* of Austria); and Malta, according to the 1981 Declaration of the Government of Malta on Neutrality (the concluding documents of the Madrid summit of the CSCE in 1983 have taken this into account).

And now Ukraine. In order to understand this phenomenon correctly, it is necessary to examine the history behind the idea of Ukraine's neutrality and the evolution of the concept. It should suffice to recall the historical context in which the adoption of the Declaration of State Sovereignty took place, when for the first time mention of Ukraine's neutrality was made. Ukraine was then still a part of the USSR. Evidently, for Ukraine neutrality meant separation from the union and, in connection with its declared nuclear-free status, an intention to secede from the Soviet Union's imperial structure. After the collapse of the USSR and Ukraine's declaration of independence, confirmed by the referendum of 1 December 1991, neutrality meant an avoidance of attempts to revive the union's center and a shift toward European structures.

The Commonwealth of Independent States was created in Minsk in December 1991. Attempts on the part of certain political forces to transform the CIS into a new union structure with a strongly defined center were made in the early stage of this organization's formation. These were followed by yet other attempts to maintain a united army under the banner of the United Armed Forces, in order to stave off division of the properties of the former USSR and their assets and liabilities and make the countries joining the Commonwealth swallow the bitter pill of a common military bloc structure (the Treaty on Collective Security, signed on 15 May 1992 in Tashkent).

In the latter case, Ukraine, abiding by the principle of neutrality, refused to enter the structure of the military bloc. Statements to that effect, containing the term *pozablokovist* ("remaining out of blocs"), have since been made by the president of Ukraine and leading figures of the Ministry of Foreign Affairs and the Ministry of Defense.

The important point here is how to understand neutrality in general, and the neutrality of Ukraine in particular, in the context of the processes of economic and political integration in Europe.

Today it may be affirmed that in relation to the changes in Europe that have occurred since the end of the Cold War and the rupture of the bipolar bloc structure, the concept of "classical" permanent neutrality, as it had been conceived by the creators of the Hague Convention at the beginning of the twentieth century, no longer exists. Pure neutralism, that is, neutralism for the sake of neutralism, in the face of growing and deepening integrational processes on the continent and ever-increasing interdependence at global and regional levels, would mean drifting away from the general course of world events, toward isolationism and autarky. Testimony to this fact is borne by the examples of Austria, Finland, Sweden, and Switzerland, which speak of their neutrality in quite different ways. Yet these same countries have declared their interest in participating in the processes of integration in Europe through affiliation with European-based organizations, including those of a military-political nature.

It is necessary, therefore, to take a fresh look at the neutrality of Ukraine. Ukraine does not need neutrality for the sake of neutrality, but as a means to achieve its main national interest: absolute sovereignty and independence, consolidation of statehood, provision of territorial integrity and inviolability of borders, and political stability and economic prosperity. Evidently Ukraine's goals will not stand in the way of the general direction of the processes taking place on the European continent. There is no contradiction between the Ukrainian policy of neutrality and Ukraine's interest in cooperating with the European organizations, including NATO, the member states of which have similar aims.

The debates on the principal directions of Ukraine's foreign policy that are taking place both within and without the Supreme Rada of Ukraine give sufficient grounds to affirm that Ukraine is in favor of NATO membership for the new Central and East European states. This issue is of immediate relevance to Ukraine.

An opinion poll conducted by SOCIS-GALLUP on the eve of the NATO summit in January 1994 provides interesting data. Over twelve hundred people above fifteen years of age were questioned. The only question posed was, "Do you consider that Ukraine should join NATO to ensure its security?" to which 51.4 percent answered in the affirmative (54.7 percent of Ukrainians and 45.9 percent of Russians; 61.9 percent of entrepreneurs; 58.6 percent of students; 55 percent of people with higher education; and 51.1 percent of peasants and workers). Those who considered NATO membership unnecessary for Ukraine totaled 20.8 percent; and 26.9 percent had not yet formed an opinion on this issue.[13]

Let us now reflect on various possible scenarios that may occur in the event a positive decision is reached at the NATO summit by the member states in favor of revision of the future structure and composition of NATO.

First Option

The NATO council at its session decides to accept new members (Poland, the Czech Republic, Hungary, and Slovakia). A natural question arises: What would be the reaction of the other countries in the eastern part of the continent, especially Russia? The answer is contained in the letter from President Yeltsin to the leaders of the chief European states, published in November 1993 in the documents of the Federal Intelligence Service of Russia. This document, titled "The Prospects of a Wider NATO and the Interests of Russia," states:

> As a result of the enlargement of NATO and the fact that its biggest military group, possessing colossal offensive capacity, has entered the areas lying in

direct proximity to the Russian borders, there is a need for Russia to rethink all
its defense concepts, reform its armed forces, reappraise operative theater military actions, involve additional infrastructure, dislocate huge military contingents, and change operative military plans and the nature of combat training.[14]

Ukraine, on the other hand, is amenable to the possible entry of certain East
European states into NATO and the opening of its frontiers to the west, but it
worries about Russia's stance and the situation that might then ensue along the
eastern boundary of Ukraine, which would pose a real threat to the national
security of Ukraine.

Second Option

Ukraine, along with other countries of Central and Eastern Europe, joins NATO.
This option is less probable. Russia's reaction would be the same; it might even
be more negative. A typical remark on this issue was made by one of Russia's
defense experts, General G. Dmitriev:

> Poland, the Czech Republic, Slovakia, Hungary, and even Ukraine, all dream-
> ing of joining NATO, should understand that if they really do so, they would
> immediately fall under the orbit and aims of the strategic nuclear forces of
> Russia, with all possible consequences that are thereby entailed.[15]

As is evident, the possible consequences of the first and second options may
lead to an aggravation of the current military-strategic and political situation at
the subregional, regional, and even global levels and would pose a real threat to
the national security of Ukraine.

Third Option

NATO increases its membership by admitting countries of Eastern and Central
Europe, including Russia. This is the least probable option. In this case, NATO
not only would lose its initial function as a defensive union and its effectiveness
as a military-political organization but would also be transformed into an organization with a principally different stature—an all-European system of collective
security. New preconditions would be needed for the creation of such a system,
although it may result from a gradual, painstaking movement in this direction.

The most probable and optimum option is the one adopted in Brussels on
10–11 January 1994. It is already being translated into action within the framework of relations between the integrated West and its Eastern neighbors. It
envisages the gradual spread of influence of NATO and other integrated West
European organizations into the East, attracting countries from the latter region
into associated cooperation with West European institutions—a tendency that
would cater to the national security interests of Ukraine.

Examples of such cooperation, first of all, may be the North Atlantic Cooperation Council, formed in 1992, of which Ukraine is a member, as well as implementation of the new initiative, the Partnership for Peace, as proposed by President Clinton, which contains new ideas and forms of cooperation between NATO and the East European countries but at the same time does not extend the composition of this organization. Anatoly Zlenko, Ukraine's minister of foreign affairs, put his signature on the Partnership program on 8 February 1994. It is worth mentioning that Ukraine is the first among the CIS states to join this program. Speaking on the occasion, the chief of Ukrainian diplomacy said:

> By approving the program Partnership for Peace, Ukraine reiterates its fundamental political priorities and the choice it has made to return to Europe, from which it was artificially severed, as well as its choice to join the family of European nations.[16]

Creation of an "integration area" in the subregion would correspond to today's reality and cater to the national interests of the Central and East European states. Preliminary attempts have been made in this direction by the countries entering the "Group of Four" (Hungary, the Czech Republic, Slovakia, and Poland). Ukraine's initiatives for the creation of a zone of stability and security in Central and Eastern Europe are timely and, in terms of future prospects, fruitful. This idea, in certain aspects, coalesces with approaches proposed earlier by the president of Poland, Lech Walesa, and the prime minister of France, Édouard Balladur, and in some ways Ukraine's initiatives also suit the all-European context, the Helsinki Final Act, and other documents of the CSCE. It should be stated that this idea does not aim at the formation of any military-political body in the subregion. The "bloc syndrome" of the Warsaw Pact era and its consequences are all too familiar. The formation of certain mechanisms for political deliberations and coordination within the framework of Ukraine's implementation of its initiatives, however, would be a correct and concrete step toward the creation of a subregional and, ultimately, all-European system of international security.

The introduction of the Parliamentary Assembly of Black Sea Economic Cooperation in the southern periphery of the European continent holds promise and conforms to the interests of Ukraine's national security. The fall session of its assembly in Kiev, from 29 November to 1 December 1993, was good proof of the fact that its member states (including Russia, Ukraine, Turkey, and Greece, among others) strive for not only economic but political cooperation as well.

The idea of creating a union of Danube basin states based on common economic interests and tied together by this massive water channel deserves special attention. The current importance of this idea lies in the fact that the majority of the states of the Danube basin, including Ukraine, suffered heavy losses as a result of UN sanctions against Serbia.

The Return of Ukraine

Today a new geopolitical configuration is forming in the vast territory of the European continent, and Ukraine is a part of it. It is developing under the influence of two opposing tendencies: the process of disintegration and decentralization of the totalitarian system and the creation of new regional and subregional integration "fields."

The current political process in Europe demonstrates that, step by step, the European political arena is turning into a bipolar geopolitical structure, with NATO and the European Union at one end and Eurasia, with Russia and its clear areas of influence and interests as a center at the other. Ukraine has to make a decisive strategic choice with regard to its moves in the new geopolitical environment. The choice is evident. Ukraine should "return" to Europe, to the family of civilized nations. Ukraine must do so independently, and not "at the tail of the Moscow fleet," moving toward an integrated Europe. This does not mean that Ukraine should neglect its interests in the East. Normal interaction with Russia and the CIS states is one of the preconditions of Ukrainian integration into Europe. But to clearly identify its place in civilized Europe and its national interests and to guarantee its security, Ukraine should come out of Russia's "zone of vital interests." A qualitatively new situation has emerged in Ukraine's relations with its Western partners. It is characterized by the following factors:

- The generally favorable public opinion of the West toward Ukraine as a result of its latest foreign policy moves, including the signing and ratification of the Tripartite Agreement on the fate of nuclear arms in Ukraine's territory and the signing of the document on Ukraine's participation in the Partnership for Peace;
- Concern over Russia as a result of the December 1993 elections to the State Duma of the Russian Federation, the acceleration of Russia's imperial ambitions, and the disenchantment with economic reforms in Russia (evidenced by resignation of leading reformers); and
- Concern over the economic and political situation in Ukraine, especially the virtual stoppage of reforms; the acute economic crisis (as President Clinton stated, "The United States recognizes that it is very important to be supportive as Ukraine tries to reform and get through this period of economic transition"[17]); the social and political tension during elections; and the Crimean poll results and the threat to the territorial integrity of Ukraine.

Opinion in favor of aid to Ukraine in order to thwart social upheaval and a military-political confrontation in Ukrainian-Russian relations is gaining ground. This opinion is being formed against the backdrop of the aggravated Yugoslavian crisis. A consensus on preventing the conflict rather than regulating should it occur is dominant.

In this regard, How can the West help? For one, the West should freeze relations with Russia and, after a definite strategic reshuffling of material resources, initiate (parallel to Russia) a large-scale system of aid to Ukraine. It is not "Ukraine instead of Russia" but "Ukraine together with Russia," as parallel recipients of aid. Such a policy would gradually shift the West from a clearly expressed pro-Russian orientation.

The West should also be definite about the prospects of its aid to Ukraine. There are several spheres of priority where Western aid would best be applied. One is agriculture.

Agriculture can truly pull Ukraine out of an economic dead end. The prevalent kolkhoz structures need changing. Investments, new agrarian technology, and fuel are necessary, but the return for these changes would be received in the course of a year (maximum). Ukraine does not demand a place in the European agrarian market as a competitor. The traditional market for sale of its agricultural products is Russia, which is not only a huge market but a long-term one (even during the most favorable periods of history Russia could not fully avail itself of food grains). It is difficult for Russia to exert pressure on Ukraine, having been tied so long to its food-grain market. To recall the New Economic Policy experience, the agrarian expansion of Ukraine might stabilize (to a certain extent) the finance system. Bread coupons (similar to those issued in 1924–25) are a reality. The stabilization and elevation of agriculture do not need large credits.

The need for creating a stabilization fund for the Ukrainian currency, the *hryvna*, is fully understood by Western partners. It is impossible to save Ukraine's economy without this fund. The mechanism is well known. The experience of international financial institutions in this sphere is quite rich.

Providing technical aid to the private sector and small business community of Ukraine for the creation of a management infrastructure is another priority. The private sector, in competition with Russian business, needs to defend its own interests and the interests of the state, which in turn must defend small business. There is hope that the state legislature of Ukraine will protect Ukrainian business. Western experts can be involved in preparing and implementing such legislation. Representatives of nonstate entrepreneurial bodies, who could collect up to one-third of the votes of the electorate in future elections, constitute a constructive majority in the parliament and are capable of pulling Ukraine out of a crisis. The left and right extremist wings in the parliament will be engaged in sorting out relations between themselves and will, therefore, hardly do anything constructive. This circumstance would serve as an additional stimulus for Western partners in helping the nascent middle class, which is interested in the continuation of democratic and market reform.

Unlike Russian entrepreneurship, traditionally inflamed by the superstate "Russian idea," the middle class in Ukraine is more pragmatic and, along with the West, would defend the national values of Ukraine. The independence of Ukraine is one of the main conditions for its existence.

Table 1

Prospects for NIS Integration into World Economy

	Population (in millions)	Chances of Integration with World Economy	Potential Areas of Breakthrough in the World Market
Large States:			
Russia	148.5	high	crude oil and gas, mineral resources, high-technology products, service sector
Ukraine	51.9	medium	certain types of raw materials and industrial products, agriculture
Uzbekistan	20.7	high	gold, certain types of mineral resources, certain industrial items, agriculture
Kazakhstan	16.9	high	crude oil and gas, mineral resources, metallurgy, metal manufacturing
Belarus	10.3	medium	certain types of industrial goods, including high-technology goods
Small States:			
Central Asia			
Tajikistan	5.4	low	agriculture
Kyrgyzstan	4.4	low	agriculture
Turkmenistan	3.7	high	crude oil and gas, agriculture
Caucasus			
Azerbaijan	7.1	high[a]	crude oil and gas, agriculture
Georgia	5.5	high[b]	certain types of mineral resources, agriculture, tourism
Armenia	3.4	low	agriculture
Baltics			
Lithuania	3.7	low	agriculture
Latvia	2.7	medium	agriculture
Estonia	1.6	low	agriculture
Moldova	4.4	medium	agriculture

Source: Official national statistics; remarks of experts.
[a]In case the armed conflict with Armenia comes to a stop.
[b]In case the internal situation is stabilized.

Table 2

Foreign Debt Situation of Ukraine (in billion Ukrainian karbovantsi)

	Debtors		Creditors		Balance (+, −)	
	1 Sept. 93	1 Oct. 93	1 Sept. 93	1 Oct. 93	1 Sept. 93	1 Oct. 93
Armenia	3.1	4.0	4.6	7.0	−1.5	−3.0
Azerbaijan	32.0	45.2	19.2	25.6	12.8	19.6
Belarus	118.2	148.7	100.2	157.9	18.0	−9.2
Georgia	11.6	12.9	4.6	9.9	7.0	3.0
Estonia	4.9	6.9	4.7	9.0	0.2	−2.1
Kazakhstan	41.3	64.3	46.4	49.4	−5.1	14.9
Kyrgyzstan	10.2	11.2	5.4	6.5	4.8	4.4
Latvia	26.6	22.7	18.0	28.9	8.8	−6.2
Lithuania	122.6	27.1	27.2	27.9	95.4	−0.8
Moldova	25.3	28.9	17.1	33.9	−8.2	−5.0
Russia	2,046.2	2,880.9	7,775.8	6,603.3	−5,729.6	−3,722.4
Tajikistan	5.5	12.3	7.3	15.7	−1.8	−3.4
Turkmenistan	34.8	35.3	497.9	470.0	−463.1	−434.7
Uzbekistan	54.8	58.4	24.8	29.0	30.0	29.4
Total	2,537.1	3,358.8	8,553.2	7,474.3	−6,016.1	−4,115.5

Source: Author's own data; Ukrainian Institute of International Relations; Taras Shevshenko University, Kiev.

Table 3

U.S. Financial Aid to CIS Countries (Financial year 1992–93)

	Population (as % of total CIS population)	Total Aid (in million U.S. $)	Percent	Per Capita (in $)
Armenia	1.20	188.0	8.11	55.04
Kyrgyzstan	1.60	95.9	4.14	20.99
Georgia	1.95	106.5	4.95	19.12
Turkmenistan	1.34	54.6	2.36	14.23
Moldova	1.56	54.9	2.37	12.31
Belarus	3.63	118.5	6.11	11.42
Russia	52.36	1,448.0	62.46	9.68
Kazakhstan	5.99	82.4	3.55	4.82
Tajikistan	1.99	15.9	0.69	2.80
Ukraine	18.19	137.2	5.92	2.64
Uzbekistan	7.57	16.3	0.70	0.75
Azerbaijan	2.61	0.1	0.00	0.01
Total	100.00	2,318.3	100.00	8.12

Source: Author's own data; Ukrainian Institute of International Relations; Taras Shevshenko University, Kiev.

Table 4

Net National Product Decline Rate in CIS Countries
(in percent price index as of 1990)

	1991	1992	Change from 1990 (%)
Russia	−15	−19	69
Ukraine	−8	−13	80
Kazakhstan	−10	−15	77
Uzbekistan	−19	−20	65
Belarus	−11	−13	78
Azerbaijan	−19	−25	67
Moldova	−18	−26	61
Kyrgyzstan	−23	−11	68
Turkmenistan	−23	−10	81
Armenia	−32	−34	45
Tajikistan	−25	−34	50
CIS as a whole	−14	−17	71

Source: Data collected by B. Bolotin, Institute of World Economy and International Relations of the Russian Academy of Sciences.

Table 5

Economic Risk in Ukraine

Factors	Value	Weight	Significance
General state of the economy during coming 12 months (1 = very good, 10 = very bad)	10	0.10	1.00
Growth of gross national product (GNP) at comparative prices for coming 12 months (1 = significant growth, 10 = drastic fall of more than 10%)	10	0.05	0.50
Expected risk in GNP (1 = significant growth, 10 = sharp fall)	8	0.05	0.40
Growth of industrial output in coming 12 months (1 = more than 10% growth, 10 = more than 10% decrease)	10	0.10	1.00
Growth of investment in coming 12 months (1 = more than 10% increase, 10 = more than 10% decrease)	9	0.10	0.90
Growth of consumption demand for coming 12 months (1 = more than 10% increase, 10 = more than 10% decrease)	8	0.05	0.40
Common inflation (1 = more than 5%, 10 = more than 100%)	10	0.05	0.50
Dynamics of inflation for coming year (1 = sharp control, 10 = sharp spending)	7	0.05	0.35
Availability of finance from abroad (1 = available, 10 = very difficult to obtain)	9	0.05	0.45
Labor situation (1 = surplus cheap labor, 10 = deficit of labor)	1	0.05	0.05
Quality assessment of workforce (1 = high, 10 = skilled labor absent)	3	0.05	0.15
Monetary policy (1 = moderate, 10 = tough)	2	0.05	0.10
Fiscal policy (1 = stimulates demand, 10 = tough)	5	0.05	0.25
Tax level (1 = relatively low, 10 = extremely high)	7	0.05	0.35
Dynamics of tax level (1 = would decrease, 10 = would increase)	4	0.05	0.20
Development of energy power complex (1 = more than 10% development, 10 = more than 10% fall	9	0.10	0.90
Total	112	1.00	7.50

Note: For comparison, economic risk in the United States is 4.10 and in Russia 7.00.

Source: Author's own data; Ukrainian Institute of International Relations; Taras Shevshenko University, Kiev.

Table 6

Sociopolitical Risk in Ukraine

Factors	Value	Weight	Significance
Threat to stability from abroad (1 = nil, 10 = extremely high)	6	0.03	0.18
Stable government (1 = absolute, 10 = minimum)	8	0.10	0.80
Nature of official opposition (1 = constructive, 10 = destructive)	3	0.05	0.15
Influence of underground opposition (1 = nonexistent, 10 = threat of revolution)	2	0.04	0.08
Evaluation of social stability (1 = absolute, 10 = intense tension)	7	0.10	0.07
Relations between workers and management (1 = cooperation, 10 = persistent strikes)	5	0.04	0.02
Value of employment level for coming 12 months (1 = absence of unemployment, 10 = covers more than 25% of active population)	6	0.15	0.90
Evaluation of distribution of gross income (1 = equal, 10 = differentiated within society)	7	0.07	0.49
State attitude toward foreign investment (1 = stimuli and guarantees, 10 = strict restriction)	6	0.10	0.60
Risk of nationalization without compensation in full (1 = practically absent, 10 = quite high)	5	0.02	0.10
Probability of armed conflicts with neighbors (1 = absent, 10 = inevitable)	8	0.12	0.96
Attitude of local bureaucracy toward foreign investment (1 = supportive and effective, 10 = corrupt and disruptive)	7	0.07	0.49
Involvement of state in economy (1 = minimum, 10 = constant and decisive)	9	0.07	0.63
State ownership of economy (1 = highly restricted, 10 = absolute)	3	0.04	0.12
Total	82	1.00	6.40

Note: For comparison sociopolitical risk in the United States it is 2.76 and in Russia 6.87.
Source: Author's own data; Ukrainian Institute of International Relations; Taras Shevshenko University, Kiev.

Table 7

External Economic Risk in Ukraine

Factors	Value	Weight	Significance
General balance-of-payment situation with dollar zone (1 = normal, 10 = substantial problems)	8	0.10	0.80
Balance of trade with dollar zone for coming 12 months (1 = highly positive, 10 = acutely negative)	8	0.10	0.80
Growth of exports to the dollar zone for coming 12 months (1 = more than 10% increase, 10 = more than 10% decrease)	6	0.05	0.30
Growth of imports from dollar zone for coming 12 months (1 = more than 10% increase, 10 = more than 10% decrease)	6	0.05	0.30
General balance-of-payments situation with ruble zone for coming 12 months (1 = highly positive, 10 = acutely negative)	8	0.10	0.80
Growth of exports to ruble zone for coming 12 months (1 = more than 10% increase, 10 = more than 10% decrease)	6	0.05	0.30
Growth of imports from ruble zone for coming 12 months (1 = more than 10% increase, 10 = more than 10% decrease)	6	0.05	0.30
Official restrictions on capital mobility (1 = free mobility, 10 = mobility prohibited)	7	0.05	0.35
Dynamics of official restrictions on capital mobility (1 = quite simplified, 10 = quite complicated)	6	0.05	0.30
Dynamics of restrictions on trade with the dollar zone in coming 12 months (1 = quite simplified, 10 = highly complicated)	6	0.05	0.30
Balance of trade with ruble zone for coming 12 months (1 = quite positive, 10 = highly negative)	8	0.10	0.80
Dynamics of trade restriction with ruble zone for coming 12 months (1 = quite simplified, 10 = quite complicated)	5	0.05	0.25
Dynamics of exchange rate of karbovanets for coming 12 months (1 = more than 20% increase, 10 = more than 20% decrease)	10	0.10	1.00
Change in world prices of oil (1 = more than 20% increase, 10 = more than 20% decrease)	5	0.10	0.50
Total	95	1.00	7.10

Note: For comparison, economic risk in Russia is 5.20.

Source: Author's own data; Ukrainian Institute of International Relations; Taras Shevshenko University, Kiev.

Notes

1. See for example, Samuel P. Huntington, "The Clash of Civilizations?" *Foreign Affairs*, vol. 72, no. 3 (summer 1993); Karen Dawisha and Bruce Parrott, *Russia and the New States of Eurasia: The Politics of Upheaval* (Cambridge: Cambridge University Press, 1994); Ilya Prizel, "Ethnicity and Foreign Relations: The Case of Ukraine," Working Paper no. 22, Russian Littoral Project, University of Maryland and Johns Hopkins University (June 1993); *The Political and Strategic Implications of the State Crises in Central and Eastern Europe* (Luxembourg: Institute for European and International Studies, 1993); Ian J. Brzezinski, "European Security and Ukraine" (paper presented at the National Institute for Strategic Studies roundtable on "Ukrainian Security: Modern Perspectives," 10 January 1994); "Ukraina ta mizhnarodnie spivtovarystvo," Dopovid', *Politychna dumka*, 1993, no. 1; Roy Elison, "Pytannia bezpeky u vidnosinakh Ukrainy zi Skhidn'oiu, Tsentral'noiu ta Zakhidn'oiu Evropoiu," *Politychna dumka*, 1993, no. 1.

2. O.S. Vlasiuk, "Natsional'ni interesy Ukrainy ta ikh prioritety: Formal'ni vysnovky za rezul'tatamy systemnoho analizu [documentary material]" (Kiev, 1994).

3. "O sotsial'no-ekonomicheskom sostoianii Ukrainy za deviat' mesiatsev 1993 goda: Dannye Ministerstva Statistiki Ukrainy," *Delovaia Ukraina* [Business Ukraine], no. 83 (November 1993); and Volodymyr Lanovyi, "Interv'iu s prezidentom Fonda vosstanovleniia ekonomiki Ukrainy eks-vitse Prem'erom Ukrainy V. Lanovym," *Kievskie vedomosti*, 28 December 1993.

4. *Kievskie novosti*, 14 January 1994.

5. *Washington Post*, 6 March 1994.

6. Erik Whitlock, "Ukrainian-Russian Trade: The Economics of Dependency," *RFE/RL Research Report*, 29 October 1993, p. 39.

7. *Izvestiia*, 5 January 1994.

8. See *Natsional'na bezpeka Ukrainy: Istoriia i suchasnist'* (Kiev, 1993), pp. 48–52.

9. *Holos Ukrainy*, 10 October 1993.

10. Huntington, "Clash of Civilizations?"; William Wallace. *The Transformation of Western Europe* (London: Printer, 1990).

11. See, for example, L. Freedman, P. Hassner, D. Senghaas, S. Silvestri, and C. Zaldivar, *War and Peace: European Conflict Prevention*, Institute for Security Studies, Western European Union, Challiot Papers 11 (October 1993).

12. "Dekliaratsiia pro derzhavnyi suverenitet Ukrainy vid 16 lypnia 1990 roku," *Ukraina na mizhnarodnii areni* (Kiev: Zbirnyk dokumentiv, 1993), p. 10.

13. *Kievskie vedomosti*, 19 January 1994.

14. *Izvestiia*, 26 November 1993.

15. *Moskovskie novosti*, 21 November 1993.

16. *Holos Ukrainy*, 19 March 1994.

17. *New York Times*, 5 March 1994.

7

Belarus's Foreign Policy Priorities and the Decision-Making Process

Vyacheslau E. Paznyak

The case of Belarus's foreign policy formulation is similar to that of some other newly independent states (NIS). Major political forces were almost taken by surprise by the short-lived coup of August 1991, whose failure, destined by the developments in Russia, triggered the process of obtaining sovereignty. No elaborate scenarios of independence had existed by the time the Declaration of Sovereignty was adopted.[1] The spontaneous disintegration of the Soviet Union, coupled with the emergency integrative process (the formation of the CIS), created, at least initially, the political oxymoron of the CIS, whose unique function was to offer a means of cooperative disintegration. The shaping of Belarus's foreign policy, lacking adequate institutional, conceptual, technical, and personnel capabilities, has been mainly spontaneous and reactive. Belarus has had to solve the very complex external tasks that have besieged it since independence, almost simultaneously and en masse.

On 27 July 1990, the newly formed Supreme Soviet of the Belorussian Soviet Socialist Republic[2] adopted the Declaration on State Sovereignty, which defined full state sovereignty of the Belorussian SSR as "supremacy, independence and absolute state power of the Republic within its territory, validity of its laws and independence of the Republic in foreign relations," and declared "the determination to establish a law-based state."[3] However, it is only in the aftermath of the failed coup that the republic's parliament mustered the majority required to give the declaration the status of a constitutional law (25 August 1991) prior to the adoption of the new constitution.

Several provisions of Article 10 of the declaration are of special importance. First, Article 10 guaranteed Belarus the right to establish armed forces, as well as internal security forces and state and public security agencies controlled by the Supreme Soviet. Second, the consent of the Supreme Soviet was required for the deployment of foreign military units and the establishment of bases and installa-tions on Belarusian territory. Another provision of the declaration set the unprec-edented goal of making Belarus a nuclear weapon–free zone and a neutral state.[4] Belarus's Minister of Foreign Affairs, Piatr Krauchanka, speaking in the general debate at the forty-sixth session of the UN General Assembly, offered perhaps the first approach to setting forth a hierarchy of national interests in foreign relations. Listed as "Foreign Policy Principles and Priorities of the Republic of Belarus," they included: (1) achieving genuine independence and sovereignty; (2) interacting in the creation of a common economic space within a new com-munity of sovereign states; (3) mobilizing international support for the solution of the Chernobyl problem; (4) transforming Belarus into a nuclear weapon–free zone and neutral state; (5) integrating Belarus into the Pan-European process; (6) creating conditions for the formation of market structures in Belarus for its economic development; (7) ensuring ecological security; and (8) ensuring free interaction of world cultures.[5]

The primary task of overcoming the information "blackout" of Belarus in the world community is being solved. By August 1994, the republic had received official recognition as an independent state from 123 countries. It has established diplomatic relations with 97 countries. Twenty-one embassies have been opened in Minsk. The young state has become a member of over twenty international organizations.[6] It has joined some basic international arrangements and institu-tions, to which it had not been party before. Belarus has been consistent and fairly successful in its search for diplomatic recognition by the majority of states as well as in establishing normal working relations with its neighbors and more distant states.

On 2 October 1991, the Supreme Soviet adopted the text of the Declaration on the Foreign Policy Principles of the Republic of Belarus, which affirmed adherence to the principles of the Charter of the United Nations and the Univer-sal Declaration of Human Rights, and the international obligations assumed by Belarus under its international agreements. The declaration also proposed that the CSCE participants open talks on the elimination of nuclear weapons and declare Europe a nuclear-free zone.[7] At the forty-sixth UN General Assembly session, the Belarusian delegation also spoke in favor of concluding a treaty banning all nuclear weapons tests.[8] In addition, Belarus's parliament has become the first among the three concerned states of the former Soviet Union (FSU) to accede to the Nuclear Nonproliferation Treaty and to ratify the START I Treaty, as well as the Lisbon Protocol. The process of withdrawing strategic nuclear forces from Belarusian territory to Russia is under way, the CFE Treaty was and is being thoroughly implemented, and the Chemical Weapons Convention was signed. Overall, Belarus has lived up to its commitments concerning its nuclear weapon–free status.

On 10 December 1991, the Belarusian parliament, by an absolute majority, denounced the 1922 Treaty on the Formation of the Union of Soviet Republics and ratified the Agreement on the Establishment of the Commonwealth of Independent States. Sixty-nine percent of those polled in the republic approved of the commonwealth agreements.[9] Belarus seeks to play an active role in the CIS and Pan-European politics, while in compliance with its declared neutral status. Though this neutrality does not allow it to join military alliances or become involved in hostilities elsewhere, it does provide allowances for mediation in resolving conflicts. However, neutrality was not viewed unanimously as an end in itself. For some policy makers, it has either been a "sacred cow," never to be renounced, or an instrument for consolidating sovereignty, after which Belarus's status could be revised, depending on the situation. For others, it was just a mistake that would be corrected in favor of a military alliance within the CIS.[10]

The Role of Institutions in Foreign Policy

The legal and institutional mechanisms for foreign policy making are in the formative stages. Until the new constitution was adopted on 15 March 1994, the provisions of the old Soviet-era constitution were formally followed, while the existing structures have been transformed and expanded. According to the old Soviet constitution of Belarus, the Supreme Soviet was the supreme body of state power, was responsible for legislation, and had the authority to define the main foreign policy objectives and make key foreign policy decisions.[11] Between sessions, the functions of the Supreme Soviet were delegated to the Presidium of the Supreme Soviet, which was accountable to the former, was elected from among the Supreme Soviet's deputies, and was headed by the chairman of the Supreme Soviet. The Presidium was responsible for coordinating the work of the standing commissions of the Supreme Soviet, ratifying or rejecting international treaties, nominating and dismissing the republic's diplomatic representatives, accrediting foreign diplomatic representatives, and so forth.[12]

Upon independence, changes were introduced. Compared to his predecessors, the chairman of the Supreme Soviet received limited new authority to sign international agreements and remained more a parliamentary speaker.[13] New advisory positions on international and national security affairs were introduced. The International Relations Department was established within the apparatus of the Supreme Soviet in order to manage mainly technical and procedural matters. The new structure of the Supreme Soviet standing commissions featured several specialized commissions designed to meet the international needs of the newly independent state. They included the Commission on International Affairs and Foreign Economic Relations, the Commission on National Security, Defense, and Combating Crime, and the Commission on National Policies and CIS Affairs.

A new body, the Security Council of the Republic of Belarus (SCRB), was formed in November 1991 to deal with issues of national security. Intended to be the highest coordinating collective political body, the SCRB was created to define the republic's military policy in the fields of security, strategy, and military organization and to protect the republic's sovereignty and its defense potential, ecology, and citizens' rights and freedoms.

Until the first president of Belarus was elected, the SCRB was presided over by the chairman of the Supreme Soviet; his deputy was the council's vice chairman. The Security Council also included the prime minister (chairman of the Council of Ministers), the chairman of the Supreme Soviet Commission on Security, Defense, and Combating Crime, the prosecutor-general of the Republic of Belarus, the minister of defense, the chairman of the State Security Committee, the minister for internal affairs, the minister for communications and information technologies, the minister of transportation, the chief of the Belarusian Railways Department, and other officials at other levels.[14] The SCRB was to meet at least twice a year, but, since its primary objective has been to take operational measures against external threats, and none have been perceived to exist, the few meetings held focused mainly on organizational matters and discussion of national security doctrine drafts.

The Council of Ministers, being the supreme executive and administrative body of state power, has been implementing Belarus's foreign political activities (with the introduction of the presidency, it has been superseded by the Cabinet of ministers). In 1993–94, the Department of International Political and Economic Affairs and the Department of Citizens' Rights, Public Security, and Defense Matters were created within the apparatus of the Council of Ministers. This was obviously intended to enhance the established nomenklatura's control over sensitive national security and international issues and was done in response to the developing confrontation between Prime Minister Vyacheslau Kebich and the chairman of the Supreme Soviet, Stanislau Shushkevich, as well as the prime minister's team and the parliamentary opposition and dissenters. These two departments not only tried to supervise the relevant ministries and parliamentary commissions but inevitably paralleled some of their functions.

The Department of Citizen's Rights, Public Security, and Defense Matters was subsequently reorganized into the State Secretariat for Combating Crime and National Security and later into the Directorate for Coordinating the Activities of the Administrative Bodies of the Council of Ministers (in fact for controlling the Ministry of Internal Affairs [MVD], the KGB, and the armed forces). The heads of this body became notorious for imposing their opinions on foreign policy and national security issues.[15] The ambitions of the State Secretariat for Combating Crime and National Security were brought to light in an open letter to Chairman Stanislau Shushkevich and Prime Minister Vyacheslau Kebich by the former KGB chief Eduard Shirkouski and the former minister for internal affairs Vladimir Yahorau, both of whom were later forced to resign.[16]

The Ministry of Foreign Affairs is charged with the practical organization and implementation of both domestic laws and regulations and instructions pertaining to foreign political activities and international arrangements. Before the proclamation of independence, the staff of the Belarusian Ministry of Foreign Affairs numbered forty-five people. There were Departments of International Organizations, International Law, Information, and Protocol, as well as a Secretariat. In mid-1992, the number of ministerial personnel amounted to nearly one hundred, but the estimated target is around two hundred. The growth in responsibilities, however, necessitates further restructuring. One of the options under discussion is to reorganize the existing Departments for International Security and Disarmament, International Treaties and Law, and some others into directorates, as well as to create new ones, such as Directorates of International Economic Organizations, North America, Europe, developing countries, the CIS, and others.

The activities of the Belarusian Foreign Ministry during the initial period of independence were concentrated on establishing diplomatic relations with foreign countries, conducting arms control talks, probing opportunities in international organizations, and, generally speaking, learning about the external world and Belarus's place in it. In response to an acute shortage of specialists, in September 1992, the Department of International Policy was organized at the Belarusian State University in Minsk. In 1993, the specialization of students in international relations and international economic relations was initiated at the Belarusian State Linguistic University and the Belarusian State Economic University. Reportedly, there is some international assistance in the training of Belarusian diplomatic cadres. The country was included into the corporate program of the Washington-based Council for International Diplomacy intended for government officials. However, it seems that government officials may have fewer opportunities, at least in terms of time, compared to university students.

A conflict developed between the speaker of parliament, Shushkevich, and the foreign minister, Krauchanka, as a result of inconsistencies and failures on the part of the Foreign Affairs Ministry,[17] as well as Shushkevich's encroachments on foreign policy in the struggle to reduce its dominance by the pro–prime minister party (including Krauchanka), which had pushed forward joining the CIS collective security treaty. The ministry faced allegations of gross mistakes, an inability to formulate an adequate foreign policy concept, and a disregard for the political directives of the Supreme Soviet and its Presidium.

The mutual "misunderstanding" on the part of the Ministry of Foreign Affairs and the chairman of the Supreme Soviet, as well as the latter's ambiguous stand on accession to the Treaty on Collective Security,[18] resulted in the fact that, after the treaty was "signed" in May 1993, the signing had to be confirmed again later in the year. Another instance of "misunderstanding" occurred in Ashkhabad, when the Belarusian premier refused to sign several documents relating to the treaty, though there was nothing to prevent the signing. Nevertheless, the principal question still remains: Will the rest of the parties to the Treaty on Collective Security agree to the reservations the Belarusian parliament pledged to make during its ratification? If there is no such agreement, debates on the treaty are likely to be resumed.

The Ministry of Defense, whose former leadership struggled to keep the armed forces out of politics and politics out of the armed forces, has narrow functions with regard to foreign policy. The role of the ministry (particularly the Directorate for Treaties and Legal Matters) is to execute the parliamentary decisions on arms control and military cooperation within the CIS and with North Atlantic Cooperation Council members. Still, the position and the arguments of the military establishment in the debate over the CIS collective security system have shown that it undoubtedly has influence in the foreign policy process. In addition, public criticism by the chief of the Defense Ministry's Press Center, Colonel Vladimir Zametalin (who later was appointed press secretary of Prime Minister Kebich), against the political course pursued by the parliament shows that the problem requires permanent attention.[19]

Along with the Ministry of Foreign Affairs and some other agencies, the State Security Committee (KGB) retains an important role in providing analysis for foreign policy decision making. The objectives of the KGB that are relevant to the foreign policy process are outlined in the Temporary Regulations on the State Security Committee, adopted on 15 January 1992.[20] They include: obtaining intelligence on foreign political, economic, defense, scientific, technological, and ecological problems for the purpose of informing the government of Belarus; gathering information about foreign intelligence, the intentions of foreign security services, and specific intelligence actions aimed at undermining the sovereignty and territorial integrity of Belarus; and safeguarding the republic's economic interests.[21]

The process of laying down a legislative basis for Belarus's security interests has not yet been completed. The foreign policy guidelines (the first attempt to draft a comprehensive foreign policy program) prepared by the Foreign Ministry were heavily criticized by Shushkevich and returned to the drafters for revision. The second draft, prepared jointly by the Foreign Ministry and the Commission on International Affairs and Foreign Economic Relations early in 1994, has not yet been discussed and is doomed to yet another revision because of the adoption of the new constitution, the election of the first president, the ensuing reformulation of domestic and foreign policies, and reshuffles in the government.

The Political Debate in the Foreign Policy Process

For the moment, one can sketch several "strategic logics" being espoused in the domestic debate on Belarus's prospective foreign political strategy.

"Symbolic Logic"

This logic rests on the symbols of "Slavic kinship" and a "Slavic triangle" (Belarus-Russia-Ukraine), which stress a similar attitude among the peoples of these three states.[22] Pan-Slavists, now united into the International Slavic Congregation (Slavianskii sobor), proceed from the premise that a dangerous Western geostrategic threat exists for the "Slavic civilization," and the only chance for survival, according to the Belarusian political party Slavianskii sobor "Belaia Rus'," "is the creation of a political, military and economic union of all Slavic nations from the Balkans to the Pacific."[23]

The "symbolic logic" also has a counter aspect in the image of an imperialistic Russia, obsessed with expansionist designs as well as extrapolating the historical conquest and Russification of Belarus onto the present.[24] These symbols are emotionally overcharged and thus prone to irrational solutions lacking rational pragmatism. A sober consideration of the centrifugal sovereignization of the Slavic states in Eastern Europe discards the idea of a Pan-Slavic civilization as a delusion. The same may be said about the idea of the "Slavic triangle," which would mean for Russia a hardly desirable shrinkage of its territory back to the borders of the fifteenth century, and may simultaneously provoke suspicions about the hegemonic intentions of Slavs.

Geopolitical Logic

The dismantlement of the line of separation and confrontation between East and West precipitated a radical shift in the European and global geopolitical balance. The European context features three important points: (1) the breaking apart of former socialist East European states from the former Soviet sphere and their drifting toward the West; (2) the shifting of some geostrategic functions (both from the Western and Russian vantage points) that had previously been provided by the former East European socialist countries onto the newly independent states, as well as a strategic restitution through the emergence of the "New Eastern Europe"; (3) the tendency toward a restoration of the former role of Central Europe, or Mitteleuropa (that was prominent approximately until the period of World War I) as an "ebb-and-tide" zone, or a zone of potential instability and contest, between East and West. According to this logic, these lands are destined to be subordinated to either the East or the West, and control over them is the key to controlling all of Eastern Europe.

The status quo is possible only by creating a belt of independent states from Finland to the Black Sea (a version of the "buffer zone").[25] In an anti-Russian version, a "cordon sanitaire" must cut off Russia from other European states. Since 1989, the idea of creating a Baltic–Black Sea political-economic association (commonwealth) that would unite Belarus, the three Baltic states of Lithuania, Latvia, and Estonia, Ukraine, and Moldova has been discussed in Belarusian political circles.[26] A major proponent of this idea has been the Belarusian Popular Front. Originally, the prospective association was viewed as a collective mechanism for gaining sovereignty through secession from the USSR and resisting economic pressure from Moscow, while at the same time avoiding economic dependence on the West. In this way, the chances for independent development and for entrance into the West European markets were to be ensured. This new association was seen as being viable both because of geopolitics and the historical experience of the Grand Duchy of Lithuania shared by its members. In addition, the similarities in their cultures and economies would make it more natural.[27]

After the implosion of the USSR, the sovereignization of the former Soviet republics, and the formation of the CIS, the Belarusian Popular Front has emphasized the necessity of the Baltic–Black Sea Association (BBSA) as a counterbalance to the huge Eurasian Russia and as a safeguard of sovereignty. Meanwhile, the CIS is perceived as an unstable, dangerous, Russia-dominated formation to be kept at an arm's length by East European states.[28]

The political debate on Belarus's participation in associations also includes broader proposals. The Belarusian Social-Democratic Party ("Hramada") has voiced support for a midpoint somewhere between complete separation from the CIS and membership in the BBSA. It suggested that the best path for Belarus would be not to sign the CIS statute but, rather, to become an associated member and cooperate in the economic field only. Instead, Belarus could initiate a new international organization, something like a smaller European Community, that could be joined by some former Soviet republics, namely, the Baltic states, Ukraine, and Moldova, as well as former CMEA countries such as Poland, the Czech Republic, Slovakia, Romania, and Bulgaria.[29] The National-Democratic Party of Belarus, which unites the radical section of the Belarusian Popular Front, does not exclude the possibility of creating the BBSA, but without Russia. However, this party supported the notion that Belarus should secede from the CIS and avoid any alliances for a while.[30]

Two conferences concerning the prospects for the BBSA were organized in Minsk during 1990, with the participation of parliamentary delegations from Latvia, Lithuania, and Belarus, but, though several joint resolutions were passed,[31] there have been no breakthroughs since. The governments of the various newly independent states have been preoccupied with domestic problems. At the same time, centrifugal tendencies within the FSU have continued. Besides, the original idea was promoted by forces in opposition to the former (or successive, as with Belarus) governments, therefore, it could not be equally accepted at an official level by all prospective parties for a number of reasons.[32] Meanwhile, Belarusian diplomacy focused on laying down basic principles for its relations with its neighbors, as well as establishing working diplomatic links with these neighbors.

The idea of a subregional military-political alliance incorporating or omitting Belarus has also been expressed by political forces and individual politicians and analysts from other states. In an interview with the Warsaw weekly *Zprost*, Zbigniew Brzezinski recommended that Poland initiate a new regional political alliance, uniting Poland, Ukraine, the Czech Republic, Slovakia, and Hungary, which would act as a counter to Russian power.[33] A similar proposal, although without reference to countering Russia, was made by Polish President Lech

Walesa when he spoke in favor of a NATO-II as a common security system for Poland, Hungary, the Czech Republic, Slovakia, and the Baltic states to ensure the inviolability of their borders and to prevent border conflicts.[34] The abundance of projects such as these at least proves that some sort of strategic uncertainty in the region exists and cautions against hasty actions.

The Logic of European Self-Identification

"Return to Europe" was a buzzword for both the government and the opposition shortly after the initial wave of sovereignty, but it has been wishful thinking so far. Although geographically Belarus never ceased to be a part of Europe, Belarus's political, economic, and cultural integration into Europe is still a problem. The political image of a unified Europe is tempting, but it may have to remain a distant vision, given the disintegration in Eastern Europe and the "defenses" raised by Western Europe intended to cool East European hopes for early membership in existing European structures. The process is also complicated by gaps in economic and social development, as well as great differences among the countries' cultural, religious, and political values.

The "Bridge Logic"

The role of a "bridge" is being contended for by many of the newly independent states that emerged from the collapsed Soviet Union. But the metaphor of a "bridge," however attractive, has two serious flaws. First, it implies a passive role as a station for interaction between external actors. Second, it lacks originality and seems commonplace. "Bridgeomania" does testify to the desire of these new states to quickly reserve for themselves the most advantageous positions in the new Eurasian political landscape. In this case, however, supply exceeds demand. With respect to Belarus, its western and eastern "bridges" (the CIS and subregional alignments in Central Europe) are still being formed. Therefore, as of now, as a functional strategy, it cannot be distinctly outlined.

A "bridge" (ideally a neutral one) is useful, and perhaps essential, when sides are separated. The hypothetical scenario of a unified Europe, with transparent borders and free circulation of people, goods, capital, and information, may prompt other, possibly more preferable options. The idea of "bridge construction" that views Minsk as the "Eastern Brussels of the common European home," the coordinating center of the CIS, and the initiator of an East European Economic Community may remain popular for some time.[35] This presents Belarus as a link between the CIS, Central Europe, and Western Europe, and perhaps, as a prospective "bridgehead" for developing relations between China, the countries of Asia and the Pacific region, and Eastern Europe. Belarus's landlocked position, as well as its inadequately developed transport, communications, banking, and service infrastructures, will impede the realization of such a concept.

The prerequisites for a "bridge" role that do exist may be enhanced, however, by consistent efforts at economic and political integration. The geopolitical and geostrategic position of Belarus would theoretically enable it to be an axis state, to promote its national interests, and to have political, economic, and military influence in the region.[36] But an axis state, by definition, would have to be an independent state, not a client state. It would necessarily require maintaining good relations with Russia while reducing the level of economic, military, and political dependence on it, meaning Belarus would have to escape from Russia's direct control.

The role of an axis state for Belarus implies that it is of a key strategic and military importance for Russia, that the weakening of Russia's control and especially the deterioration of its bilateral relations along its western frontiers would severely damage Russia's position in its zone of traditional preeminence. Conversely, this would strengthen the positions of Russia's potential rivals. Some political forces in the West and in Eastern Europe might be interested in drawing Belarus away from Russia with the aim toward further weakening the latter and creating a "buffer zone," safeguarding Central and Western Europe from hypothetical relapses of Russian expansionism.

As opposed to the complex relations between Russia and the Baltic states and Ukraine, Belarus has been the only state on Russia's western littoral (besides Scandinavian nations) to maintain loyal relations with it. But, as in previous centuries, Belarus may again become a potential ground for a geostrategic contest among neighboring states. Therefore, the geopolitical position of Belarus as an objective axis should be supplemented with an adequate foreign policy. In other words, a potentially key role may be realized through a strategy that would incorporate two initial provisions: maintaining good relations with neighboring states and performing the function of the regional balancer-state, and an active guarantor of a positive status quo and regional balance of power. This balancer-state role, which logically follows from Belarus as an axis and its sought-after neutral status, integrates rational points from the aforementioned "strategic logics."

Logic of Events

At present, Belarus, like other newly independent states, faces formidable tasks in defining its foreign policy strategy and national security doctrine. Belarus's foreign policy is determined, on the whole, by both external and internal policy-shaping factors. The republic is a part of regional and global international systems that include geographic, ideological, and military aspects. Belarus has never possessed sufficient resources to exert a decisive influence on the course of its development. Conversely, economic and political developments in such states as Russia, Ukraine, and other former Soviet republics are having a considerable impact on the formulation and pursuit of Belarusian foreign policy.

Belarus's internal policy-shaping factors are dependent on the specific qualities of the post-totalitarian period. Because some of the international community's primary requirements for Belarus's domestic development have not been met, its opportunities in the external sphere have also been affected.[37] Belarusian society is only at the early stages of social and political transformation. The most important political, legal, and ethical norms that regulate social relations are being reshaped and transformed, but they are far from firmly established. Furthermore, uncertain and unstable social processes produce similar uncertainty and unpredictability among the political outputs, including foreign policy decision making. This becomes even more serious when combined with similar problems on the entire territory of the former Soviet Union.

The development of a state's foreign policy strategy and priorities is also influenced by its actual, as well as perceived, threats and national interests. Thus, the policy-shaping factors are being shaped themselves by such sociopolitical determinants as the external policy orientations of the ruling political elite, as well as the main political forces (parties, movements, voluntary associations), their arrangement and degree of influence; the dominant predispositions of the populace; the availability (or lack) of public consensus on foreign policy strategy; and the ability of the ruling elite to ensure a substantial level of agreement.

Developing any substantial consensus on the foreign policy direction, generally speaking, would depend on the legitimacy and recognition of the government's authority. Of crucial importance is whether the government has an elaborate and optimal strategy, and whether this strategy has comprehensibility and appeal to the requirements, aspirations, and perceptions of a public majority. In other words, a foreign policy strategy, as a part of the general strategy of national development, must proceed from an adequate perception of national interests, on the one hand, and must formulate and represent them with maximum precision, on the other hand. Unfortunately, both the crystallization of national interests in the Belarusian society and their theoretical formulation by political elites have been rather languid.

Discussions over the relevant issues have often been emotional, and the "battleground" has been delimited by the two extremes: radical nationalism and Soviet internationalism.

Aside from visible disagreements over the future direction of national development in society and the parliament, which showed in its procrastination over decisions on the basic provisions of the new Constitution, other factors have impeded progress in working out a viable foreign political strategy.

These have included a paucity of foreign policy specialists; difficulties in pooling interests to form a creative independent community; a continued closed foreign policy decision-making process; a still-budding tradition of public debate on foreign policy; attempts by the state to control the press; and the unpreparedness of many of the newly formed parties for generating foreign policy concepts or for their sophisticated discussion.[38] The situation started to change for the better in May 1992. The National Center for Strategic Initiatives and, later, the

university-based Center for Strategic and International Studies and the Belarusian Center for Strategic Studies were established. In addition, the Development
and Security Research Institute of Belarus was formed in 1993.

But to date, the newly formed nongovernmental structures can hardly boast
impressive results from cooperation with governmental agencies. As the then
First Deputy Foreign Minister Georgii Tarazevich acknowledged, the newly independent Belarusian state "does not have that much experience in cooperating
with independent research structures."[39]

Just like all other former Soviet republics, Belarus has to solve a number of
similar problems in its domestic and foreign policies. Without establishing a
clear-cut hierarchy among these problems, they can be listed as follows: (re)cre-
ating an independent state and consolidating sovereignty and national security;
formulating national interests and foreign policy priorities; determining a foreign
policy doctrine; defusing social and economic crises; gaining greater political
and economic independence; diversifying foreign relations and overcoming
asymmetrical interdependence; providing external support for domestic transfor-
mations; creating an independent image and achieving a meaningful status and
role in regional and global contexts; forming a legal basis for relations with
neighboring states, within the CIS as well as with other members of the international community; organizing an infrastructure of foreign missions and providing
logistical support; solving problems related to the accession to the system of
international arrangements and institutions and realizing their corresponding
commitments; reducing armaments; reforming the defense sphere; building up
the military forces; and developing ties with Belarusians living abroad (foreign
diaspora) and protecting their interests. Belarus's interests seem to boil down to
the stabilization of the CIS, the efficient utilization of its potential, the gradual
harmonization of the republic's regulatory and legal relationship with the European Union, and an upgrade of its political, economic, and social standards to the
level of the developed nations with a view to joining West European structures.

The foreign policy of Belarus is experiencing acute problems that are symp-
tomatic of a crisis, largely as a consequence of crises in other spheres of society.
The content of the foreign policy debates among the contending forces has been
determined by the general struggle around the national development strategy.
Meanwhile, foreign policy itself has, on many occasions, become both a battlefield and a means of confrontation. In addition, the confrontation between the
leaders of the Council of Ministers and the Supreme Soviet produced a negative
effect on the situation. As a result, the important foreign policy factor of leadership has been undermined, and the external activities of different agencies have
been disrupted and inadequately coordinated.

Moreover, the national security doctrine is, likewise, yet to be adopted. This is
a result of an ideological crisis in the young state, in which the idea of national
sovereignty ("national idea") has been unable to take deep root superceding the
old ideology. Mass consciousness and state structures have been very cautious

and doubtful toward the "national idea." Meanwhile, the absence of an ideological and political consensus in society as to the direction of further development leads to an ideological rupture and conflict between the official policy and its popular perception.

A certain paradox, as well as a predicament in the foreign policy process, lies also in the reality of Belarus's geostrategic situation. Belarus, not being a power center itself, is located between two European power centers. Clearly, a "Belarussocentric" model of relations with the outside world would not fit the real context. At the same time, taking into account that fact, the actual foreign policy of Belarus should proceed from its national interests, placing it in the center of "world creation." Regrettably, the rather vague visions of the true Belarusian national interests are not conducive to the pursuit of an adequate foreign policy. Even though being fairly activist, Belarus's foreign policy has lacked creative initiatives that match the changing international environment. Quite often it has been reactive, which can be explained by an explicit or implicit "verify-with-Russia" dependent style of decision making. Foreign policy formulation has also been closed for the "uninitiated" majority, meaning predominantly closed and far from democratic, which holds true for the entire political system of Belarus.

The last two years have not been too eventful in the way of theoretical or conceptual innovations. The Supreme Soviet and the "party of the Council of Ministers" both spent their energy on circular debates over several issues. They focused on the CIS economic union, the CIS Treaty on Collective Security, and the Belarusian-Russian monetary union. The Council of Ministers and its supportive parliamentarians have been consistently attached to the idea of solving economic problems through closer ties with Russia, on the basis of the existing needs (Belarus is dependent on Russia for oil, gas, and raw materials) and mutual interests. These efforts also rest upon the persisting common Soviet "social genotype," the social and cultural affinity of the two peoples, not to mention Belarus's economic dependence and weak ethnic mobilization. Thus, no new ideas emerged in the field of foreign policy during the presidential elections. Domestic problems were at the forefront. The anticorruption radicalism of presidential candidate Aliaksandr Lukashenka was balanced with familiar references to closer relations with Russia.

Changing Decision-Making Patterns:
New Structures, Same Priorities?

The new constitution laid down the basic principles and legal and organizational framework for Belarus's foreign policy. Article 18 of the constitution reads that, in its foreign policy, the country "proceeds from the principles of the equality of states, nonuse of force or threat of force, inviolability of borders, peaceful settlement of disputes, noninterference into internal affairs, and other universally recognized principles and norms of international law. The Republic of Belarus aims at making its territory a nuclear-free zone and the state a neutral one."[40] With the election of the first president, Belarus has become a presidential republic. The president is both the head of state and the chief executive, and, according to Article 100 of the constitution, he takes measures to safeguard sovereignty, national security, and territorial integrity; represents Belarus in relations with other countries and international organizations; conducts negotiations; signs international treaties; and appoints and dismisses diplomatic representatives to foreign countries and in international organizations.[41] No radical changes in Belarus's foreign policy were declared, simply some corrections and a few changes of phraseology.

Russia remains a priority. Greater attention will be paid to the development of relations with the neighboring states and the CIS member countries. At the same time, efforts will be made to avoid losing momentum in relations with Western Europe, the United States, Japan, and others. The foreign policy of Belarus will be focused on creating conditions for the advancement of external economic relations to overcome the economic crisis and carry out reforms. The national interest has been defined as the single criterion of foreign policy.[42]

A new stage in the development of the Belarusian state and its foreign policy has begun. The same problems of elaborating the strategic concept of international activities and viable mechanisms for its realization remain.[43] Despite the multifaceted crises that Belarus has faced, sovereignty and the political situation have been temporarily stabilized, at least until economic hardships and new parliamentary elections provide further aggravation.

Notes

1. Belarus became the eighth of the fifteen Soviet republics to declare sovereignty.
2. Replaced by "Belarus" on 19 September 1991.
3. Letter, UN Permanent Representative of the Belorussian Soviet Socialist Republic to UN Secretary General, 6 September 1991, Annex, Declaration of State Sovereignty of the Belorussian Soviet Socialist Republic adopted by the Supreme Soviet of the Belorussian Soviet Socialist Republic on 27 July 1990, unofficial translation, A/46/427, p. 1.
4. Ibid., p. 6.
5. See *Statement by Piatr K. Krauchanka, Minister of Foreign Affairs of the Republic of Belarus in the General Debate at the Forty-sixth Session of the United Nations General Assembly* (Minsk: Belarus Publishing House, 1991), pp. 21–30.
6. *Zviazda*, 22 July 1994; *Narodnaia gazeta*, 16 August 1994.
7. Letter, UN Permanent Representative of Belarus to UN Secretary General, 18 October 1991, Annex, Declaration of 2 October 1991 by the Supreme Soviet of Belarus on the foreign policy principles of Belarus, A/46/582, p. 2.
8. "Statement by P. Krauchenka," *Sovetskaia Belorussiia*, 2 November 1991.
9. *Znamia iunosti*, 13 December 1991.
10. These views of neutrality were apparent in the parliamentary debates on the defense doctrine and, indirectly, in the draft of the new constitution of Belarus, which featured no mention of a neutral status. See "Konstitutsiia (osnovnoi zakon) Respubliki Belarus'," *Narodnaia gazeta*, 22 August 1992.

11. *Konstitutsiia (osnovnoi zakon) Belorusskoi Sovetskoi Sotsialisticheskoi Respubliki,* (Minsk: Belarus Publishing House, 1980), p. 36.

12. Ibid., pp. 39–40.

13. See Stanislau Shushkevich, "Ucht'em velikii opyt Rossii," *Komsomol'skaia pravda,* 21 June 1994.

14. See "Resolution of the Supreme Soviet of the Republic of Belarus on the Creation of the Security Council of the Republic of Belarus" (in Belarusian), *Vedomosti Viarkhounaga soveta respubliki Belarus,* nos. 1, 5 (January 1992), pp. 9–13.

15. See, for example, Gennadii Danilov, "Belarusi sleduet peresmotret' svoiu pozitsiiu v otnoshenii Dogovora SNG o Kollektivnoi Bezopasnosti," *Sovetskaia Belorussiia* (March 1993).

16. See E. Shirkousky, V. Egorov, "O nekotorykh voprosakh gosudarstvennogo ustroistva Respubliki Belarus'," *Narodnaia gazeta,* 26 January 1994.

17. For example, the thoughtless and unsuccessful race for a seat at the UN Security Council and the considerable increase in Belarus's payments to the UN, to mention a few. For a more scrupulous account, see Valerii Tzerpkalo, "Tvortsy novogo shuma ... ," *Sovetskaia Belorussiia,* 18 December 1993.

18. See Mycheslau Hryb, "Pochemu ne priniaty ogovorki ... ," *Narodnaia gazeta,* 1 June 1993.

19. See V. Zametalin, "Korabl' tonet ili ego toplat?" *Vo slavu rodiny,* 8 December 1993.

20. The Law on the KGB is expected to be adopted in 1995.

21. See "So shchitom, no bez mecha?" an interview with a KGB official, *Sovetskaia Belorussiia,* 15 April 1992.

22. See, for example, Il'ia Leviash, "Na rasstoianii litsom k litsu," *Evropeiskoe vremia,* no. 2 (1992).

23. See *Sovetskaia Belorussiia,* 12 September 1992.

24. See, for example, a controversial article by Zianon Paz'niak "O russkom imperializme i ego opasnosti," *Narodnaia gazeta,* 15–17 January 1994.

25. H. Mackinder, *Democratic Ideals and Reality: A Study in the Politics of Reconstruction* (New York, 1919), pp. 157, 158. Cited in Elgiz Pozdniakov, "Geopoliticheskii kollaps i Rossiia," *Mezhdunarodnaia zhizn',* nos. 8–9 (1992), pp. 10–11.

26. The idea was first put forth in 1916 at an international congress in Losanna by a leader of Belarusian National Revival, Anton Lutskevich.

27. See, for example, Zianon Paz'niak, "Al'ternativa vsegda sushchestvuet ... ," *Narodnaia gazeta,* 23–30 October 1990.

28. See Zianon Paz'niak, "Belarus' i dorozhe," *Narodnaia gazeta,* 29 October 1992.

29. See Aleg Trusau, "Tsi stane Minsk 'stalitsai' BChS?" *Narodnaia gazeta,* 20 January 1993.

30. See "Belorus'—Eto zvuchit gordo," *Sovetskaia Belorussiia,* 25 January 1992.

31. See "Vremia skazat' pravdu," *Sovetskaia Belorussiia,* 15 October 1991.

32. It is indicative that an American specialist on the Baltic states, A. Plakan, voiced skepticism about their possible unification in some form even among themselves. See "Poka kazhdyi sam po sebe," *Sem' dnei,* no. 1 (1993).

33. Cited in *Krasnaia zvezda,* 5 January 1993.

34. See Lech Walesa, interview, *New Times,* no. 45 (1992).

35. See, for example, former Minister of Foreign Affairs Piatr Krauchanka's pronouncement cited in *USA Today,* Supplement, 8 February 1993, p. 11.

36. For a discussion of the concept of an "axis state," see Zbigniew Brzezinski, *Game Plan: A Geostrategic Framework for the Conduct of the U.S.-Soviet Contest* (Boston, MA: Atlantic Monthly Press, 1986).

37. Belarus's full membership in the Council of Europe, an influential political inter-governmental organization uniting about thirty countries, is contingent on the democratization of the political system and economic reforms. Meanwhile, no free multiparty parliamentary elections have been held to date, and privatization has hardly begun.

38. One will be disappointed to discover that not a single political party in Belarus has come up with a full-fledged and consistent foreign policy concept. Those who have come closet are the Belarusian Popular Front and, understandably, the communists.

39. See *Femida*, no. 50, 13 December 1994, p. 3.

40. Constitution of the Republic of Belarus, *Polymia*, (Minsk Publishing House, 1994), p. 14.

41. Ibid., pp. 18–19.

42. See President Aliaksandr Lukashenka, "My spadziaemsia na kanstruktiunae supra-tsounitstva z usimi palitychnymi silami," *Zviazda*, 29 July 1994; Mycheslau Hyrb, "Zneshniia politika buduets'sa na padstavakh natsyianalnaga intaresu i natsyianalnai biaspeki," *Narodnaia gazeta*, 16 August 1994; also, new Minister of Foreign Affairs Uladzimir Sian'ko, "My ne planuem radykalnykh zmen u zneshniai palitytsy," *Zviazda*, 9 August 1994.

43. This was accentuated by the chairman of the Supreme Soviet, Mycheslau Hryb, in his speech before the heads of diplomatic and consular missions of Belarus abroad. See Hryb, "Zneshniia politika buduets'sa na padstavakh natsyianalnaga intaresu."

8

Dimensions and Orientations in the Foreign and Security Policies of the Baltic States

Peeter Vares

The Creation of Foreign and Security Policies in the Baltics

After a fifty-year interval, the Baltic states are once again in charge of their international policies. During the period of Soviet rule, they, like all the other republics of the Soviet Union, were not allowed to participate in the formulation of foreign policy. While Baltic foreign ministries did exist, they had only a symbolic function—staffed by only five or six people, they were allowed minimal cultural and trade contacts with Western countries and limited inter-Communist Party ties within the Soviet bloc. They had to report to the USSR Ministry of Foreign Affairs on every move they made and served as cover organizations for the KGB.

The creation of more substantive foreign policies in the Baltic republics actually began before they gained independence in August 1991.[1] In 1989–90, the emerging political parties voiced their first visions of the future of the Baltic states, which generally speaking boiled down to sovereign democratic states that enjoyed friendly relations with all countries of the world. By that time, under the pressures of perestroika and glasnost, the Soviet authorities had been compelled to loosen their grip on the foreign contacts of the union republics. The adoption in 1990 of declarations of independence by the Supreme Councils of Lithuania (11 March), Estonia (30 March), and Latvia (4 May) accelerated their entry into the international community.

Their first moves were to pursue the following three aims: first, to recall the attention of the international community to the forgotten Baltic states and their strivings toward independence; second, to gain international support and assistance in this fight for independence; and third, to join different international organizations that could eventually facilitate the achievement of independence.

They have succeeded in the first two aims, due to the Baltic lobby in foreign countries, numerous trips abroad by Baltic politicians, and the bloody events of January 1991 in Lithuania and Latvia, which highlighted the independence fight of the Baltic states in the eyes of the international community. They have almost completely failed, however, in the third aim. International bodies were not yet ready to accept the Baltics without the consent of Moscow—they still considered them part and parcel of the Soviet Union. The policies of major world powers toward the Baltics were greatly influenced by the U.S.-Soviet dialogue as well as the Gorbachev syndrome,[2] making the Western attitude toward the Baltics less resolute and causing them to maneuver between Moscow and the Baltic capitals.

The first foreign policy acts of the still Soviet-occupied republics were the establishment of horizontal ties with each other. These ties took the form of the Agreement on Economic Cooperation Between Latvia, Lithuania, and Estonia (signed on 12 April 1990) and the adoption of the Declaration on Unity and Cooperation, which renewed the Treaty on Unity and Cooperation and the resulting declaration (signed by Estonia, Latvia, and Lithuania in Geneva on 12 September 1934) and also created a Council of the Baltic States to assist in the full restoration of independence. The abortive communist-military coup in the USSR on 19–21 August 1991 precipitated the disintegration of the Soviet Union and made immediate independence possible for Estonia, Latvia, and Lithuania. The Baltic states gained diplomatic recognition from nearly fifty countries in three weeks, thus achieving a new qualitative level in the sphere of their international activities.[3] In comparison, the analogous process in the 1920s took two to three years.[4]

The Baltic societies, however, were not prepared for independence. Their domestic situations were characterized by enormous confusion, and while the Balts were eager to rejoin the international community, few of them had been able to study international relations. They wanted to establish rule of law in their states, but could only refer back to the little international law that the Moscow authorities had considered necessary for the periphery. They had to create security policies for their countries, but no local Balt had ever been involved in strategic or security studies. The only thing that the Balts did not lack was enthusiasm, but it could not compensate for their ignorance. There were too many unadopted laws, uncreated institutions, and absent systems, which were needed immediately. Baltic politicians were then unprepared for independent foreign policy formulation, let alone the charting of security policy perspectives.

There were even difficulties regarding the question of who should direct and influence foreign policy, and to what extent. The Popular Front, the Parliamentary Committee on International Relations, the Ministry of Foreign Affairs, the prime minister, and the chairman of the Supreme Council could all lay claim to that right. A simplistic, unprofessional approach to the selection of the foreign ministry staffs (i.e., qualifications based on enthusiasm, radicalism, and, in some cases, "diplomatic heritage") as well as the subjective evaluation of the capabilities of the few competent local experts in the field of international relations, formerly connected with Soviet diplomacy, contributed to a situation in which the new foreign services failed to assume the role of regulator of the foreign policy formulation processes. This state of affairs was also caused by the new decentralization of foreign contacts, mirroring the processes under way in the Baltic societies themselves.

With a substantial enlargement of foreign ministry staff, numerous enthusiastic amateurs rushed to fill the outwardly attractive vacancies in the foreign services. Inexperienced people lacking any diplomatic background were appointed to one important post after another. The new foreign policy leaders seemed to share the old Soviet mentality dictating that only a loyal party functionary (even if inexperienced) could successfully formulate foreign policy (Communist Party members were, of course, excluded) and that a public competition was not a prerequisite for selecting people for diplomatic careers as in most advanced countries.

Of course, tremendous difficulties were experienced in building the foreign services. Low wages hurt recruitment of the most capable internationally minded people, who, as a rule, went into the business sector. Standing vacancies were a common phenomenon in the foreign ministries of the Baltic states. People with a minimal knowledge of foreign languages could easily get a decent post. Life was full of trials for those who had already started their diplomatic careers earning their living abroad either stamping visas or lecturing on the Baltic states, as well as for those who lived abroad apart from their families for economic reasons.

To fill the lacuna in the Balts' knowledge of foreign languages, young Canadians, Australians, British, and Americans of Baltic origin were employed by the ministries. Initially, they worked mainly as translators; when they were used elsewhere (owing to the lack of personnel), they often failed because, as a rule, they did not know the local situation. They later recieved higher-level appointments. The staffs of the foreign ministries of the Baltic states, absorbed in routine, were not prepared to make foreign policy analysis. Many of the functionaries capable of doing so became engaged in interparty fights and election campaigns. The small Baltic legations abroad also failed to fill the gap; instead, they delivered generally poor or no analysis.

Could people with higher professional qualifications have been found in the Baltic states? It probably would have been possible: in 1918–20 the posts of the key diplomats representing the interests of the Baltic states in the international arena were filled exclusively by authoritative and experienced politicians regardless of their former connections with tsarist Russia's government institutions.[5]

The Baltic foreign ministries did not succeed in making the lives of the foreign diplomats in the Baltic states easy either. The mushrooming foreign embassies got an exceptionally uncooperative reception in the whole Baltic region. The working conditions provided for them left very much to be desired, making it difficult for them to carry out their duties for months.

The impact of the Soviet lifestyle was felt for quite a while. The atmosphere surrounding foreign policy formulation in the Baltic states greatly resembled that in the Soviet Union in the first perestroika years, when Soviet domestic policy was constantly debated and heavily criticized, whereas foreign policy was almost never subjected to public discussion and was presented by the mass media as faultless.

The number and gravity of domestic problems influenced foreign policy formation to a considerable extent. The first and foremost problem was the struggling Baltic economies, but the presence of the former Soviet troops in the Baltics was also undoubtedly a significant source of pressure. Each Baltic state also had its own pressure groups. In Estonia, the pressure groups consisted of the Estonian Congress, an alternative legislative body that ceased its activities in September 1992, and groups concerned with the Russian question in northeastern Estonia. In Latvia, they were the Latvian Citizens' Congress as well as the huge Russian-speaking population. In Lithuania, it was the Polish minority.

Despite the complex problems of international communication, the international community was impressed by the apparently active foreign policies of the Baltic states. Such an impression was created by the large number of invitations the Baltic states received from leaders and communities of other countries and the eager responses by the republics to these invitations. At times, it created a distorted picture of their aims. For example, the numerous exchanges of visits between the Baltic states and Asian countries formed an illusion that Baltic interests rested with the Far East or Southeast Asia.

The reactive nature of Baltic foreign policy formulation became immediately obvious whenever the republics were confronted with tasks that could not be dealt with in an improvised manner, when thoroughly considered policy decisions were to be made. The foreign policies of the Baltic states needed to be painstakingly worked out, a task that evoked little or no enthusiasm on the part of the Ministries of Foreign Affairs. A number of research institutions or other entities involved with international relations or foreign policy had appeared, and their services could be used, if wanted, by the appropriate authorities, though the academics could not claim to have personal experience themselves. None of them, however, had adequate contacts with their foreign ministries to influence foreign policy formulation. The institutions created by political parties were endowed with a major drawback—the party framework seldom guaranteed them objectivity.

The inclusion of the Baltic states in the international community turned out to be a difficult process. Few priorities were determined as to which international organizations and treaties should be joined first and why, and with which states basic international agreements should first be concluded.

The unpreparedness of the foreign policy apparatus and the resultant rather primitive, inflexible policies created an impression that those in charge of foreign policy in the Baltic states were often sailing with a broken compass. The

Baltic governments, however, did not acknowledge this. They even seemed ambitious to see their countries play a more significant role in international relations.

The same could practically be said about the formation of security policy in the Baltic states. Since there were no government institutions immediately upon independence that could address global military security problems, such questions were placed under the jurisdiction of the Ministries of Foreign Affairs and entrusted to one or two functionaries without any specific military background.

Estonia was the last of the Baltic countries to create a Ministry of Defense (13 April 1992). Latvia preceded Estonia, while Lithuania had already formed a Ministry of the Home Guard. Although inexperienced, their staffs at least consisted of people on whom had been conferred the first military ranks of the republics and who were going to be the new military leaders. Unlike the first independence years of 1918–20, Baltic officials were rather reluctant to use the skills and experience of the Balts who had served in the Soviet military. However, due to an absence of choice, many of those with Soviet military experience did manage to get responsible posts in the ministries—only to be ousted later.

Foreign Policy Options

The Baltic states' preferred foreign policy options were publicly voiced even before the republics became independent. Eight major directions could be considered: (1) Baltic-Nordic relations; (2) relations within the Baltic Sea States Council; (3) Baltic states and the New Hansa concept; (4) inter-Baltic cooperation; (5) Baltic-U.S. relations; (6) Baltic relations with Russia and other republics of the Commonwealth of Independent States (CIS); (7) the Baltic states as a gateway between the East and the West; and (8) Baltic–European Union relations.

The first key point is that the Baltic states adopted a Western orientation. This was based predominantly on the historical links the Baltic states have always had with Europe. However, to a great extent, it was also due to the need of the Balts to obtain substantial financial aid from the West, both because of the failure of perestroika and because of strong prejudices against Russia and everything Russian. The changes that had taken place in Europe and the world—namely, the disappearance of East-West confrontation, the new balance of political forces, and the new geopolitical realities—contributed to the strengthening of the Western orientations of the Baltic states. However, it became clear that it would not be easy to transform the political interest of the Western countries regarding the Baltic states into an economic interest, a major concern for the newly independent Balts.

The West, in fact, could open new perspectives for them in the fields of economics, trade, international aid, and cooperation. Nevertheless, two main problems became apparent. While formally they are not developing countries, the Baltic states, in reality, needed just as much economic aid. In addition, the basis for economic cooperation between the Baltic states and the West had not been worked out by either side, and the speedy establishment of such a basis remained rather questionable. Because of the insufficient economic relationship with the West, the Baltic states moved toward integration with each other on an equal footing in order to mutually reinforce their positions—a characteristic tactic of small countries that was also evident in the 1920s, when the Baltic states considered different variants of regional unions, from some conception of a Baltic-Scandinavian space to a minimal three-party agreement confined to the Baltic states.

The first impulse for the Baltic states in rejoining the international community was the emotional-romantic Nordic attraction. The Nordic countries had given the Balts full support long before they became independent. In the spring of 1990, Iceland offered itself as an intermediary in the negotiations between Moscow and the Baltic republics. Admittedly, it was not very successful, since an intermediary must be neutral toward both conflicting parties and recognized as such by them—Iceland had from the very beginning sided with the Balts. Nevertheless, it was a demonstrative and practical step in proving that the Baltic question was no longer "the domestic affair" of the Soviet Union.

A common political achievement inspired by the Nordic countries was the opening of Baltic information bureaus in a number of Nordic countries at the end of 1990. These information bureaus later became the prototypes for Baltic diplomatic legations. The Baltic and Nordic foreign ministers met each other at an official level as early as December 1990, when other countries would not have undertaken such a challenge to the USSR. The moral and material help the Nordic countries provided greatly reinforced the Nordic-Baltic dimension. It also gave rise to some serious worries in the Nordic countries, the most apparent being the underdevelopment of any accountable apparatus for receiving aid in the Baltics and the uncertainty that the aid was being properly utilized. In fact, neither Nordic officials nor Baltic politicians managed to work out a reliable framework for two-way Nordic-Baltic cooperation. However, they were united by common political, security, and environmental interests.

The interest of the Baltic states in the Baltic Sea area is also quite natural. The Baltic states joined the Council of Baltic Sea States (created in March 1992 and uniting Denmark, Sweden, Finland, the St. Petersburg region, Estonia, Latvia, and Lithuania, as well as the northern parts of Poland and Germany, as coastal allies) primarily because the formation of a new regional union implied the equality of all its participants and, second, because the participation of both Germany and Russia in the council would decrease the possibility of either raising claims on Baltic territory, although they did not rule out a unified action against the Baltic states within this framework. The council, in fact, became a convenient place to settle controversial matters between the Baltic states and Russia and a forum to rebuff Russian allegations of human rights violations in the Baltic states.

The New Hansa concept did not have any concrete ideology as its basis; rather, it symbolized the necessity of restoring historical regionalism and developing the intermediary functions of the Baltic states. Baltic public opinion was favorably inclined toward the Hanseatic ties but was not immediately ready for the reassertion of German influence in the Baltic region. Although the project never got off the ground, Germany did become one of the most important political partners of the Baltic states as of 1993.

Paradoxically, inter-Baltic cooperation has been regarded by Baltic officials and Baltic public opinion as, if not the least important, then at least one of the less significant options among the foreign policy alternatives of the Baltic states. The Balts have, in fact, never flocked together—either in ancient history, in the independent interwar years of 1920–40, or in the Soviet period. During the interwar period, the Baltic states were not particularly interested in concluding alliances with each other, and the presidents of the three states never held any joint meetings.

The Soviets were more interested in uniting the Balts, viewing the Baltic republics as the "Soviet West." At the same time, they have always feared Baltic unity and have tried to dilute the notion of the "Baltics" by integrating them with either Karelia, the Leningrad region, Belarus, or Kaliningrad. Only once did the Balts work closely together—during their struggle for independence against the central Soviet leadership in the perestroika years.

The international community has always been inclined to treat the Baltics as a united entity or, at least, as three countries united by common problems. Riga was often considered a regional center, although Estonia and Lithuania have never recognized its leading role. Their different historical, ethnic, religious, and linguistic backgrounds do not favor the spiritual unity of the Baltic states. The similar structures of their economies do not contribute to intensive economic cooperation; rather, they make them competitors. Various efforts at cooperation have been made, including the revival of the traditions of the rather unsuccessful Baltic Union of 1934–40 (announced in 1990); the regular meetings of the Baltic presidents, prime ministers, and ministers of foreign affairs that make up the Council of the Baltic States, and the parliamentary delegations that form the Baltic Assembly; and the Baltic Council of Ministers with its secretariat. The Baltic states have made common efforts to coordinate foreign and security policies, but so far they have contributed little to any kind of political and economic rapprochement.

Because of the closed nature of society during the Soviet period, the Baltic populations did not deem it necessary to learn foreign languages. The Moscow leadership did not favor it either—the teaching of French, for example, was banned for years in Baltic schools. Estonia was, perhaps, best off, due to the nearby Finnish television with its numerous programs in foreign languages. Of course, the similarity of Finnish and Estonian played a role. The Balts have now become aware that a comprehensive knowledge of foreign languages is an important prerequisite for joining the international community and informing the world about Baltic problems.

The general absence of interest in each other does not favor the creation of infrastructures and networks embracing all of the Baltics, although this is a matter of paramount importance not only for the Baltic states themselves but for the nearby international community as well.

No joint agreement has been reached on the creation of a common telephone communications network. The Baltic republics are handling separate deals with various international companies competing for contracts. No efforts have been made to create a joint Baltic airline system, such as SAS for Scandinavia or SABENA for the Benelux countries, which, according to Western experts, would be the only reasonable approach.

The Baltics could have served as a crossroads for Europe, if not for the Soviet regime, long ago. The international community has always contemplated the Baltics as an important transit route to Europe. Several years ago, the grand Via Baltica transit road project, which would both link Finland, Estonia, Latvia, and Lithuania to Eastern Europe and improve inter-Baltic connections, was launched. It has met with several problems, however. First, the Soviet Union impeded its implementation, then enthusiasm for it subsided among the Balts because the construction did not promise any immediate profits, and now the project has become popular again. Via Baltica is scheduled to be opened by 2010. Until then, the Baltic states have to put up with the poorly maintained inter-Baltic roads, which lack adequate services. The time-consuming transportation route created by the Soviets—the Chaika railway connection between Tallinn, Riga, Vilnius, and Minsk intended for inter-Baltic connections—has been replaced by the Baltic Express, which goes as far as Warsaw and is used extensively by Baltic and Polish smugglers. Still, disagreements among the Baltic states can be encountered at practically every step.

It is not without reason that the Baltics have looked to the United States as a potential advocate for their advancement into the international arena. After the Soviet occupation of the Baltic states in 1940, the U.S. administration implemented the Stimson doctrine and pledged never to acknowledge the annexation. In the postwar years, American administrations kept to this word and continually reiterated the Balts' right to independence. However, the "white ship"—American relief so much waited for by the Balts—never arrived. During Gorbachev's rule, when the Baltic states expected a lot from the United States, its position was rather ambiguous. The Baltic states were again naive enough to think that the U.S. administration would exert every possible (including military) pressure on the Moscow authorities to help them exit the USSR. True, pressure was exerted repeatedly by the U.S. Congress both before and after independence, and the U.S. administration has provided the Baltic states with financial aid, but the Baltics seemed to be of little importance to the United States, being beyond its sphere of interests.

The geopolitical position of the Baltic states endows Russia with an essential role. Their eastern experience had been not only bitter but tragic. Exhausted by the half-century socialist experiment, the Baltic states could not imagine that even a radical transformation of the East would offer them some optimism for a future partnership. The constant economic instability of Russia does not favor closer contacts, and even though the Baltic policies toward Russia may be detrimental to them, they care little—emotions have taken the upper hand. A major reason for this has been the stationing of Russian troops on the territories of the Baltic states. The withdrawal of the Russian troops became an extremely live issue right after the restoration of independence. The Balts have reiterated the inadmissibility of the continued presence of foreign troops on the territories of independent states. From the very start of the negotiations with Russia, the Balts were not ready to compromise on the matter, and they did not agree to carry out discussions on the status of the Russian troops. On 14 June 1992, the Lithuanians held a referendum concerning the withdrawal of Russian armed forces from the country's territory by the end of 1992, as well as compensation for damage caused by the army's presence. Of the voters who turned out, 90.79 percent voted yes. Sergei Stepashin, chairman of the Defense and Security Committee of the Russian Supreme Soviet, however, qualified the expression of the will of the people in a referendum "as not a civilized method" and called the demand for the army to leave Lithuanian territory a violation of the human rights of the soldiers.[6]

Russian officials had long considered it impossible to withdraw the troops by the autumn of 1992, as the Balts demanded, insisting on 1997 at the earliest. The actions of the Russian troops challenged all international norms of behavior. Without informing the governments of the Baltic republics and without their approval, the troops redeployed themselves and continued to hold artillery exercises on land and sea targets, causing damage to the local environment. Moreover, they carried out illegal business activities—selling weapons and land (which they did not own) and cutting down forests. The increasing tensions and the political deadlock formed between the Baltic states and Russia came to a head in the form of armed skirmishes with Russian military units, particularly in Estonia, during the summer of 1992. The Russians used such skirmishes skillfully. The 15 July 1992 session of the Russian Supreme Soviet accused the Baltics of escalating actions against Russian troops in the region, obstructing their removal, and delaying the solution of technical problems associated with withdrawal.[7] In response, the Balts have attempted at every opportunity to gain international support for their demands.

Under the pressure of international public opinion, Russia completed the withdrawal of its troops from Lithuania by 31 August 1993 and from Latvia and Estonia by 31 August 1994. The Baltic states reached agreements with Russia on the matters of social guarantees for the retired Russian officers and their families. An agreement was also reached to sell some Russian warships to Lithuania so that the latter could create a fleet of its own. The money received from.

the Lithuanians was to be used to build houses for the Russian officers, whereas Lithuania would provide its own builders and construction materials.[8] Russia reserved control of the Skrunda radar station in Latvia for five years in return for rent, and remained in Paldiski (Estonia) for another year to dismantle the two nuclear submarine training reactors. All three Baltic states had to face huge damages inflicted on their environment by the half-century presence of the Russian troops.

The territorial claims of Latvia and Estonia on Russia are another matter that aggravates their relations. References by the Balts to the peace treaties concluded with Russia in 1920 in Tartu and Riga, respectively, and the territorial settlements fixed by them produce a negative reaction on the part of the Russian negotiators. For them, history starts on 12 June 1990, when Russia, which they do not consider the legal successor of either "Soviet Russia" or "the Soviet Union," adopted the Sovereignty Declaration. The Balts, in their turn, do not seem to realize that territorial conflicts have always been among the world's most long-lasting and difficult problems to solve, and they will probably not get a quick solution to their border dispute with Russia. Stressing their discontent with Russia's obstinacy, they have demonstrated their benevolence toward Russia's immediate neighbors, Ukraine and Belarus. Lithuania has taken the lead in such relations.

The transformation of the Baltic states into a gateway between East and West was debated for years by the Baltic communities abroad. As far back as 1970, Rein Taagepera, an Estonian-American political scientist, developed the idea. In fact, the Baltics have always been a bridge—though very often they served as a rug for others to wipe their feet.[9] This once popular idea, however, lost favor in the Baltic states. Regardless of numerous statements by Baltic officials about such a necessity and of assertions that the East-West boundary passes along the eastern frontiers of the Baltic states, there is in reality a susceptibility toward Western proposals and an indifference toward the East. The West remains sufficiently stable, whereas the situation in the East is much less predictable. In addition, the bridge metaphor presupposes good relations with both parties, which is not the case with the East.

In their wish to become Europeans, the Baltic authorities have undertaken measures toward rapprochement with the European Community (EC). However, they did not have a clear understanding of the problems arising with this connection. For quite a long time, Baltic politicians behaved naively while discussing this option. They seemed not to have known that many of the countries currently part of the European Community had queued up for years in order to become members. The first steps toward the EC were the signing on 11 May 1992 of trade and cooperation agreements with the European Community and the obtaining of most-favored-nation (MFN) trading status from the EC. The Baltic states also signed a political declaration with the EC, declaring their shared ideals and pledging foreign policy coordination. In order to facilitate economic reforms, the

European Community adopted on 23 November 1992 a decision to provide the Baltic states with a seven-year loan amounting to 220 million ECUs (100 million to Lithuania, 80 million to Latvia, and 40 million to Estonia). The progress toward joining the EC (now the European Union) became more concrete in 1994. Government commissions were formed in the Baltic states to develop the bases for eventual integration. In July, the European Union signed free trade agreements with the Baltic states that come into force in January 1995. Urgent steps have further been taken to prepare association agreements by the end of 1995.

Foreign Policy Successes

In the Soviet Union, it was typical that every major international event that took place in the country or in which the USSR participated was hailed as a success for Soviet foreign policy. Something similar happened for quite a while in the Baltics. The first meetings of key Baltic officials with world leaders, both abroad and at home, and both before and after the restoration of independence, were exuberantly welcomed by the Baltic mass media as a sign of the growth of the prestige and importance of the Baltic states. The joining of global international organizations such as the UN and UNESCO and negotiations within regional organizations such as NATO, the Council of Europe, and the Nordic Council were also regarded as successful outcomes of Baltic foreign policy. In the Soviet case, it was a mere political trick, whereas in the Baltic states, it was an expression of satisfaction with a completed foreign policy event.

The real successes of the foreign policies of the Baltic states, however, lie elsewhere. The main ones scored may be attributed to the preindependence period. One of the first was the cooperation between the Baltic states in their struggle for independence begun in 1988 and symbolically characterized by the "Baltic chain" arranged by the Popular Fronts of the Baltic republics on 23 August 1989. The "Baltic chain" greatly promoted the Baltic cause in the international arena and contributed to the disclosure of Soviet policy toward the Baltics. Then followed the long-awaited official Soviet acknowledgement of the existence of the secret protocols attached to the Molotov-Ribbentrop Pact— achieved by the persistent efforts of Baltic politicians. Another major success was the Lithuanian resistance to the blockade organized by the USSR in the spring of 1990. Thanks to the courageous fight of the Lithuanians, the international community became better aware of the essence of the Baltic question. The handling of the bloody events in Lithuania and Latvia in January 1991 was even more effective in winning the sympathies of the outside world. An overwhelming success was gained when Estonian leaders initiated a lightning visit to Tallinn by Yeltsin on 12 January 1991. The visit brought the crisis to an end and helped inform the world about the Soviet government's adventurist policies in the Baltics. The declarations of independence adopted by the Estonian and Latvian Supreme Councils on 20 August 1991, on the second day of the coup, crowned the foreign policy successes of the preindependence period. Still one more success could be added—in January 1990, an Estonian School of Diplomacy was created in Tallinn, which up to now has remained the only one of its kind in the Baltics. Thanks to its enthusiastic and serious activities, the Estonian Ministry of Foreign Affairs was the first to recruit people with more or less professional training for its foreign service.

The postindependence successes of the foreign policies of the Baltic states are still rather modest. Domestic problems have taken an upper hand in Baltic politics. Beyond any doubt, the withdrawal of Russian troops could be qualified as the major success of that period, but this success was achieved only through the diplomacy of the Western powers, particularly the United States.

Security Policies of the Baltic States

There has been a consensus about the source of potential threats to the Baltic. "I stress, only Russia and no other state is our potential enemy. Our secret services should be directed against Russia," said Andrejs Krastins, vice chairman of the Supreme Council of Latvia, at a meeting with the editorial board of the Riga newspaper *Diena* as far back as July 1993.[10] The officials of the other Baltic states have been less explicit in their public statements about Russia as an enemy.

Russia is generally regarded as a threat to the Baltic states for a variety of reasons:

1. The post-perestroika situation in the Commonwealth of Independent States, particularly in Russia, is fraught with serious potential dangers for the independence of the Baltic states. Setting aside the extremely hostile statements of Vladimir Zhirinovsky, the leader of the Russian Liberal Democratic Party who threatens to reconquer the Baltic states, many chauvinists have emerged in Russia who, while fighting for the retention of the Kurils within Russia, draw parallels with the Baltic states as age-old Russian territories.

2. The international community seems to recognize the "natural right" of Russia to have specific interests in the post-Soviet countries, parallel to the idea that Latin America is the private domain of the United States. The West is frightened by the Yugoslav precedent of interethnic cataclysms on the territory of the former USSR and seems willing to leave the peacekeeping functions to Russia, which, in principle, knows the characteristic features of these regions better.[11] Estonia has been the first to protest against Russia's intentions to exercise such a role on the territory of the former USSR. Estonia's foreign minister, Trivimi Velliste, voiced that position at the CSCE foreign ministers' meeting in Rome on 30 November 1993, characterizing it as "letting the goat into the orchard."[12] The CSCE still decided not to extend any financial support for these purposes and suspended the debate until better times.

3. The former Soviet republics are a convenient springboard for the satisfaction (albeit partial) of Moscow's chauvinistic ambitions. Russia would like to restore the place of the Baltic states as a "window into Europe" for itself, since it is through the Baltic ports that the shortest sea transportation lines from Russia extend into Northern and Western Europe. Thus, the official Russian policy toward the Baltics is characterized by endeavors to preserve its influence (direct or indirect) in this region.

4. The main points of the "Basic Provisions of the Military Doctrine of the Russian Federation" (approved by the Russian Federation Security Council and adopted by presidential decree on 2 November 1993), while determining the potential threats to Russia, also include factors that directly concern the Baltic states. These include: (1) the territorial claims of other states to the Russian Federation and its allies; and (2) the suppression of the rights, liberties, and legal interests of the citizens of the Russian Federation in foreign countries.[13] The Baltic states have been accused of these "sins," and Russia has expressed its readiness to punish the Balts for any of them in the future. For that purpose, the 76th Guards Airborne Division is located in Pskov, and a SPETSNAZ (Special Designation Brigade) at Pechory, ready to arrive at a crisis point in the Baltics within some fifteen minutes.[14]

The question of how to guarantee the security of the Baltic states came up mostly right after the Baltic states regained their independence. Neutrality was the only security policy option that was occasionally talked about in the Baltics prior to independence. It was initially considered in a purely political sense, as it indicated a relatively distant position from the powerful eastern neighbor. The Popular Fronts of Estonia, Latvia, and Lithuania met in Tallinn in May 1989 and issued a joint statement that the Baltic nations "aspire for sovereignty in a neutral, demilitarized Balto-scandia."[15] Thereafter, that idea was rarely taken up again. The renewed references to the sad experience of small countries during World War II suppressed most of the talk about becoming neutral states. It was emphasized that the neutrality of the Baltic states lasted less than two years at the end of the 1930s and was of no help to them. The revision of neutrality among Western neutrals made the Balts even more cautious in advocating that option for themselves. The appeal to neutrality was typical behavior for newly formed small states in the twentieth century, but neutrality could, under new conditions, be an efficient means of providing guarantees for the security of the Baltic states if they had armed forces that would stand against aggression from a big power. However, they do not have, nor will they ever have, such armies. There were a few hints at the possibility of joining the nonaligned movement, but the topic received no further attention. The Baltic states do not consider themselves Third World countries and, after all, due to the radical political changes taking place in the world at the end of the 1980s, the movement has lost its previous significance.

Baltic leaders made a special point of obtaining information about Nordic security. The possibility of Baltic-Nordic cooperation on security and defense matters has occasionally been taken up by both parties. The Estonian and Latvian authorities even developed an idea of a possible Baltic-Nordic regional security scheme. The matter, however, disappeared from the agenda, since the inequality of the parties was far too great. Besides, the Nordic countries had all developed separate security and defense policies. However, the Scandinavian experience of defending their states and nations was of great interest to the Baltics because of the numerous similarities between the Nordic and Baltic states.

The Baltic leaders turned their sights toward NATO, which, in conformity with its new action program toward Eastern Europe, was ready for contacts with the Baltic states. Thus, in December 1991, a political declaration on joint activities of NATO and the Baltic states within the North Atlantic Cooperation Council (NACC) was signed in Brussels, which, the Baltic authorities hoped, would help them solve the most pressing problem of their military security—eventual admission to NATO, thus removing the Baltic states from the Russian sphere of interest. It would also link them more tightly with the West, though not necessarily meaning that NATO bases would have to be located on Baltic territory. Besides, NATO membership would enable the Baltic states to rebuild and modernize their defense forces.[16] Commenting on NATO relations with the Baltics, the late Manfred Wörner, NATO secretary general, had stated, "We don't exclude future membership . . . but it is not on the agenda."[17]

The Baltic authorities came gradually, but rather unwillingly, to the understanding that NATO, in fact, was not going to admit any new members in the near future. At the same time, the Baltic authorities encountered NATO's willingness to help them with advice. NATO representatives participated actively in different conferences in the Baltic states on the present situation in Europe and in the Baltic region, the development of Baltic strategic interests, Baltic-CSCE relations, and Baltic cooperation in international security. When NATO came up with the Partnership for Peace (PfP) initiative toward the East European states, the Baltic states joined it in 1994.

At the same time, Baltic politicians are looking for security guarantees in Europe. In their endeavors to join the European Community, the Baltic states were attracted by the EC's plans to turn the Western European Union (WEU) into its defense arm. At first, the Balts even ignored the fact that they lacked their own efficient national armies, which is a precondition for membership in the WEU, since it pools its members' capabilities. However, in 1994, the WEU offered the Baltic states associated partnerships, which were accepted. Still, the WEU will be able to take care of the security of the Baltic states only after they join the European Union, which is not likely to happen any earlier than at the turn of the century.

Many debates have taken place concerning the buildup of the Baltic national armies. All three Baltic states are presently strengthening their armed forces; however, there is little consensus as to how these forces should be shaped. Due to the lack of legislation regulating their functioning, progress in this area has been very difficult. Lithuania was the first to create military structures; since September 1991, the army has been fully functional. The army is now approximately 6,000 men strong, and it is expected to have 20,000 officers and servicemen in the future.18 The number of men in the military forces of Latvia is 26,000. The minimum size of the Defense Army in Estonia has been fixed at approximately 2,000 men. In addition, 1,500 should serve in the Border and Coastal Guard, 300 in the Militarized Interior-Defense Unit, and 200 in the Rescue Service. Nominally, the armed forces of the Baltic states may be used only in the event of foreign aggression. In addition, in order to enhance the defense capabilities of the Baltic republics, the prewar voluntary popular armed organizations are being reestablished. The restoration of the voluntary paramilitary units, which are to reach a scale of tens of thousands of men just as they did in the prewar period, creates, in fact, a great deal of confusion and misunderstanding.

The Baltic states have quite unexpectedly encountered serious problems with the draft—conscripts avoid fulfilling their military duty. This widespread phenomenon can be accounted for by a revulsion to military service acquired during Soviet times, when youngsters serving in the Soviet armed forces were cruelly treated. Another serious problem for the Baltic armies is the lack of basic weapons and ammunition. The Baltic states will not be able to afford armaments in the near future. Hopes of obtaining some compensation or weapons from Russia for the armaments expropriated from the Baltic states in 1940 are rather tenuous. The Balts are becoming ever more aware that, contrary to their expectations, nobody is going to donate arms to them, and they will probably have to buy the necessary armaments with their own rather meager financial resources.

Public opinion in the Baltic states is rather ambiguous on the subject of rearming. People feel that the aspirations of today's Baltic military are, first and foremost, associated with a nostalgic wish to restore something approximating the prewar Baltic armies, which in 1940 turned out to be incapable of defending their countries against the Soviet invasion. According to the prevailing public view, the Baltic states hardly need large armies, since, in the case of major hostilities, they could still be defeated in a couple of hours. On the one hand, the national security of the Baltic states can hardly be secured by military means. At the same time, a minimum level of military defense is needed in order to give a degree of credibility to the policy of independence.

Baltic military cooperation is a rather controversial topic. It is impossible to create efficient defense structures and forces from the limited economic bases available. There is little teamwork among the various governmental institutions in each Baltic state to reach an agreement on the multiple aspects of state security, such as political, economic, social, environmental, and defense aspects. Civilian monitoring of the armed forces, police, internal security structures—a must in a democratic country—is mostly unknown and ignored in the Baltic states. The military leaders manipulate the military information passed to the press— only two or three correspondents in each of the Baltic states are authorized to write about the military problems of their countries. To complicate these problems, military officials have even been involved in suspicious arms deals. As in the prewar years, Baltic politicians talk a great deal about the need to pool the armed forces of the three states. The failure to do so in 1940 made the loss of Baltic independence inevitable.

The pooling of Baltic military forces remains quite questionable for the future. "We were friends. Now we are rivals," said Estonian Premier Mart Laar in late 1993.[19] Nevertheless, their precarious national positions have emphasized the necessity to coordinate national activities. On 13 September 1993, Estonian Defense Minister Jüri Luik, Lithuanian Defense Minister Audrius Butkevičius, and Commander of the Latvian Defense Forces Dainis Turlais signed a Declaration on Baltic Security and Defense Cooperation. Emphasizing the necessity to exchange information and to create common air-defense systems as well as joint activities in defense of land, sea, and airspace, the declaration was an important decision and a clear deviation from previous isolated policies.[20] On 17 December, the prime ministers of Estonia, Latvia, and Lithuania met in Vilnius, where they agreed to exchange military attachés, intensify their military cooperation, coordinate training of Baltic defense forces, acquire weapons and ammunition in accordance with NATO standards, and even plan for the tightening of their eastern borders. Estonia proposed the creation of a unified Baltic defense organization similar to NATO.[21] In order to develop further the idea of Baltic military cooperation, they decided to form a Baltic Battalion. At the meeting of the heads of general staffs of the Baltic states, held on 15–16 February 1994 in Riga, it was agreed that the battalion's structure should consist of the staff, three cover-force units, one rear unit, and one headquarters unit. The battalion was designed to include about one thousand men, and English was chosen as its operational language.[22] The Baltic Battalion will complete its training in 1995 and will be attached to the UN peacekeeping forces.

In their search for the best and most efficient security policies, the Baltic states have to face a complicated reality—the period of isolation from international relations has been extensive and has left its imprint on the local people. Since there is no adequate model to follow, the case to be solved is unique.

The Baltic states have always desired to "enter Europe," but fate has always made them provinces of a bigger power. Isolation has been the foreign policy tradition of independent Estonia since the interwar period. Perhaps the new, yet fragile, initiatives of contemporary Baltic cooperation and coordination of activities could indicate the beginning of the modern era. To gain this goal, the Balts must first and foremost overcome their domestic and international feuds, divergences, political discords, and provincial mentalities. The Baltic states must become qualitatively new nations, sharing the basic principles of the modern developed and democratic international community. On the basis of these standards, it would be possible to elaborate long-lasting, intelligent, and wise policies favoring international security, peace, and well-being.

Notes

1. W. Clemens, "The Republics as International Actors," *Nationalities Papers*, vol. 19, no. 1 (spring 1991), p. 75. See also T. Alatalu, "Estonian Foreign Policy in 1991, Before the Declaration of Independence," *Monthly Survey of Baltic and Soviet Politics* (November 1991), pp. 2–7.

2. Michael Mandelbaum, "Coup de Grace: The End of the Soviet Union," *Foreign Affairs, America and the World, 1991/1992*, vol. 71, no. 1 (1992), pp. 172–73. See also Dimitri K. Simes, "America and the Post-Soviet Republics," *Foreign Affairs*, vol. 71, no. 3 (summer 1992), p. 74.

3. Estonian weekly newspaper *Baltic Independent*, 27 September–3 October 1991.

4. Toivo U. Raun, *Estonia and the Estonians* (Stanford, CA: Hoover Institution Press, Stanford University, 1987), p. 124.

5. Eesti Välisdelegatsioon, *Eesti Entsüklopeedia*, vol. 2 (Tartu, 1933), pp. 842–43.

6. *Baltic Observer* (Latvia), 25 June–1 July 1992.

7. *Baltic Observer*, 23–29 July 1992.

8. *Argumenty i fakty*, nos. 29–30 (August 1992).

9. Bronis J. Kaslas, "The Baltic Nations," in *The Quest for Regional Integration and Political Liberty* (Pittston, PA: Euramerica Press, 1976), pp. 8–9.

10. *Nezavisimaia gazeta*, 24 July 1992.

11. P. Vares, "Russia—Opportunities, Risks and Threats," in *Venäjän ja Baltian tulevaisuudennäkymät: Mahdollisuudet ja uhkat. Valionneuvoston kanslia* (Helsinki, 1992).

12. Estonian daily newspaper *Päevaleht*, 6 December 1992.

13. *Izvestiia*, 18 November 1993.

14. Andrei Raevsky, "Development of Russian National Security Policies: Military Reform," Research Paper no. 25. (New York: UNIDIR, 1993), p. 21.

15. Statement issued by the Baltic Assembly, Tallinn, May 1989, published in *Popular Front of Estonia* (Tallinn: Valgus, 1989), p. 5.

16. *Päevaleht*, 17 November 1991.

17. *Baltic Observer*, 22–28 October 1992.

18. *Baltic Observer*, 30 July–5 August 1992.

19. Estonian daily newspaper *Postimees*, 23 December 1993.

20. *Päevaleht*, 14 September 1993.

21. Estonian weekly newspaper *Baltic Independent*, 17–23 December 1993.

22. *Päevaleht*, 22 February 1994.

III

The Southern
Newly Independent States

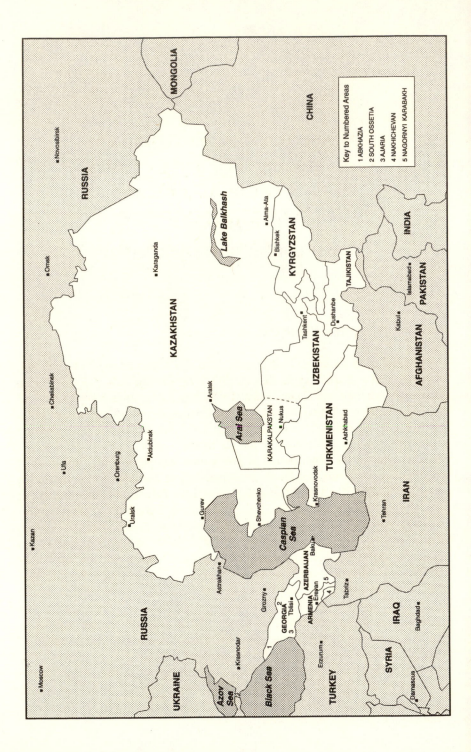

Key to Numbered Areas

1 ABKHAZIA
2 SOUTH OSSETIA
3 AJARIA
4 NAKHICHEVAN
5 NAGORNYI KARABAKH

9

The Sociopolitical Environment Conditioning the Foreign Policy of the Central Asian States

Kemal H. Karpat

Introduction: General Considerations

The purpose of this study is to deal with the broad historical, political, cultural, territorial, and national factors that condition the foreign policy of the Turkic states of Azerbaijan and Central Asia. Tajikistan, due to its unsettled situation, will be given less attention, although much of what follows applies to that state, too. It should be noted from the beginning that independence came for all the ex-Soviet republics, and especially the Turkic states, suddenly and rather unexpectedly, without the usual period of preparation that permits the formation of proper public and national opinion, leadership cadres, communication networks, and so forth, free from the influence and mentality of the old dominating center. Thus, during the first two years of independence the Central Asian states formulated their foreign policies in close relation to internal developments in Russia, all the while attempting to gain recognition from as many foreign states as possible in order to distance themselves from Russia. Consequently, this study will devote considerable attention to those events in the Russian Federation that affected the course of political life in Central Asia. The foreign policy of the Turkic states is part and parcel of their emergence as national states, and the two are viewed as such in this study. In fact, the foreign policy of the new nations in Central Asia is part of the founding process, much the way the foreign policy of Ataturk in 1920–23 was part of the founding of the Republic of Turkey. The founders of the national states have considerable freedom to decide their future foreign policies, but also a high degree of limitation imposed by Russia, due to their past association with the Soviet Union, which continues in the Commonwealth of Independent States (CIS).

The disintegration of the Soviet Union in 1991 and the transformation of the union republics into independent territorial nation-states have raised a series of basic conceptual, philosophical, and practical issues, both for the Russian Federation and the new states. The first and paramount issue was the redefinition of nationhood, national identity, territorial borders, and national interest according to the new realities. Paradoxical as it may appear, history places the Central Asian states in a better position than Russia as far as some of these points are concerned. Throughout the socialist period Moscow and the Russian Federation—although largely led by ethnic Russians—acted as the ideological and administrative seat of a supposedly classless society composed of a great variety of ethnic groups. These groups, of course, were denied the freedom to express their national political consciousness. The nationality policy applied to the Muslim republics aimed primarily at fragmenting the universal Islamic community, the *ummet*, an imaginary, ideal concept rather than a reality. The Soviet regime feared its neighbors, the old spokesmen for this *ummet*: primarily Iran, and, somewhat less, Turkey. The latter abolished the caliphate in 1924 and abandoned the pretension of commanding the Muslims' political allegiance. However, the abolition of the caliphate in Turkey did not eliminate overnight the Islamic traditions and cultural outlook of the Central Asians, acquired over centuries, or their habit of regarding Istanbul as their national Islamic center, second only to Mecca and Medina. For Central Asians and other Muslims of Russia, the hajj to Mecca without a stop in Istanbul was considered incomplete.[1] At various dates, mainly from 1924 to 1936, Central Asia was divided into a variety of administrative-territorial units in order to break down the *ummet*'s territorial unity by identifying each ethnolinguistic group with a territory.

The Soviet nationality policy, as is well known, emphasized ethnicity as the foundation of political identity and made the vernacular the distinguishing element of nationality of the major ethnic groups. This policy was in essence an almost ideal blueprint for speeding up nation formation in Central Asia and Azerbaijan (the nationality policy there brought together the various old Azeri khanates, such as Shirvan, Kuba, and Shusha). Meanwhile, the supposedly supranationality policy of the Soviets greatly expanded the usage of the Russian language and generalized many elements of the Russian political-communist culture, while the leaders refused to call the Soviet Union a Russian state. The Soviet policy resembled the Ottoman efforts in the nineteenth century to create an Ottoman nation out of diverse ethnic groups. This Ottoman policy strengthened the national identity of the members of various ethnic groups while holding back and neutralizing the national identity of the ethnic Turks. Hence Turkish nationalism did not acquire its distinct marks until the twentieth century, while Russian "nationalism" emerged in the nineteenth century as a means to assimilate the tsar's non-Russian subjects. One might further note numerous striking parallels in the nationality problems, changes in the political regimes, and economic policies of the Ottoman and Russian empires and the Republic of Turkey and the Soviet Union. (All this could be made the subject of an illuminating historical study.)

The basic problem for Russia today is to become a true nation with an identity and culture of its own. The Russian state must decide whether it wants to achieve economic, spiritual, and cultural self-fulfillment first for the Russians as a people, or continue to view its "Russian-ness" as intrinsically bound to the domination of other ethnic and national groups. This domination prevented the emergence of a Russian identity independent of the domination of others. The state became in fact the vehicle to indoctrinate the Russians with messianic dreams and use them as the docile tools of an expansionist state. If Russia desires honestly to become an authentic Russian nation-state without the psychological need to dominate other nations, this attitude can profoundly affect the internal and external policies of the Central Asian states. The issue deserves more scrutiny than we can give it here. Suffice it to say that the search by the Russians for "superpower" status implies the restoration of the old structure. The fall of many world empires—Ottoman, Habsburg, British, French—since 1918 has left lasting wounds, but nowhere do the imperial memories appear as deeply rooted in the popular psyche as in Russia.

The situation in the former Soviet Union must be placed in the proper perspective in order to better appraise the situation of the Central Asian states. The entire history of Russia has been made and unmade by the state, that is, a power group, not by the nation or society. The case is proven by events in 1991. The disintegration of the Soviet Union in 1991 was preceded by the collapse of the center, that is, the Soviet state, which was embodied in the Communist Party and its numerous policy-making bodies, much in the way that the end of the monarchical state had brought about the end of the tsarist regime in 1917. The collapse of the communist state compelled the Russians to realize overnight that they were an inchoate nation, an amorphous body of people without a distinct political identity deriving from a true national state of their own.[2] The absence of a true governing Russian nation in a multiethnic structure is typical of the traditional type of empires of which the Soviet Union was the last surviving prototype, despite claims to the contrary. Of course, the Soviet government further complicated the situation by actually adopting the European colonialist formula of the metropolis-colony dichotomy in its military and economic relations with the periphery, while striving to Russify and "denationalize" the Muslims through the policy of atheism, which could undermine Islam as a source of national identity more than the weakening of Orthodoxy undermined the Russians' sense of national identity. While Russian colonists poured into every economically promising crevice of the vast Soviet territory, they remained distinguished from Central Asians and Muslims in general by their dominant political-economic status and their language and Orthodox faith. The Russians acted as the dominant social class, but also as the supporting human basis of the state rather than as the representatives of a Russian nation. The issue was aggravated further by the fact that the non-Russian Europeans were considered also "Russians," although ethnically and linguistically they never considered themselves as such. Thus, in the ultimate analysis, "Russian-ness" in Central Asia was determined by one's association with the "center-state," which in turn conferred status. In practice, the real difference between the "outsiders" and the indigenous population was determined by religion. Indeed, no Muslim Tatar, Chechen, Turk, or Persian, for example, however high his education, achievement, or position, could ever qualify as a "Russian" or "European" unless he converted to Christianity and became fully Russified in manners and spirit. These are known issues, but they need to be reviewed to understand better the meaning of the political transformation of Central Asia and the current psychological-legal position of the Russians in the area. The Russians, in short, are viewed as the tools of an oppressive alien state rather than the bona fide members of a normal nation, and they are treated as such.

The disintegration of the Soviet center, that is, the party-state, left largely intact and capable of reorganizing and reactivating themselves the very institutions that helped the center govern the periphery. Among these institutions of the center, the armed forces, the Ministry of the Interior, and the KGB occupy the first rank. It is these bodies that are now striving to re-create the old center, both by using the CIS as their tool and by casting themselves as defenders of the "civil" rights of the Russians living in the old Soviet republics. These two issues increasingly occupy a central place in the foreign relations of the old republics with Russia.

The CIS, about which there will be further discussion, is the potential vehicle capable of transforming the old extensive imperial center-periphery relationship into a new selective, harmonious economic and military relationship between the Russian Federation and the old republics. But the CIS can also be easily used by Moscow to dominate the ex-republics by assuring for itself the utmost benefits and fewest liabilities. At the moment the power instruments of the old communist state, that is, the army and the KGB in Russia, are in the process of developing a new relationship with the old Central Asian and Caucasian periphery. It should not be forgotten that the ex-Soviet army, although reduced in size, remains a formidable force, and it, the KGB, and the relevant ministries are indoctrinated with a heavy dose of nationalism, which, for lack of a truly persuasive and binding Soviet nationalism, had to borrow its symbols, heroes, and spirit from the Russian messianic nationalism used by the tsarist regime throughout its expansionist existence. Nationalism in Russia today emanates from the military, the KGB, and various civilian groups. The current weakness of the "national" political institutions of the Russian Federation, such as the parliament and constitution, the slow progress of privatization and the market economy, and public apathy have induced the leaders, including Boris Yeltsin and his prime minister, to court the power instruments of the old Soviet state, especially the armed forces. In this context one can point out that Yeltsin's brutal elimination of the old parliament in October 1993—amidst applause from the West—and the election of a new one in which the conservative-nationalist forces have the numerical superiority have greatly increased the influence of the army and other irredentist forces. The outcome of this struggle cannot be predicted with accuracy, although one can venture some views. The USSR was brought down primarily because of the economic weight and political oppression of the state organs, especially the army, operating through the Communist Party. A restoration of the old state by the instruments of the state can only bring to power and give additional privileges and authority to the military, the KGB, and other antidemocratic forces. The restoration of the old order can only hasten its fall in a much more dramatic and, socially speaking, costly manner than the fall of the USSR. The Soviet regime sought to save the tsarist empire with internal reforms. There is no other regime to save what is left of the communist empire but democracy, if it can be implemented at all.

The Vestiges of the Soviet Union

The foreign policy of the Central Asian states is conditioned simultaneously by the challenges and developments taking place in the Russian Federation (including efforts to re-create the old union) and the ethnic, cultural, economic, and historical forces within their own territories unleashed by independence and national statehood. The CIS forms the main axis of the foreign policy of the Central Asian states. Consequently, Central Asian foreign relations are conditioned by a set of circumstances that have no parallel in world history, except probably to a limited measure in France's relations with its former colonies in Central and West Africa. The restoration of the Russian Foreign Ministry to its previous policy-making status is an omen of things to come. The Foreign Ministry in both the tsarist and Soviet eras has played a major and generally successful role in projecting abroad selected images about the intentions and policies of the state. Its leading personnel have always been selected from among the exceptionally well-educated and sophisticated Russians and Russified non-Slavs whose psychological understanding of the West, including the United States, was repeatedly proven by their adroit ability to manipulate the Western press and the public. No Russian foreign policy could be carried out without the input of the Foreign Ministry. Consequently, the Foreign Ministry has been called to carry out the new foreign policy of the Russian Federation, whose objectives were defined in part in circles of the armed forces. The former republics became the central target of the "near abroad" policy, indicating that they were still regarded as part of the "internal" empire rather than truly independent nation-states. The rapid transformation of the Russian Foreign Ministry (including Andrei Kozyrev) from an institution promoting a Western-type democracy, respect for the independence of other nations, the market economy, and close relations with the West (it is the most Westernized segment of the Russian bureaucracy) into an advocate of a nationalist policy toward the near abroad, including Central Asia, is worthy of some discussion. As the USSR began to disintegrate, Yeltsin issued a decree on 18 December 1991 making the Soviet Foreign Ministry and all its assets an institution of the Russian Federation; one week later he placed Deputy Prime Minister Gennadii Burbulis in charge. Andrei Kozyrev, who had been in office since November 1990 and who was Yeltsin's protégé, kept his place, evincing a truly intriguing ability to survive, given the harsh criticism leveled at him.[3] At this early stage it seemed that Russia was ready to accept and conduct regular relations with the new nations, as indicated by the creation of a new department to oversee relations with the members of the Commonwealth of Independent States (created late in 1991). Meanwhile, the Russian Foreign Ministry decided to upgrade its information services. This move was undertaken primarily to answer state critics who had severely censured Kozyrev and even asked for his resignation because they saw Russia's foreign policy as too accommodating to the West and ready to accept as a fait accompli the new political configuration of the former Soviet Union. In fact, early in 1992 Kozyrev made a tour of the CIS nations and established diplomatic relations with Turkmenistan, Tajikistan, and Moldova. Both Yeltsin and Kozyrev opposed the creation of a special ministry to deal with the CIS countries, as proposed by the state counselor Sergei Stankevich, an advocate of an active near abroad policy. The Security Council of the Russian Federation, headed by Iurii Skokov, also had endorsed the idea of a special ministry to deal with the near abroad (Skokov would be dismissed eventually). Skokov asked for Kozyrev's resignation, while the latter accused the proponents of an intensive near abroad policy of being "national patriots" and "neo-Bolshevists"[4] and defended a good-neighbor policy with the former Soviet republics. The conduct of relations with the near abroad was left ultimately to the Foreign Ministry. The decision represented a victory for Yeltsin and Kozyrev and was received with deep relief by all the ex-republics, for it neutralized the ultranationalists. Obviously Yeltsin and Kozyrev's initial accommodating attitude toward the former union republics came as much from domestic power considerations as from fear of alienating the West. However, ultimately late in 1993 the growing pressure of the nationalists and the army, coupled with a loss of popularity by Yeltsin, led him and Kozyrev closer to the position held by the advocates of a strong near abroad policy.

We have devoted considerable attention in the above pages to developments in Russia because they are part of the general process that seeks to define the content and scope of the postcommunist Russian nation and will in turn play a crucial part in the foreign policy of the Central Asian nations.

The Russian Federation is engaged in a search for a definition of the Russian nation, its territorial scope, cultural content, and relations with the state and a true perception of its own history, while seeking to introduce democracy and a market economy. In contrast, the Central Asian nations, unbelievable as it may seem at first sight, appear to be in a relatively better situation as far as formal territory and definition of nationality are concerned. The breakup of the Soviet Union left the Turkic states with a well-defined territory (however artificially drawn initially) and a national identity, which, although imposed from above, rested on concrete and genuine ethnolinguistic bases, and on a historical background suitable to the formulation of a national history.[5] Already several Kazakh, Uzbek, Azeri, and other "national" histories based on rather interesting cultural, anthropological, and economic data encompassing the old tribal federations, traditional khanates, and so forth, have appeared in print.[6] The first demand of scholars and visitors from the area to the West is for printed information on the history of their "national" states, the naive assumption being that their "nation" had been in existence for centuries and that the statehood gained in 1991 was a belated recognition of a historical fact. This preoccupation with old history is essentially part of the comprehensive process of decolonization taking place in the political, cultural, and economic spheres of activity of the Central Asian states. The Soviet era is dismissed as an accidental phase of national life. The more positive aspects of the Soviet era, such as increased literacy, the rise of modernist elites, medical services, road and rail infrastructure, and communications are judged from a national perspective, as both the tsarist and communist regimes are viewed as colonial and imperial structures that delayed—rather than speeded up—the nation-formation process. Also, one cannot ignore the fact that half of the population of Central Asia, in fact over 50 percent in Tajikistan, deals in agriculture and has preserved its traditional culture and modes of life, as did most of the native lower-income urban groups. The issue has a basic relevance to the process of nation formation, as the indigenous culture of the lower classes may become the source of national culture. The situation appears to be rather confusing in Tajikistan, which lacked a true ethnic Persian foundation, since the accepted culture was the Islamic-urban culture centered in linguistically cosmopolitan cities, while in the countryside the tribal-ethnic culture of the Uzbeks dominated (it should not be forgotten that most of Tajikistan was administered from Bukhara until the Soviet era).

For the first time in their history the Central Asian states are in possession of a well-defined area and are identified with a modern type of political structure, namely, the territorial national state, in which, to repeat, the nation and the state formally coincide. The source of national identity is ethnicity based on language, and indeed ethnicity and language appear to define national territorial statehood. Other forms of identity appear to be secondary to ethnonational identity, at least for the time being, since ethnicity in Central Asia is open to wide interpretation. If ethnicity is defined not solely by language but as a mode of life comprising all the elements of material and spiritual culture, then a language-based view of ethnicity and nationality appears to be rather narrow. In any case, the old forms of identity emanating from clan, tribe, region, religion, and ethnicity appear to have realigned themselves, politically speaking, in a hierarchical order, topped by the territory-bound "national" ethnic identity, at least among the ruling elites.

The conservative modernists and nomenklatura elites seem to be united in accepting the primacy of the national-ethnic identity, primarily toward others. At the same time, the Central Asian governments strive to promote the idea that Central Asia is a cultural whole—that is, it shares a common culture, history, and religion—but is divided into a series of political-administrative units that give recognition to the prevailing linguistic, regional, and geographic differences. The desire to harmonize the particular with the general and universal is reflected in the foreign policy of the Central Asian states in the form of regional organizations, mainly economic, while the older generation often invokes the union of Turkestan.

It is in the context of the special circumstances that attended the process of nation formation in Central Asia and Azerbaijan that Islam acquires its true function, not solely as a source of spiritual nourishment for individuals but as the cultural foundation of the emerging national culture and language. A broad, almost universal concept of cultural ethnicity was based on Islam, while linguistic and tribal identity coexisted with it in a subordinate capacity. Today national identity based on language-rooted ethnicity is promoted by the government and has the upper hand over Islamic cultural ethnicity. In a speech dedicated to the "Strategy of the Formation and Development of Kazakhstan as a Sovereign State," President Nazarbaev declared that a "nation cannot exist without a state system . . . in its turn the disappearance of a nation leads to a senseless existence of its state." The progress of the state was bound to the "revitalization of the national culture and language and the restoration of the spiritual-cultural roots of Kazakhness . . . [and] on the creation of the necessary requisite conditions for the Kazakhs who were forced to leave their country to come back." After defining Kazakhstan as an open, peace-loving, and democratic state, respectful of the sovereignty of other states and possessing a multistructured market economy, Nazarbaev touched upon the "complicated ethnopolitical and legal" nature of Kazakh society by defining it as a sovereign ethnic-national Kazakh entity with deep national roots and traditions and a multiethnic political community.[7] Obviously Nazarbaev strived to find a formula that would allow him to culturally transform the country into a Kazakh national state while recognizing the rights of other minorities, especially the Russians. So-called fundamentalist Islam, on the other hand, rejects the entire concept of territorial national statehood and language-based ethnicity and thus appears at odds with both the historical evolution of the Central Asian states and their current political-social situation and aspirations. The Central Asian states pursue a "secular" policy not so much because of the separation of politics and religion, which is a rather debatable concept, but because the very survival of each of the newly constituted independent states depends on the preservation of national-ethnic identity and territory. The rise of ethnicity as the mark of national identity raises a series of disturbing questions concerning the freedom of ethnic subgroups in each republic, since each possesses scores of other ethnic groups. Thus the Karakalpaks in Uzbekistan—about a million—consider themselves closer to the Kazakhs than Uzbeks and looked to

Moscow in the past to balance the authority of Tashkent. There is of course the view that "cultural ethnicity" is different from "political ethnicity." In other words, the minor ethnic groups in Kazakhstan would accept the fact that the state is politically Kazakh and that all have citizenship, while the minority groups would enjoy full linguistic, religious, and cultural freedom, although this formula may not work well in a unitary centralized state.

The Foreign Policy of the Central Asian States

The Central Asian republics moved swiftly to national independence in 1991 through a series of popular independence referendums, followed by presidential elections that gave the governments a legitimate foundation of power.[8] The Soviet Union, hitherto considered a superpower with immense military capabilities, disintegrated at a speed unknown in world annals because the state mechanism (the Communist Party) that had kept the union together was abolished and left its main organs—the army, the KGB, and so forth—without direction, although these bodies underwent some disintegration. Unlike other states that emerged with independence from the disintegration of the Ottoman, Habsburg, and West European empires, the Central Asian states gained their freedom and sovereignty without prolonged struggle or bloodshed. The demonstrations in Almaty (note the recent Kazakhization of the name from the Russian Alma-Ata) in 1986, the bloody occupation of Baku in 1989, and the subsequent gaining of new strength by the Azerbaijan Popular Front and its demonstrations indicated the presence of popular will to achieve some freedom from Moscow. These events played some part in conditioning the judgment of both the Russians and the Central Asians toward their own capabilities as well as the real strength of the union. The Central Asians believed, or were made to believe, that the might and durability of the union were so overwhelming that any open opposition to it would remain effectless. However, the defeat of the Soviet troops in Afghanistan and Moscow's inability to definitively curb the political ferment in Azerbaijan, Kazakhstan, and Uzbekistan produced doubts about the invincibility of the center. A psychological milestone was thus passed. But once independence was declared and Moscow acquiesced to it, Central Asian sovereign national statehood became a fait accompli. The Russians believe that they were unjustly deprived, by a combination of rapidly evolving circumstances, foreign pressure, and unpreparedness, of the fruits of five hundred years of national struggle and conquest. The perceptions of both sides about the circumstances leading to the disintegration of the Soviet Union had a profound impact on their foreign policies.

The Russians faced a certain psychological difficulty in treating the new states as truly independent and still regarded relations with them as a sort of internal question, while the Central Asians, after a short period of hesitation, came to regard the concept of near abroad as a device to be used by diehards to defend and restore the old union. Thus the first and primary foreign policy objective of the Central Asian states was to accept every possible means, including new organizational agreements such as the CIS, both to settle the common problems inherited from the old union and to thwart Russia's efforts to reestablish the old status quo. The Central Asian states used international recognition as a key device to consecrate their independence.

Turkey was among the first states to recognize first Azerbaijan and then the Central Asian states. The United States in turn extended quick recognition of and established diplomatic relations with Kazakhstan and Kyrgyzstan in January 1992 and with Turkmenistan, Uzbekistan, and Tajikistan in February 1992, and set up embassies in each state shortly thereafter. Today Uzbekistan and Kazakhstan have been recognized by some 130 states and have established diplomatic relations in some 70 countries, the remaining three states having won recognition from some 100 to 130 states and have established diplomatic relations with some 40 to 60 states. All the Central Asian states and Azerbaijan have become members of the United Nations and its affiliates, the International Monetary Fund (IMF), the World Bank, the Conference on Security and Cooperation in Europe, the Organization of the Islamic Conference, and so forth.

It is essential to note that already by 1989 and 1990 practically all the Central Asian states, taking advantage of glasnost and perestroika, had held a variety of national congresses and conventions—described as "scientific conferences"—that dealt with the revival of the national culture and history. Already a variety of taboos dealing with national history had been pushed aside and national figures such as Ismail Gaspirali of the Crimea and Abdurrauf Fitrat of Uzbekistan, long condemned as bourgeois nationalists, were rehabilitated. Many of the so-called scholarly conferences to which foreigners were invited sought to revise the Soviet views on some key "national" issues, such as the famines and the forced sedentarization of the tribes in Kazakhstan in the 1930s, the Russian occupation of Central Asia in the 1860s, and the place of the Jadidists (modernists) in national history. These feverish preindependence nationalist activities did not aim at independence or separatism but played a key role in preparing the national elites for seizing the opportunity of independence when it actually presented itself. However, the search for the roots of national history and national culture had been going on in a variety of forms since the early 1970s, and glasnost and perestroika merely helped intensify and generalize this search. In this context it is essential to note that the search for national historical roots was carried out not on behalf of a common homeland such as Turkestan, except for a few diehards, but on behalf of the specific republic with which the researcher identified himself/herself. The fact that one historical or literary figure was claimed simultaneously by several republics was either ignored or accepted as being valid during the old ages, "when we all lived together." The process of rebuilding the national history turned the old religious figures into "national heroes who perpetuated our language and literature." For instance, the first Ahmed Yesevi conference was held in 1990 in Kentau, some fifteen miles from the town of Turkistan (the former Yesi), where the *pir* or *baba* lies in the mausoleum built by Tamerlane, and which is the site of a university bearing his name. He was described as a literary figure who established the basis of the Kazakh language and literature, although Yesevi was a Sufi and hardly aware of his nationality.[9] In sum, the Central Asians sought first to develop an authentic image of their national history and culture, which helped consolidate the national independence when it came. The search for the authenticity of the nation, culture, language, and faith in the years preceding independence should yield excellent clues in explaining how unexpected independence and national sovereignty were quickly internalized. The fact that the Russians were always regarded as undesirable aliens and rulers helped internalize independence not as a political value or principle but as a practical method to get rid of Moscow's presence. It should be noted that, notwithstanding the degree of Russification among elites, the rural, and grassroots lower urban classes in Central Asia preserved a high degree of cultural authenticity lacking in Turkey and even Iran.

National independence and sovereignty are the indispensable conditions to promote the interests of the territorial national state. Foreign policy is the means to defend and promote the national interest abroad and secure international support to perpetuate independence and sovereignty. It is carried out by an experienced staff and ministry organized for the purpose. The Central Asian people had practically no experience in foreign relations and hardly possessed the bureaucratic organization and professional staff capable of meeting the challenge of foreign relations. In fact, the Central Asian states seemed to lack the very concept of foreign policy as a basic and indispensable instrument for promoting the national interest.[10] All the "foreign ministers and ministries" of the old union republics, notably those of the Central Asian states, had no visibility and least of all the necessary authority to engage in even the most innocuous foreign relations, while their "embassies" in Moscow often served as hostels for their natives visiting the center. The foreign policy experience of the Central Asian states prior to Russian occupation was negligible. It is true that many of the old petty Central Asian khanates had periodically dispatched emissaries to Istanbul to plead with the caliph, the head of the Muslim community, for some help or to secure the sanction to legitimize some usurped throne.[11] In fact, during the nineteenth century the Bukharan and Khivan emirs had what one may call permanent representatives in Istanbul whose residence or "embassy" was the famous Uzbek lodge (it was open to all the Central Asian Muslims), which is still standing in Üsküdar, on the Asiatic side of Istanbul. However, the *şeyhs* of the lodge, acting as diplomatic envoys, together with numerous other religious and political delegations coming from Central Asia, were the personal representatives of the Khivan or Bukharan rulers and not the state itself. They, like other overseas Muslim dignitaries, were regarded as part of the religious establishment of Istanbul. These earlier Turkish relations with Central Asia, which broadened until 1917 to include a number of intellectuals, including many Jadidists who came to study in Istanbul, obviously cannot be ignored. However, these relations among ruling emirs and sultans can never be regarded as the equivalent of true interstate relations. Central Asia experienced true interstate relations only after 1991.[12]

Central Asian states rapidly won international recognition and membership in international bodies and established embassies and consulates abroad, despite financial constraints. The diplomatic offensive was due, as implied, on the one hand to the need to strengthen their precarious independence and sovereignty, and on the other to use it to offset the concentration of the armed forces and economic power in Russia's hands. It is therefore quite understandable that the Central Asians focused their foreign relations, first, on securing international recognition, and second, on neutralizing (so far successfully) the threat posed by the power instruments, for example, the armed forces of the old union. It should be mentioned also that the establishment of widespread foreign relations sought by the Central Asian states, in addition to securing them the international protection that comes with diplomatic recognition, had the virtue of ending the political, cultural, and scientific isolation of this area by placing it in the stream of world communication. Most Central Asian intellectuals, similar to their modernist counterparts in other Islamic countries, see the West as the fountainhead of contemporary civilization—not Russia or the Russians, as they were compelled to believe during the Soviet regime. Consequently, the Central Asian states' rapid opening up to the West is motivated as much by the need to strengthen and safeguard their sovereignty as by a genuine yearning to establish direct and permanent communication with the authentic sources of today's dominant civilization and thus put a permanent end to their isolation.[13] The practical implications of this basic political-philosophical leaning toward the West are evident in some key decisions. First, there is the decision of Azerbaijan and all the Central Asian states (except Tajikistan) to adopt the Latin alphabet as the chief means of written communication. Second, there is the relatively friendly treatment accorded to Western business corporations and investors, despite bureaucratic red tape of various types and interest-motivated personal manipulations. For instance, the Kazakh government accorded to the Chevron Corporation and its partners the concession to exploit the Tengiz oil field in a relatively short time, while prior to independence the Soviet officials procrastinated (by inflating their terms) for a long time. Today, some seventy American corporations, including such giants as Mobil Oil, General Motors, Boeing, and Philip Morris, just to mention the larger ones, are involved in Central Asia and are receiving from the governments almost "preferential" treatment, probably as a vehicle to greater U.S. interest and involvement.

The Bureaucratic Background of the
Central Asian Foreign Ministries

Unlike Russia, which inherited the experienced and sophisticated Foreign Ministry of the former Soviet Union, the Central Asian states had to recruit anew their foreign ministry staffs from whatever source was available. By early 1994 the

Foreign Ministry of Russia had stabilized (after a period of crisis, dismissals, and readmissions) at three thousand people, excepting the missions abroad, while the Central Asian foreign ministries typically include about fifty to eighty people each. The first obvious source of personnel recruitment for the Central Asian states was the indigenous people who served on the staff of the Russian Foreign Ministry, usually in minor jobs. The second and most widespread source for the Central Asian foreign ministries was the upper ranks of the native civil bureaucracy, usually the best educated and those who could converse in European languages. They included a number of indigenous young bureaucrats who had been sent after 1988 to study abroad, most to Europe and a few to the United States. Some of the graduates of the old party institutes designed to train the future party leaders also joined the foreign ministries (Nazarbaev is a graduate of such an institute in Almaty that has been transformed into an Institute of Management and Economics and was later attached to the president's office).

Turkey was one of the first countries that agreed to act as a proxy and help train the foreign ministry personnel from the Central Asian states. For instance, a Protocol in Cooperation in the Diplomatic Field, signed in Tashkent by the foreign ministries of Turkey and Uzbekistan on 5 March 1992, that is, just a few months after Uzbekistan won independence, is typical of the "diplomatic" technical aid provided by Turkey to the Turkic states of Central Asia. The protocol was based on the Friendship and Cooperation Agreement signed by Turkey and Uzbekistan on 19 December 1991 in Ankara. Similar agreements were concluded with the other states. According to the protocol, the "Turkish embassies will represent Uzbekistan and protect the latter's rights and interests in the accredited third countries, for a period of time to be mutually agreed" (Article 2). Turkey undertook to do the same in international organizations until the Central Asian states created their own foreign ministry personnel. Consequently, Article 4 of the protocol stated that "the Ministry of Foreign Affairs of Turkey will provide professional training to the Uzbek diplomats," while Article 5 stipulated further that the "Ministry of Foreign Affairs of Turkey will provide assistance and support to the Ministry of Foreign Affairs of Uzbekistan regarding diplomatic services."[14] Moreover, Turkey invited several teams of Central Asian bureaucrats, notably economists, for training that included a series of seminars and actual desk work in the appropriate Turkish offices.

It is essential at this point to review briefly the national credentials and ideological background of the indigenous bureaucrats of Central Asia, including foreign ministry personnel. It goes without saying that most of the native bureaucrats serving in the upper ranks of their domestic government were members or candidates to membership of the Communist Party. But it is probably correct to say that few of them were truly convinced communist ideologues. The top echelons of the national bureaucracy, including the foreign ministries, were educated in party schools and were obviously members of the Communist Party. Thus, one may conclude that the bureaucracy in power consists mostly of the old communist-era civil service. This view would be correct if the growing size of the native bureaucracy and some of the qualitative changes that took place after independence were ignored. The old communist cadres were the only trained bureaucrats, usually in the technical professions, available to conduct the day-to-day business of the new governments, since there were no truly "national" cadres formed yet. Instead of waiting for the emergence of "national" cadres to replace them, the ruling communist bureaucracy tried to "nationalize" itself overnight, and became ardent Uzbek, Kazakh, or other patriots. This patriotism was genuine, at least up to a point, since the indigenous bureaucracy and the intelligentsia, although sharing by necessity the communist ideology with their Russian masters, were in fact separated from them by ethnicity and religion. This communist-era bureaucracy presently ruling the Central Asian states knows from inside how the Moscow system and the KGB work and think. They also know how to manipulate their former masters. There is sufficient grounds to claim that after World War II, members of the local Communist Party branches were affected as much by rising Uzbek, Kazakh, or other localism and ethnic awareness as by communism, not so much as an ideology but as a form of political association and social behavior. All this resulted in a rather curious interplay of patron-client relationships between Moscow and native party leaders, and especially between the latter and their cronies selected on the basis of tribal, clan, or regional ties but also in the search for popular support and a sheer interest in position and income. In other words, the communist experiment in Central Asia had a lasting behavioral impact, but the same experiment evolved in a specific manner as conditioned by the ethnocultural structure of the native society and its almost total domination by Moscow.

It appears that the old party bosses of Central Asia, represented by such prominent figures as Rashidov (d. 1983) of Uzbekistan and Kunaev of Kazakhstan (who was ousted by Gorbachev in 1986 and died in August 1993), came to rely on a fairly large local constituency and their own selected bureaucrats. These leaders co-opted the upper ranks of the native population and induced them to obey the system by providing nourishment to their cultural needs (sometimes they suppressed the manifestations of established Islam, the free ulema—learned religious scholars—but left free the popular *tārikāt*—popular religious brotherhoods—that did not challenge the political system) and by adroitly using the economic resources at their disposal to distribute patronage to selected rural and urban areas. In retrospect it appears that these outwardly obedient "tools" of Moscow were instrumental in promoting the rise of a large local native intelligentsia—bureaucracy—from the lower ranks of the native society, including the traditionalist villages. They did so, partly at least, in order to dominate and govern more absolutely their own indigenous society while catering to its "national" cultural needs, which often consisted of secularized religious practices and beliefs. The center went along with manipulation of its representatives in the field, notably during the era of Brezhnev, who seemed to have viewed with some personal fondness the deference-prone Central Asians, since Moscow was interested more in acquiescence to its authority than how this acquiescence was secured. It is difficult to determine whether these native leaders were aware of the political implications of their policy of educating and creating a large native intelligentsia. (Of course, the decision taken by Khrushchev to give the natives greater access to higher education, though stemming from the need to upgrade the quality of the local workforce and industrialize Central Asia in order to defeat capitalism, had its impact in speeding up the creation of a native intelligentsia.) I asked Dinmukhamed Kunaev, a few months before his death in 1993, why some Kazakhs called him *Kazakhstan 'ın atası* (the father of Kazakhstan). In response he claimed that he tried to educate and modernize his Kazakh people, that he built Almaty into a modern city (though inhabited by a Russian majority) and tried to meet the needs of the countryside people without offending their traditions and customs. (Our conversation took place under the portrait of Kunaev's grandfather, attired in the pilgrim hajj garb, taken after the latter's return from Mecca. Kunaev said he was at once a communist, a Kazakh, and a Muslim, but believed in God). Pressed to say whether he intentionally sought to create a large body of native Kazakh intellectuals, he answered that his desire was to enlighten his entire nation. (In his memoirs, which were dictated in late 1990, Nursultan Nazarbaev is rather critical of Kunaev and his policies, but in a very measured fashion.)

The KGB appears to have become aware of the new patterns of social stratification in Central Asia. It advised Moscow to take the necessary measures to stop the ascendancy of the native intelligentsia-bureaucracy.[15] The effort to oust the entrenched local bosses started during Andropov's tenure and reached its climax during Gorbachev, who dismissed Kunaev (among others) and replaced him with a Russian, Gennadii Kolbin. This caused the first nationalist riots in Almaty, the first spark of independence in Central Asia. Significantly enough, Kazakhstan adopted 17 December 1986, the date of the riots, as the day of independence, that is, the national holiday of the country.

The native apparatchiks were often accused of corruption and nepotism and of "favoring Islam, protecting Sufi brotherhoods, or siphoning funds to unofficial mosques." As Michael Rywkin points out, "Such allegations only increased popular sympathy for the purged officials," and needless to say cemented further the incipient solidarity between the native bureaucrats and the emerging national constituency. Consequently, it is quite easy to understand, as M. Nazif Shahrani put it, the "domestic acceptance and tolerance of the old political order," that is, the old nomenklatura, despite their Leninist ideology; a large part of these bureaucrats, notably at the middle and lower levels, are "nationalized" or at least willing to appear as such.[16] In the 1986–90 period, the upper ranks of the old apparatchiks were replaced by the second echelon of leaders, all of whom, with the exception of Askar Akaev of Kyrgyzstan, had been high-ranking members of the Communist Party and are now heading their respective states. But practically all of them came from the humble ranks of the traditional society, were educated in modern schools, and preserved an awareness of their ethnic identity. The better-educated and promising native intellectuals were often given jobs in Moscow and were viewed overnight as stalwarts of the center, and thus mistrusted. Those who served in the home republic gained the aura of the good native son.

The current heads of state in Central Asia turned nationalistic once they became sure that the demise of the USSR was real. Uzbek leaders were suspicious of Gorbachev's reforms and opposed liberalization but were among the first to declare independence as early as 31 August 1991. Even Islam Karimov, who had first supported the August 1991 coup in Moscow, decided after witnessing the coup's failure to ban the party from government and education and to confiscate its property. Eventually he transformed the party into the People's Democratic Party and used it as his own power base while formally taking his legitimacy from his people; he was popularly elected president with an 86 percent majority on 29 December 1991, but once in power he ignored the most elementary norms of democracy. In sum, I believe that the nationalism of the Central Asian leaders is genuine, but with many caveats. Consequently, it is correct to state that the current leaders of the Central Asian states are supporting the creation of a national culture in their respective states, since they have come to regard such a national culture as the irreplaceable basis for the independence and sovereignty of the state and for their own power. They are also trying to maintain most of the modernistic features of the old system, including education and women's rights. The roots of this nationalism, as mentioned, are in the leaders' traditionalist family background, their relative acquaintance with cultural authenticity, their aspirations for administrative autonomy, and the need for a supporting native constituency, not to speak of their exceptionally astute, opportunistic instinct for power.[17] At the same time most of the leaders continue to view Moscow in a rather friendly manner, not only because of their previous political-ideological affinity with the old center but also because of an entrenched belief that Moscow still possesses somehow the ability to decide the ultimate fate of their republic and themselves. The fall of Abulfez Elchibey, who embraced an unequivocal Azeri nationalism directed against Moscow (and toward Iran), was a good lesson that cannot be ignored.

Independence, national statehood, and the expansion of the bureaucracy have opened great employment opportunities for the elites educated in the modern schools and have permitted, indirectly, the "national" culture of the traditional masses from which this intelligentsia originated to percolate into the upper echelons of the government. The cultural closeness of the current rulers of the Central Asian states to the masses, despite their association with the old regime, has made them relatively popular and easily electable.[18] However, not far from the surface there lies a mass of accumulated grudges against all kinds of things, including the leaders' past association with and servility to Moscow. Thus the top leadership of the Central Asian republics is caught between its desire—and that of large segments of the native population—to be free from political dependency on Moscow and its own past associations and personal-ideological ties with the Soviet center. The nationalists in the opposition parties throughout Central Asia mention continuously the leaders' old links with Moscow, and simultaneously the rulers' fear of a native nationalist backlash. This fear induces them to prove that they are genuine Uzbek, Turkmen, or other patriots while remaining in the good graces of Moscow, however contradictory it may appear. Actually the coming of independence and statehood and the shift of power and patronage away from Moscow to local cadres have split the educated elite groups in every Central Asian state into bureaucrats and intelligentsia. The former appears to be identified with the state, while the latter claims to speak on behalf of the nation and all it entails. The split is manifest in the political parties, but a study of the political parties, including the officially approved ones in the hands of the old native nomenklatura and the "unregistered" nationalist opposition parties, falls outside the scope of this chapter. Suffice it to say that the protagonists in the struggle for democracy in Central Asia presently consist of the bureaucracy and the intelligentsia, the latter hoping to attract the emerging civil groups. The bureaucracy relies on its control of the government apparatus to maintain its political supremacy, while the intelligentsia seeks the support of the indigenous masses by appealing to their traditional values and national culture. For instance, the Azat, Alash, and Zheltoksan parties (the last two unregistered) in Kazakhstan are doing exactly that, although in varying degrees of intensity and appeal to traditionalism and Kazakh ethnic nationalism. On the other hand, some leaders such as Nazarbaev have learned how to manipulate the opposition parties while successfully building their own party and bolstering their image as popular national leaders. Ultimately the question of legitimacy will decide the political fate of the new leaders and their regimes. The old communist legitimacy no longer has its old force, while the democratic legitimacy stemming from popular acceptance and the electoral system has struck no real roots, partly at least because the elections failed to improve the population's living standards.

Islam, National Identity, and Foreign Relations

Islam is one of the major sources of national identity and a factor facilitating the relations of Central Asia with other Islamic countries. It conditions also the formation of a national culture and affects the political behavior of the masses and their leaders. The issue is of capital importance, but we shall devote to it the minimum space necessary to illustrate the rather unique position of Islam in Central Asian society.

As a religious dogma, along with its institutional and legal framework, Islam has a certain uniformity and universality that provide a good common basis for understanding among Muslims. At the same time, Islam, having achieved the acceptance of the same *iman* (faith), leaves its followers totally free to adapt to and live in accordance with the social, geographic, and political environment. Islam is an individualistic religion without an organized clergy and thus allows each community to adopt the faith according to the sociogeographical situations. Consequently, Islam has adapted easily to every continent and circumstance and has become easily identified with the local culture and customs. In areas relatively remote or isolated from the orthodox centers of Islam, the identification of the faith with the local secular culture has been greater.

Russian-Soviet and Western scholars have measured the "secularization" of Muslims in accordance with their observance of the rituals of the faith, such as prayer, fasting, and abstinence from alcohol and pork. This naive understanding of Islam has led numerous scholars to claim that the hold of Islam on the Kazakhs and Kyrgyz was weak because they converted late and failed to practice the rituals of the faith. This view is echoed also by many Central Asian nomenklatura who never had the curiosity to find out how their ordinary conationals think and feel about their faith. Besides, claiming that the Central Asians are not good Muslims is likely to win them points with the Russians and Westerners.

The study of Islam both in the West and the former Soviet Union has been caught in a vicious circle. Scholars have studied Arab Islam as the archetype of the faith and regarded its various ideological manifestations as likely to occur elsewhere, too. Thus Wahhabism, which appeared in the northeastern section of the Arabian Peninsula in the late eighteenth century, has been viewed mistakenly as the prototype of all Islamic fundamentalist and revivalist movements. Consequently, developments in Islam in Indonesia, Turkey, Iran, and other countries were regarded either as replicas of Arab Islam, or aberrations if they showed peculiarities of their own. The Soviet scholars in turn adopted wholesale the Western concepts concerning Islam—especially the negative judgments—and applied them to the study of their own brand of Islam. Thus, throughout the Soviet era the folk Islam, which will be dealt with briefly below, was condemned and violently repressed as superstition, obscurantism, and reactionism.[19] The same scholars viewed the urban and better-organized manifestations of nationalism under religious garb as Muslim fundamentalism and condemned it as such. For instance, in 1985 and several times afterward, Gorbachev, following his advisors' opinion, criticized and condemned Islam (once while in Tashkent) in the most intemperate manner as obscurantism, while Kozyrev repeatedly called the attention of the West to the danger of Muslim fundamentalism in order to justify the Russian intervention in Tajikistan. The rise of this nationalism rooted in folk Islam among the Central Asian lower and middle classes was evident in the 1970s as elementary- and mid-level native schoolteachers and their pupils began to visit and repair the graves of local saints, minstrels, and historical leaders. Eventually after independence the names of these personalities were given to parks, streets, and localities. Soviet scholars condemned all the natives' searches for the roots of their identity in their own culture, of which folk Islam was an inseparable part, as a sort of Muslim fundamentalism probably inspired by Iran or Egypt, although there was little connection among them. (The Russians came to see the Afghan resistance to their invasion as a form of religious opposition rather than a national one.) The Soviet scholars' views on Islam, though heavily influenced by Western writings, were in turn adopted by the Kremlinologists often acting as experts on Central Asia, and portrayed as original and honored as such.

The acceptance and practice of Islam among Central Asian elites vary greatly. Since the overwhelming majority of these elites received an atheist education and were heavily indoctrinated with anti-Islamic propaganda, they tend to be personally neutral—if not hostile—toward any religion, although often they are the first to acknowledge its practical importance. Nonetheless, as the process of national consolidation intensifies and the new regimes' need for popular support and cultural harmony with the ruled increases, Islam is bound to gain further importance. But the religious crises may remain under control as long as religion is considered an individual matter and the state leaders' secularist postures are maintained, and as long as the religious freedom of the Russians, notably in Kazakhstan, where church attendance has increased, is not hindered. The truth is that Islam in the lands that became Russia and the ex-Soviet Union developed almost from the beginning in close association with the local culture, and found in Ahmed Yesevi (d. ca. 1166) an ideal representative who disseminated Islam in the guise of local folk religions, including shamanism. The mystical Sufi Islam, as represented both by the eleventh-century Yesevia religious brotherhood and its urban offshoot of the fourteenth century, the Naqshbandiyah, are of Central Asian origin and were, and are, popular among Turks, Persians, and Indians, but were shunned by orthodox, establishment Islam. The late president of Turkey, Turgut Özal, declared publicly that he was a Naqshbandi and did his best to honor the memory of Bahauddin Naqshbandi, the founder of the order, whose tomb near Bukhara was and is a popular shrine. The ultraorthodox Muslims reject the Yesevia and Naqshbandiyah. Even today the Saudi Arabian missionaries in Central Asia denounce unsuccessfully this local mystical understanding of Islam and the rites associated with it as being un-Islamic. From its early days to our time Islam in Central Asia and Russia as a whole was part of the daily life of its followers and entered into the fabric of various currents—Jadidism (modernism), nationalism, Pan-Islamism, Pan-Turkism—that affected the sociopolitical life of Russia's Muslims. It is only now that Russian scholars seem to have started to become aware of the unique characteristics of their Islam.[20]

Thus, if one accepts the fact that faith and local-tribal culture are intimately interwoven, notably in folk Islam (which existed as a parallel religion to that officially sanctioned by the old regime, represented by the four muftiates during the Soviet era), then it seems evident that Islam as the repository of the folk culture will become a major source of national culture. Indeed, the historical experience in nation formation during the last two hundred years indicates that the religious and nonreligious folk culture of the dominant ethnic-national group becomes the source of national culture and provides the symbols of national identity. As the case of Ahmed Yesevi illustrates, a religious mystic could be transposed into a "father" of the nation.

Today Islam in Central Asia is a source of national culture and an avenue for the political leaders to court popular support and identify themselves with the masses. It is Islam that permits a leader to tell the Muslim masses, "I am one of you." Tribal and clan affiliation can obviously buttress further the leader's iden- tification with the masses but cannot achieve it fully without the religious ingre- dient. It would be impossible for a non-Muslim Kazakh or Uzbek to become a generally accepted leader. National identity and religious affiliation—even if one is not an observant Muslim—are becoming inseparable from each other. The opposition parties in Central Asia are aware of these practical realities and when convenient have accused their presidents of atheism. The presidents in turn, contrary to some misinformed claims, have strived to prove that they are good Muslims. Thus, Niyazov of Turkmenistan and Karimov of Uzbekistan visited Mecca (and Akaev promised to) not only to ingratiate themselves with the Sau- dis but also to prove to their countrymen that they are good Muslims. To be a Muslim in Central Asia is a necessary condition for being a good Uzbek, Turk- men, or Kazakh. Fundamentalism as perceived in the West, on the other hand, does not exist in Central Asia. The fact that it is often mentioned derives from Islam's bad name in the West and thus provides a convenient excuse both for Russia and the totalitarian regimes of the area to silence their opponents and critics, Karimov of Uzbekistan being a good example. It is true that the fertile Fergana Valley, unlike other areas, has been a traditional stronghold of orthodox Islam due to a variety of geographic, historical, and political factors. The inhabi- tants of these areas, including the Tajiks, have long-standing urban and sedentary traditions that favor close identification with tenets of orthodoxy. But orthodox Islam cannot be equated with fundamentalism, if that word implies the establish- ment of a government guided by the political principles of Islam.

The Saudi and Iranian missionaries chose the Fergana Valley to disseminate their own brand of Islam.[21] The first were branded Wahhabis and the second Humeinis and registered a degree of local success due mainly to the spiritual vacuum left by Soviet atheism, but there was not a true fundamentalist move- ment. It may be correct to state that fundamentalism in Central Asia has little chance of success because ideologically its universalism and denial of ethnicity and national statehood conflict and directly challenge the basic political trend in the area: national independence and sovereignty based on ethnonational culture and identity. Islam retains its appeal among the masses because it is part of their folk culture, and because of this, it is the source of their national-ethnic identity.

Islam as a factor of international relations provided the cultural bond that linked Central Asia to the Muslim countries in Asia and Africa, particularly Turkey and Iran. The issue was best described by President Nazarbaev in his speech delivered on the eve of Kazakhstan's independence day. After stating that "Kazakhs, today, for the first time in their history have a chance to mold their statehood, [achieve] a comprehensive development of their language and culture," he declared that

> we have to keep in mind in our foreign policy the Islamic factor. We are realistic about it. We take into account the spiritual basis of Islamic culture and the importance of Islamic culture in modern life. The Islamic world has many potentials which we cannot ignore. But we also have no grounds for all kinds of talks [pleading] for strengthening or enhancing religious fundamentalism in our country.[22]

The foreign ministries of the Central Asian states are heirs to the bureaucratic cadres' cultural and ideological transformation, as mentioned before. They have to cope with, among other things, a domestic audience increasingly influenced by nationalist-populist Islam while at the same time maintaining a facade of neutrality toward Islam often disguised as "secularism" in order to soothe the apprehension of the Russians and Westerners, some of whom appear to regard any revival of Islam as a form of militant fundamentalism. Today the Central Asian states are trying to reduce the number of ethnic Russians in government service or to push them to second- or third-rate positions, although occasionally the Russians are ostentatiously awarded high ministerial positions, such as prime minister of Kazakhstan. The foreign ministries in particular seem to give priority to recruiting native intellectuals, but Russians often describe the preference given to the natives as a form of nationalistic and religious discrimination.

Today, the foreign policy of the Central Asian states is largely in the hands of the presidents of the countries, due, partly at least, to the need for a single consistent policy line. Practically all major decisions, from the appointing of senior officials and ambassadors to granting concessions to foreign companies and concluding treaties, are decided by the president. In some reported cases, the president decided who should be allowed to enter or leave the country. In a notorious case, Baymirza Hayit, a scholar of Uzbek origin living in Germany since 1944, was invited as a guest of honor by the Uzbek Academy of Sciences, but was asked by the president to leave the country in twelve hours. Apparently the KGB persuaded Karimov to oust the well-known anticommunist scholar. The foreign ministry and its resident staff, together with newly established offices or institutes of strategic studies or strategic planning, assist the president in the formulation of foreign policy and help him carry it out. The concentration of foreign policy prerogatives in the president's hands is normal and expected in a presidential form of government—and the de facto regimes that prevail in Central Asia are presidential. Central Asian foreign relations have acquired an escalating importance in tandem with the rising ominous nationalism of Moscow. In some cases even the parliaments of Kazakhstan and Kyrgyzstan have become involved in foreign policy matters, although so far such involvement seems to be an exception rather than the rule. Nevertheless, the parliaments of Kazakhstan and Kyrgyzstan have successfully blocked their presidents' agreements to send troops into Tajikistan to put down the civil war there. Meanwhile, the upgrading of the quality of foreign ministry personnel continues at a feverish pace. Uzbekistan has established in Tashkent under French auspices a Université de Diplomatie et Economie Mondiale dedicated to training future Uzbek diplomats. Incidentally, the rector (president) of the university is the Uzbek minister of foreign affairs. Meanwhile, the European Community—now the European Union—has already appointed representatives to Uzbekistan and plans to have two representatives in each country with the purpose of providing both advice and financial support for the development of the energy sector, human resources, food production and distribution, privatization, and communication. Also, many Central Asian professionals who have worked in Moscow with foreign enterprises have been given high positions in the foreign ministries or hired as foreign policy advisors to the presidents. The foreign ministry structure is in constant evolution, and no definitive assessment is possible until it takes a more definitive shape. One of the major handicaps to the development of a truly modern foreign service personnel is the lack of hard currency. Consequently, the Central Asians may be forced to use Moscow's old facilities for training their diplomats and expose them to undesirable indoctrination. Aware of this situation, the Central Asian states are looking for other training opportunities.

The CIS, Central Asia, and the Armed Forces

The armed forces are the indispensable attribute of national sovereignty. They express the national will to exist and provide the actual means to secure that existence. There cannot be an independent sovereign state without its own armed forces. The Central Asian republics did not have their own armies, except for some paramilitary units organized for various police functions. The creation of native armed forces is obviously one of the most complex and difficult problems faced by the new states. President Nazarbaev has described very well his republic's need for armed forces:

> [Kazakhstan's] main goal is the defense of the sovereignty and the territorial integrity of the country. As a sovereign state Kazakhstan considers the maintenance of its defense capacity to be one of the most important state functions and the common cause of all the people living in the republic. Consequently Kazakhstan will do whatever is necessary together with other states to build an all-around system of international security. [Consequently] the formation of our own armed forces, the army of the Republic of Kazakhstan, must be completed in a short time.[23]

In the following section we shall attempt to provide an overall assessment of the tug-of-war between Russia and the new states that ended in the formation of national armed forces in each of the CIS states. National independence for the new states meant escaping from the security arrangements made by Moscow and establishing their own security policies and national armies with or without Moscow's cooperation. The division of the Soviet armed forces could assure each state a number of military units; the troops on their soil would become a part of the national army. Yet the reality proved to be immeasurably more difficult than they thought.

The ties between the Central Asian states and Russia, developed over one hundred years, are deep and multifaceted. They cannot be severed or altered overnight, notably in matters of economy and defense. Consequently, in matters of defense the Central Asian states are bound to remain dependent on Russia for a number of years to come. So far none of the Central Asian states possess armed forces capable of fighting even a small-scale war. The Central Asians view China and its enormous population as a far greater threat to their existence as an ethnic group and a state than Russia. China, in turn, is keenly aware that the existence of a series of independent Turkic states at the border of East Turkestan can only stimulate the nationalist aspirations of the Uigurs. The Chinese conquered for the last time the land of the Uigurs in 1877, when they put an end to the independent state of Yakub Bey and renamed the country Sinkiang in 1884. The Uigurs vividly remember these events. China has refused to recognize twelve frontier points with Kyrgyzstan and reportedly claimed a part of eastern Kazakhstan. The potential territorial claims of China, however remote they may appear at this time, are a source of great anxiety throughout Central Asia and an unheralded but ever-present reason for the new republics to maintain friendly relations with Russia, the only power that can cope with the military might of China. It is probably for this reason that Kazakhstan has curtailed the entry of the Chinese into the country and scaled down their sizable investments.

Thus the Central Asian states are placed in the uneasy situation of fighting the Russian nationalist efforts to bring them under Moscow's authority while seeking Russia's economic support and military protection to assure the very national independence and sovereignty that Moscow appears to threaten. The CIS was the partial result of this situation. It was seen as an organization that could and needed to take care of the problems shared by the republics of the former Soviet Union, including the settling of conflicts. It was established in Minsk on 8 December 1991 by Russia, Ukraine, and Belarus and was soon joined by the Central Asian states.[24] The CIS developed several policy-making bodies, such as the Council of Presidents and the Council of Prime Ministers, with additional bodies created later, such as the Councils of Defense, Foreign Affairs, and Intelligence.[25] Its membership has oscillated; in October 1992 Azerbaijan dropped out (at the time the number of members was reduced to ten since the Baltic states and Moldova stayed out) but came back in 1993. The CIS command structure, if it can be called that at all, came out in May 1992. The Treaty on Collective Security was signed on 15 May 1992 in Tashkent and reaffirmed by a series of military agreements in the draft CIS Charter, signed on 22 January 1993, by only six member of the CIS: Russia, Kazakhstan, Uzbekistan, Kyrgyzstan, Tajikistan, and Armenia. Turkmenistan stayed out but signed a series of bilateral military agreements with Russia, making it a de facto member. The number dropped to five and rose again in 1993 with the addition of Azerbaijan and Georgia. Ukraine, Moldova, and Azerbaijan did not sign the Treaty on Collective Security because they saw it as a re-creation of the old center.

The basic purpose of the CIS, according to Russia, was to maintain the unity of the strategic and general purpose forces of the Soviet Union and to preserve the ruble zone. It is true that after the coup of 1991, Yeltsin ordered a reorganization of the Soviet Defense Ministry and established a new command team under Marshal Evgenii Shaposhnikov that remained in place after the dissolution of the USSR. The well-established Russian tradition of maintaining the continuity of the military establishment was thus preserved. The armed forces of the former Soviet Union were formally placed under the command of the CIS Council of Heads of State, but in reality they remained an all-union institution and a supranational organization, being in fact, as Stephen Foye put it, an independent actor or a "twelfth CIS state."[26] The CIS members agreed to coordinate their foreign policies, open their frontiers to free movement of citizens, and cooperate on transportation, but soon all these agreements—notably the ones concerning the common economic space, foreign policy, and the armed forces—went awry. In May 1992, faced with opposition from Ukraine on a variety of military issues, Russia decided to establish its own armed forces, as did the other CIS members. Meanwhile, Russian cities decided to treat the citizens of the former USSR not residing permanently in Russia as foreigners and/or as stateless persons (Russia had passed a citizenship law on 1 September 1991 allowing any Soviet citizen to take Russian citizenship within three years if he/she had not taken another republic's citizenship). The constantly changing language and policies of the CIS reflected new views taking shape in Russia. The term "near abroad" began to be used increasingly in 1992 with regard to the Russian Federation's policy toward the former Soviet republics and the status of the ethnic Russians and those who identified ethnically and culturally with the Russians living on the territory of the former Soviet republics. The total number of people who fall into this category amounts to about 25 million, of whom close to 10 million live in Central Asia, mostly in Kazakhstan. The issue was first formulated by Iurii Skokov, the head of the Foreign Policy Commission of the Security Council of the Russian Federation.[27] Skokov argued not only about the rights of the Russians living in the near abroad but also about the need for Russia to counter the aspirations of the United States to be the only world leader. He was dismissed from his position, but on 1 December 1992 Kozyrev's Foreign Ministry issued a fifty-eight-page document outlining Russia's foreign policy and strived to clarify his own position toward the near abroad. He accepted the concept, while he avoided defining it as part of Russia's foreign relations. Arguing that the term referred to internal unity, he ominously avoided discussion of Russia's policies and intentions toward the Central Asian states. Actually the near abroad concept, which included the Russian state's obligation to defend the rights and interests of Russians—and those identified culturally with Russia—was a basic part of the Russian General Staff's military doctrine.[28] Russia's concern for the Russians living in the countries of the near abroad is to some extent natural, but the solutions proposed are hardly acceptable. The truth is that independence—at least in Central Asia—unleashed the unavoidable process of decolonization. It was not carried out based upon a well-designed plan, but resulted from processes of national independence and nation formation. The Russians in Central Asia have occupied, by force of their better education and control of political power, the best economic and administrative positions in the country. They have treated the native population in a contemptuous manner and seldom bothered to learn their language, culture, and traditions. Today, the ethnic Russians face the loss of these colonial privileges and have to bow before their former subordinates. Yet it is the nationalists in Russia proper who have championed the rights of the Russians living in the near abroad for their own expansionist goals rather than the colonists themselves, although the latter's complaints are growing. Actually the treatment of the Russians in the near abroad or Central Asia has been far more lenient and considerate than the treatment accorded to other peoples regarded rightly or wrongly as part of a formerly dominant ethnic group. For instance, the newly independent Balkan states, under the advice of Russia, forced out millions in 1877–78 and thereafter from their ancestral lands because supposedly they were "Turks" who had been associated with the previously ruling Ottoman government, a nonnational structure that was labeled "Turkish" for the sake of expediency. The "ethnic cleansing" by Serbs in Bosnia is the continuation of this old policy. So far in Central Asia there has not been any violence directed at Russians, or legislation aimed at depriving them of their property and civil rights. In fact, Kyrgyzstan and Kazakhstan have gone out of their way to urge the Russians to stay, and have assured their safety in every way. Kazakhstan has passed a law punishing ethnic-national discrimination, while Kyrgyzstan has established a special agency to deal with ethnic problems.

On the other hand, all the Central Asian states have raised their native tongues to the constitutional status of state languages and have refused to grant the Russian language an equal status, despite the fact that it is still the main medium of communication among the native elites. Only in Kazakhstan has the Russian language been upgraded to the rank of the language of interethnic communication. Moreover, all the Central Asian states have adamantly refused to grant ethnic Russians dual citizenship, despite Russia's repeated demands, the latest pressure coming from Russian Foreign Minister Andrei Kozyrev during his recent trip through Central Asia. Only the president of Kyrgyzstan has promised to grant dual citizenship to ethnic Russians, but he may be overruled by his legislature. The loss of superior status, the need to learn the hitherto despised native languages, as well as the psychological malaise resulting from all this have compelled many Russians, Ukrainians, and Germans, notably the former command cadres, to move out of Central Asia, although Kazakhstan and Kyrgyzstan received in 1993 considerable numbers of Russians exiting from Tajikistan. Anyway, the Central Asians see in Russia's efforts to maintain the privileged status of its citizens the proof of the Russians' perennial love for empire and fear it as such.[29] The bulk of the working Russian population is made up of blue- and white-collar workers, and they can be easily replaced by natives, thus indirectly helping lower the high unemployment rate among natives. But the Russians living in Central Asia include also highly qualified technicians and specialists who had run the industrial plants, and their departure, although not regretted, since there was little if any social intercourse between the indigenous population and the "Europeans," has created serious management problems—notably in Kyrgyzstan, where Akaev issued public pleas to the Russians to stay in the country.

It is not evident yet what measures would suffice to soothe the Russians and persuade them to abstain from separatist endeavors or seek the intervention of the Russian Federation.[30] Meanwhile, there has been a rather muted campaign to persuade the native intelligentsia—whose preferred medium of communication is Russian—to speak their native tongue, especially in Kazakhstan, where a sizable percentage of the urban population does not know their own mother tongue. The truth is that, aside from Uzbekistan's partial exemption, practically all the Central Asian states lack modern and up-to-date facilities to teach their own languages. There are relatively few people among the young generations, especially in the cities, who possess a full literary command of their native languages—which lack, among other things, scientific and technical terminology.

The discussions about the fate of the armed forces of the CIS progressed amidst the rising Russian outcry about the fate of the Russians abroad. As mentioned before, on 15 June 1993 the joint military command of the CIS was abolished due to Russia's failure to use the CIS to control militarily and otherwise the territory of the former Soviet Union. Shaposhnikov, the commander of the joint armed forces of the CIS, was appointed secretary of the Russian Security Council to replace Iurii Skokov, the architect of the near abroad views and the proponent of a CIS ministry that would have downgraded the Foreign Ministry.[31] The Russians gave as a reason for their action the economic burden of supporting all the CIS forces. Actually, the CIS armed forces agreement had become redundant. Already Azerbaijan, Ukraine, and Moldova had decided to create their own armed forces. In the spring of 1992 Kazakhstan assumed control of the military personnel, installations, and property of the CIS armed forces installed on its territory, and in August 1992 created its own border troops and planned to create its own navy. In March 1993, Nazarbaev concluded a wide-ranging defense agreement with Russia on military cooperation and the setting of joint defense zones extending to the territory of both countries. Incidentally, in

June 1992 Kazakhstan passed a law on organs of national security to replace the old Soviet KGB—actually to create a Kazakh security organ having more or less the functions of the old, including extensive authority to "ensure state and public interests." Uzbekistan adopted a law in the summer of 1992 to create an army of land and air units. The Uzbek army backed the communist side in the Tajik civil war, providing troops and supplies. At the same time, as though to assert its military power, it conducted military operations in the Osh districts of Kyrgyzstan, apparently without obtaining prior permission. This is, in fact, further evidence of Uzbekistan's perennial effort to assert some sort of dominion over its smaller neighbor. The fact that the Uzbek government declared openly that Russia was Uzbekistan's chief guarantor of security and stability invites suspicion that Uzbek bullying may have Russian support.[32] The Turkmen government signed in mid-June 1992 a document with Russia, in which Russia agreed to assist Turkmenistan in establishing a national army and to provide equipment, training, and funding. The army was to be under joint Turkmen-Russian command and would not engage in operations without joint consent. By April 1993 a total of sixty thousand troops were stationed on Turkmen soil, fifteen thousand under direct Russian command.[33]

Kyrgyzstan claimed that it was a country without an army or military or defense personnel, despite the fact that 78 percent of the population, according to a survey, wanted to have an army. Yet in June 1992 President Akaev issued a decree assuming jurisdiction over all the troops found on the national soil, while the Kyrgyz vice president, Feliks Kulov, described Kyrgyzstan's military doctrine as "armed neutrality," and Russian troops assumed responsibility for guarding the Kyrgyz borders. Tajikistan's armed forces are to a very large extent Russian and remain under Russian command, despite the relative peace that has prevailed for the past year. The rather complex civil war in Tajikistan and the massive Russian involvement there render difficult an analysis of the country's future.[34]

In sum, the Central Asian states have managed to create the nucleus of national armed forces,[35] but whose command structure is still largely Russian and whose equipment, ammunition, and so forth are supplied or bought largely from Russia. The command structure of the old union army was 90 percent Slavic (80 percent Russian); the current command structure of the Central Asian states is probably still 60 percent Slavic, although the native percentage is increasing fast. A number of states have promoted the junior native officers to higher ranks and have given them command positions. A fairly large number of Central Asian officers—three hundred from Turkmenistan and probably as many as a total of fifteen hundred—are being trained in Turkey or by Turks; already a number of them have assumed command of their troops. The Pentagon has also concluded agreements concerning the training of the Central Asian armies. The nationalization of the army in Azerbaijan occurred mainly after Elchibey won the presidential election of 7 June 1992 with a 60 percent majority (Gaidar Aliev was barred from running for office because of age) and embarked on a major drive to Turkify the country by coming closer to Turkey while abandoning membership in the CIS. Azerbaijan, due to the Karabagh war, has built a rather sizable army, which, although still lacking fighting power, is bound to be the largest and most experienced armed force of all the Muslim states in the former Soviet Union. (We have not dealt with the disposal of strategic nuclear missiles, which gave Kazakhstan much-needed publicity and world attention, as seen in U.S. Vice President Al Gore's visit to the country in December 1993 and President Nazarbaev's very important visit to Washington in mid-February 1994. The issue is important but is a one-time event, unless Kazakhstan refused ultimately to dismantle its nuclear arsenal—as the Iranians claimed in late January 1994 in reports that were rebuffed by Kazakhstan. In any event, the Kazakh Supreme Soviet ratified the country's accession to the START I Treaty.)

The Economic Factor in Central Asian Foreign Relations

The importance of the economic factor in determining Central Asian relations with Russia is too overwhelming and will not be dealt with here in any detail. Suffice it to say that the economic and fiscal ties of Central Asia to Russia developed over one hundred years and made the two sides dependent on each other, although as usual Russia had the upper hand.[36] All Central Asian countries were included in the ruble zone.

The privatization of the economy became linked from the very start to political issues that in turn were tied to the broader questions of national interest and identity. An outright privatization would have definitely enhanced the already superior economic position of the ethnic Russians by making them owners of the enterprises and land they operated as administrators. Moreover, liberalization and privatization could disturb the existing setup, lower living standards, and create social unrest. But economic liberalization and privatization also had the potential of creating a new national sphere of economic activity and propertied middle classes within each republic, which, if successful, could consolidate the national identity and sovereignty.

The economic policies of the Central Asian states are far from acquiring their final shape. They remain heavily controlled by the state, with Kazakhstan and Kyrgyzstan having adopted some privatization. Inflation and scarcity of goods are rising, in part at least because Russia failed to meet its financial obligations, including the financing of the pension fund. In fact, Russia has complained that it is asked to bear the financial burden caused by the Central Asians' transition to independent statehood and a market economy. Meanwhile, the Central Asian states refused to accept the heavy conditions imposed by Russia in order to keep them in the ruble zone; they objected that these conditions would, among other things, impose limitations on their freedom and undermine their long-range economic potential. The long-brewing dispute reached the breaking point over Central Asian participation, against Russian objection, in a summit meeting of the Economic Cooperation Organization (ECO), consisting of the five Central Asian states, Azerbaijan, and also Afghanistan, Iran, Turkey, and Pakistan, the last three being the founding members. Russia saw the meeting, held in July 1993, as a major step toward the creation of a Muslim common market and warned the Central Asian states that they had to choose between the ECO and economic union within the CIS. Already Russia, although a member, was apparently unhappy with the Turkish-initiated Black Sea Economic Project, which included all the states bordering the Black Sea and also Azerbaijan and Greece. Meanwhile, after some hesitation Kazakhstan and Kyrgyzstan decided to speed up their transition to privatization and a market economy and opened up further their borders to foreign capital, although it is not quite clear how they intend to carry out their privatization by selling shares or vouchers. The issue is further complicated by the presence of the vast kolkhozes and sovkhozes in Kazakhstan that cannot be easily turned over to and operated by private individuals. A recent survey of the situation by the World Bank, when published, should give illuminating insights.

Kyrgyzstan, without major economic resources of its own, pins its hopes on tourism to turn the country into the Switzerland of Asia; it has received rather generous loans from international financial organizations, due partly at least to its good democratic record. Meanwhile, Uzbekistan decided to adopt its own plan of development—some described it as following the Chinese or the Chilean (Pinochet) models—of keeping more or less intact the statist economic structure while permitting only a limited degree of privatization. President Islam Karimov paired his economic statist policy with a repressive stand toward the opposition parties, first Birlik and then Erk (the latter party seceded from Birlik because it believed in cooperation with the government). Resource-rich Turkmenistan has followed a somewhat different policy under the direction of President Saparmurad Niyazov. He became first secretary of the party in 1985 when the previous leader was ousted and then in 1991 renamed his old party the Democratic Party; after declaring independence on 27 October 1991, he was popularly elected president on 21 June 1992. Turkmenistan has agreed to open its gas and oil resources to foreign companies for exploitation, hoping to establish markets abroad.[37] It has recently agreed to an extensive economic-commercial exchange with Iran. All in all, despite variations in style and degree of commitment to a market economy, the Central Asian states, headed by Kazakhstan—except for impoverished Tajikistan—have sought to establish economic relations with a variety of foreign countries while maintaining their old ties with Russia and hoping to draw benefits by staying in the ruble zone. (The Russians did not hesitate to exploit when suitable the image of helpful "big brother" that the old communist regime had cultivated in Central Asia.)

Eventually all this maneuvering by Russia and Central Asia about securing for themselves the greatest benefit came to a sudden end in 1993, as all the Central Asian states—except Tajikistan—found themselves outside the ruble zone and had to issue their own currency. The Kyrgyz government, under the advice of the IMF, introduced its own currency, the *som,* and caused a sharp reaction from Uzbekistan, leading to a temporary border closure. Then other states introduced their own currencies (the *sum* in Uzbekistan, the *tenge* in Kazakhstan, and the *manat* in Turkmenistan and Azerbaijan; they all gave one name, *kıyin,* to the fractions). The Central Asian states cannot maintain their independence and sovereignty for long without an economic union of some kind. Historically, Central Asia existed as an economic whole even when divided into khanates and republics. The Russian administration wisely accepted this fact when it established in 1867 the Turkestan governate that comprised all of Central Asia (most of Kazakhstan was under another administrative division). The Stalinist policy of using each republic to specialize in a given product, for example, cotton in Uzbekistan, certainly undermined the possibility of forming an economic union in the region but did not entirely destroy it, or at least the concept of it. The need to establish economic unity in Central Asia was proposed by President Nazarbaev as early as 1990. Since then the heads of the Central Asian states have met at least eight times to discuss the establishment of a common market.

Expulsion from the ruble zone has forced the Central Asian states to seek their own remedy. Meetings between the leaders of Kazakhstan, Uzbekistan, and Kyrgyzstan have resulted in a formal agreement to establish a common market to support each others' currencies and oppose the growing Russian economic and strategic pressure.[38] Russia asked for equity holdings and a share in the output of natural resources—about 10 percent of the oil and gas pumped out of Kazakhstan, Turkmenistan, and Azerbaijan—and has delayed the payment for goods, including coal taken from the area. It seems that Turkmenistan and Tajikistan are drawing closer economically and militarily to Russia, although the final outcome of all this maneuvering is not clear yet. The Uzbek-Kazakh agreement was to become effective on 1 February 1994 and in the year 2000 turn into an economic union. It is interesting to note that Karimov issued a decree on 22 January 1994 that covered a wide range of industries subject to privatization as a means to expedite the union, this after he approached the IMF on 21 January 1994 for credits while opening the door to foreign investments. These measures were preceded by agreements of Kazakhstan and Uzbekistan to cut down their imports from Russia, while Karimov stated that the two countries had the capacity to satisfy each other's needs; the expectation was that Iran and Turkey would help fill the gap. Meanwhile, both Kazakhstan and Uzbekistan have made drastic changes in the administration of their fiscal and economic institutions.

In effect, today all the Central Asian states aspire to establish their own armed forces and have their own national currencies (which have lost value, but so far less than the ruble), thus meeting some of the outward conditions of national independence. Meanwhile, Russia has used every possible orthodox and unorthodox means and has drawn the two ultranationalist countries of the Caucasus, Azerbaijan and Georgia, into its own military and economic orbit.[39] It is too early to judge whether the difference in attitudes taken by Russia toward these two areas actually heralds her future policy, namely, to establish a firm influence and presence in the Caucasus (President Yeltsin just signed an agreement that leaves three major military bases in Georgia in Russian hands) while maintaining a loose grip on Central Asia.

Conclusion

The foreign policy of the Central Asian states is developing along with the efforts to build the basic institutions necessary for an independent state, such as a national army and bureaucracy. The creation of an authentic national culture and identity rooted in the national history, which is being slowly rewritten in light of the perception of the past and aspirations, is an inseparable part of state building. Consequently, the foreign policy of the Central Asian states reaches beyond the technical confines of normal relations among states and acquires a basic role in the construction of the national territorial state. In this context one can say that the current foreign policies of the Central Asian states may leave permanent marks upon the character, attitudes, and orientation of the emerging national structures. There are at least three major tasks related to foreign policy that may determine the evolution of the internal and external policies, as well as the character, of these states.

The first task is to overcome the past subordinate associations of Central Asia with tsarist Russia and the Soviet Union. There is no question that tsarist and communist Russia played a decisive part in undermining the traditional Central Asian society and forcing it socially, politically, and territorially to assume its current shape. The indigenous culture, including Islam, was thus forced to mold itself (without losing its authentic spirit, at least at the grassroots level) according to the sociopolitical conditions imposed on it from above. The Russians defined independently their own role in creating a modern political and institutional superstructure sustained by a very traditionalist infrastructure. Had the Russians started their "reformist" endeavors by tackling the traditional rural and tribal structure not with compulsory brutal sedentarization, collectivization, and frontal attacks on the traditional family, as done by Stalin in 1927, but by instituting better and more efficient market relations in villages, the results might have been different. The old traditional structures in villages and tribes were incorporated into a variety of Soviet agricultural production units and governed with an iron hand. Nazarbaev in his childhood recollections provides exceptionally insightful passages concerning the treatment of Kazakh villagers by the Russians and communists. In one passage he describes how his father Abish (according to the tribal tradition the eldest son took the father's name, so Nazarbaev's tribal name is Nursultan Abish) was forced to join the kolkhoz but managed to take care of his family by raising apples in his backyard, which he and his son marketed in Almaty. The Russians directing the kolkhoz soon asked Abish not to sell his apples on the market but to surrender the entire crop to the kolkhoz. In response Abish cut his beloved apple trees, and afterward the family lived on the edge of starvation. No leader who remembers so vividly his family's sufferings can be expected to cherish the old system, even though it brought him to prominence.

The key question concerning the Central Asian republics' relations with Russia is the extent to which Moscow is able to shed its imperialistic historical national identity and regard its former subordinates as equals. In other words, the question is whether Russia can redefine its national identity without making the subjugation and rule of other nations its essential psychological ingredient. By the same token one can pose the same question to the old native communist nomenklatura ruling the republics, who in the past accepted wholeheartedly Moscow's supremacy and obediently fulfilled its instructions, in exchange obtaining position, income, and prestige. As mentioned in the text, some of the native leaders acted with a sense of national responsibility during the Soviet era, but others labored to please Moscow at any price so they could retire and live comfortably there. It will be the task of Central Asian foreign policy makers to persuade the Russians to get rid of their self-devised historical image as the "big brother," as Stalin euphemistically expressed it. The same foreign policy makers will face the task of inculcating the natives with a sense of independence toward everything Russian and confidence in their own abilities to decide the course of their national future.

The second task of the foreign policy of the Central Asian countries concerns their own historical, linguistic, and religious "near abroad" and the possibility of becoming members of a large ethnic, cultural, or religious union. This "cultural near abroad" consists first of Turkey, which has an infinite number of historical, cultural, and religious ties with Central Asia, and second of Iran. Pan-Turkism and Pan-Turanism as policies for uniting all the Turkic peoples were never popular in Central Asia or even among ordinary citizens of Turkey. They were reserved in 1908–18 to a small group of Azeri, Tatar, and Turkish intellectuals. On the other hand, Pan-Islamism as a form of nationalist union with Pan-Turkist features was born in Russia in 1880–1920. It was envisaged as the only practical device to liberate Muslims from Russian rule. Iran subtly appeals to a form of Pan-Islamism but relies largely on its own self-made image as the fountainhead of a Persian culture, and occasionally language, which it describes as dominant throughout the area. Iran hopes that somehow, someday, the Central Asians will be lured back into this Persian world dominated by Shi'i fundamentalist Iran. Afghanistan, Pakistan, and the Arab countries, in that order of importance, can appeal to the Central Asians mainly on the basis of shared Sunni Islamic ties. On balance, neither Pan-Turkism, nor the Persian historical culture, nor unity of faith can rival in attraction and loyalty or supersede national statehood and the identity that emanates from it. On the contrary, the attraction of nationhood will grow stronger. It will be the task of the Central Asian foreign policy makers to steer their countries away from regional or global associations based on historical, cultural, and linguistic ties, while using the same ties to consolidate their national independence and sovereignty. Regional associations for economic and self-defense purposes are always possible.

The third task of the foreign policy of Central Asia is the global one, or, to be more precise, the overall "civilizational" orientation of their states. The Russian and Soviet concepts of modernization, or "progress," as they usually defined it, took the West as a model, the contrary views of the Slavophiles notwithstanding. The Russian modernists took the science and technology from the West but ignored its democratic humanitarian, political, and cultural aspects, notably its liberal political pluralism. The beginning of modernism among Russia's Muslims had a Western orientation more in terms of values and aspirations than institutions—as was the case among the Ottoman modernists. The Soviet regime tried to nip in the bud the Muslims' yearning for contact with the fountainhead of contemporary civilization by prohibiting contact with Europe and by telling the Central Asians that Russia was the true source of civilization and that their highest level of aspiration should be education in a Russian institution and the mastery of the Russian language. Today, most of the intellectuals in Central Asia would like to establish strong, permanent, and genuine ties with the West. The decision by all the Central Asian Turkic states to abandon the Cyrillic alphabet and accept the Latin alphabet by 1995 is the most convincing proof of their intention to join the civilization of the West. The main ideological difference between Turkey and Iran stems from this point. Turkey wants to cement its alliance with the Central Asian states by moving them fully into the sphere of Western civilization, while Iran wants to keep them in the oriental Islamic sphere of civilization, which it hopes to reshape according to its own Shi'i fundamentalist revolutionary image. This choice of civilization—which is really a political rather than a cultural choice—does not imply the abandonment of the Central Asians' religion, traditions, language, and customs, but the valuation and reconstruction of all these through a set of new values and philosophy within the confines of a national territorial state, which is, incidentally, a Western form of political organization.

It is difficult to determine at this stage whether the Central Asian foreign services possess the personnel with the necessary knowledge, sophistication, and skill to carry out the above tasks to a successful conclusion. At first glance the situation is not very encouraging. Foreign policy decisions, from the simple to the most important, are made by the presidents of the republics, while the foreign ministers act more as employees and delegates than executives with defined responsibilities of their own. The foreign ministries do not yet have established traditions of service or possess the proper strategic philosophy, although there is evidence that serious attempts are being made to overcome these shortcomings either by establishing foreign service schools or by sending personnel for training abroad. The old dependency on Moscow for training and the view that the average citizen is ignorant of international relations, if preserved, may inhibit the development of an independent-thinking foreign policy staff. The recently elected parliaments, notably in Kyrgyzstan and Kazakhstan, do take from time to time an interest in foreign policy issues, especially in opposing attempts to maintain or increase the government's dependency on Moscow. The parliaments are bound to reflect more and more the opinion of the public, if the political parties become truly representative of the views and interests of various social groups. The nationalist intelligentsia is becoming increasingly interested in foreign issues, often in a rather extreme manner, but so far its impact on government decisions is barely felt. In the ultimate analysis the intelligentsia's input as well as the influence of the public on foreign policy matters is dependent on the democratization of the entire political system. It is premature, in fact impossible, to expect the Central Asian countries to produce overnight a full-fledged democratic system. However, a slow start must be initiated before the current authoritarian regimes become ossified and the leaders permanently entrenched in power. The Kazakh experiment, while far from being ideal, represents a good start, as does Kyrgyzstan. On the other hand, Elchibey's short-lived experiment in true democracy, although nipped in the bud, has set a precedent that may still bear fruit in the future.

The progress and the creative endeavors of a new nation are often stimulated by the memory of past achievements. Such memories nurture the national consciousness and the collective ego and become the incentives for future creative endeavors. Central Asia as a whole occupies a very distinguished place in the Muslim world as the citadel of intellectual achievement. Proportionate to its size, it has produced the largest number of theologians (Bukhari, Hamadani), philosophers (Farabi, Ibn Sina [Avicenna]), mathematicians (Kwarizmi, Ulugh Beg), poets (Navai), and hundreds of other scholars and writers. In the era of nationalism these Central Asian luminaries have been appropriated by Arabs and Persians. The Central Asian creativity in all intellectual and artistic fields lasted from the eighth to the seventeenth centuries. It was an unparalleled period of achievement, when Central Asia was at the crossroads of world cultures. National independence and sovereignty should enable Central Asia to link itself again to the rest of the world, and thus end its isolation from the real sources of civilization and regain its past creative prowess. This is the unique and vital foreign policy mission facing the Central Asian states, the awareness of which may inspire them to rise to the challenge.

Notes

1. The issues are discussed in Dale Eickelman and James Piscatori, eds., *Muslim Travellers: Pilgrimage, Migration and the Religious Imagination* (Berkeley: University of California Press, 1990).

2. For a discussion of what is "Russian" and who are the "Russians," see Paul Goble, "Russia and Its Neighbors," *Foreign Policy*, no. 90 (spring 1993), pp. 79–88.

3. See Suzanne Crow, "Personnel Changes in the Russian Foreign Ministry," *RFE/RL Research Report*, vol. 1, no. 16 (17 April 1992).

4. Ibid.; see also idem, "Russia Prepares to Take a Hard Line on the Near Abroad," *RFE/RL Research Report*, vol. 1, no. 32 (14 August 1992).

5. See Kemal H. Karpat, "Central Asia Between Old and New," *Central Asian Survey*, vol. 12, no. 4 (1993), pp. 415–25.

6. For the new history textbooks, see Murakthan Kani, *Kazaktyn Köne Tarikhy* [The old history of the Kazakhs] (Almaty: Zhalyn, 1993). This is a reprint of the original, which appeared in 1987 in Arabic script in Sinkiang in China; it is based on Arabic, Persian, and Chinese sources. See also Ermukhan Bekmakhanov, *Kazakhstan v 20–40 gody XIX veka* (Almaty: Qazaq universiteti, 1992). This book was initially published in 1947 and was banned by the Soviet authorities.

7. *Kazakhstanskaia pravda*, 15 May 1992.

8. See reports in *Presidential Elections and Independence Referendums in the Baltic States, the Soviet Union and Successor States* (Washington, DC: Commission on Security and Cooperation in Europe, 1992).

9. The conference was organized by the first secretary of the Kentau district but was presided over by the vice prime minister of the Kazakh republic. The forty-odd communications read at the conference dealt almost entirely with the literary aspects of *Divan-i hikmet*, the chief work of Yesevi (d. ca. 1166) compiled by his followers in the fifteenth century. The fact that Yesevi was basically a religious figure, and that he used the Turkish language of the time only as a medium to express his religious beliefs, though of basic importance, was conveniently ignored. This writer presented one of the two communications that dealt with Yesevi's religious ideas and his Sufi order. The communication was ignored. However, at a second Yesevi conference held in Ankara in 1992, much debate centered on his theological contributions, although the Central Asian participants still preferred to discuss Yesevi's literary work. I could not attend, though officially invited, the third Yesevi conference, held in Almaty in November 1993. Yesevi's busts have appeared in various Central Asian countries and his name has been given to streets and squares that formerly bore the name of Russian and Soviet heroes.

10. The issue was debated in an international conference, "The Opening of the New Turkic Republics to the Outside World: Problems and Solutions." The conference was organized by the Turkish Institute on Foreign Relations with the assistance of TIKA (Turkish Agency for Cooperation and Development) and was held in Ankara on 11–12 December 1992.

11. The correspondence between the Ottoman caliph and the Central Asian and Azerbaijani khanates from the sixteenth to the late nineteenth centuries is being published by the General Directorate of the Turkish Archives. See, for instance, *Osmanlı Devleti ile Azerbaycan Türk Hanlıkları Arasdndaki Münasebetlere Dàir Arşiv Belgeleri*, vol. 1, 1578–1914, and vol. 2, 1575–1918 (Ankara, 1992, 1993). The significance of this correspondence is in Kemal H. Karpat, *Islamism-Panislamism: The Remaking of State, Society and Religion in the Late Ottoman Empire* (forthcoming).

12. One of the few attempts to study the foreign policies of Central Asian states is by Martha Brill Olcott, "Nation Building and Ethnicity in the Foreign Policy of the New Central Asian States" in *National Identity and Ethnicity in Russia and the New States of Eurasia*, ed. Roman Szporluk (Armonk, NY: M.E. Sharpe, 1994).

13. The ambassador of Turkmenistan in Ankara, who participated in the foreign relations conference of 1992 (see note 10), claimed that in one year his country was recognized by one hundred states and had established relations with sixty of them, and that his country had "firmly decided to utilize all the diplomatic means available" to break away from isolation. He claimed that the foreign policy principles of his country were the defense of the national interest, an open door, neutrality, noninterference in the affairs of other states, and avoidance of ethnic strife. Relations with Russia were to be on a bilateral

basis and no different from other nations. According to the ambassador, Turkmenistan viewed as natural the public's revived interest in Islam (the number of mosques went from 5 or 6 to 150) but wanted to avoid religious conflicts. The mullahs did not know Arabic and did not possess the proper knowledge of Islam, hence the need for an enlightened teaching of Islam and Islamic history.

14. The texts of numerous agreements concluded by Turkey have been distributed by the Turkish authorities to various institutions. The quotation was taken from a text distributed to the Central Asian Center of the Bilkent University. These and all other agreements have been published in the *TC Resmi Gazete*, the official legal review of the government. See *TC Resmi Gazete*, 13 and 17 July 1991; 25 November 1992; 23 January 1993; 24 January 1993; etc.

15. Even after independence the KGB continued to monitor closely the cultural and political developments in Central Asia. The Yesevi conference mentioned in note 9 was directed by an academician who many said was part of the old Soviet secret service. A Turcology conference held in Kazan in 1992 was attended by the head of an institute of ethnography from Moscow who intended to study the "ethnic situation in Kazan," that is, the various non-Tatar groups who were opposed or could be made to oppose the incumbent government. He was described by other participants as being in the KGB.

16. Michael Rywkin, "Post-USSR Political Developments in Former Soviet Central Asia," *Nationalities Papers* (fall 1992), p. 98; also M. Nazif Shahrani, "Islam and the Political Culture of 'Scientific Atheism' in Post-Soviet Central Asia: Future Predicaments," in *The Politics of Religion in Russia and the New States of Eurasia*, ed. Michael Bourdeaux (Armonk, NY: M.E. Sharpe, 1995).

17. It should be noted that the heads of Turkmenistan and Uzbekistan are married to Russian women and reportedly speak Russian at home, as do much of the ruling elite throughout Central Asia, without, however, identifying themselves with Russia or rejecting their own culture and identity.

18. Rywkin wrote that successive purges affected three sets of officeholders, with the new appointees sharing the fate of their predecessors within a year or two of their initial appointment. The most important consequence of the purges was that local Muslim party officials, because of the "suffering" at Moscow's hands, became "rehabilitated" in the eyes of their compatriots—a development that took on key significance at the moment of independence. Rywkin, "Post-USSR Political Developments," p. 99.

19. Soviet scholars can sometimes provide exceptionally illuminating information on Islam in Central Asia and the Caucasus even though their purpose is to criticize and downgrade it. S.P. Poliakov, an anthropologist, regarded traditionalism, that is, the continuity of the local culture, even when fused with Soviet ingredients, as the chief characteristic of the rural mass culture. He regards Islam as the most powerful factor in the continuity of tradition, which in turn prevented the adoption of Soviet modes of life. In Poliakov's view, the mullahs (rural religious men) and folk Islam became the mainstay of religion after the Soviets destroyed the established Islam. Traditionalism even manifested itself in a petit bourgeois mode of production where buying and selling of land in villages followed the rule of *adat* (customary law) and the *şeriat* (religious law). Poliakov feared that perestroika (he wrote the book in 1989) would undermine all the progress registered by Central Asia during the Soviet-imposed reform. A detailed critique of the book is necessary to demonstrate the false Soviet understanding of Islam as well as the author's Marxist dogmatism, which was in fact a convenient "scientific" cover for his Russian chauvinism. Sergei P. Poliakov, *Everyday Islam: Religion and Tradition in Rural Central Asia*, ed. M.B. Olcott (Armonk, NY: M.E. Sharpe, 1992).

20. See A.V. Malashenko, "The Eighties, A New Political Start for Islam," *Russian Social Science Review*, vol. 32, no. 2 (March–April 1993), pp. 74–94.

21. Some of the most extensive information on Islam and fundamentalism in Central Asia can be found in the field reports of Ahmed Rashid, a Pakistani journalist. See *Far Eastern Economic Review*, 19 November 1992; *Herald* (November 1992); and *Nation*, 13 November 1992.

22. *Central Asian Desk*, compiled by Eric Rudenshold of the International Republican Institute-Almaty (5 January 1993), pp. 4–5.

23. *Kazakhstanskaia Pravda*, 15 May 1992.

24. Ann Sheehy wrote that Ukraine saw the CIS as "a civilized means of divorce"; Ann Sheehy, "The CIS, A Shaky Edifice," *RFE/RL Research Report*, vol. 2, no. 1 (1 January 1993), p. 37. Actually the CIS proved to be far more resourceful, thanks to Russia's efforts to make it the vehicle of restoration of a Russian empire.

25. Jan S. Adams, "Will the Post-Soviet Commonwealth Survive?" Occasional Papers (Columbus: Mershon Center, Ohio State University, 1993.

26. Stephen Foye, "The CIS Armed Forces," *RFE/RL Research Report*, vol. 2, no. 1 (1 January 1993), pp. 42.

27. John Lough, "The Place of the 'Near Abroad' in Russian Foreign Policy," *RFE/RL Research Report*, vol. 2, no. 11 (12 March 1993), pp. 21–26.

28. *Voennaia mysl'* (special edition), nos. 4–5 (1992), cited by Lough, "Place of the 'Near Abroad.'"

29. Aleksandr Prokhanov, known in the past as a liberal and a critic of the communist regime, declared late in 1992 in a speech given at Columbia University that if fascism was necessary to revive the empire he would vote for the fascists. *Current Digest of the Soviet Press*, (155/25) (1993), p. 1.

30. I asked a Kazakh nationalist intellectual, the leader of a political party, to describe the political behavior of Russia. His description: (1) Russia has always been the judge of its own actions; (2) whatever Russia does or thinks, its actions and thoughts are always right and moral; (3) Russia always portrays itself as the party that makes a sacrifice (*zhertva*) of itself for others, and as the party that is taken advantage of; (4) any land that Russia sets its foot on becomes by almost a sort of divine order Russia's blessed soil and motherland; (5) the fault with everything that goes wrong in Russia belongs to others: Jews, Germans (fascism), Americans (imperialism and exploitation), ungrateful minorities, and so forth.

31. Foye, "CIS Armed Forces"; and *RFE/RL Research Report*, 2 July 1993.

32. Bess Brown, "Central Asian States Seek Russian Help," *RFE/RL Research Report*, vol. 2, no. 25 (18 June 1993).

33. Ibid., p. 86.

34. A fairly comprehensive account of Tajikistan is in Olivier Roy, *The Civilian War in Tajikistan: Causes and Implications* (Washington, DC: U.S. Institute of Peace, 1993).

35. Except in Tajikistan, the chief commanders of the Central Asian armed forces are all natives, as follows: (1) Kazakhstan: Col. Gen. Sagadat Nurmagamatov (b. 1924), educated at Frunze Military Academy, active in the Soviet armed forces; (2) Kyrgyzstan: Major Gen. Dzhanybek (b. 1943), educated at Frunze Military Academy; (3) Turkmenistan: Lt. Gen. Dantar Kopekov (b. 1950), attended Turkmen KGB school; (4) Uzbekistan: Lt. Gen. Rustam Akhmedov (b. 1943); (5) Tajikistan: Major Gen. Aleksandr Shishlianikov (b. 1950) (from Brown, "Central Asian States"; Brown has compiled additional data on these commanders). During the fighting in the latter part of 1992, the Russian 201st Motor Rifle Division in the country was commanded by Tajik General M. Ashurox, who ordered his troops not to become involved in the fratricidal struggle.

36. See Boris Z. Rumer, *Soviet Central Asia: "A Tragic Experiment"* (Boston: Unwin Hyman, 1989).

37. Bess Brown, "Central Asia: The Economic Crisis Deepens," *RFE/RL Research*

Report, vol. 3, no. 1 (7 January 1994). Much of this information is also found in the *Kazakhstan Today Bulletin*, a monthly publication appearing in Almaty, and the *Central Asia Monitor* (January 1993).

38. Message from CENASIA Bitnet discussion group, 1 February 1994.

39. The Russian foreign minister, A. Kozyrev, has stated repeatedly that the Caucasus is essential to the security of Russia and that his country's position in that area has been assured during centuries of struggle.

10

Regional and Global Powers and the International Relations of Central Asia

Mohiaddin Mesbahi

Among the most important ramifications of the collapse of the USSR were the emergence of the new states of Central Asia and the Caucasus and the resultant geopolitical shift, modifications, and challenges in the Eurasian landmass's international relations. Several factors make the future of Central Asia's external dynamics particularly challenging. First, the geographical contiguity of Central Asia with the Middle East/Southwest Asian region has automatically enhanced the geopolitical significance and sensitivity of the region for both regional players (Iran, Turkey, Russia, China) and extraregional players (the United States, Western Europe). This once obscure and isolated part of greater Central Asia now once again constitutes the bridge between the Middle East and the Eurasian heartland. The emerging geopolitical interdependence between the Central Asian/Caucasus region and the Middle East, though still in its formative stage, will be a key element in shaping the thinking and policies of major players in the future.

Second, the significance of this geographical contiguity has been complemented and magnified by the region's "natural" cultural, ethnic, linguistic, and Islamic confluence with the Middle East/Southwest Asia. It is in fact this apparent Islamic characteristic or Islamic geocultural link that has, at least for the immediate future, given such prominence to Central Asia's geopolitical considerations. The addition of a considerable landmass between the shores of the Black Sea and the border of China's Xinjiang region populated by 60 million Muslims, all bordering the Islamic Middle East and South Asia, could only magnify the already significant preoccupation of the international community, especially the West, with the so-called Islamic factor.

Third, Central Asia and the Caucasus, even in the absence of the Islamic factor, will be a major testing ground for the ultimate shape that Russian foreign policy will take in the post-Soviet period. To a considerable degree, Russia's historical claim to being a unique Eurasian state, with all its modern implications, including its status as a great power, depends on its geopolitical status vis-à-vis its southern periphery. All the trappings of post-Soviet, postimperial Russian foreign policy, namely, the management of relations between the "center" and the former "periphery," are encapsulated in Russia's relations with the new independent states in Central Asia and the Caucasus. Russia's relations with these states will not only be an indication of Moscow's general attitude toward other newly independent states but will also reflect Moscow's self-perception as to the magnitude, scope, and proper place of Russia in the post-Soviet world.

Fourth, the new states of Central Asia, like those of the Caucasus, also constitute a testing ground and microcosm for some of the key questions and concerns of the post-Soviet world. Issues such as ethnoterritoriality and its multiple manifestations (ranging from self-determination to ethnic cleansing), nation building, underdevelopment, postcommunist transition, nuclear proliferation, and ideological extremism are all characteristic of the emerging new states and as such will not only preoccupy scholars but, given their clear policy ramifications, also the policy makers and the international community. (For example, what happened in Bosnia has also been repeated, though in a different form and obviously with less international fanfare, in Tajikistan, Nagorno-Karabagh, Abkhazia, and other regions.)

Finally, one might add the potential economic significance of the region, especially its relatively rich oil and gas resources in the Caspian basin, Kazakhstan, and Turkmenistan, as further indications of the importance of the region. The economic importance of regional states as producers of raw materials, however, should be considered in the context of the region's structural underdevelopment, the severely restrained purchasing power of its population, and thus, its limited short-term potential as a market. The combination of these factors places Central Asia, and especially its emerging external relations, at the heart of the discussion of the geopolitics of Eurasia and the Middle East.

In this chapter, the author will discuss some of the fundamentals of this emerging geopolitics by addressing the external relations of the region in the context of the attitudes of key regional players; more specifically, the region's relations with Russia, Iran, and Turkey will be emphasized. Within this context, reference will be made to the United States, China, and Afghanistan. Though regional actors such as Pakistan, India, Saudi Arabia, Israel, and others have also been active, emphasis is given to actors whose geographical contiguity and/or national interest signifies a direct and immediate impact on Central Asia's international relations. This chapter will provide a conceptual framework for the international relations of the region and the concerns and policies of key players rather than give a descriptive account of these relations.

Turkey and Central Asia: Opportunities and Constraints of the New "Turkic World"

Few other countries in the region seemed to have benefited as greatly, at least potentially, by the breakdown of the Soviet Union as Turkey, a country with the unique characteristic of being a Middle Eastern Islamic state with a strong European, secularist orientation. While Turkey's geopolitical, religious, and historical legacies have provided the regional and rational basis for its establishment as a key Middle Eastern player, its strong desire for European orientation and inclusion has been the underlying theme in Turkish foreign policy for most of this century. Although this consistent and determined effort in Europeanization facilitated Western military, economic, and political support, it has fallen short of fulfilling Turkey's ambition of inclusion in the European Community and to some extent has led to the relative marginalization of Turkey's role as an effective regional actor. In fact, the Gulf War and Turkey's preoccupation with its aftermath (the negative economic and ethnic implications), as well as the ongoing reluctance of Europe to embrace Turkey, have not only pointed to its unavoidable Middle East entanglement but, more importantly, have given rise to psychological and cultural suspicions that regardless of Ankara's efforts, Europe on "cultural" grounds will not embrace Turkey.

Thus the breakdown of the Soviet Union and the emergence of independent states in the Caucasus and Central Asia have presented Turkey with a potentially unprecedented historical opportunity to explore a completely new horizon in its foreign policy. For the first two years after the collapse of the USSR, the conventional wisdom pointed to multidimensional (i.e., ethnic, linguistic, and cultural) ties between Turkey and the region as a solid foundation for an influential, if not a dominant, position for Turkey in shaping Central Asia's external relations. Furthermore, Turkey's success story as a modern, secular "Turkic model" was presented as an alternative sociopolitical and economic model for Central Asian states in transition to the postcommunist world. Turkey, with the clear and purposeful support of the United States and Europe, and with the initial cautious acquiescence of Russia, has presented itself as a viable alternative to, and neutralizer of, the "Iranian Islamic model," which has been feared by so many in the region. Turkey's vision of itself as the embodiment of a model worthy of emulation in Central Asia was both the emotional and conceptual force behind the optimism of the early months of its ambitious foreign policy agenda in Central Asia. Ankara clearly hoped that while maintaining its long-term strategic orientation toward the West, it could clearly enhance its position by acting as the leader of the new independent states in Central Asia. Turkey's leadership and influence, if accepted by Azerbaijan and the Central Asian states, would have clearly benefited Turkey's overall security position in the Caucasus vis-à-vis Russia and would have enhanced its value for the Western world, providing a flexible and powerful foreign policy leverage for Turkey's regional and global posture.

A wide and multidimensional strategy has been pursued by Turkey to implement its Central Asian vision. The establishment of formal diplomatic relations with the new states was followed by numerous framework agreements (approximately 170) concluded between Turkey and the Central Asian states. Among the Central Asian states, Turkmenistan and Uzbekistan have been the major focus of Turkey's foreign policy. These are followed by Kazakhstan, Kyrgyzstan, and Tajikistan. While Kazakhstan's importance in Central Asia prompted early emphasis on relations with this republic, Almaty's preference for maintaining a closer relationship with Russia and Nazarbaev's sensitivity over the issue of any Pan-Turkic design in the region led to moderation of earlier ambitions of a full-fledged Kazakh-centric policy by Ankara. The failure of ambitious projects such as the operation of several Kazakh oil fields, the construction of a multibillion dollar thermal power plant, and the export of Kazakh oil via Turkey all clearly indicated the limitations in Turkish-Kazakh relations. While Turkey's relations with Uzbekistan seemed more promising, similar considerations and limited economic potential, as well as Uzbekistan's preference for structural ties with Moscow, have imposed certain limitations on long-term and significant openings for Turkey.

Among the Central Asian states, Turkmenistan may offer Turkey a more substantial economic possibility, especially in the area of energy. The key project in this context is the major gas pipeline routed from Turkmenistan through Turkey's territory (via Iran or the Caspian Sea). While progress on this project has gone beyond the usual formal proclamations, the Turkmen gas pipeline deal is not without its constraints. A similar and equally serious deal has been contemplated between Iran and Turkmenistan that might complicate the Turkish deal or eventually lead to the participation of Iran in the Turkish project, since the Iranian territory provides the most economically feasible alternative route for the pipeline. Recent high-level negotiations between Iran and Turkmenistan indicate a serious prospect for Iranian participation in this important project.[1]

What characterizes Central Asian–Turkish economic relations is their constrained and sporadic nature, and thus their limited strategic impact on overall Turkish–Central Asian relations. Perhaps more promising for Turkey is the series of infrastructural links in the areas of energy, transport, telecommunications, and education, which, if pursued judiciously, might provide a long-term and substantial basis for Central Asia's relations with Turkey.[2] In this regard, the promotion of in-depth cultural ties through the expansion of educational links (e.g., ten thousand scholarships for Central Asian students) and the promotion of Turkish (with the Latin alphabet) as the lingua franca of the new states,[3] as well as domination of the media (especially through television), Turkish broadcasts (Eurasia Channel), and technical dependency (Intelsat satellite), may prove more effective than existing economic ties and even diplomatic efforts. In this context, the future Latinization of the alphabet in Central Asian languages will be a critical factor. Though the general official tendencies of these states have been a preference for Latin over Arabic script, none have made a real national commitment to institute the change, especially in view of the continuing need for the Cyrillic alphabet and the continuing importance of Russian.

Turkey's opportunities and advances in Central Asia, however, are not without constraints. To begin with, the biggest disadvantage for Turkey is its geographical distance from Central Asia. The sheer distance and lack of real contiguity has been and will continue to be a major handicap.

Second, Central Asia, contrary to conventional perceptions, does not present a uniformly ethnic Turkic world. Not only are there variations among the Turkic peoples (including linguistic barriers within the Turkic languages), but there are also profound cultural differences between Turkish cultural messages and characteristics and the "Sovietized," isolated, and autonomous Turkic cultural heritage and traits of Central Asian peoples. Nominal similarities and vague historical memories should be weighed against the considerable impact of the Soviet legacy and the ethnic and regional peculiarities of the cultural enclaves of Central Asian societies. Furthermore, there are also Tajik people and others who belong to the Iranian cultural world.

Third, Turkey's attraction is also counteracted by three fundamental realities and problems associated with the post-Soviet Central Asian debate over the choice of a transitional model. The first problem is the vagueness of the Turkish model and its particular attributes and, more importantly, its relevance to the Central Asian sociopolitical and economic realities. Second, the slow dynamics of structural changes in Central Asia indicate the resiliency of the Soviet model and the elites' cautiousness toward drastic experimentation, especially with market-oriented, democratic models. Finally, the "Turkish model," if presented as a "ready-made" import, may ironically prove alien, especially to the general public, who may perceive it as another foreign imposition. For a mass political culture that is already too sensitive toward other dominant models (i.e., Soviet) and resentful of the Russification of its existing life, another model that may profess to copy from another alien culture (i.e., Western) may not be a way to political salvation.

Fourth, Turkey's success in Central Asia, notwithstanding cultural and political ties, to a large extent depends on its ability to provide a significant package of economic aid, investment, and technological know-how for underdeveloped Central Asia. Turkey has done well economically, but it is not an economic giant capable of dealing with the extent of the demands generated by the economically deprived "Turkic world" of Central Asia. "They want everything from chewing gum to blue jeans," complained a Turkish businessman.[4] It is not a coincidence that the substantial, high-profile diplomatic activities and the political and cultural exchanges between Central Asia and Turkey lack a proportional economic dimension. For example, South Korea surpasses Turkey in volume of trade and investments in the key Central Asian republics of Kazakhstan and Uzbekistan,[5] and the troubled and neighboring Nakhichevan has received substantially more aid from Iran than Turkey.

Fifth, there are certain domestic and external risks involved in Turkey's pursuit of an aggressive Pan-Turkic foreign policy.[6] Domestically, a hyper Pan-Turkic nationalism has already generated extreme emotionalism, resulting in undue pressure on the government to perform well in achieving its foreign policy goals in Central Asia.[7] Externally, an aggressive Pan-Turkism has caused alarm in Iran, which could possibly lead to the reemergence of the old Perso-Turkish struggle of the Ottoman period. This rivalry could potentially be explosive, if Turkey and Iran find themselves engulfed in ethnic conflicts in the Caucasus (i.e., Nagorno-Karabagh) or in Central Asia in the event of an Uzbek-Tajik dispute.

Excessive Pan-Turkism or Turkish activism in Central Asia will not be welcomed by Moscow. While Moscow's concern over the "Islamic factor" and Iranian influence has resulted in its guarded support for, or toleration of, Turkey's influence in Central Asia, Russia will oppose a sustained political and, especially, a significant military influence by Turkey in Central Asia. Moscow's determination to prevent the expansion of the Western strategic and military reach in Central Asia and the Caucasus will be a particular consideration in Russia's attitudes toward the extent and nature of Turkey's role in the region, especially in view of its membership in NATO. Furthermore, Moscow is not interested in seeing any supranational ideology, be it Pan-Islamic or Pan-Turkic, become dominant in its Central Asian backyard. This sentiment is shared by key Central Asian states, including Kazakhstan and Uzbekistan, two states with their own Asiatic ambition of becoming the center of regional gravity. The Central Asian states, while welcoming relations with Turkey, are wary of too close a connection that might negatively impact their sensitive relations with Moscow. Turkey's relations with Central Asia will thus be decided by a symbiosis of its potential and its constraints, the mix of which will also be subject to ever-evolving dynamics beyond its control.

Iran and Central Asia: Opportunities and Constraints in the "Muslim North"

Iran, even in the absence of the Soviet threat and its historical value as a buffer, continues by reason of geography to occupy a critical role in the region. This factor, regardless of other considerations, has placed Iran at the heart of the geopolitics of the Central Asian/Persian Gulf region. Geography makes Iran one of the most important contiguous neighbors of Russia/the CIS (Commonwealth of Independent States), and especially Central Asia in the "southern flank." It borders Azerbaijan and Armenia, shares the Caspian Sea with Russia and Kazakhstan, and has a long border with Turkmenistan. Iran, like Turkey, has followed an activist policy toward both Central Asia and the Caucasus.

Iran's geographical position presents Central Asia with the significant potential of developing an outlet to the open sea through the Persian Gulf. Grandiose agreements along the lines of building a modern version of the Silk Road have been signed between Iran, Turkmenistan, Kazakhstan, and China. (Russia/the CIS might, after all, have an outlet to a warm-water port!) The ambitious gas pipeline project, with an estimated cost of $12 billion, to carry Turkmen and Iranian gas to Europe via Iran, Azerbaijan, and Turkey is a further indication of Iran's transit value in addition to its economic interest in Central Asia.

Iran's initiative in providing the political support for the inclusion of the Central Asian states in the Economic Cooperation Organization (ECO), which took place during the February 1992 summit in Tehran, was the beginning of Iran's diplomatic offensive in this area. In addition, Iran has sponsored the Organization of Caspian Sea Littoral States with the cooperation of Turkmenistan, Kazakhstan, Azerbaijan, and Russia and has participated in the Ashkhabad summit, which brought together the CIS's "Asian bloc" and the presidents of Turkey, Iran, and Pakistan. Iran's special relationship with Tajikistan underscored the significance of "Iran's cultural world" in attracting the Persian-speaking republic in spite of the fact that the Tajik population is predominantly of Sunni persuasion. Iran has also signed more than 150 economic, transit, political, and cultural agreements in Central Asia and is active in providing aid to Tajikistan, Turkmenistan, and Kyrgyzstan.

A nine-day tour of Central Asia in October 1993 by Iran's president, Hashemi Rafsanjani, signified the continuous Iranian interest in the region. Numerous agreements and protocols were signed in areas of cultural exchange, trade, energy, banking, and transportation with Kazakhstan, Uzbekistan, Kyrgyzstan, and Turkmenistan. In Kazakhstan, a thirteen-article agreement was signed by Rafsanjani and Nazarbaev, according to which in addition to the establishment of transportation links between the two countries through air, railroad, and sea freight, the two sides agreed on cooperation in space technology. Emphasizing a bilateral effort to enhance cooperation in the ECO and the Organization of Caspian Sea Littoral States, Iran and Kazakhstan signed an oil agreement envisioning the export of two to five million tons of crude oil to Iran beginning in 1994.[8] According to Nazarbaev, Iran will soon become a major importer of Kazakh farm products and a key transport link in Kazakhstan's access to the Persian Gulf.[9]

In Uzbekistan, after meeting with the Iranian president and signing a number of agreements on trade, energy, and transportation, Islam Karimov, the Uzbek president, referred to the visit as signifying "a new page" in the relationship between the two countries.[10] As the key advocate of an "anti-Islamic" strategy in Central Asia, Karimov's attitude toward Iran has so far been at best cautious, when not hostile. Championing the cause of secularism, the Uzbek leadership repeatedly pointed to the Islamic threat emanating from Iran and Afghanistan in the post-Soviet period, with particular reference to Tajikistan. While the real "culprit" seemed to be the instability of the Afghan-Tajik border, Uzbekistan has not been able to overcome the temptation of occasionally utilizing its anti-Iranian rhetoric for both domestic and external purposes. It is worth mentioning that Tehran, in spite of the domestic criticism that the Iranian press leveled against the Foreign Ministry,[11] has so far overlooked this aspect of the Uzbek posture and has continued to cultivate the further expansion of relations. The Iranian reluctance to take the Uzbek posture seriously might indicate a level of commitment to a patient policy and Tehran's hope for an eventual atrophy of the notion of the Iranian threat, not only in Uzbekistan but in the region as a whole.

In Kyrgyzstan, President Askar Akaev, who had shared similar perceptions of Iran, termed the visit of the Iranian president and the opening of the embassy in Bishkek a "unique event" in the history of his country.[12] Among a package of thirteen documents signed between the two countries, the provision of Iranian credit to establish a joint project for the supply of three hundred to four hundred megawatts of electricity via the Turkmen city of Mary to the Khorasan Province, and the Iranian commitment to provide credit (through the Islamic Bank) for building a number of hydroelectric stations in the Narya River, are the most significant.[13]

Turkmenistan perhaps occupies the most important place in Iranian foreign policy priorities in Central Asia. As a neighboring state (both by sea and land) with a similar cross-border ethnic makeup and a special relationship with Russia in areas of security, Turkmenistan is Iran's key strategic Central Asian neighbor. In addition to its strategic importance, Turkmenistan presents Iran with the most practical and significant prospects for economic cooperation, especially in areas of energy and transportation linking Central Asia to Iran and the Persian Gulf. The recent visit by Rafsanjani reflected these two important components of relations between Ashkhabad and Tehran. According to a memorandum of understanding, the two countries agreed to the construction of a Turkmen-European gas pipeline, with a maximum capacity of thirty-one billion cubic meters per year, to pass through the northern part of Iran.[14]

The construction of the Sarakhs-Mashhad railway is at the heart of the project of revitalization of the new "Silk Road," which will connect the Central Asian railroad network, Europe, and the Persian Gulf via Iran. More than 160 kilometers of the railroad hve been constructed, and the project, according to recent reports, will be operational in 1996.[15] Iran and Turkmenistan have also agreed to use the Caspian Sea Littoral States Organization as an effective framework for multilateral cooperation and the establishment of a regime for tackling the issues of sovereignty over the resources of the Caspian Sea. More specifically, the two sides opposed any unilateral decision by any member state to undertake resource exploitation.[16] This announcement in the recent communiqué was a clear response to a recent Kazakh initiative for exploration of oil in the Caspian Sea that would involve key Western oil companies.[17] Beyond economic, cultural, and diplomatic activities, so far the key parameter that has defined Central Asia's relations with Iran has been the role of Islam, or more particularly, the controversies and discussion surrounding the ideological intent of Iranian foreign policy in the region. This issue has been the undercurrent of Iranian–Central Asian relations since the collapse of the USSR, and thus demands further exploration.

The "Islamic factor" has been the most critical component of Iranian foreign policy since 1979 and will continue to affect Iran's position in the new geopolitics of the region more than any other issue. Seldom has a country with such relatively limited resources been the object of such intense fear of ideological and political influence by so many diverse actors—Russia, Turkey, India, Saudi Arabia, Israel, the United States, and the new Central Asian republics, to name just a few. Real or imagined, exaggerated or not, the "Islamic factor" has become the defining concept in relations among Iran, the CIS, and other states in the region.

The inability of Iran to mechanically export its revolution abroad for the last thirteen years; the specific obstacles facing Iran and influencing Islam in Central Asia, including the fact that the absolute majority of the Central Asian population is Sunni; the fact that more than 90 percent of the agreements signed between Iran and the Central Asian republics are of an economic nature; and the fact that Saudi Arabia and Pakistan are more active than Iran in Islamic religious propagation in Central Asia probably point to a degree of exaggeration, if not hysteria, over the seemingly unlimited Iranian ability to export Islamic revolution on such a large and grandiose scale.

Central Asia's attitudes toward Iran have thus been affected to a large extent by the complexity and limitations imposed by the "Islamic factor" over bilateral relations. Fear and rejection of the "Iranian model" are being aired by all the Central Asian leaders. In fact, the political fight against the Islamic opposition in Central Asia is being carried out with the effective use of the threat of the "Iranian model." Not only has this fight justified the political repression of pro-Islamic forces in Central Asia, but the struggle against "Islamic fundamentalism" has also been a selling point of these republics in relations with the Western world. Conscious of the U.S. concern over this issue—a point reiterated by American officials visiting the region—the Central Asian leaders are eager to capitalize on their anti-Islamic, "pro-secular" stand to achieve a closer relationship with the West and especially to obtain economic aid. "Kazakhstan will act as the barrier to the path of Islamic fundamentalism," declared President Nazarbaev.[18] Ironically, none of the Central Asian republics are truly democratic, and their presidents are all former Communist Party members, yet they act as champions of democracy against the "threat of Islam," in the same way dictatorships of the Third World appealed to and obtained aid from the West in their fight against communism.

The Tajik civil war and the dynamics of the Russian, Central Asian, and even Western reactions to it were a microcosm of the so-called Islamic factor. Military intervention in Tajikistan by Russia, Uzbekistan, and the CIS, in spite of the complexity of the civil war, was nevertheless reduced to a war against Islamic fundamentalism that was nurtured and supported by its external sources, Iran and

Afghanistan. The consolidation of a Russian military and political presence and the enhancement of Uzbekistan's role as "regional policeman" in Central Asia (especially vis-à-vis Tajikistan and Kyrgyzstan) were accompanied by Western acquiescence. While the role of militant groups inside Afghanistan in providing support or shelter to Tajikistan's pro-Islamic forces was the only real "external dimension" of the Tajik conflict, Iran was given much more prominence in shaping the Islamic debate on Tajikistan. During the recent visit of President Rafsanjani, the issue of Tajikistan played a prominent role in diplomatic negotiations in all the Central Asian capitals. In all the communiqués issued during the visit, the issue of Tajikistan and promises of "nonintervention" in the internal affairs of that country were predominant.[19] Most significant was President Karimov of Uzbekistan's suggestion that Iran, along with other states of the region, should participate in the conflict resolution. In this regard, Uzbekistan's suggestion of establishing a "standing committee on security cooperation and stability in Central Asia," with headquarters in Tashkent, has been welcomed by Tehran.[20] Iran's mediating role in the Tajik civil war in early 1994 resulted in a modest though potentially significant breakthrough when the opposition agreed to participate in multilateral negotiations with the Tajik government in Tehran. Thus the Central Asian states, while continuing to raise questions about the Iranian Islamic impact in the region, are willing to utilize Iran's diplomatic weight and Tehran's Islamic credentials to settle regional conflicts, especially the ongoing civil war in Tajikistan.

Iran and Central Asia: The Russian Factor

Though a complete discussion of Russian-Iranian relations is beyond the scope of this chapter, it is important to note the impact and relevance of this relationship for Central Asia's relations with Iran. For example, Russian policy in Central Asia is to some degree being formulated and conceptually driven and articulated by the Islamic factor and the influence of the Iranian model. Russia's relations with Iran have also been negatively affected by Iran's Islamic character, an issue not new to their relationship, since the concern over Iran's brand of Islamic revolution and its possible impact on Moscow's interests predate Yeltsin's Russia and go back to the Brezhnev era. Russia has a major stake in the overall containment of the ideological threat of Islam both in Russia itself and in Central Asia. On this issue, while the Russian leadership, especially the Foreign Ministry, follows the U.S. perspective and lead on containment of Iran, more centrist forces within the foreign policy establishment—though concerned over the Islamic factor—advocate a more subtle policy toward Tehran.[21] Moscow fears the implications of the total alienation of Iran and is cognizant of the fact that a more balanced Moscow policy in Central Asia (and also the Persian Gulf) needs a more balanced policy toward Tehran. Yeltsin's policy toward Iran, though lacking the relative warmth of the last three years of the Gorbachev era, has maintained the key aspects of the relationship, including the important and controversial agreements on arms sales to Iran. The approximately $2 billion arms package to Iran reportedly includes T–72 tanks, high-performance MiG–29s, SU–24s, surface-to-air missiles, and three submarines. According to recent reports, a $1 billion sale was estimated for 1992.[22]

Warmer relations with Iran are also part of an independent policy that Moscow intends to adopt in the Middle East, one that might contradict U.S. policy preferences.[23] The coldness of the initial phase of relations with Iran under Yeltsin may have come to an end. Relations with Iran, and especially on the issue of arms sales, have become a noticeable indication of a subtle tension between Russia and the United States and their respective policies in the Persian Gulf. The decision of the Russian government to sell three submarines (Kilo-class) to Iran in spite of the U.S. government's opposition was an important indication in this context. Even the threat of linking the U.S. humanitarian aid package to the termination of Russian arms sales to Iran was politely ignored by Moscow. Yeltsin's apparent criticism of Piotr Olegovich Aven, Russia's minister of foreign economic affairs, as the main culprit in entangling Russia in the Iran arms deal, seemed a diplomatic maneuver designed to deflect U.S. criticism. According to a Russian Foreign Ministry official, the sale of arms to Iran was one of the obligations left to the Russian government by the treaties signed between the former USSR and Iran under Gorbachev. He also pointed to the financial significance of the arms deal, especially the sale of submarines, which alone will exceed "the worth of U.S. aid by three or four times."[24]

A commentary by the Radio Moscow Persian program delivered a blunt critique of the U.S. position on the arms issue, discussing U.S. inconsistency in, for example, sales of arms to Saudi Arabia: "The Americans should not hope that Russia will relinquish its interests in its deal with Iran, namely in the sale of arms to that country because of Washington's anti-Iranian stance."[25] *Le Monde* recently reported a more substantial arms package deal worth $11 billion that might include "12 TU–22M supersonic Backfire Bombers and 100 combat aircraft, including 48 MiG–29s, 4 MiG–31s, 24 MiG–27s, and 2 IL–76 airborne warning and command/control radar aircraft."[26] In addition to arms sales, the possibility that Russia might build a nuclear reactor in Iran worth $300 million has been an issue of concern for the United States.[27]

It is important to note that the issue of arms sales to Iran, regardless of its true scope, should be analyzed or considered within the broader context of Russia's financial need and its determination to remain competitive in the area of arms exports. The fact that the United States has taken a leading role in arms sales to the Middle East has also undermined the moral weight of America's call for Russian restraint. The Russian leadership in fact has recognized and is resigned to the existence of a level of tension between Russia and the United States on the issue of arms sales, a tension clearly noticed and predicted in the draft version of Russia's foreign policy concept developed in November 1992.[28] Moscow's determination to enhance its position in the Persian Gulf was reiterated in a recent announcement by Aleksandr Shokhin, Russia's deputy prime minister, concerning Russia's upcoming arms deals with some Persian Gulf states, including the United Arab Emirates, Qatar, and possibly Kuwait, which include an array of sophisticated weapons such as T–80U tanks, S–300PMU VI air defense missiles, and SU–35 fighter planes.[29]

In addition to these arms deals, Russia will resume its naval presence in the Persian Gulf in the near future, a fact underscoring the renewed Russian interest in its southern flank. A more visible Russian political presence in the Persian Gulf will not only be consistent with Moscow's desire to remain engaged in the region but will further facilitate Russia's relations with Central Asian states. Moscow will attempt to cultivate the support of the Persian Gulf states in resolving Central Asian issues, including containment of Iranian/Islamic influence, a dynamic that further points to the interdependence of the geopolitics of Central Asia and the centrality of Iran's position in this context. Beyond their financial significance, the arms sales to Iran have a political role in maintaining a "correct" though not a close relationship between Russia and Iran. Iran remains the most strategically important country in the "southern flank" and an important balance against Turkey. Russia's interest in the Caucasus, especially in defense of Armenia and in checking the excessive influence of Turkey in the region, will be best served by a better relationship with Iran. A recent report on the Russian national security concept for 1994 portrays Iran as Russia's partner in South Asia. The report advocates the "maintenance of a certain balance" between Turkey and Iran, especially as "the West would obviously give preference to Turkey as a member of NATO."[30] Moscow is also carefully watching the little-noticed but potentially significant relations developing between Ukraine and Iran.[31] In addition to an ambitious three-thousand-kilometer pipeline project (a joint project involving Iran, Azerbaijan, and Ukraine),[32] Tehran and Kiev have signed several agreements for arms sales to Iran, including tanks, bombers, and possibly submarines.[33]

Moscow's influence in Iran will also be instrumental in "regulating" Iranian–Central Asian relations. Lack of overt hostility toward Iran might also relieve Moscow of the pressure of Iran's Islamic propaganda campaign against Russia and will help to improve the image of Russia as being more evenhanded toward Islam.

An overview of Central Asian–Iranian relations in the last two years points to several key characteristics and constraints. First, the key preoccupation of Iran in the region has been and will remain regional stability. As the most contiguous regional power, and one that would be significantly affected by the spillover of ethnic conflict, stability is paramount. The multiethnic nature of the Iranian state has injected an "ethnic encirclement" component to the Iranian foreign policy thinking that will continue to inform Tehran's policy toward Central Asia and the Caucasus.

Second, the desire for stability is accompanied by a determination to remain involved in regional politics, avoid deliberate or imposed isolation, and affect the key dynamics of the region's interstate relations that have a direct impact on Iranian interests. Iran's activism will be pursued through bilateral (i.e., state to state) and regional/multilateral (i.e., ECO, Caspian Sea Littoral States Organization) cooperation. The key instrumentalities of Iranian foreign policy will focus on Iran's advantageous position as a transportation link and its diplomatic weight in conflict resolution and regional stability.

Third, Iran's policy toward Central Asia, and for that matter, toward the newly independent states of the former USSR, remains to a considerable degree "Moscow-centric." Iran's determination to break the U.S.-led containment strategy in the Persian Gulf region, the need for an alternate source of arms, the need for a balance of power against Turkey, and Russia's sheer geopolitical power dictate such a focus. Russia's and Iran's mutual needs in regulating both Caucasian and Central Asian geopolitical subsystems will inform Iran's policy in Central Asia. The challenge to Russian-Iranian relations, however, will be the degree to which Moscow follows the U.S. lead in relations with Iran, and the scope and depth of Russia's desire for a neoimperial reassertion in Central Asia and the Caucasus. An overt pro-U.S. policy against Iran and/or an aggressive policy toward Central Asia will complicate the relations between Moscow and Tehran, possibly rekindling a dramatic shift in Iranian–Central Asian relations. The most important characteristic of this shift will be Iran's utilization of its "revolutionary credentials" as a countervailing instrument in Central Asia and the Caucasus.

Fourth, cognizant of its own limitation in exporting its "revolutionary" model and aware of the supersensitivity of all regional actors, Iran will emphasize the cultural rather than the political aspect of its Islamic credentials. A survey of the content of Iranian–Central Asian relations indicates a marked emphasis on cultural ties and activities that are devoid of a direct political dimension.[34] This emphasis on "cultural Islam" it is hoped will reduce the anxiety of Central Asian states while helping to maintain Iran's unique characteristic as an Islamic state.

Finally, as in the case of Turkey, Iranian policy in the region and Central Asian expectations from Tehran will be informed by the twin realities of Central Asian life: the continuous dependency on Russia and Iran's limited economic capability to provide a significant alternative source of security for the new states.

Afghanistan: The Impact of a "Nonstate Actor"

Among the regional actors, Afghanistan occupies a particularly unique and important place. This importance results not from the deliberate ambitions of Afghanistan as a state in influencing the international politics of Central Asia but from the withering away of its statehood and the resulting fluidity of the

Afghan factor as it affects Central Asian dynamics. Afghanistan, a fragmented polity with multiple sovereignties (a condition that may not change in the near future), should be treated essentially as a nonstate actor. It provides various groups of Afghan mujahideen with a staging ground to infiltrate neighboring Tajikistan and make their influence felt through various cross-border ideological (Islamic) and ethnic solidarities. Afghanistan has been the source of material and ideological support for the Islamic and democratic anticommunist tendencies in the ongoing civil war in Tajikistan. It has also been the "safe haven" of thousands of civilian refugees and armed groups belonging to the Islamic/democratic coalition that lost the power struggle to the pro-Moscow, pro-communist faction in Dushanbe in late 1993.

Afghanistan provided both the Russian and the Uzbek governments with the justification for their regional and extraregional security concerns and their military and political intervention in Tajikistan and in Afghanistan itself. The entire political logic behind the Islamic threat, in Russia's current threat perception and foreign policy formulation, has focused on the Tajik post-Soviet experience and the assertion that the Tajik opposition is fundamentally externally inspired and sustained. While Iran's role has been repeatedly mentioned or implied, it is the Tajik-Afghan cross-border activities that have provided the Russian leadership with its ammunition on both the regional and global level to justify Russia's military presence in Tajikistan, especially in the border areas. According to Kozyrev, the Tajikistan-Afghanistan border constitutes "the border of the CSCE," "the border of the civilized world" on behalf of which Moscow is compelled to perform a stabilizing politico-security role.

Uzbekistan's role in the Afghan-Tajik dynamics has also been significant.[35] In fact Uzbekistan has been a key regional supporter of the Russian military activities in the ongoing Tajik conflict. While the Russian military, including the 201st Rifle Division and the border guard, provided the bulk of military support, the Uzbeks have played an important role, both in their paramilitary backing for the pro-communist factions and more significantly, in Afghanistan by bridging behind the opposition's logistic route. This bridging, which has enjoyed Russian support and blessings, has focused on political and material support for General Abdul Rashid Dostam, the pro-Uzbek Afghan military leader whose early defection in 1991 precipitated the collapse of the Najibullah regime in Kabul. General Dostam controls both a significant part of northern Afghanistan and a considerable amount of Russian-made weaponry left behind in the aftermath of the Soviet withdrawal. He has been supported, at first covertly and now overtly, by the Uzbek regime as a countermeasure against operations staged from Afghanistan by the Tajik opposition. This support has continued in spite of repeated official complaints by Rabbani's government in Kabul.[36] Small Uzbek boats have repeatedly used the Amu Darya River to penetrate Afghan territory and supply arms to friendly Afghan groups.[37]

The Russian-Uzbek intervention in Tajikistan and its spillover into Afghanistan point to an important element of continuity in the relevance of Afghanistan for Central Asian dynamics in the post-Soviet period. Of the key Soviet motivations for intervention in Afghanistan in the 1980s, one has survived the collapse of the Soviet Union and communism, namely, the concern over the ethnoreligious instability of Central Asia. Russia has continued to attach great geopolitical and security significance to Central Asia's border with Afghanistan—a significance that has encouraged a range of policies, including direct and indirect military presence and intervention. It is interesting to note that while the Soviet military presence in Afghanistan lacked any international acceptability, the current Russian-Uzbek operation in the Tajik-Afghan theater has enjoyed and probably will continue to enjoy international acceptance or acquiescence from major regional and international actors (possibly with the exception of Iran).

It is worth mentioning that the impact of Afghanistan as a nonstate actor goes beyond its immediate impact on Tajikistan and Central Asian security and political dynamics and also includes the involvement of the Afghan mujahideen in other regional conflicts throughout the former USSR, especially the Caucasus. Afghan volunteers have been fighting alongside Azeri forces against Armenia inside the occupied territories of Azerbaijan since mid-1993 and could possibly become involved in any prolonged anti-Russian war in the North Caucasus, especially in the Chechen Republic. The growing tension between the Dudaev regime and the increasingly heavy-handed policies of Yeltsin in the Chechen Republic have led to the possibility of an "internationalized" conflict that might include participation of "Muslim volunteers" from regional Islamic countries, including Afghanistan. Chechen officials reportedly have already established a direct connection with Ahmed Shah Masud, one of the key leaders of the Afghan mujahideen, and the two sides have considered the possibility of military training of Chechen soldiers by the mujahideen.[38]

Global Powers and Central Asia:
Russia, the United States, and China

A general review of Russian–Central Asian relations, both in concept and policy, since the collapse of the Soviet Union indicates a clear Russian desire and determination to protect its historical politico-strategic interest in the region. A detailed discussion of Russian policy in Central Asia is beyond the scope of this study and has been dealt with elsewhere,[39] but what is clear is that notwithstanding the Soviet collapse and the emergence of new independent states, Russia has been able to recover lost ground and fill the strategic vacuum in the region. Two years since the collapse of the Soviet empire, Russia has been able to consolidate its position in Central Asia through such measures as the Treaty on Collective Security, signed on 15 May 1992 in Tashkent, and a series of bilateral security agreements with the new states. "The post-union space has been preserved, with the Russian Federation managing to retain the role of leading power capable of not only persuading others, but also dictating its will if necessary."[40] Thus, the entire border of the former Soviet Union with the states of the traditional "southern flank" (i.e., Iran, Afghanistan, Turkey) remains within the realm of Russian and CIS strategic reach.[41] The treaty-bound presence of Russian troops in the border republics points to a major element of strategic continuity in the midst of incredible changes in the region.

What are the key ingredients of this apparent continuity? Why can Russia, in the midst of its own deep political and economic crisis, still count on the preservation of its historical interests and influence in Central Asia and the Caucasus? The answer to this question lies in the enduring military, economic, and political legacies of the Soviet Union. On all three levels, military, economic, and political, while the Russian "center" has been severely weakened, it still outweighs the Central Asian and Caucasian "periphery." Between the Russian "center" and its Asian "periphery" there exists a level of structural dependency/interdependence that will not be ended overnight.

Militarily, Russian foreign policy is increasingly driven by the belief that Russian security is inherently linked with the security of its Asian periphery, and thus the vigorous protection of Russia's historical geopolitical environment will remain fundamental to Russia's foreign and security policy. In fact, a careful reading of Russian thinking and policy points to the emergence of what could be termed the Russian Monroe Doctrine in Central Asia and the Caucasus. The draft version of Russia's "foreign policy concept," developed in November 1992, called the protection of the "Commonwealth's outer border" an urgent task in Russian foreign policy. The document also clearly warns other international actors, regional or otherwise, that "Moscow will vigorously oppose all attempts to build up the political, military presence of third countries in the states adjoining Russia."[42]

This "strategic denial"[43] to "third countries" accompanies, and fits conveniently within, Moscow's vision of Russia's role as the sole guarantor of security in the territory of the former Soviet Union.[44] In an important speech to the Civic Union on 28 February 1993, Yeltsin reiterated that "stopping all armed conflicts on the territory of the former USSR is Russia's vital interest. The world community sees more and more clearly Russia's special responsibility in this difficult undertaking." Cognizant of charges of neoimperialism and also of the importance of the UN in the post–Cold War world, Yeltsin went on to ask for international endorsement and legitimization of Russia's interest, stating that "the time has come for distinguished international organizations, including the UN, to grant Russia special powers as a guarantor of peace and stability in the region of the former USSR."[45]

The Russian military has to overcome enormous political, financial, and organizational difficulties to be able to perform its function in Moscow's overall strategy.[46] Yet Russian military activism in Tajikistan and similar efforts in other regions, including the creation of the North Caucasus Military District, indicate the commitment of the Russian military to perform its role.[47]

It is important to note that Russian policy in Central Asia, contrary to the conventional wisdom advocated by many Western analysts, has little to do with the controversy between "democratic" and "nationalist" elements in Moscow (a controversy now further fueled by the strong showing of the conservative elements such as Zhirinovsky in the recent Russian parliamentary elections). Whether expressed by Foreign Minister Andrei Kozyrev, "the democrat," who perceives Russia's role as the civilizer of the "primitive Asian wing,"[48] Vladimir Lukin, the "postmodern" Russian ambassador to the United States, who has called for a firm hand in the Asian periphery,[49] or Evgenii Primakov, the "realist" head of Russian intelligence, who perceives Central Asia as located squarely within Russia's legitimate sphere of influence,[50] the vision of Russian foreign policy in Central Asia carries the same message. A democratic Russia, while more flexible and "softer" in approach, will display a vision of, and attitude toward, Central Asia similar to that of its tsarist and Soviet predecessors.[51] What is also particularly important is that even some of the "new" and laudatory additions to Russian foreign policy concepts, such as "support for human rights," are now couched in a flexible language primarily to emphasize protection of Russian minorities in the former republics, including those living in the Central Asian states.[52]

The Soviet economic legacy and the continuing interstate dependency further perpetuate Russia's dominant position. Not only do the new states still need each other and Russia for their ongoing flow of production and trade (on average 25 to 30 percent of the production decline in Russia and the republics is due to broken economic ties!), but equally significant, the similarity of the challenges facing economic reforms in Russia and the Central Asian states points to a level of convergence in the economic models of these states in their postcommunist transition. As the enthusiasm over Russia's experiment with overnight market transition through "shock therapy" fades into the background and Russia's new cabinet attempts a more centrist economic policy, Central Asian states find their gradualist, conservative approach toward economic reform vindicated, and may have in fact acquired a new conservative model partner in Moscow.

Chernomyrdin's "market with a human face,"[53] Nazarbaev's "socio-market economy,"[54] Karimov's "market with strong social policy" with the state as the "main reformer,"[55] and Nyazov's "socialist-market without ideology" all indicate a degree of economic interdependence/convergence not only on economic ties but also on the level of intellectual consensus for post-Soviet transition. Free from the ritualistic ideological baggage of communism, Russia and Central Asia still share some of the socialist legacies of the Soviet experience.

The political dimension of structural dependency/interdependence between Russia and the new states follows a similar pattern. As Moscow's democratic hype and its claim of becoming an agent of democratic change in the former USSR fade, the Central Asian authoritarian elite may find in the new Russia not only vindication of their political model but also a new model partner. The conflict between President Yeltsin and the Russian parliment was not a struggle between democrats and nationalists; rather, it was a struggle to determine who will rule Russia, a process that will perhaps dominate relations with the new parliament. The predominant political model preferred for Russia by most of the active political groups, irrespective of their differences, essentially values stability and a strong state as key requirements of socioeconomic reform and security. In this there is little disagreement between the Central Asian capitals and Moscow. Thus, the relative level of convergence between the Russian and Central Asian economic models in the post-Soviet transition phase follows parallel political models required to implement reforms. Furthermore, a shared political vision on the key threat to the existing order, namely, an "Islamic threat," also provides a significant common area of interest between the Central Asian elite and Moscow.[56]

The military, economic, and political dimensions of Russian–Central Asian interdependence seem even more significant if analyzed in the context of real alternative sources of competition from outside. Much has been written about the United States, Turkey, Iran, China, and others in relation to Central Asia and their attempts to fill the vacuum left by the Soviet collapse.

Theoretically, the United States and China are the two great powers that can challenge Russian dominance. Practically, however, neither power is either willing to pose or capable of presenting a real challenge. The U.S. objectives within the region include the maintenance of stability, containment of the "Islamic threat," promotion of a market economy and democracy, access to key raw materials (especially oil), and prevention of nuclear proliferation. The U.S. commitment to implement these objectives is limited, however, since Washington has focused on the most important elements, which include maintenance of stability and containment of the "Islamic threat" and nuclear proliferation (in the case of Kazakhstan). On these objectives, the interests of the United States and Russia coincide, and in view of the limited U.S. investment, an acquiescence to Russia's role, especially in maintaining stability, has characterized the U.S. policy in Central Asia (the case of Tajikistan was a clear example in this regard).[57] U.S. attempts to promote democracy and a market economy have been sporadic[58] and largely unsuccessful, since they either have been rebutted by Central Asian states or efforts have been overshadowed by acquiescence to continued postcommunist and secular authoritarianism in the region out of fear of Islamic fundamentalism.[59] The limited economic assistance by the United States and its Moscow-centric policy in this regard have further diminished the scope of direct U.S. influence in the region.

China is another regional power whose contiguity, significant size, thriving economy, and powerful military make it a potential competitor for Russia and a major player in Central Asia. China's relations with the new Central Asian states occupy an important place in shaping the post–Cold War regional order. The fact that China had already accelerated its economic interaction with the Soviet Central Asian republics by the late 1980s and its swift diplomatic recognition of the new states in early 1992 indicated the importance that Beijing attaches to the future of its interests in the emerging Central Asia.

The official Chinese foreign policy position has been developed throughout the numerous diplomatic interactions between Beijing and the Central Asian states and was particularly articulated during the April 1994 Central Asian tour by Chinese Premier Li Peng, who led the largest Chinese delegation thus far in his visit to Uzbekistan, Kyrgyzstan, Turkmenistan, and Kazakhstan. During this extensive and highly publicized visit, the Chinese premier emphasized the four principles of Beijing's relations with the Central Asian states: peaceful coexistence, common prosperity, freedom of choice (referring to the model of transition), and promotion of regional stability.[60] In pursuing these principles, China's operational strategy incorporates several general themes: promoting Xinjiang's ethnoterritorial security by forging an understanding with Central Asian states for mutual cooperation against separatist and religious movements; using Xinjiang's economic magnet for regional economic cooperation and possibly integration; confidence-building measures through reduction of military presence and, more specifically, resolution of border disputes; and a careful balance between China's Central Asian objectives and policies and its relations with Russia, a balance that, in view of bilateral considerations and global balance-of-power calculations, will reflect the strategic importance that Beijing attaches to its critical relationship with Moscow.

Chinese policy in the region since the collapse of the Soviet Union indicates a cautious and gradual policy, a posture reflective of complex and potentially explosive issues that link China's own inner Asia, primarily Xinjiang, and the new Central Asian states.[61] Issues of ethnicity and religious revivalism, in addition to the lingering problem of border disputes, are key problems that define the security parameters of China's relations with Central Asia.[62] One may add to this the problem of drug trafficking,[63] Central Asian concerns over the implications of China's nuclear testing, and Chinese economic projects on Central Asia's border that may cause environmental problems.[64]

Chinese apprehension over the increased pressure of religious sectarianism and cross-border ethnoterritorial tensions on Central Asia's border with Xinjiang, coupled with the increasingly problematic nature of the national and religious dynamics of Xinjiang itself, has contributed to China's cautious policy in the area. China's entire strategy in the region is driven by the thesis that economic prosperity will be the only viable answer to ethnic and religious conflict. Accordingly, China's relations with Central Asia have emphasized a gradual regional economic cooperation between the Central Asian states and Xinjiang.[65] In this regard, a relatively extensive trade and economic interaction between Central Asia and Xinjiang has been launched, especially in the areas of light industry, technical assistance, and communication links, comprising more than 250 joint ventures and cooperative enterprises between the two regions.[66]

China's strategy, however, has to deal with the ironic dilemma that further economic integration of Xinjiang with Central Asia may only accelerate ethnic and religious affinities, leading to separatist tendencies and ethnic conflict.

On broader issues of security, the Central Asian states (Tajikistan, Kazakhstan, and Kyrgyzstan) that have inherited the Sino-Soviet territorial dispute, given their newly acquired sovereignty, will have more difficulty in making territorial concessions to China. Further, they have decided to approach border negotiations with China collectively, alongside Russia, under the "CIS" joint commission umbrella. Building on Soviet-Chinese diplomatic efforts on border issues, the post-1992 border talks resulted in modest though politically significant progress in the reduction of border tension, including confidence-building measures such as the creation of "zones of decreased activities."[67] This progress on territorial issues includes the first official border demarcation treaty between Kazakhstan and China (Xinjiang-Kazakh frontier)[68] and initial understanding on Sino-Kyrgyz and Sino-Tajik borders. Two factors, however, will continue to affect the future or final resolution of border issues between China and the Central Asian states. First, while the breakdown of the Soviet Union has provided a better diplomatic opportunity for border negotiations, it has ironically introduced a potentially new obstacle, namely, the difficulty for the newly independent states to make major territorial concessions to their big neighbor, concessions that, given nationalistic feelings, could be particularly costly at home. Second, Central Asian reliance on Russian/CIS collective security protection was a clear though implicit message to China as to the limits of Beijing's strategic reach, pointing to another element of geopolitical continuity in the Central Asian region.

Conclusion

The realities of relations between the new Central Asian states and key actors such as Iran, Turkey, the United States, China, and others indicate that, given the enormity of Central Asian needs and the military, economic, and political limitation of these actors, Russia's chance of being the most important player remains promising. Therefore, will the 1990s witness the reassertion of Russia's dominant center in its Asian "periphery?" Are there any mitigating factors that might signal that Russia will not be able to repeat the remarkable imperial comeback of the post-1917 period?

One might argue that the presence of such a formidable superpower as the United States, competition from Iran, Turkey, and China, the Russian economic crisis, and the nationalistic-Islamic fervor of the new states have formed a powerful combination that will not allow the reassertion of Russian dominance. Indeed, these are formidable challenges. Yet Russia has not been unfamiliar with similar obstacles in the past, and in fact, Russia's power base, both at home and abroad is, in 1994, much more favorable than it was in 1917.

The key mitigating factor against Russia's reassertion of dominance in the long term will be domestic and subjective in nature, namely, the absence of a dynamic, forward-looking neoimperial vision and zeal. Russia's "great power ideology" lacks the religiously based "third Rome" theory of the tsars and the equally fanatical Marxian-utopian conviction of the Bolsheviks. The most devastating implication of the current Russian crisis is not only its economic problems but also the emergence of a national psyche that is largely shaken by doubts about its glorious past and is devoid of real hope and vision for the future. The "messianic"/"civilizing" elements of the Russian Euro-Atlanticist view is defeatist in nature, since it looks primarily to the West for salvation and inspiration. And the Realpolitik component of the Russian neo-Eurasianist perspective is inherently cynical and lacks ideological conviction, and thus it is not equipped with the visionary impulses required to supplement and inspire Russia's objective (i.e., military and economic power). Gorbachev's "new political thinking" was too little and too late an attempt to revitalize the needed ideological backup of the empire.

Will Russia's nationalism provide the ideological substitute for communism? The outdated, nostalgic, and inherently exclusivist currency of Russian nationalism, which presently inspires nationalist-communist factions in Russia, will be a dangerous and poor substitute, as it will engulf Russia in a bloodbath of various civil wars at "home" and wars of national liberation in its "nearby foreign parts," including Central Asia. In the absence of an all-embracing visionary ideology and in the context of the current deep crisis, Russia's policy in Central Asia must rely on ordinary instruments of power, that is, military superiority and diplomacy of accommodation and maneuver, a symbiosis that may prove inadequate for a repetition of the post-1917 imperial revival.

While Russia will have the overall capability and conducive circumstances to perpetuate its centrality for Central Asia, other regional players cannot be denied their participation in shaping and influencing the international relations of the region as a whole, notwithstanding their own constraints and limitations. With the exception of Russia, China will remain the most powerful regional power able in the long run to affect Central Asia's geopolitical dynamics; indeed, the real challenge of domination for Central Asian states, among the new players, may not be Iran or Turkey, but China. Though China's policy toward the region so far indicates a gradualist and "correct" attitude, more forward-looking regional ambitions cannot be discarded. Xinjiang's ethnoterritorial tension and the destabilizing impact of the fast pace of economic development, if combined with similar cross-border trends in Central Asia, may forge the "Chinese domino" in inner Asia. In this scenario, a weak Russian presence in Central Asia will prompt a more activist, if not interventionist, policy by China. It is not, thus, surprising that intra–Central Asian stability will remain a key concern for Beijing and that the "stabilizing" role of Russia as a "peacemaker" in the region (i.e., Tajikistan) will be tolerated, if not welcomed by, China.

Several themes will continue to inform China's relations with Central Asia. First, these relations simultaneously entail useful windows of economic opportunity and the risk of cross-border ethnoreligious and territorial conflicts. Second, the key domestic and cross-border threat, as perceived by both China and the Central Asian states, will continue to be Islamic ethnonationalism. This shared vision of the threat will be an important area of mutual security and political cooperation between China and Central Asia. Third, in view of the CIS security framework and Russia's determination to protect its regional interests, Sino-Russian relations will be a significant arbiter in relations between China and Central Asia. Finally, trade and economic cooperation will continue to be the engine of growth in Sino–Central Asian relations. The increasing expansion of border trade and economic activities, if unhampered by political brakes, could lead to some level of regional economic integration in the Xinjiang–Central Asian region.

Among the regional actors, Turkey will continue to enjoy a hospitable environment for political, cultural, and economic interaction. While emphasizing the central cultural theme of Turkicness, Turkey will downplay the earlier grandiose notion of creating a "Turkic world" in any institutional political form. In this regard, the limitations imposed on Turkey by absence of territorial contiguity will remain a structural impediment.

Turkey will continue to present itself not only as a "model" but also as the most effective political and diplomatic outlet for Central Asian states to the Western world. Its membership in NATO and its historically close relationship with the United States will remain an asset. The significance of Turkey's Western connection, however, will be measured by the degree of its utility for the new Central Asian states, especially in view of the fact that the road to bilateral interaction with the West need not necessarily go through Turkey. This is particularly noteworthy in areas of real interest to the West, namely, energy, where in fact Western (especially U.S.) oil companies, with the support of their respective governments, have made considerable inroads without Turkey's participation, and at times in spite of it. Furthermore, other regional Middle Eastern actors, such as Israel, have presented the value of their "good offices" in Washington as a bridge to Central Asia. Israel, in particular, not only has a much more legitimate case in terms of its effectiveness in Washington, but it has also enjoyed the luxury of being able to present Central Asia with its historical reputation in technical assistance in the areas of agricultural development and environmental issues. Some of the recent U.S. developmental aid to Central Asia, including pilot projects in the areas of agriculture and water, are in fact operated by Israel.

Finally, as it was argued earlier, Turkey's effectiveness in the eyes of the Central Asians depends on its overall image not only as a successful economic model but also as an effective regional political player. In this regard, Turkey's record as a powerful state in shaping its own immediate environment, namely, the Transcaucasus, will be compared with those of Russia and Iran and will be an important indicator in shaping its overall image in Central Asian capitals. So far, the perception of Turkey's effectiveness, especially in its claims of leadership of the Turkic world, given its performance in Azerbaijan and particularly in the Nagorno-Karabagh conflict, has been mixed. Not only could Turkey not utilize the presence of the staunchly pro-Turkish government of Elchibey in Azerbaijan to consolidate its position in the Transcaucasus, but it furthermore indicated its own limitations when it could not save Elchibey's regime from being overrun by the "Moscow-oriented" regime of Gaidar Aliev in June 1993. Furthermore, and more significantly, in spite of rhetorical solidarity and political support, Turkey almost became a nonfactor in preventing the Armenian military and political advances in the war against Azerbaijan. In addition, Turkey's historical friendship with the United States did not prevent Washington from taking a clearly pro-Armenian stand in the Azeri-Armenian conflict.

Like Turkey, Central Asia (and the Caucasus) will continue to present a significant foreign policy front for Iran in the 1990s and beyond. While Iran's historical regional focus has been toward its Arabian south, if the new states emerge as full-fledged nation-states, the new northern front might acquire an equally significant place in Iranian foreign policy.

Iran's contiguity and strategic location will be the defining factors in Iranian–Central Asian relations. While Iran can capitalize on its geographical linkage, both economically and politically, it will also have to bear the negative consequences of all the irredentist and especially ethnoterritorial and political conflicts of the new states, ranging from Tajikistan to Nagorno-Karabakh. As one of the most attractive and logical regional refugee hubs, Iran has been the main recipient of refugees from all the regional conflicts, including the wars in Afghanistan, Iraq, and, more recently, the Transcaucasus (more than 100,000 Azeri refugees are sheltered by Iran either inside Iranian territory or on the Azeri-Iranian border). Territorial instability, enhanced by a complicated ethnoreligious factor, will be a predominant Iranian consideration in its relations with Central Asia and the Caucasus.

Regional conflicts will not serve Iranian interests, and thus Tehran will promote conflict resolution in Central Asia and the Transcaucasus. Both in the Tajik civil war and in the Nagorno-Karabagh conflict, Iranian diplomacy reflects this fundamental concern. The effectiveness of Iranian conflict resolution attempts, however, will be measured against regional receptivity toward Iranian mediation and diplomacy. In Tajikistan, both Russia and the Central Asian states have guardedly welcomed Iranian mediation whereby Tehran has provided the conduit for participation of the Tajik opposition in the inter-Tajik negotiations. Given Iran's cultural affinity with Tajikistan and the Islamic overtone of its political dynamics, this republic will continue to occupy a special place in Iranian policy toward Central Asia. In the Nagorno-Karabagh conflict, the core of the Iranian dilemma will be to maintain a balance in its relations with the two neighboring states of Armenia and Azerbaijan. This dilemma not only has the potential to complicate Iranian border security, but it may further have domestic repercussions in view of the large Azeri-Iranian population and small but historically significant Armenian minority. Although historical religious and ethnic considerations dictate a pro-Azeri foreign policy, Azerbaijan's tempered attitudes toward Tehran and considerations over Turkish and Russian influence in the region have resulted in a difficult but generally "evenhanded" Iranian policy toward Armenia and Azerbaijan.

Central Asia also presents Iran with an important opportunity to break out of its regional isolation in the south, that is, the Middle East. This is particularly critical in view of continuous U.S.-Iranian hostility and Washington's containment policy, which has focused on Iran in addition to Iraq. While the overall direction of the U.S. containment policy against Iran has been stretched to cover Central Asia—as Washington clearly prefers and advocates a distance between Central Asian states and Tehran—Iran will look to Central Asia as a necessary breathing space in the north.

The competitive relationship between Iran and Turkey is viewed as a significant factor shaping Central Asia's international relations. What is not clear, however, is the operational or real significance and substance of this competition. While both Ankara and Tehran have jockeyed for position in the region, given their limitations and the enormity of Central Asian needs, the region has so far accommodated both and avoided the stark choice of selecting between the two. At times the competition seems more ethereal than detrimental, and more the reflection of the anxiety of the two regional newcomers and the willingness of the new states to manipulate. This is not to suggest the absence of competition for political or economic influence, especially in view of the international preference for Turkish influence over Iranian, but to indicate the existence of opportunities or conditions of parallel interests and cooperation. In this regard, regionalization regimes, especially ECO and cross-border business activities, including regionwide gas and oil pipelines that go through both Iran and Turkey, may in the long run overshadow or at least tame the competitive aspect of the relationship.

As far as the ideological competition between "models" is concerned, their long-term relevance for Central Asia lies less in their unique national origin, that is, Turkish or Iranian, than in their general and essential message. The attractiveness of the "Turkish model" for Central Asian development strategies consists of two general factors: its secular characteristics, which appeal to the Central Asian advocates of varying post-Soviet models (i.e., socialism with a human face, state capitalism, free market, etc., as they all essentialize the secular nature of their strategies), and its success in political and social mobilization against any Islamic alternative, Iranian or otherwise. This is particularly important, not only for the current Central Asian leaders but, perhaps more significantly, for those native political forces, including the opposition, that are weary of any nonsecular alternative for political and social development. In other words, if the Turkish model is of any long-term significance, this significance lies in its advocacy for the separation of church and state, a debate that has already preoccupied most of the Muslim societies around the world and will similarly be a source of struggle in Central Asian societies in the future.

The allure of the "Iranian model," as is the case in the "Turkish model," for Central Asia's future has less to do with its peculiar "Iranian-ness" than what it generally implies. The essential characteristic of the "Iranian model" is its rejection of secularism (the separation of church and state) as a product of an alien political culture and civilization (i.e., Western, including Russian). The long-term influence of the "Iranian model" has thus to be measured by the extent to which Central Asian societies face the central issues of the role of Islam in shaping their sociopolitical dynamics. The role of Islam as such has been categorically rejected by all Central Asian leaders and in fact is legally banned in the constitutions of all five Central Asian states. Islam as an ideology, however, will continue to have an appeal for those political forces that either through conviction or convenience tap into religion as the organizing force of social or political mobilization. The significance of Iran in this context will not only be its ability to provide useful support for such movements, but more significantly, its continuing presence as a functioning Islamic state. In other words, it is not the particularities of the Iranian model that might make it relevant for Central Asia. The Iranian model in fact is peculiar to its own sociopolitical history and culture and as such cannot be either imported or mechanically emulated. A decade of flirtation with the idea of exporting revolution to neighboring Iraq proved the bloody futility of such an endeavor.

The Islamic alternative should be analyzed within the general framework of political struggles throughout the Islamic world, of which Central Asian societies—as "deficient," "isolated," and "secularized" as they are in this regard—are part and parcel. Thus, the discussion over which model will win in Central Asia, Iran's or Turkey's, should be "denationalized." The long-term impact of these models in Central Asia would be better understood in the context of the essential dichotomy of their secular and nonsecular messages and in the future struggle of these two trends in the region, a struggle that has similarly been waged in most other Islamic societies in recent years.

In Central Asia, as in most other postcolonial Islamic regions of the world, secularism is in power, and there is little indication that in the short run this hegemony can be effectively challenged. In this context, Central Asian leaders in their fight against Islam as a particular force will be supported by major regional and international actors, including the United States, Russia, China, and Turkey. For secularism to maintain a strategic hegemony it needs, in a Gramscian sense, a societal consensus.[69] To forge this consensus these states have to fashion an alliance with those sociopolitical opposition forces and classes that essentially share a preference for secular polity and fear an all-embracing political Islam. This alliance could possibly only come with genuine democratization and power sharing, a task that has so far proven to be too challenging for the ruling elite. In the absence of this hegemonic consensus, and in view of Central Asia's nondemocratic tradition and the current practices of its leaders, an "Islamic model," though not necessarily as a strategy for development, could be utilized as an effective tool for political mobilization and change.

Notes

1. See ITAR-TASS, 18 August 1994, in *FBIS Daily Report: Central Eurasia*, 18 August 1994, p. 35. Turkey, in addition to bilateral economic projects, has also been active in providing credit and economic aid to the new Central Asian states, totaling $850 million.

2. For a discussion of these ties and a good overview of Turkey's foreign policy in Central Asia, see Philip Robins, "Between Sentiment and Self-Interest: Turkey's Policy Toward Azerbaijan and the Central Asian States," *Middle East Journal*, vol. 47, no. 4 (autumn 1993).

3. In contrast to Azerbaijan, the Turkic dialects of the Central Asian states are not readily compatible with Istanbul Turkish.

4. Alan Cowell, "Turks Find Demand, but Few Deals So Far in Central Asia," *New York Times*, 4 August 1992.

5. For example, South Korea's second-largest conglomerate, the Daewoo Group, is carrying out a joint venture with Uzbekistan to produce 10,000 automobiles per year in Tashkent, which far outweighs similar investments by Turkey in the republic. The same is true for the German Mercedes-Benz target production of 200,000 vehicles (mostly trucks) in Tashkent.

6. This is rather significant in view of the fact that one expects that Turkey will be willing to enhance its political position in Nakhichevan in competition with its main rival, Iran.

7. For an interesting discussion of this issue, see Shireen Hunter, "The Muslim Republics of the Former Soviet Union: Policy Challenge for the United States," *Washington Quarterly* (summer 1993), pp. 57–68; and Robins, "Between Sentiment and Self-Interest."

8. For reports on Rafsanjani's visit to Kazakhstan, see *FBIS Daily Report: Central Eurasia*, 27 October 1993, pp. 63–64.

9. Ibid.

10. Interfax, 18 October 1993, in *FBIS Daily Report: Central Eurasia*, 19 October 1993, p. 75.

11. A recent editorial criticized the Foreign Ministry for ignoring the hostile attitudes of the Uzbek government, especially Karimov's attitude toward Iran and the Uzbek role in undermining the Iranian effort in resolving the Tajik conflict. See "Why Go to Tashkent," *Tehran Times*, 11 August 1994.

12. *FBIS Daily Report: Central Eurasia*, 22 October 1993, p. 72.

13. Ibid., pp. 70–71. Among other notable events of Rafsanjani's trip was his extensive talk with the association of Kyrgyz ulema and his participation in the evening prayer in the Bishkek mosque.

14. Voice of the Islamic Republic of Iran (Tehran), 14 October 1993, in *FBIS Daily Report: Central Eurasia*, 20 October 1993, p. 72.

15. During his recent Central Asian tour, President Rafsanjani and his counterparts repeatedly referred to this project. See, for example, coverage of his trip in *FBIS Daily Report: Central Eurasia*, 2 October 1993, pp. 70–72, and 26 October 1993, pp. 70–73.

16. *FBIS Daily Report: Central Eurasia*, 26 October 1993, p. 72.

17. On this issue, Russia shares the concern of Iran and Turkmenistan. Though Russia has not taken an official position, Russian sources have expressed serious reservations about Almaty's unilateral move, invoking not only the Caspian Sea Organization's provisions but existing treaties between Russia and Persia (pre-1917) and the USSR-Iran as the only existing legal base of action. See Boris Vinogradov, *Izvestiia*, 9 December 1993, p. 3. The major oil consortium created for this $500 million project includes the Kazakh "Kaspiishelf," AGIP (Italy), British Gas (Britain), the joint British Petroleum and Statoil (Norway), Mobil Oil (United States), Shell (Holland), and Total (France).

18. See ITAR-TASS, 23 May 1992, in *FBIS Daily Report: Central Eurasia*, 27 May 1992, p. 52.

19. See, for example, *FBIS Daily Report: Central Eurasia*, 25 October 1993, p. 67; 21 October 1993, p. 72; 19 October 1993, p. 76.

20. *FBIS Daily Report: Central Eurasia*, 21 October 1993, p. 71.

21. For a discussion of the views of different "schools of thought" in Russian foreign policy toward the Islamic factor, see Mohiaddin Mesbahi, "Russian Foreign Policy and Security in Central Asia and the Caucasus," *Central Asian Survey*, vol. 12, no. 2 (1993), pp. 182–90.

22. Dushanbe Radio, 23 July 1992, in *FBIS Daily Report: Central Eurasia*, 27 July 1992, pp. 60–61.

23. A Russian national security concept for 1994 recognizes the significance of relations with Iran in spite of U.S. concerns. See "Russian National Security Concept for 1994," *Obozrevatel'-Observer*, 14 December 1993.

24. Interfax, 8 October 1992, in *FBIS Daily Report: Central Eurasia*, 8 October 1992, p. 15.

25. Radio Moscow (in Persian), 25 September 1992, in *FBIS Daily Report: Central Eurasia*, 28 September 1992, p. 10.

26. Cited in *Foreign Systems Research Center-FSRC Analytical Note*, 28 October 1992, p. 1. *Izvestiia* has reported that in addition to the purchase of new aircraft, Russia might provide spare parts for Soviet-made Iraqi airplanes now at Iranian disposal. Cited in the same source.

27. *Keyhan Havai*, 21 October 1992, p. 4.

28. "Frictions might emerge after all in the areas where Russia is competitive (arms exports for instance)." From the draft quoted in Interfax, 2 November 1992, in *FBIS Daily Report: Central Eurasia*, 2 November 1992, p. 12.

29. Shokhin argued for the maintenance of a military-technical balance in the region and recovery of Russia's lost position in the Middle East arms market. *Rossiia*, no. 58 (14 December 1993), pp. 1, 7. See also the interview with Viktor Posuvaliuk, director of the African and Middle East Department of the Russian Foreign Ministry, on the same subject, ITAR-TASS, 16 December 1993, cited in *FBIS Daily Report: Central Eurasia* 17 December 1993, pp. 50–51.

30. "National Security: Russia in 1994," *Obozrevatel'-Observer* (special supplement), 14 December 1993.

31. For an expression of the Russian concern on this issue, see Vladimir Mikheev, "Ukraine Chooses Foreign Economic Partners According to Principle of Reliability," *Izvestiia*, 12 February 1992, p. 5, in *FBIS Daily Report: Central Eurasia*, 21 February 1992, pp. 78–79.

32. For details on the pipeline agreement, see interview with Ukrainian gas industry official M.P. Koval'ko, in *Pravda Ukrainy*, 5 May 1992, p. 3.

33. *Izvestiia* cites a report from Reuters that Ukrainian First Deputy Prime Minister Konstantin Masik has stated that Ukraine "can supply Iran with arms as part of a four-year deal worth $7 billion." Ukraine's severe energy needs make the arms deal with Iran a

practical measure. Pressure from the United States, however, may modify the nature and scope of the arms deal. The issue of arms deals with Iran was raised, for example, by U.S. Vice President Gore in his meeting with President Kravchuk during his December 1993 visit to Ukraine. At issue was the report of an $800 million arms deal with Iran.

34. Book fairs, art exhibitions, artistic displays, and so forth are characteristic. Obviously these efforts are "Islamic" in nature, yet they are carefully scanned for their non-politicized content and emphasis on Islamic cultural and scholarly dimensions. For the most recent manifestations of these efforts, see the details of cultural ties established between Iran and Central Asian states, including Kyrgyzstan, covered in *FBIS Daily Report: Central Eurasia*, 21 October 1993, pp. 70–72; 25 October 1993, pp. 65–66. It is worth noting that on purely Islamic aspects, Saudi Arabia, Pakistan, and Afghanistan are more active than Iran.

35. For a detailed discussion of the Russian-Uzbek role in Tajikistan's civil war, see Mesbahi, "Russian Foreign Policy."

36. Abdul Wahab Asefi, Afghanistan's ambassador, has repeatedly complained about Uzbekistan's "active support" in the internal affairs of Afghanistan, especially of paramilitary organizations such as Dostan's against the Afghan government. ITAR-TASS World Service (in Russian), 11 August 1994, in *FBIS Daily Report: Central Eurasia*, 12 August 1994, p. 9.

37. ITAR-TASS, 9 August 1994, in *FBIS Daily Report: Central Eurasia*, 10 August 1994, p. 47.

38. Turan (Baku), 12 August 1994, in *FBIS Daily Report: Central Eurasia*, 12 August 1994, pp. 20–21. According to the minister of press and information of the Chechen Republic, Movladi Udugov, Mas'ud has expressed the readiness of the Afghans to participate in a jihad against any Russian aggression.

39. Mesbahi, "Russian Foreign Policy."

40. *Nezavisimaia gazeta*, 8 December 1993. In the same vein, Boris Yeltsin's remark on the independence of the Chechen Republic, "there can be no question of any kind of its sovereignty outside Russia," seems to point to the same sentiment. *Komsomol'skaia pravda*, 8 December 1993.

41. For the view of the Russian military on the issue of the CIS border, see General Andrei Nikolaev (commander in chief of the Russian Federation border troops), "The Military Aspects of Insuring the Security of the Russian Federation," *Mezhdunarodnaia zhizn'*, 9 September 1993, pp. 16–20; and Boris Gromov (Russian deputy defense minister), "Peacemaking Is Not Just the Concern of the Military," interview, *Krasnaia zvezda*, 27 November 1993, p. 3. For a general discussion, see Mesbahi, "Russian Foreign Policy," pp. 181–215.

42. Interfax, 2 November 1992, in *FBIS Daily Report: Central Eurasia*, 2 November 1992, p. 12.

43. For different versions of Russian views on this "strategic denial," see "Basic Provisions of the Military Doctrine of the Russian Federation: Russia's Military Doctrine" (official draft), *Rossiiskie vesti*, 18 November 1993, pp. 1–2; Aleksei Arbatov, "The West Will Not Defend Russia Against the West," *Novoe vremia*, no. 44 (October 1993), pp. 22–26; "National Security: Russia in 1994"; "The Position of Russia and Its National Interest" (report by the United States and Canada Institute), *Rossiia*, no. 1 (4 January 1994), p. 5.

44. On Russia's role as "peacekeeper" and "stabilizer," see "Position of Russia and Its National Interest," p. 5; Andrei Kozyrev, "The Guideline Is Russia's Interests: The New Tasks of Russian Foreign Policy," *Rossiiskie vesti*, 9 February 1994, p. 3. For similar views expressed by Central Asian leaders, see the interviews of Nazarbaev, Nyazov, and Karimov with Kazakh Radio Network (Almaty), 31 January 1994, in *FBIS Daily Report:*

Central Eurasia, 1 February 1994, pp. 1–2; and 22 February 1994; and Interfax in *FBIS Daily Report: Central Eurasia*, 25 February 1994, pp. 37–38.

45. For the text of Yeltsin's speech to the Civic Union, see the Russia Television Channel (Moscow), 28 February 1993, in BBC *Summary of World Broadcasts*, 2 March 1993, pp. B1/B3.

46. For a discussion of complexities facing the Russian military in performing this new role, see the interview with Gromov, "Peacemaking Is Not Just the Concern of the Military," p. 2.

47. For Grachev's comments on the role of the Russian army in regional conflicts and also the North Caucasus Military District, see interviews with Russia Television Channel, 28 February 1993, in BBC, *Summary of World Broadcasts*, 3 March 1993, p. C2/1; and ITAR-TASS, 26 February 1993, in ibid., 1 March 1993, p. B7/B8.

48. See Andrei Kozyrev, interview, *Le Monde*, 8 June 1992, pp. 1–5, in *FBIS Daily Report: Central Eurasia*, 9 June 1992, pp. 14–16. Also see Andrei Kozyrev, TASS, 26 March 1992, in *FBIS Daily Report: Central Eurasia*, 27 March 1992, pp. 19–20; and Evgenii Gusarov, "Towards a Europe of Democracy and Unity," *Rossiiskaia gazeta*, 5 March 1992. The Russian foreign minister makes the point that European republics of the former USSR are in the CSCE sphere and will belong to the civilized world. On the other hand, "the Asian republics belong to a different world and although at first they had illusions, they back-pedaled when faced with the reality of Asia. Those republics realized that it was better to conclude the political and military alliance with Russia in one form or another."

49. In an interview with Ostankino Television, Ambassador Lukin advocated that in addition to leverage in the security arena, Moscow should utilize its economic leverage in the "near abroad." See Vladimir Lukin, interview, in *FBIS Daily Report: Central Eurasia*, 13 December 1993, pp. 71–72.

50. *International Affairs* (Moscow), nos. 4–5 (April–May 1992), p. 82; and Sergei Shevykin, "Evgenii Primakov Stirs the Waters: World Reaction to the Russian Foreign Intelligence Service Report," *Nezavisimaia gazeta*, 30 November 1993, p. 1, in *FBIS Daily Report: Central Eurasia*, 1 December 1993, p. 2.

51. For a general comparison of existing consensus on this issue, see Arbatov, "The West Will Not Defend Russia"; "Basic Provisions of the Military Doctrine," pp. 1, 2; Nikolaev, "Military Aspects of Ensuring Security," pp. 16–20; "Position of Russia and Its National Interests," p. 5; and Kozyrev, "Guideline Is Russia's Interests," p. 3.

52. See, for example, Sergei Ordzhonikidze (deputy representative of the Russian Federation at the UN), "Report to the UN General Assembly," cited by ITAR-TASS in *FBIS Daily Report: Central Eurasia*, 13 December 1993, pp. 69–70; Lukin, interview, pp. 71–72; and Kozyrev, "Guideline Is Russia's Interests."

53. See Viktor Chernomyrdin, interview, ITAR-TASS, 5 January 1993.

54. See Besenbay Iztelevov (Kazakh minister of economics), interview, *Izvestiia*, 30 January 1993. According to Nazarbaev's own projection, the state will remain in control (ownership) of 60 to 70 percent of the industry and agriculture of Kazakhstan for the forseeable future. Nazarbaev, interview, *Profil*, 13 December 1993, reported in *FBIS Daily Report: Central Eurasia*, 13 December 1993.

55. See Islam Karimov, interview, *Rossiiskaia gazeta*, 24 February 1993.

56. The reference to the "Islamic threat" now constitutes a recurrent theme in Russian foreign policy discussions. For a recent expression of this issue, see Andrei Kozyrev's comments on "religious extremism," which were made during his visit to China in January 1994, *Izvestiia*, 29 January 1994, p. 4; and Kozyrev, "Guideline Is Russia's Interests." For a conceptual discussion on the Russian view of the Islamic threat, see Mesbahi, "Russian Foreign Policy," pp. 184–85, 188–90. It is interesting to note that Russian

officials have consistently used international settings to emphasize the Islamic threat. During the historic handshake between Arafat and Rabin in Washington, Kozyrev could not resist overshadowing the significance of the PLO-Israel accord by reminding the audience of the more important and dangerous conflict brewing in the southern periphery of Russia as a result of Islamic extremism, that is, Tajikistan and Afghanistan. CNN special report, monitored by the author.

57. The U.S. position on Russia's "peacekeeping" role in Central Asia, and especially in the Tajik case, has been recently moving toward Russia's suggestion that these forces should operate (as UN troops) under the UN (or the CSCE) mandate, a position advocated by Russia since mid-1992. The visit of Rosemarie Forsyth, a U.S. National Security Council official and head of a State Department delegation to Tajikistan on 15 December 1993, and the meeting with General Boris P'iankov, commander of the CIS peacekeeping forces in Tajikistan, was the latest development in this regard. See *FBIS Daily Report: Central Eurasia*, 17 December 1993, pp. 81–82. For Russia's official view, see Andrei Kozyrev and Douglas Hurd, "Europe Will Not Enter CIS 'Hot Spot,' Nor Will It Give Russia a Free Hand," *Izvestiia*, 14 December 1993, p. 3. The article clearly indicated the proximity of the official views of Russia and Great Britain on this issue.

58. The U.S. selective approach in support of democracy in Central Asia has been a source of tension; for example, while supporting Kyrgyzstan as the bulwark of democracy in Central Asia and giving it most-favored-nation status, the United States has singled out Uzbekistan for occasional criticism. See the coverage of Vice President Gore's trip to Central Asia in *FBIS Daily Report: Central Eurasia*, 14 December 1993, pp. 76–97.

59. Occasional U.S. support for opposition groups in Uzbekistan, such as Birlik, has been bluntly rebutted by Uzbek leaders. For an interesting account of this issue, and the "quiet diplomatic war" involving a rather frank encounter between Strobe Talbott (U.S. ambassador to the CIS) and President Karimov, see *Izvestiia*, 16 September 1993. Also see James Critchlow, "Uzbekistan and the West: Time for a New Departure," *Central Asia Monitor*, no. 5 (1993), pp. 17–21.

60. For coverage of Li's trip, see *People's Daily* (overseas edition), 20 April 1994.

61. For an overview of China's relations with Central Asia, see Lillian Craig Harris, "Xinjiang, Central Asia and the Implications for China's Policy in the Islamic World," *China Quarterly*, no. 133 (3 March 1993); and Gerald Segal, "China and the Disintegration of the Soviet Union," *Asian Survey*, vol. 32, no. 9 (September 1992).

62. See Harris, "Xinjiang, Central Asia," especially pp. 119–23.

63. "Increase in Drug Trafficking," *Holos Ukrainy*, 15 July 1993, p. 5, in *FBIS Daily Report: Central Eurasia*, 20 July 1993, p. 40; and Vladimir Berzovskii, *Rossiiskaia gazeta*, 25 November 1993, p. 2.

64. "Protestors Demand End to PRC Nuclear," in *FBIS Daily Report: Central Eurasia*, 6 May 1993, pp. 52–53; "Xinjiang Turks Threatened with Extinction," *Gunaydin* (Istanbul), 24 May 1990, in *FBIS Daily Report: Central Eurasia*, 30 May 1990, p. 72. Following his recent visit to Beijing, President Nazarbaev of Kazakhstan announced that the issue of Chinese nuclear testing in Lobnor had been raised with Chinese leaders and that Beijing had expressed its readiness for negotiations on banning the tests. ITAR-TASS, 19 October 1993, in *FBIS Daily Report: Central Eurasia*, 20 October 1993, p. 84.

65. In this regard, China's economic relations with Kazakhstan have been most significant. With a $500 million trade turnover (22.4 percent of Kazakhstan's foreign trade), China now constitutes Almaty's number one economic partner. *FBIS Daily Report: Central Eurasia*, 20 December 1993, p. 85.

66. *People's Daily* (overseas edition), 25 March 1993.

67. At the end of the seventh round of talks between China and the "CIS" Joint Commission, both sides agreed to establish a 200-kilometer stability zone of "decreased

activity along the border." *FBIS Daily Report: Central Eurasia*, 4 December 1992, p. 2; and *People's Daily* (overseas edition), 30 November 1992. See also J. Richard Walsh, "China and the New Geopolitics of Central Asia," *Asian Survey*, vol. 33, no. 3 (March 1993).

68. *FBIS Daily Report: Central Eurasia*, 28 April 1994, p. 70; and 29 April 1994, p. 60.

69. The concept of hegemony in this context implies the consolidation of power and stability by the dominant sociopolitical forces, not through coercion but by developing a general consensus among various groupings around one or several central themes. These themes define the fundamental interests and preference of the society and are reflected in its institutions, including the state, organs of power, education, and civil society. The ability to forge a general consensus on the preference for secularism (separation of church and state) in Central Asia will be a key factor in avoiding the typical dichotomy character- istic of the current struggle between states and Islam in most Islamic societies. For a general view on the issue of "hegemony" and "consensus," see John Hoffman, *The Gramscian Challenge: Coercion and Consensus in Marxist Political Theory* (Oxford: Basil Blackwell, 1984).

11

Emerging Patterns in the International Relations of Central Asia

Mark N. Katz

Developments in the newly independent states of Central Asia have engaged the attention of policy makers and scholars both in the region itself and far beyond it. This is because the future course of Central Asia's international relations will affect the interests of many nations outside the region.

There are several reasons why this region is of concern to the outside world. First, it borders on three nations or regions that have often had antagonistic relations with one another, i.e., Russia, China, and the Islamic world. Second, it is potentially a very important region economically, due primarily to its enormous wealth in oil, gas, and other natural resources. Third, the region has become important due to the fear or hope (depending on one's point of view) that it might be susceptible to Islamic fundamentalism and revolution. And fourth, Central Asia has become important because others think it is important; the region has become an arena where several nations hope to extend their own influence, and fear the consequences of their opponents doing so.

Much has already been written about the international relations of the newly independent Central Asian states. For the most part, however, this analysis has focused on the foreign policies of outside powers toward this region. The states of Central Asia tend to be treated as relatively passive actors in the foreign policy field, but outside powers seeking to pursue their various goals in the region will succeed only to the extent that domestic politics in the region allow them. An outside power is likely to be influential in any given Central Asian state only if the group enjoying political predominance there allows it to be. The groups that are, or become, politically predominant in the five Central Asian states, then, will have a crucial effect on their countries' relations with the rest of the world.

Outside powers, of course, play an important role in assisting various groups to gain, retain, or regain power. Hence, it is important to understand the goals of important outside powers toward the region, as well as how capable they are of pursuing these goals. But it is also important to understand how the evolution of domestic politics in each of the Central Asian republics can affect their relations with outsiders.

At present, there appear to be three possible paths that the political evolution of Central Asia might take. The first is the preservation of the status quo, in which the former Communist Party apparatus, however renamed, continues to exercise a monopoly on power. The second is the evolution of pluralist democracy, which does not rule out political participation by former communists or by Islamists. The third is the emergence of radicalized Islamic regimes in the area that are both anticommunist and antidemocratic.

This chapter will examine Central Asia's political evolution as well as the foreign policies favored by both ruling and nonruling parties in the region. It will then examine the foreign policies toward Central Asia of important external powers in order to explore how they might affect the region's political evolution. Last, there will be a discussion of how both the political evolution of the various Central Asian states and the foreign policies of external actors toward them interact and may affect the region's international relations.

Central Asian Political Evolution

There has been a significant degree of variation in the political evolution of the five Central Asian republics since they became independent.

Kyrgyzstan has made the most progress along the path toward pluralist democracy. Nonruling parties have been allowed to operate relatively freely, the press is free, and the Kyrgyz government has demonstrated a commitment to the protection of human rights.[1]

In *Kazakhstan*, the former Communist Party elite continues to dominate both the government and the media. Two nonruling parties have been allowed to register, and the activities of others are tolerated to some extent. There is also a significant degree of press freedom. While the Kazakh government has acted primarily to preserve the political status quo, it has also displayed some willingness to allow gradual progress toward democratization.[2]

Uzbekistan's government appears firmly committed to preserving the status quo through continued rule by communist apparatchiks, not only in Uzbekistan, but in Tajikistan as well. Only one real opposition party, Erk, was allowed to register; its candidate ran unsuccessfully for president in December 1991. After that, however, the government made the activity of all opposition parties illegal. The media is also very tightly controlled.[3]

Turkmenistan's government is even more firmly committed to preserving the status quo of continued rule by the renamed Communist Party. Unlike the situation in Uzbekistan, where some opposition party activity was permitted for a time, such activity has not been tolerated at all in Turkmenistan. The press is also very firmly controlled by the regime.[4]

Tajikistan has experienced a brutal civil war. While this civil war is, in one sense, a dispute among various regions of Tajikistan, it can also be seen as a conflict between forces wishing to preserve the status quo and forces seeking to bring about political change. The forces seeking change claim that they want to bring pluralistic democracy to Tajikistan, while those opposing them claim that these forces seek to establish an antidemocratic, radicalized Islamic regime. At independence, it was the former communists, or forces seeking to preserve the status quo, who were in power. By mid-1992, they had become so unpopular that they were driven first to sharing power with and then ceding all power to the forces seeking change. By the end of 1992, however, the forces seeking to preserve the status quo had regained power forcibly. The civil war continues, however, with the involvement of Russian and Uzbek armed forces.[5]

Central Asian Foreign Policies

Ruling and nonruling parties in Central Asia, as well as everywhere else, pursue or advocate foreign policies within the specific domestic political context in which they operate. Yet even though they may disagree on domestic issues, there are often some areas of agreement shared by ruling and nonruling parties in the foreign policy sphere. For instance, both ruling and nonruling parties seek broad recognition for their country, as well as foreign aid, investment, and trade. Additionally, both ruling and nonruling parties usually seek to maximize their country's independence and avoid foreign dominance.

Nevertheless, the disagreements between ruling and nonruling parties on domestic issues have an important effect on their respective approaches to foreign policy issues. For ruling parties in Central Asia, the primary domestic political goal is to remain in power. They all pursue a foreign policy that they believe assists them in doing so. Similarly, the primary domestic political goal for nonruling parties in Central Asia is to gain or share power. The foreign policies they advocate or pursue are ones they hope will help achieve this objective.

The above statements, of course, are generalities that are true for the foreign policies of ruling and nonruling parties in all countries. What are the specifics with regard to Central Asia?

Ruling Parties

Despite their differing attitudes toward political evolution in their respective countries, the ruling parties in all five Central Asian republics have pursued remarkably similar foreign policies. In contrast to Ukraine, the ruling parties in all five Central Asian republics have chosen not to maintain large defense establishments themselves but to rely primarily on Russia to provide them with security. Apart from Armenia, only four Central Asian republics (Kazakhstan, Kyrgyzstan, Tajikistan, and Uzbekistan) signed the 15 May 1992 Commonwealth of Independent States (CIS) Treaty on Collective Security with Russia. This agreement specifically forbade the signatories from joining alliances directed at other signatories. Through this treaty, the Central Asian signatories agreed to maintain an exclusive security relationship with Russia and not to ally militarily with any nation outside the CIS. Although Turkmenistan did not sign this treaty, it did sign a bilateral security agreement with Russia in June 1992, which also established an exclusive military relationship between the two countries.[6]

Why those ruling parties seeking firmly to maintain the status quo (in Uzbekistan and Turkmenistan, and the former communists in Tajikistan) would seek a close military relationship with Russia is clear: they want Moscow to help them stay in power. (Why Russia would want to do this will be addressed later.) A similar motive may be present for the ruling party in Kazakhstan. Here, however, the situation is complicated by the ethnic situation in that country.[7] Any effort to rapidly replace the predominantly Russian military establishment with a predominantly Kazakh one might increase secessionist sentiment within the Russian population predominant in northern Kazakhstan.

The motive for the democratizing government in Kyrgyzstan to ally with Russia is also comprehensible. Kyrgyzstan is surrounded by larger, more powerful neighbors whose governments are either hostile to or ambivalent toward democracy. Because of its remote location, it is highly doubtful that meaningful security assistance would be available from the Western democracies if Kyrgyzstan's democracy were threatened. An alliance with a democratizing Russia, then, is probably the best external guarantee for the preservation of democratization in Kyrgyzstan. The Kyrgyz government, of course, has no influence over whether or not Russia remains a democracy. If it does not, Moscow is not likely to exert much effort to preserve democracy in Kyrgyzstan; it might even help to destroy it.

In its brief period in office, the democratic/Islamic government in Tajikistan called upon Russia to intervene in the civil war there.[8] It seems to have hoped that a democratizing Russia would have an interest in defending a democratizing government in Tajikistan as well as in preventing the communist apparatchiks from returning to power. This hope, however, proved to be unfounded.

In addition to the military sphere, the foreign policies of the five Central Asian republics have been similar in other respects. All have joined the Conference on Security and Cooperation in Europe (CSCE) as well as a host of other international groupings. All have sought good relations with the West (meaning here not just the United States and Western Europe, but also Japan and South Korea), China, Iran, Pakistan, Saudi Arabia, Turkey, and even Israel, as well as others.

Even those status quo Central Asian governments that have most loudly denounced all opposition parties as being Islamic revolutionaries (whether the charge was accurate or not) have sought friendly relations with the Islamic Republic of Iran. The most striking example of this was the visit of Uzbekistan's President Karimov to Tehran in November 1992 to improve relations with that country; his visit coincided with the Uzbek-assisted suppression of the democratic/Islamic government in Tajikistan.[9]

There appears to be a twofold incentive for Central Asian governments to have good relations with Iran: (1) to dissuade Iran from undertaking actions hostile toward them; and (2) to raise concern among the many Western and Middle Eastern nations that fear that "Iranian influence is rising in Central Asia" and thus induce them to provide assistance to Central Asia—much as many Third World nations played on Western fears of expanding Soviet influence to obtain aid from the West during the Cold War.

But while seeking good state-to-state relations with Iran and other Muslim governments, the status quo regimes in particular have tended to denounce opposition parties as being Islamic and revolutionary, even if they are not.[10] In addition to its domestic political implications, this policy appears designed to deflect or mute criticism by the West and by Russian democrats of status quo regimes' internal policies. The fact that status quo regimes denounce as Islamic revolutionary nonruling parties suggests that these regimes may calculate that Western and Russian democratic fears of Islamic revolution coming to Central Asia will outweigh their desire to foster democracy in the region. And, to the extent that the West and Russia fear Islamic revolution, status quo regimes hope that external pressure to democratize will be minimized.

Nonruling Parties

In addition to the ruling parties, there are a host of nonruling parties in Central Asia that pursue a variety of political goals. There are parties that are primarily democratic, others that are primarily nationalist, and still others that are primarily Islamic. These different programs, however, are not necessarily mutually exclusive.

Each of these parties tends to gravitate toward those states with which it shares common views of what is a desirable political order. Islamist parties tend to seek support from Iran, Saudi Arabia, and Pakistan. Secular nationalist parties in the republics with ethnic and linguistic links to Turkey often see Turkey as a role model. Democratic parties seek sympathy for their cause from Western as well as other democracies.

In the immediate postindependence period, however, these nonruling parties were not hostile to external powers whose internal political structures were different from the ones they sought to build in their own republics. For example, the Islamic parties were not implacably hostile toward the United States and the West. Nor were the democratic parties implacably hostile toward Iran. On the other hand, these Central Asian nonruling parties were not so enamored with the idea of the foreign country they admired having a particularly strong influence in their republics. Secular nationalist parties, for example, which saw Turkey as a model to emulate, did not want their republics to become subordinate to Turkey. Similarly, Islamist parties did not necessarily want to see their republics become subordinate to Iran or establish an Iranian-style Islamic republic.

This last point is worth elaborating. A staff report of the U.S. Congress's Commission on Security and Cooperation in Europe noted that while many people describe the Alash Party in Kazakhstan as extremist, "its leaders maintain they favor a multi-party democracy and are opposed to fundamentalism and dictatorship of all kinds."[11] The cochair of Alash, Saltanat Ermekova, stated, "If an Islamic regime came to power in Kazakhstan, we would be the first to fight it."[12] Little is known about opposition parties in Turkmenistan, but according to one report they tended to look toward Turkey and the democratic parties in Russia as models.[13]

In a series of interviews published during the summer of 1992 (i.e., before the return to power of the communists) in the Tajik weekly *Tojikiston*, leaders from many political parties indicated a desire for close relations with Iran, with which Tajikistan has cultural and linguistic ties. Often, however, the leaders also indicated a desire for broader relations with the outside world, or for limiting ties with Iran to some degree. The leader of the Rastokhez National Front, Tohir Abdujabbor, said that his party seeks close ties with Iran, but that "we are ready to establish industrial and economic ties with any country that is so inclined." On the role of Islam, he said that "the government system, the state organs, and the prosecutor's office must not interfere with people's lives, nor have anything to do with ideology."[14] The founder of the Democratic Party of Tajikistan, Shodmon Yusuf, called for a Tajik-Iranian alliance, but he also called for freedom of religion.[15] Even while in exile in Tehran during 1994, Yusuf denied that his party favored the creation of an "Islamic society."[16] Two officials of the Islamic Renaissance Party called for the creation of an Islamic government but specified that such a government must have a parliament and leaders "chosen by the people." They called for close relations with other Muslim countries but stated, "We are not funded by any other country and we are completely independent."[17]

What this shows is that while Islamist parties opposed the preservation of the status quo, they did not necessarily support the establishment of a radical, antidemocratic Islamic regime. Alash, for example, advocates the establishment of a pluralist democracy, while several parties in Tajikistan envisioned an Islamic government being democratic. Those who fear these parties, however, claim that such moderate statements are merely propaganda intended for Western consumption and that their true aim is to establish antidemocratic, Islamic regimes.

Except for Russian nationalist groups (mainly in Kazakhstan), different nonruling parties in Central Asia have tended to have similar views about states outside the region. Just as Russia is seen by the ruling parties as an ally acting to help them stay in power, it is viewed as an opponent by nonruling parties seeking change. Nonruling parties in general have hoped that the concern for democratization on the part of Western countries would lead them, as well as democrats in Russia, to support their efforts to bring about political change. Nonruling parties see a whole host of countries—Western, Asian, and Muslim—as potential sources of aid, trade, and investment. Finally, Muslim governments are seen not only as supporters of change but also states to be kept at arm's length to a certain extent. Nonruling parties in Central Asia do not want to see their countries go from domination by Russia to domination by any other state.

There has, however, been a change in the foreign policy outlook of some nonruling parties following the reimposition of communist rule in Tajikistan as well as the political crackdown in Uzbekistan. Their hopes that Russian democrats would support parties seeking democratic evolution have been dashed. Hopes that the United States and the West would also provide assistance in bringing about political change have also been disappointed. A leader of the exiled Democratic Party of Tajikistan, Dust Muhammad Dust, stated, "It is a bitter irony that the West would prefer the old 'communist' guard to stay in power simply because the only alternative, in their perception, is Islamic fundamentalism. Nothing could be further from the truth."[18] Shukhrat Ismatulaev of the Birlik Party in Uzbekistan warned, "When democratic organizations are suppressed, the initiative can pass to extremists, and a peaceful course can [no longer] be the way to control dissatisfaction."[19]

In other words, when nonruling parties seeking peaceful political evolution are crushed, the opposition may become radicalized and dominated by leaders who seek to establish an antidemocratic Islamic republic. This may well be happening. The anticommunist democratic/Islamic parties in Tajikistan appealed for help from the West, and even from Russia, during the autumn of 1992, when they were trying to prevent the communists from returning to power. Since then, however, what remains of these democratic/Islamic parties are receiving the bulk of their assistance from extremist Islamic groups in Afghanistan.[20] Similarly, while the Uzbek government crackdown may have ended the activities of the two main democratic parties, Erk and Birlik, Muslim fundamentalist groups in Uzbekistan are apparently still active—and may also be receiving assistance from extremist groups in Afghanistan. As Bess Brown of the RFE/RL Research Institute put it, "The repression of the democratic Uzbek nationalists may prove to have removed an important moderating force from the political scene, and the country may find its conservative communist leadership facing an Afghan-supported Islamic insurgency that would finish off hopes for rapid integration into the outside world."[21]

External Powers and Central Asia

This section will examine the foreign policies toward Central Asia of the major relevant external powers. Which outcome in the domestic struggle within Central

Asia do the policies of these outside powers support, and how strong is that support? These important external actors include Russia, the United States and the West, Muslim states, and important non-Muslim Asian states. It must, of course, be kept in mind that nations do not pursue foreign policies monolithically. Often, a nation's foreign policy is ambiguous. This may be the case because there are different groups struggling for power and competing foreign policy visions are a part of their overall rivalry. Ambiguity may also occur even when a government is firmly controlled by one group that deliberately pursues a dual strategy.

Russia is still the most influential external power in Central Asia. As was mentioned before, Moscow has close ties with all the existing governments. It continues to maintain tens of thousands of troops in the region and to have close economic ties with it. The foreign policy of Russia's hardline communists and ultranationalists toward Central Asia is fairly clear. Seeking to preserve the power of the former bureaucrats and limit democratization in Russia itself, they also support the preservation of the status quo regimes in Central Asia as well as Russia's predominant influence there.[22]

While opposed to the hardline communists and the ultranationalists on most domestic issues, Yeltsin and the democrats also generally support the status quo regimes in Central Asia. Even Andrei Kozyrev—the reformist foreign minister who has been highly criticized by the conservatives—has defended Russian intervention in the Tajik civil war by claiming that it is needed to halt "the spread of Islamic nationalism."[23] Russia's democrats do indeed genuinely fear that Islamic nationalism will spread throughout Central Asia and into the predominantly Muslim regions of Russia itself. They may also maintain this position so as not to allow Russia's conservatives to credibly accuse them of being insufficiently nationalist. Russia's democrats, in other words, see preserving Moscow's influence in Central Asia to be important for domestic political reasons in Russia.

Russian democrats, then, also support the preservation of the status quo in Central Asia. In the summer of 1993, Moscow sent an additional ten thousand Russian troops to guard Tajikistan's border with Afghanistan, from where the opponents of Tajikistan's restored communist regime receive arms and sanctuary. These Russian border troops have even launched raids into Afghanistan. On the other hand, fears in Russia have reportedly arisen about the possibility of Moscow being dragged into another costly guerrilla war, as it was in Afghanistan. Apparently fearful that Russian troops will become involved in another quagmire similar to the Soviet intervention in Afghanistan, Russia has cooperated with Iran and other states in organizing talks between the warring parties in Tajikistan.[24]

Thus, while Moscow has been willing to undertake some military action in order to preserve the status quo in Central Asia, it is not clear whether the democrats or the nationalists in Russia would be politically able to undertake a prolonged and/or expanded effort to do so. In other words, Russian commitment

254 MARK N. KATZ

to preserving the status quo in Central Asia is relatively firm if the effort needed to do so is relatively modest. The more difficult the task becomes, however, the more doubtful Russia's commitment to preserving the status quo may become. And in 1994, Afghan-based Tajik rebel forces stepped up their attacks against Russian troops based on the Afghan-Tajik border.[25]

The *United States* government has actively promoted democratization in Central Asia. As was the case with other former Soviet republics, American recognition of the newly independent states of Central Asia occurred only after they agreed to abide by CSCE principles. Washington has praised Kyrgyzstan and Kazakhstan for the progress they have made toward democratization, and has criticized the lack of such progress in Uzbekistan, Turkmenistan, and Tajikistan.

Yet while Washington would ideally prefer democratization to the status quo in the region, it definitely prefers the status quo to the possibility of Islamic revolution. Thus, despite its tense relations with the status quo regimes, Washington seems prepared to work with them, as well as Russia, to prevent the coming to power of Islamic fundamentalist forces. Many in Washington—often outside the administration—warn that encouragement of democratization may be the best way to dampen the popularity of Islamic revolutionaries.[26] But in practice, Washington has been unwilling to press the status quo regimes very hard to democratize. Nor is it likely that the United States could or would do much itself to protect the status quo regimes if they were seriously challenged by Islamic revolutionary forces.

Western Europe, Japan, and *South Korea* would all welcome democratization in Central Asia, but they are less vocal about promoting it than the United States. Central Asia's economic potential is of more importance to these countries than either its political development or its strategic importance.[27] They are willing to work with all the existing regimes, whether democratizing or firmly status quo, and would definitely prefer not to see Islamic fundamentalist regimes come to power in the region.

Japan, South Korea, and most of Western Europe were able to quickly establish good working relations with the revolutionary regime in Iran soon after the downfall of the Shah. If Islamic revolutionary regimes came to power in Central Asia, it is probable that Japan, South Korea, and most of Western Europe would be able to establish friendly relations with them, too. For external powers with primarily economic interests in the region, the maintenance of order under any regime that allows them to trade and invest peacefully is preferable to civil war or other forms of disorder that would make these activities difficult or impossible. Thus, while Western Europe, Japan, and South Korea can be said to favor the status quo in Central Asia, they are not wedded to it.

China has one important security concern with regard to Central Asia: Beijing does not want to see the independent states of the region support the secessionist efforts of their ethnic kinsmen, the Uigurs, in Xinjiang—the Chinese province that borders the region. China has sought to forestall this by offering economic incentives to the newly independent states—which are not eager to annoy their more powerful neighbor anyway.[28]

The Chinese government probably prefers the status quo ex-communist regimes in the area to either democratizing or Islamic revolutionary governments. Beijing, however, has displayed a willingness to peacefully coexist with democratizing Kyrgyzstan. And just as it enjoys good relations with revolutionary Iran, Beijing may well be able to establish friendly ties with Islamic regimes in Central Asia—especially if they have hostile relations with Russia and the West. Thus, while China prefers the status quo, it is primarily concerned with preserving it only in Xinjiang—a task Beijing can probably accomplish whether or not the status quo in Central Asia is maintained.[29]

Iran has an Islamic revolutionary regime and would like to see this form of government spread to other predominantly Muslim states, including those in Central Asia. But Iranian foreign policy is complex. The Iranian leadership is confident that Islamic revolution will occur in these countries in the long run. In the meantime, Tehran seeks to establish good relations with the existing governments of the region, including those that are anti-Islamic. The Iranians fear that a premature effort on their part to promote Islamic revolution could lead to a nationalist, anti-Iranian backlash in the region that would only enhance the influence of the United States, Turkey, and other rivals of Tehran. Thus, Iran reportedly did little to assist the democratic/Islamic forces in the Tajik civil war.[30] Tehran apparently feared that the victory of these forces in Tajikistan, the one Central Asian state with predominant cultural links to Iran, would alienate the four other states in the region with predominant cultural links to Turkey.[31]

On the other hand, if status quo regimes in Central Asia become unpopular and Muslim opposition to them grows strong and turns to Tehran for support, Iran would be in a good position to assist them. Iran, then, would prefer Islamic revolutionary regimes to come to power in Central Asia but realizes that this is unlikely to occur soon. Aside from Islamic regimes, Tehran probably prefers to see firmly anti-Islamic status quo regimes in Central Asia rather than democratizing ones. For an authoritarian status quo regime that does not permit a democratic opposition to arise may serve as a better incubator of an antidemocratic Islamic revolutionary opposition than would a democratizing government that would allow nonruling parties to bring about change without resorting to violence.

Iran, however, is not the only country whose actions support Islamic revolution. While strife-torn *Afghanistan* does not have a unified government, most of the various factions there are Islamic. The democratic/Islamic forces in Tajikistan have been receiving military assistance from various groups in Afghanistan. It is also reported that Gulbuddin Hekmatyar, the radical Islamic Pushtun leader, is providing them with military aid.[32] This assistance seems to be going to the Islamic revolutionary elements within the Tajik opposition, thus strengthening them vis-à-vis the democrats, who had been stronger during their brief period in office.

Pakistan has sought to establish good relations with the existing Central Asian governments. But Pakistan is also the primary supporter of Hekmatyar in Afghanistan. If reports that he is aiding the Tajik opposition are true, he is probably doing so with Islamabad's blessing. Pakistan's policy toward the region, then, may be similar to Iran's: it is willing to work with the status quo regimes, but able to support Islamic revolution when the opportunity arises. Despite its ambitions to play an important role in Central Asia, however, Pakistan's ability to do so may be quite limited due to its relative poverty.[33]

Saudi Arabia is a conservative Muslim state that opposes Islamic revolution. It has provided assistance, especially in the form of revitalizing Islam, in the hope of limiting the influence of Iran and other revolutionary Islamic regimes and has offered its own version of Islam as a nonrevolutionary model for Central Asians.

But Saudi Arabia's policy toward Central Asia is somewhat complicated. It opposes Islamic revolution, but it also opposes democratization—which the Saudi royal family does not wish to see spread to the Middle East. The Saudi government is more comfortable with the status quo regimes of the region, but its own efforts to promote Islam may actually undercut these efforts. Many of the missionaries and other aid workers sent over by Saudi Arabia are, in fact, Islamic zealots whom Riyadh prefers to send out of the kingdom. And just as with many of the young Saudis who went to help the Afghan mujahideen when they were fighting against the Soviets, many of those sent to Central Asia have an Islamic revolutionary agenda that they hope to implement not only in Central Asia but in Saudi Arabia itself. In addition, many wealthy Saudis provide generous financial assistance to Islamic revolutionaries throughout the Muslim world, including Central Asia. Some do this unwittingly, thinking only that they are somehow "helping Islam." Others, however, oppose the Saudi monarchy and support Islamic revolution elsewhere in the hope that its success in other Muslim nations will increase the prospects for it in Saudi Arabia itself.[34] Thus, while the Saudi government may support the preservation of the status quo in Central Asia, both its own actions as well as those of some of its citizens may serve to undercut the status quo and promote Islamic revolution.

Turkey is a Western-oriented, secular, democratic state. It has sought to extend its influence in Central Asia as well as to limit that of Iran there. But while the Turkish government favors democratization, it also fears the spread of Islamic revolution. Like the United States, then, it prefers the existing status quo regimes to the prospect of Islamic revolutionary ones.[35]

The very existence of democracy in Turkey, however, serves as a model for those ruling and nonruling parties in Central Asia that also favor democratization. But democracy is not completely secure in Turkey. There have been occasions when the army has seized power. There is also a growing movement that wishes to see the secular state replaced with an Islamic regime. If either the army or an Islamic revolutionary government came to power in Ankara, Turkey would no longer work to promote democracy in Central Asia. The strong showing of Islamic forces in the Turkish municipal elections of 27 March 1994 has resulted in Russia increasing its cooperation with Turkey's secular national government. The Russians apparently fear that the rise of Islamic forces in Turkey could influence the political evolution of Central Asia as well as the Muslim regions of the Caucasus.[36] Despite its cultural links to four of the five Central Asian republics and its desire to play a large role there, Turkey's ability to affect the political evolution of Central Asia is limited by its geographic distance from the region. In addition, although Turkey's economy has grown significantly in recent years, it is not in a position to provide large-scale economic assistance to Central Asia.

The Correlation of Forces

Apart from certain Muslim states, most external powers support the existing governments in Central Asia, whether they are democratizing or firmly status quo. Except for Russia, however, external support for these Central Asian governments is not particularly strong. Russia is probably the only government willing and able to intervene militarily in support of the existing Central Asian governments. There may, however, be a limit to how much the Russian public is willing to tolerate military intervention there if it appears that a quagmire of Afghan proportions is developing. On the other hand, with the exception of support from various factions in Afghanistan to Islamic forces in Tajikistan and possibly elsewhere, external powers that want to see political change of one sort or another in Central Asia are not working especially vigorously to bring it about. Thus, despite press accounts describing active rivalry among external powers for influence in the region, the political evolution of Central Asia may actually depend more on the relative strength of the various competing internal forces there.

What can be said about the prospects for each of the possible directions— maintenance of the status quo, democratization, Islamic revolution—in which Central Asia might evolve politically both in the short term and the long term? This question requires a discussion of the relative strengths and weaknesses of the ruling and nonruling parties in Central Asia that are pursuing these alternative political paths as well as the effects of the foreign policies pursued by external powers in the region.

Maintenance of the Status Quo

In the short term, status quo regimes consisting of ex-communists can easily maintain themselves in power, especially with Russian help. The ruling parties have the power to deny nonruling parties the ability to legally and peacefully compete for power. And in case of armed struggle with their opponents, the ex-communists either possess greatly superior forces, or, as in the case of Tajikistan, can call upon external allies who do.

In the long term, however, the prospects for the survivability of the hardline status quo regimes are probably poor. This statement can be made with some confidence simply based on the fact that the demand for democratization has spread to many countries throughout the world where it has never or rarely been present before. Many dictatorial regimes, including communist ones once thought to be invulnerable, have fallen. Most of the rest are on the defensive. It simply defies all credibility to believe that the people of Central Asia are somehow different from people everywhere else, and that Central Asians prefer the status quo, prefer to be ruled by communist apparatchiks, than to make decisions for themselves. And while Russian military assistance may help status quo regimes remain in power, it will not necessarily make them more stable. Indeed, popular discontent with status quo regimes may well be inflamed by the perception that they are the puppets of a foreign power. Finally, if a status quo regime weakens and civil war erupts, Russian military involvement may not be sustainable if it becomes unpopular with the Russian public. And without Russian assistance, the survivability of an unpopular status quo regime is highly doubtful.

Democratization

To the extent that governments in Kyrgyzstan and, to a lesser extent, Kazakhstan have permitted democratization, the populace has embraced it. But where Central Asian governments do not permit democratization, it appears to have no real prospect for occurring in the short term.

In the long term, the prospects for Western-style democratization in nations with status quo regimes are open to question. While Islamic revolution appears to be far less popular than Western-style democracy among Central Asians now,[37] the forces seeking democracy could suffer serious disadvantages vis-à-vis the forces seeking Islamic revolution if civil war erupts. In a situation where Moscow was aiding a status quo regime in a war that was unpopular in Russia, Islamic states were aiding the Islamic revolutionaries, and no one was helping the democrats, Islamic revolutionary forces may be in the best position to come to power after the downfall of the status quo regime. This might be avoided if the status quo regime permitted democratization to occur peacefully—but it is highly doubtful that any of them will do this any time soon.

Islamic Revolution

Hardline, Iranian-style Islamic revolution appears unlikely in the short run not only because the existing governments and Russia are strong enough to defeat it but also—indeed mainly—because it simply is not a particularly popular ideology in Central Asia now.

If Western-style democratization is not allowed to occur peacefully, however, the prospects for Islamic revolution may increase. This could occur, as was mentioned before, if outside powers were aiding Islamic revolutionaries and no one was aiding the democrats. But the popular appeal of Islamic revolution within Central Asia might increase if its proponents are successfully able to persuade enough people that (1) Russia and the West do not want democracy to come to Central Asia and hence support the former communists' stay in power; (2) Islamic revolutionary states opposed to Russia and the West are Central Asia's "true friends"; and (3) Islamic revolution is "true democracy"—something that all revolutionaries claim about their ideology. In a situation where an unpopular, foreign-backed dictatorship is strong enough to suppress democratic opposition, Islamic revolution may look increasingly appealing to a populace that is impatient for change and disillusioned with Russia and the West. This might also be an opportunity for Islamic revolutionary governments to become involved and extend their influence, just as the Soviet Union used to do with Third World Marxist revolutionary movements at the time that the unpopular regime they were fighting against was weakening.

Conclusion

This analysis suggests that while status quo regimes are likely to remain in power, their ability to do so in the long term is highly doubtful. Such regimes tend to become unpopular domestically. And while there is some external backing for these regimes, it may prove to be relatively limited. The general publics in Russia, the United States, and the West have shown in the past that they cannot be counted on to support involvement in protracted conflict to prop up unpopular regimes abroad. It is highly doubtful that this will change in the future.

But if status quo regimes are unlikely to last in Central Asia, it is still very much an open question whether liberal democracy or Islamic revolution will come there. It is obviously too early to judge in which direction Central Asia's political future will evolve.

Ironically, the most important factor in shaping Central Asian public opinion about the relative merits of liberal democracy and Islamic revolution may be the attitude of the status quo regimes. If these governments recognize that their ability to remain in power over the long term is probably limited, they themselves are likely to prefer democratization to Islamic revolution. Under democracy, the supporters of the current status quo would have a chance to participate in free elections. They may actually win such elections and remain in power. But even if they lose, they can at least remain as a loyal opposition party with the prospect of winning subsequent elections—as the former communists have done in Lithuania, Poland, and Hungary.

If an Islamic revolution succeeds, however, the supporters of the current status quo regime recognize that they will probably not be allowed to play any significant political role after falling from power. A status quo regime recognizing its own mortality, then, is likely to work to bring about democratization, since its supporters are likely to fare better under it than if Islamic revolution succeeds. Russia, the United States, and the West may be able to help bring about democracy if the status quo regime invites their assistance in effecting a transition.

On the other hand, those status quo regimes that think they can retain power indefinitely without democratizing may actually serve to strengthen the prospects for Islamic revolution. While status quo regimes can easily suppress their democratic opponents, they are unlikely to avoid becoming increasingly unpopular domestically. People impatient for change may see externally armed Islamic revolutionaries as more capable of deposing the hated status quo regime than unarmed democrats receiving no meaningful foreign support.

As Islamic revolutionary opposition to the status quo regime grows, the latter may realize that it probably cannot survive without instituting reform. But such efforts may come too late. The attempt to institute democratization by a status quo regime when it has become extremely unpopular may be seen as a sign of weakness that may only serve to accelerate armed opposition on the part of the Islamists who not only wish to oust the regime but also prevent their democratic opponents from being able to come to power through peaceful means. Neither Russia nor the West is likely to be willing or able to successfully intervene if conditions deteriorate to this extent. On the other hand, even limited outside assistance from external Islamic revolutionary regimes may prove decisive at this stage in assisting Central Asian Islamic revolutionaries achieve their aims.

Some might argue that democratization in Central Asia is extremely risky. They argue that if the status quo regimes allowed democratization, this may simply lead to Islamic revolutionaries coming to power via elections. This, of course, is possible. But even if it did occur, the likelihood that the Islamists would be under the influence of external Islamic powers appears less if they came to power by democratic means, without Iranian or Afghan help, than if they came to power through armed struggle with foreign assistance.

While it is possible that an Islamic revolutionary party could come to power through electoral means, this does not appear likely. It is highly significant that in those Central Asian states where democratization has proceeded the furthest—Kyrgyzstan and Kazakhstan—Islamic parties have not attracted much of a popular following. The truly ominous case is Tajikistan, where the democrats held the upper hand in the anti–status quo coalition that ruled there briefly in 1992, but where the Islamic revolutionaries appear to be gaining the ascendancy within the opposition after the forcible return to power of the communist apparatchiks.

Notes

1. *Implementation of the Helsinki Accords: Human Rights and Democratization in the Newly Independent Republics* (Washington, DC: Commission on Security and Coopera-

tion in Europe, 1993), pp. 170–77; and U.S. Department of State, *Country Reports on Human Rights Practices for 1993* (Washington, DC: U.S. Government Printing Office, 1994), pp. 941–47.

2. *Implementation of Helsinki Accords*, pp. 189–204; Department of State *Country Reports*, pp. 934–41; and James Critchlow, "Letter from Almaty," *Central Asia Monitor*, 1994, no. 2, pp. 9–13.

3. *Implementation of Helsinki Accords*, pp. 205–21 and Department of State *Country Reports*, pp. 1137–45.

4. *Implementation of Helsinki Accords*, pp. 178–88 and Department of State *Country Reports*, pp. 1108–12.

5. *Implementation of Helsinki Accords*, pp. 222–32 and Department of State *Country Reports*, pp. 1076–86. For coverage of the civil war, see the "Events in Tajikistan" section of *Central Asia Monitor*, beginning with issue no. 3 (1992).

6. Robert V. Barylski, "Central Asia and the Post-Soviet Military System in the Formative Year: 1992," *Central Asia Monitor*, 1992, no. 6, p. 24.

7. For a detailed study of this issue, see Philip S. Gillette, "Ethnic Balance and Imbalance in Kazakhstan's Regions," *Central Asia Monitor*, 1993, no. 3, pp. 17–23.

8. See "Civil War in Tajikistan," *Central Asia Monitor*, 1992, no. 5, p. 8; and "Events in Tajikistan," *Central Asia Monitor*, 1992, no. 6, pp. 2, 4.

9. Christopher J. Panico, "Uzbekistan's Southern Diplomacy," *RFE/RL Research Report*, 26 March 1993, pp. 42–44.

10. Bess Brown, "Central Asia," *RFE/RL Research Report*, 22 April 1994, pp. 14–16.

11. *Implementation of Helsinki Accords*, p. 191.

12. Ibid., p. 199.

13. It also appears that what little freedom they were permitted occurred under Gorbachev, before Turkmenistan became independent. Jim Nichol, "Turkmenistan: Basic Facts," *CRS Report for Congress* (93–322 F), 16 March 1993, pp. 2–3.

14. Shahrbanou Tadjbakhsh, "The 'Tajik Spring of 1992,'" *Central Asia Monitor*, 1993, no. 2, p. 23.

15. Ibid., p. 24.

16. "Interview: Shodmon Yusuf and Rahim Musalmanian Ghobadiani," *Central Asia Monitor*, 1994, no. 3, p. 10.

17. Ibid., pp. 25–26.

18. Quoted in Marat Akchurin, "Tajikistan: Another Bosnia in the Making?" *Central Asia Monitor*, 1993, no. 3, p. 9.

19. Quoted in Tadjbakhsh, "Tajik Spring of 1992," p. 14.

20. The extent to which various Afghan groups may be providing military assistance to the Tajik exiles in their country is not clear. For a discussion of this and related issues, see Shahrbanou Tadjbakhsh, "Tajikistan: From Freedom to War," *Current History*, April 1994, pp. 173–77.

21. Bess Brown, "Tajik Civil War Prompts Crackdown in Uzbekistan," *RFE/RL Research Report*, 12 March 1993, p. 6.

22. On the foreign policy of Russia's right wing, see Vera Tolz, "The Burden of the Imperial Legacy," *RFE/RL Research Report*, 14 May 1993, pp. 41–46.

23. "The Empire Strikes Back," *Economist*, 7 August 1993, p. 36.

24. So far, however, there has been no progress in achieving a peaceful resolution to the conflict. Tadjbakhsh, "Tajikistan: From Freedom to War."

25. Margaret Shapiro, "Violence in Tajikistan and Georgia Spurs Russia's Fears of a Quagmire," *Washington Post*, 16 June 1994.

26. There is a growing literature on the United States and Central Asia. See David Hoffman, "Power Competition in Central Asia," *Washington Post*, 14 February 1992;

"Congressional Hearing: United States Policy Toward Central Asia," *Central Asia Monitor*, 1992, no. 2, pp. 21–31; James Rupert, "Dateline Tashkent: Post-Soviet Central Asia," *Foreign Policy*, no. 87 (summer 1992), pp. 175–95; and James Critchlow, "What Is the U.S. Interest in Central Asia's Future?" *Central Asia Monitor*, 1992, no. 5, pp. 27–29.

27. On Central Asia's foreign economic ties, see Sheila Marnie and Erik Whitlock, "Central Asia and Economic Integration," *RFE/RL Research Report*, 2 April 1993, pp. 34–44.

28. Bess Brown, "Central Asia: The First Year of Unexpected Statehood," *RFE/RL Research Report*, 1 January 1993, p. 29; and Keith Martin, "China and Central Asia: Between Seduction and Suspicion," *RFE/RL Research Report*, 24 June 1994, pp. 26–36.

29. Some, however, claim that China aims not just to retain control of Xinjiang, but to "bring Central Asia under eventual Chinese domination" by sending large numbers of Chinese to live and settle in the region. According to one estimate, over 500,000 Chinese have recently moved into Kazakhstan, 100,000 to Uzbekistan, and 75,000 to Kyrgyzstan. Henry R. Huttenbach, "Post-Soviet Central Asia and the China Factor," *Analysis of Current Events* (Association for the Study of Nationalities), 1 May 1994, p. 2.

30. The chairman of the Democratic Party of Tajikistan complained about the lack of assistance to the Tajik democratic/Islamic coalition not only from Russia and the West but Iran also. "Interview: Shodmon Yusuf," p. 11.

31. Panico, "Uzbekistan's Southern Diplomacy," pp. 43–44. See also Shireen T. Hunter, "Central Asia and the Middle East: Patterns of Interaction and Influence," *Central Asia Monitor*, 1992, no. 6, pp. 13–14.

32. "Events in Tajikistan," *Central Asia Monitor*, 1993, no. 3, p. 5. See also Bess Brown, "Central Asian States Seek Russian Help," *RFE/RL Research Report*, 18 June 1993, pp. 87–88.

33. Hunter, "Central Asia and the Middle East," pp. 14–15.

34. Steve Coll and David Hoffman, "Radical Movements Thrive on Loose Structure, Strict Ideology," *Washington Post*, 2 August 1993.

35. Hunter, "Central Asia and the Middle East," pp. 12–13.

36. Elizabeth Fuller, "Turkish-Russian Relations, 1992–1994," *RFE/RL Research Report*, 6 May 1994, pp. 9–10.

37. Richard B. Dobson, "Islam in Central Asia: Findings from National Surveys," *Central Asia Monitor*, 1994, no. 2, pp. 17–22.

12

The Institutions and Conduct of the Foreign Policy of Postcommunist Kazakhstan

Oumirseric Kasenov

After the dissolution of the Soviet Union, Kazakhstan became an independent actor in the international system. Considering the peculiarities of the history of Kazakhstan, its geopolitical situation, its present economic and social development, and the threat of ecological disaster, we can define the main priorities of Kazakhstan's foreign policy as follows: strengthening state sovereignty, integrity, and inviolability of borders; protecting economic interests and sovereignty over natural resources; ensuring free access to external markets; and preventing ecological disaster.

In order to ensure national security, it is important to analyze those processes that might threaten state sovereignty, integrity, and inviolability of the borders of Kazakhstan. Such threats could arise as a result of the aggravation of the social, economic, political, ethnic, demographic, and ecological situation in Kazakhstan and in neighboring states.

Controversial interstate relations might become the source of conflicts. That is why a mechanism of dialogue and cooperation with neighboring states must be created. The stability of the region and confidence among states can be achieved if mutual interests and security are taken into account.

At the apex of Kazakhstan's threat hierarchy are two geographically proximate states, Russia and China. Each possesses great economic and military potential, including nuclear weapons. If one of these states should put forward territorial claims on Kazakhstan, serious defense problems would arise.

The borders of Kazakhstan are quite open and unprotected. Kazakhstan is separated from other states by sea (the Caspian) only for a small portion of its borders. It is too complicated a task to defend Kazakhstan's borders, since they do not have any natural barriers.

Kazakhstan has formed its own armed forces, but it is obvious that Kazakhstan's armed forces will never be comparable to those of Russia or China. Therefore, it is clear that Kazakhstan will be able to defend its sovereignty and territorial integrity only in alliance with other states.

Kazakhstan prefers not to get into situations that require the use of armed forces to defend its sovereignty and territorial integrity. The solution to this problem lies mainly in political methods, economic mutual interaction with neighbors, and effective foreign policy. There are many states in the world whose security is provided precisely through policies of good-neighborliness rather than armed force.

Therefore, in the bilateral and multilateral negotiations in which Kazakhstan participates (or may participate), it must obtain guarantees of different levels of security (military, economic, ecological, etc.) in return for the promise not to resort to military force, or the threat of military force, in any form, including the use of the territory, territorial water, or airspace of neighboring states.

Similarly, external economic relations are a matter not only of internal development but of security as well. Economic interdependence should ensure national sovereignty, as in the example of Russia and Kazakhstan. Russia depends on Kazakhstan for raw materials and food, and in turn Kazakhstan depends on Russia for manufactured goods. A higher level of bilateral relations will lead to a higher level of interdependence and, consequently, a lesser threat of confrontation and conflict.

But economic interdependence must be bilateral, because the weaker side would be under a permanent threat to its economic security. Kazakhstan now depends very much on Russia for the supply of manufactured goods, oil products, and consumer goods. All of its communications go through Russian territory. Normal operation of the Kazakh economy would be undermined if Russia stopped the supply of manufactured goods, oil, and oil products or blocked communications.

Kazakhstan is landlocked and has no access to the open sea (except the Caspian Sea). For further development of trade with other countries, Kazakhstan needs to ensure the right to access to the sea through bilateral negotiations and agreements, otherwise it will depend permanently on its neighbors. Such dependence will undermine not only its economic but also its political sovereignty.

The formation of economic cooperation among members of the Commonwealth of Independent States (CIS) might be a natural basis for the realization of the "Eurasian economic space." The association of Europe and the Asia-Pacific region with the participation of the CIS would turn the Eurasian economic space not only into a zone of world economic cooperation but a zone of security as well.

The removal of the Iron Curtain greatly increased the efficiency of railway lines and air routes between Europe and the Asia-Pacific region. The position of Kazakhstan between Europe and Asia makes it possible for Kazakhstan to act as a bridge. For this purpose, Kazakhstan recommends the full use of the Trans-Asian Railway, from Beijing to Istanbul via Almaty, and the construction of international airports in Almaty and Aktaū (in western Kazakhstan), which are situated midway between the airports in Shannon, Ireland, and Singapore. The acquisition by the Central Asian states, located deep within the Asian continent, of an exit to the seas and oceans to the south through the territory of neighboring states has extraordinary significance for the strengthening of their independence and economic development.

One of the main characteristic features of our time that has not been given sufficient attention yet is the ecological interdependence of countries. The biosphere is a "unique and indivisible empire" that cannot be preserved without international cooperation. Today, humanity is threatened not only by nuclear dangers but also by ecological pollution, which does not recognize any borders: acid rain, for example, which has become commonplace in Europe and North America, and salt storms, which are caused by the shriveling up of the Aral Sea in Kazakhstan. The Aral Sea plays a dramatic role in the preservation of Kazakhstan's biosphere. The most important aim of Kazakhstan's ecological policy is the organization of large-scale, effective international cooperation in saving the sea.

The ecological policy of Kazakhstan is to pursue multilateral and bilateral agreements with the republics regulating actions in the ecosystems in the region. For the republics of Central Asia and Kazakhstan, the main problem is the use of the waters of the Amu Darya and Syr Darya, which flow into the Aral Sea. Kazakhstan can use the experience of the Danube Commission, Rhine Commission, and joint Canadian-American Commission on the Great Lakes as a guide. It is imperative for Kazakhstan to overcome bureaucracy in the field of environmental protection, to adopt ecological laws, and to forecast the ecological consequences of economic reforms. Moreover, it also needs to thoroughly analyze its natural resources, correlate them to the world's natural resources, and assess the influence of the ecological situation in one region on the ecological situation of other regions.

Although Kazakhstan is a multinational state, it was the Kazakhs who gave the state its name because it was created along primordial Kazakh ethnic lines. Nevertheless, Kazakhstan formulates and carries out a foreign policy that expresses the interests of the state as a whole rather than of any particular ethnic group, including Kazakhs.

Kazakhstan is not only a multinational state but also a multireligious one. Kazakhs confess Islam, but a significant part of the population confesses Christianity and other religions. Because Islam is not so deeply rooted in Kazakhstan, its influence is not as strong as it seems to some observers in the West. Nevertheless, Kazakhstan takes into consideration the "Islamic factor" in its foreign policy strategy, to an appropriate degree. For Kazakhs and other peoples of Islam living in the republic, there are spiritual and cultural values connecting them with other peoples of the East. For all Kazakhs as a whole, whatever faith they profess, Islam is a part of world culture.

However, there is little chance that Kazakhstan will join some sort of association of Muslim states, such as the Organization of the Islamic Conference. First of all, the heterogeneous ethnoconfessional makeup of the population of Kazakhstan could not help but hinder this: non-Muslim ethnoconfessional communities are quite large and should be taken into account by politicians. Hence, Kazakhstan cannot be ruled by one of the main political principles of the Muslim religion—the principle of inseparability of secular and spiritual power. Nor does the dogma of Islam assist the transition to a market economy; rather, it might even impede it. Finally, with the current level of development in Kazakhstan, one can hardly speak about the introduction of the laws of Shari'ah, as demanded by the principles of the Islamic state.

The Republic of Kazakhstan is a secular state, in which all religions are separate from the state and in which creed is the private matter of its citizens. Kazakhstan does not develop its relations with foreign states and international organizations on the basis of religion, but rather on the basis of the recognized norms of international law, mutually advantageous interests, and the general interest of creating a global security system.

Taking into account its difficult geopolitical, economic, and ecological situation, and its ethnodemographic composition, what then should be Kazakhstan's foreign policy priorities?

The only possible foreign policy strategy for Kazakhstan is to have good neighborly relations. Kazakhstan should maintain special relations with Russia because of the large Russian population in the state, because of the common open borders, which extend for more than six thousand kilometers, and because of historical experience. These relations should vary to include economic, political, and military relations. In this connection, the integration process in Central Asia should not be of an anti-Russian or anti-Chinese character. The estrangement of Kazakhstan and other Central Asian states from Russia could bring about a coordinated Russian-Chinese infringement and thereby pose a threat to regional security and to Kazakhstan's sovereignty and territorial integrity.

One can distinguish among different circles in the formulation and implementation of Kazakhstan's foreign policy. The first, and the most important, is its special relations with Russia. The second is its relations with Tajikistan, Uzbekistan, Kyrgyzstan, and Turkmenistan. This circle should balance Kazakhstan's relations with Russia and China. The third circle is Kazakhstan's international relations with Turkey, Iran, and Pakistan. This circle can help Kazakhstan, as well as other Central Asian republics, in diversifying its foreign connections. Such a diversification could open a new window for Central Asian states in such regions as South Asia, the Middle East, and Western Europe. The fourth circle is its relations with China, which can provide a way to the Pacific region. The fifth circle is its relations with the United States, Japan, and Europe, which can balance its relations with Russia and China in case they resort to expansionist and hegemonist policies in the region. This is the most favorable model of priorities for Kazakhstan's foreign policy, which is currently being implemented by President Nursultan Nazarbaev, who described them in his article "A Strategy for the Development of Kazakhstan as a Sovereign State."[1]

The foreign policy of the Republic of Kazakhstan is based on the strong desire for independent statehood, and its basic purpose is to keep and strengthen state sovereignty, integrity, and inviolability of borders and to create favorable conditions for achieving economic and social progress.

Foreign Policy Decision Making

The foreign policy decision-making process in Kazakhstan is not yet regular and systematic. It has been under construction since Kazakhstan's emergence as an independent state. Many important components of this machinery are in place now; others will appear in the future. Improvement in the foreign policy decision-making process is a matter of great importance for such a young independent state as Kazakhstan as it sets out to accomplish its national goals and interests on the international scene.

The president is usually the key actor in the foreign policy decision-making process. In accordance with the new constitution of the Republic of Kazakhstan, he plays the main role in the formulation and conduct of foreign policy. He determines the main goals, directions, and priorities of foreign policy, adopts measures to implement them, represents Kazakhstan at the highest level in international relations, and signs bilateral and multilateral treaties and agreements.

He has his own foreign policy-making staff within the presidential apparatus to help him in conducting current, day-to-day foreign policy moves and activity. Of course, this staff relies on the Foreign Ministry and on other governmental bodies associated with foreign affairs.

The Council on Security of the Republic of Kazakhstan was created to deal with national security matters. The president is the chairman of this body and nominates his deputy and members of the Council of Security by special decree. Among the members are the vice president, prime minister, two state advisors, foreign minister, defense minister, interior minister, and chairman of the Committee on National Security. The main purpose of the Council on Security is to coordinate activities of different governmental bodies in the field of national security. The formation of this structure is aimed at helping the president fulfill his key tasks in managing foreign and defense policy as it relates to internal security, especially in shaping an informed and coherent policy.

The Cabinet of Ministers of the Republic of Kazakhstan sets up concrete mechanisms to implement state policies in the spheres of foreign affairs and national security. The most important role it plays is in developing military industry and its conversion.

The Supreme Council of the Republic of Kazakhstan is involved in the foreign policy and defense decision-making processes in several ways: it votes on funds for fulfillment of foreign policy and defense programs; it places some restrictions on how the armed forces of the Republic of Kazakhstan can be used; and it ratifies or rejects the main international treaties and agreements.

The foreign policy and defense decision-making processes in Kazakhstan have been aptly described, in analogy with France, as an admixture of "parliamentary and executive dominance." The president of the Republic of Kazakhstan is constitutionally and practically the one who has "supreme responsibility" in foreign and defense matters and personally implements policy in these fields. As usual, there is no serious opposition in parliament to the president in promoting his foreign and defense policies. This relatively limited role of Kazakh parliamentarians in these spheres is reinforced by the fact that oversight "hearings and fact-finding missions are not a normal part of the Kazakh parliamentary system."

The Supreme Council of the Republic of Kazakhstan, once elected, creates committees. Among them are the Committee on External Relations and Interparliamentary Ties and the Committee for National Security and Defense. The main foreign policy acts and documents pass through these committees before discussion at the plenary sessions of the parliament. The Department of External Relations of the legislative assembly helps facilitate the committees' functioning.

Before the introduction of free elections in independent Kazakhstan, the Supreme Council was subservient to the chief executive. One of the reasons for this subservience was that few of its members had specialized knowledge in foreign affairs. In fact, before 1994, there were no high-level debates on foreign policy issues in parliament. The previous parliament, for example, ratified the decision to accede to the Nuclear Nonproliferation Treaty (NPT) as a nonnuclear state without any debate. As for the new legislative assembly elected 7 March 1994, no serious change in its level of activism is expected, because of the continuing lack of specialists in international affairs among the elected members.

Mass communications media have little influence on foreign policy decision makers. Public apathy on matters of foreign and defense policy is visible enough; the mass media present no analysis or even reflection on or explanation of Kazakhstan's foreign and defense policies and its international positions, mainly because there are so few good analysts and columnists in newspapers, radio, and television.

All political parties and movements emerged on the political scene after Kazakhstan became an independent state. They pay attention exclusively to internal, not external, issues. The importance of foreign policy and its role in providing favorable external conditions for solving international issues are not so clear for them, mainly because of the lack of specialists in international affairs among party personnel, activists, and cadres.

The government machinery dominates the formulation of foreign policy and, therefore, hardly utilizes the expertise available outside official circles. It would be more effective to formulate foreign policy with the help of, say, a think tank. In this connection the first, but not last, step was made with the creation of the Kazakhstan Institute for Strategic Studies under the aegis of the president of the Republic of Kazakhstan. This institute takes part in preparing, drafting, and evaluating the most important documents, programs, and moves in the areas of foreign policy and national security.

There is a lack of not only scientific research institutes and centers but also educational ones. International relations faculties exist only in the national university al-Farabi and in Almaty State Pedagogical University, but there is no specialized institute of international relations.

There is also a serious shortage of specialized and well-educated diplomats with a knowledge of foreign languages in Kazakhstan's foreign service. After the dissolution of the Soviet Union all Kazakh diplomats who served in the Soviet diplomatic corps returned to Kazakhstan. But their number is small. The majority of Kazakhstan's diplomatic corps comes from fields other than international relations. Education in international affairs and allied subjects has to be strengthened and upgraded and its scope widened. It is important also that Kazakhstan upgrade and coordinate existing research facilities, ensuring a continuous flow of selective material for the planning of its foreign policy.

This is why Kazakhstan's government is interested in signing agreements with foreign countries for the education and training of students as professional diplomats. Indeed, this situation needs to be corrected; the void needs to be filled. In conclusion, it is evident that there is work to be done in helping parliament, the mass media, and the academic community forge a solid domestic political basis for foreign policy. As such, a foreign policy elite is only now emerging in Kazakhstan.

Nuclear Disarmament and the Security of Kazakhstan

As part of the USSR, Kazakhstan was intensely involved in the nuclear confrontation between the two opposing military-political systems during the Cold War. Even now the participation of Kazakhstan in global nuclear policy is extremely high. The Semipalatinsk nuclear test site was closed by a decree of President Nazarbaev on 26 August 1991, but other military ranges are still in operation. The space facility at Baikonur is used for not only peaceful but also military purposes. As a dangerous heritage of the former Soviet Union, 104 SS–19 intercontinental ballistic missiles with ten reentry vehicles remain in Kazakhstan.

Kazakhstan ratified the Strategic Arms Reduction Treaty (31 July 1991) between the former USSR and the United States, as well as the Lisbon Protocol, signed by Kazakhstan, Russia, Ukraine, Belarus, and the United States on 23 May 1992. But only on 13 December 1993, over eighteen months later, did the Supreme Council of Kazakhstan ratify the Nuclear Nonproliferation Treaty as a nonnuclear state.[2]

Why did Kazakhstan not immediately announce its agreement to remove nuclear weapons from its territory for liquidation and join the Nuclear Nonproliferation Treaty as a nonnuclear state? President Nazarbaev responded to this question earlier this year in Switzerland, where he was taking part in the work of the World Economic Forum. He emphasized that Kazakhstan agreed to ratify the treaty on nuclear issues only after an understanding on three points was achieved: the guarantee of nuclear states not to use nuclear weapons against Kazakhstan (such a guarantee was received, including from China); the return of the value of enriched uranium in the nuclear warheads (agreement on this was reached with the United States); and economic issues (investments in Kazakhstan and economic integration with the Western states, including with the United States). Nazarbaev noted that

> Kazakhstan never wanted to be a nuclear power, if only because 500 nuclear tests were conducted on the territory of the Semipalantinsk region, 87 of them above ground and 107 underground. Even today hundreds of thousands of people suffer and Kazakhstan has been left alone with this problem. I closed, by my decree, the nuclear testing area. In connection with all this, the desire of Kazakhstan to keep away from such weapons and not have any on its territory will be understood.[3]

The signing of the Nuclear Nonproliferation Treaty by Kazakhstan can be considered a favorable factor for the extension of the nuclear test ban treaty and the broadening of its membership.

Searching for the Eurasian Security Formula

The peculiarity of Kazakhstan's foreign policy is that it must preserve relations of equality with Russia and other states of the CIS, continue the dialogue with the West, and be diplomatically active in the East in order to overcome its former estrangement from Asia. Here, the main aim of Kazakh foreign policy is to provide for Asian security and work toward integrating it with European security.

It is obvious that the experience accumulated in Europe can be used to solve Asian problems. But this experience must not be transferred mechanically, given the difference of the situations in Europe and Asia: Europe is compact, while there is a dissociation of regions in Asia (the Middle East, South Asia, Southeast Asia, etc.); there are deep differences in the socioeconomic development of the Asian countries; and there is a great variety of civilizations and religions in Asia. Moreover, Europe, in accordance with the Conference on Security and Cooperation in Europe (CSCE) Helsinki Final Act (1975), legally acknowledged borders and territorial integrity. Asia has not done the same. There are many countries in Asia that have territorial claims on others. But all these difficulties do not exclude the possibility of using the European experience in Asia.

President Nazarbaev set forth his step-by-step plan at the forty-seventh session of the General Assembly of the United Nations for the creation of a united Asian structure of collective security and its gradual transformation into a European, and then global, system of security. He suggested, as a first step, the convocation of the Conference on Assistance and Measures of Confidence in Asia, to be followed, in stages, by the organization and development of interdependent security structures, to be in place by the year 2000.[4]

There are, undoubtedly, many complications and impediments on the path to carrying out this Kazakh initiative: the great diversity of civilizations and religions in Asia, differences in the levels of socioeconomic development of these countries, and territorial disputes and regional conflicts. But obviously the time has come to rise above conflicting interests; there is no other path to prosperity for the people of Asia except through peace and cooperation.

Two meetings of experts from Asian states have already taken place in Almaty, with the participation of representatives of the United Nations, the Conference on Security and Cooperation in Europe, the Organization of the Islamic Conference, the League of Arab States, and other organizations. The heads of a number of countries of Asia have already expressed their official support for Kazakhstan's initiative to convene a conference on assistance and measures of confidence in Asia. Kazakhstan believes that Asia, like Europe, can institutionalize negotiating mechanisms and security structures similar to those of the CSCE, not through mechanical imitation, but by taking into account the specific character and experience of Asia.

Kazakhstan in the Commonwealth of Independent States

After the dissolution of the USSR, the Commonwealth of Independent States was created, first consisting of the three Slavic republics: Russia, Ukraine, and Belarus. Then the Central Asian states, Azerbaijan, Armenia, and Moldova joined the CIS. But problems continue to plague the commonwealth. Self-interests prevail, unsettling economic competition still persists, the idea of the single ruble monetary system has disintegrated, and the common military strategic zone has been reduced to the borders of Russia.

The causes of the ineffectiveness of the CIS are the incompatibility of economic, political, and military interests, primarily between Russia and Ukraine; variations in understanding of the CIS objectives; different paths toward a market economy; and political instability in some of the CIS members. In particular, Russia is unable to become the core of the CIS, providing equal partnership among its members, mainly because of its egoistic policy toward the reallocation of former Soviet property, as well as the threat of its armed forces, its complex economic relations, and its sometimes irredentist inclinations.

Kazakhstan has encountered great difficulties in the development of its relations within the CIS. Until recently, Kazakhstan's suggestions for the strengthening of integration in the economic and military spheres had not been favorably received by the other CIS states, especially Russia. It seemed that the dissolution processes within the CIS were stronger than the integration processes.

But there are hopeful signs of late. The return of Azerbaijan and the entry of Georgia into the CIS are evidence of the lack of alternatives to the commonwealth. Today all the republics of the former Soviet Union, with the exception of the Baltic states, are members of the CIS, and measures are being taken to secure the recognition of the commonwealth and its charter organs in the international arena, including the United Nations.

On 24 September 1993 the Treaty on the Creation of the Economic Union was signed in Moscow, the first major step on the path to the economic integration of the states of the CIS on a principally different basis. The Supreme Council of Kazakhstan ratified the treaty on 13 December 1993.

The fate of the economic union and its effectiveness and viability depend greatly on the degree to which it is equally favorable to all. This is the key issue, not the issue of how many sovereign rights each state should delegate to the supranational economic union.

The realities of an interdependent world, and moreover of the interdependent republics of the former USSR, are such that the path of absolute sovereignty has no future. But at the same time, the rejection of state sovereignty in the name of economic union is also absolutely impossible.

Kazakhstan is doing everything it can to ensure that the economic union of the countries of the CIS succeeds. The re-creation of the single economic sphere that collapsed after the fall of the USSR is in all their interests. The policy of strengthening the integration process in the CIS is one of the cardinal positions of Kazakhstan, a position that it not only has not deviated from but has defended and put into practice from the moment the USSR fell and the CIS was created.

The extremely difficult economic crisis, hyperinflation, the sharp drop in the standard of living, and the failure to resolve the crisis independently opened the eyes of many politicians to the fact that the path to prosperity (at least in relative terms) lies in unity and in closer ties among the countries of the commonwealth. Of course the question here is not one of resurrecting the USSR, but of building a stronger and more effective economic union functioning on the principles of equality and mutual advantage. In the process of organizing the economic union of the CIS, much can and should be borrowed from the experience of the European Union.

Relations with Russia

After the fall of the USSR a new Russia and an independent Kazakhstan appeared on the geopolitical map of the world. The most important result of the development of their relationship was the signing of the Treaty on Friendship, Cooperation, and Mutual Assistance on 25 May 1992.[5] This was a treaty between two equal and sovereign states that had decided to give a new character to their relations.

The two years since then have shown that the transition to qualitatively new relations is not so simple and that it is greatly affected by the correlation of forces within Russia, which, to a large degree, determine its foreign policy generally, and toward Kazakhstan and the other former Soviet republics in particular. In Russia, unfortunately, many political parties and movements are banking on the resurrection of the USSR in some new form, in which one can clearly see the image of a Russian empire that had sunk into oblivion.

The establishment of equal relations between Russia and the former Soviet republics is greatly hindered by the Russian desire to continue to see these countries as exclusively in the Russian sphere of influence and geopolitical interests. Even such a dangerous tendency as Russia's willingness to use force, including the military, to protect the Russian-speaking populations and secure citizenship for them has arisen. It is obvious that, in Russia's new military doctrine (entitled "Basic Provisions of the Military Doctrine of the Russian Federation," approved by the Russian Federation Security Council and adopted by presidential decree on 2 November 1993), there is a tendency to support local wars on CIS territory. The objective of defending Russian citizens living abroad is mentioned in this doctrine.[6] It may be used as a pretext to send Russian troops to any place in the non-Russian former Soviet republics where Russians live. Also alarming is Russia's insistent requests at the UN and the CSCE for the right to install Russian forces in the hot spots of the former USSR as peacekeepers for these organizations.[7] It should be noted that the UN Charter and the principles of the CSCE prohibit the participation in peacekeeping operations of states that have a special interest in the zone of conflict.

Just as worrying was Zhirinovsky's victory at the polls in Russia in December 1993, which clearly indicates that in Russia there are politicians who wish to reestablish the empire and who are supported by a significant portion of the Russian population. If these politicians come to power, it will certainly lead to clashes and conflicts in the heart of the Eurasian landmass, undermining peace and stability on a global scale.

It was a very serious signal when Russian Foreign Minister Andrei Kozyrev promised changes in Moscow's foreign policy in accordance with the public mood after Zhirinovsky's victory. Sometime later, at a meeting with Russian ambassadors who work in the "near abroad," Kozyrev declared that "the main region of the foremost vital Russian interests were the CIS and the Baltic states, and that the main threats for them emanate from this region also." He said that Russia must not retreat from regions that were spheres of Russian interest for ages, for if Russian troops were to withdraw, the security vacuum would be filled by forces not so friendly, forces that are directly hostile to Russian interests. As a grand strategic issue for Russia's foreign policy, Kozyrev named the protection of Russians and Russian-speaking populations' rights as a state interest, recognizing Russia's responsibility to support the right to "dual citizenship."[8]

Kozyrev's comments follow on the heels of criticism for Russia's apparent lack of a firm policy on this issue. One critic was the chairman of the previous parliament's Foreign Policy Committee, Evgenii Ambartsumov, who strongly criticized Kozyrev for ignoring vital Russian interests in the near abroad and for his indifference to Russians living there.[9]

As for Kazakhstan, some Russian politicians want to divide it along ethnic lines and annex northern Kazakhstan. Andranik Migranian, the well-known political scientist and member of the Russian Federation's Presidential Council, recently published an article confirming that "there are many political forces in Russia who do not recognize the territorial integrity of Kazakhstan and existing borders between Kazakhstan and Russia and define northern Kazakhstan as a natural part of Russia because of its large Russian population."[10]

It is clear enough that the real aim of these political speculations is to organize a Russian separatist movement in Kazakhstan. Undoubtedly, such serious provocation against Kazakhstan's territorial integrity and interethnic stability may lead to a dangerous situation similar to that of the Trans-Dniester in Moldova or the Crimea in Ukraine.

It is a fact that Kazakhs in Kazakhstan make up only 42 percent of the population, with Russians making up 38 percent. There are many other nationalities in Kazakhstan. Such an ethnodemographic composition is the result of the imperial policy of tsarist Russia and its successor, the Soviet Union. It would be no exaggeration to say that the communist leaders of the Soviet empire succeeded in the Russification of Kazakhstan more than the Russian tsars did. As a result, the Kazakhs became a national minority in their homeland.

What is the significance, then, of requiring dual citizenship for Russians and a state language for speakers of Russian? Only one thing: to destabilize the whole political and interethnic situation in Kazakhstan and undermine its sovereignty.

Russia has also intensified its economic pressure on Kazakhstan, especially in the days leading up to the election of the country's first post-Soviet parliament, on 7 March 1994. Evidently, Russia wants to provoke in Kazakhstan an economic crisis that in turn will cause political and interethnic instability or at least weaken its former semicolony, which had become an independent state. The same policy is also carried out by Russia in other former Soviet republics.

One example of Russian economic pressure on Kazakhstan involves the Kazakh-American joint venture Tengizchevroil. Russia arranged transport restrictions under the pretext that Kazakh oil is full of mercaptan, sulfur compounds that can cause an odor if they leak from the pipelines. Therefore, Moscow refused to raise the annual ceiling of forty-four million barrels for Kazakh oil passing through its pipelines. As the *New York Times* reported, "The company is building a special plant to take out most of the contaminants. There are considerable suspicions that the Russians are using the issue to pressure Chevron to come to terms on a new pipeline to the Russian port of Novorossisk and to prevent Kazakhstan from feeling too independent."[11] Of course, Russia wants to be cut in on any gains from Kazakh oil. Also, it is clear enough that Russia is holding Kazakhstan hostage, using its monopoly on the pipelines to control the gas and oil from the Caspian region, including western Kazakhstan.

In the military sphere, the pressure exerted by Russia came to light when it sought Russian status for strategic armed forces left in the territory of Kazakhstan after the collapse of the USSR, the preservation of military test sites, and other objectives. As for the former secret Soviet space site Baikonur, Russia wants to preserve it as a base for Russian space operations.

It is becoming more noticeable that Russia sees its military presence in Kazakhstan and in other former Soviet republics as the main leverage by which to keep and strengthen its control over the internal situation, rather than to defend these republics from outside threats.

Only a few Russian analysts have signaled the dangers of such a policy for the future of Russia itself. Among them is Aleksei Arbatov, who emphasizes that it is wrong to think that "the weaker and less stable the other republics are, the stronger and better off Russia is." On the contrary, "a consistent policy of respect, recognition of the sovereignty of the other republics, and fair and equal cooperation in various fields would be the best way to control the centrifugal forces affecting the territories of the former Soviet Union."[12]

As for foreign observers, Zbigniew Brzezinski, in a 1994 article in *Foreign Affairs,* came to the conclusion that "Russia can be either an empire or a democracy, but it cannot be both," and cautioned that "efforts to recreate and maintain the empire by coercion and/or economic subsidy would condemn Russia not only to dictatorship but to poverty."[13]

The Kazakh people do not want to return to the empire in any case and will never agree to relinquish state sovereignty and territorial integrity. Kazakhstan recognizes Russia's interests and takes them into account in all fields of domestic and foreign policy. As indicated earlier, the first priority and main partner of Kazakhstan is Russia. Kazakhstan is ready to cooperate with Russia and develop Kazakhstan-Russian relations in all directions, and as deeply as possible. But as President Nazarbaev said, "It is impossible to tango alone. You need a partner. The desire of your partner is also necessary for more valuable cooperation."[14]

It is important to emphasize that friendly cooperation among the former Soviet republics is possible only on the basis of equality, noninterference in internal affairs, nonuse of force or the threat of force in solving existing and future interstate problems, and other principles of international law. Kazakhstan is interested in Russia's economic and political development and in strong good-neighborly relations with it. It is in this regard that Kazakhstan sees its guarantee of stable and secure development.

Relations with China

It is true that not long ago many Central Asians viewed China and its enormous population as a far greater threat to their existence, as an ethnic group, than

Russia.[15] But now, seeing rising nationalism and neoimperial moods and tendencies in Russia and in its foreign policy in the near abroad, many of them have changed their views and believe that in the near future the real threat could come from Russia.

Some Russian analysts have created and periodically emphasized the myth of the Chinese threat by pointing to growing Chinese economic power, nuclear potential, and ethnic expansion abroad. The Russian military scientist M. Gareev, while alluding to the positive foreign policy of China, cautioned that "it is necessary to take into account that in spite of the desires of some politicians, the demographic factor might be one of the most determining factors of the behavior of this state."[16] One cannot ignore the possibility that the reason for stimulating the myth of the Chinese threat is to make the Central Asian states keep their distance from China and become closer to Russia.

And what about the other myths, such as the threat of Islamic fundamentalism or Pan-Turkic nationalism, especially in the western parts of China—the Xinjiang region—where the population is mostly Turkic and Muslim? Can the emergence of independent Turkic and Muslim Central Asian states stimulate the struggle of the non-Han people for national liberation?

Ross H. Munro noticed that "relieved Chinese leaders seem to have concluded by early 1992 that neither pan-Turkic nationalism nor militant Islam was about to sweep the Central Asian republics. That in turn meant that neither force poses a serious and immediate threat to Xinjiang itself. The ruling secular elites of all five new republics made their hostility to militant Islam very clear."[17]

As for Kazakhstan and other Central Asian states, they have strictly carried out the principle of noninterference in one another's internal affairs, and therefore there is no room for such political speculations.

Over the last two years Kazakh-Chinese relations have made great progress. When Kazakhstan was part of the USSR, it had the opportunity to develop relations mainly with the Xinjiang-Uigursk autonomous region of the People's Republic of China (PRC). Having become independent, Kazakhstan is now pursuing the development of ties with all of China. The citizens of Kazakhstan received a great deal of satisfaction from the fact that the PRC was one of the first countries to recognize Kazakhstan as a sovereign state and to establish diplomatic relations with it. Kazakhstan and China have embassies and other representations in each other's countries.

An important result of President Nazarbaev's second visit to the People's Republic of China in October 1993 was the joint signing of the Declaration on the Fundamentals of Friendly Relations Between Kazakhstan and China. In this document the principles of respect for sovereignty and territorial integrity, non-aggression and noninterference in each other's internal affairs, nonuse of force or the threat of force, and equality and mutual advantage were laid out. The most important aspect of the signed declaration is that it opened up a new stage in the development of Kazakh-Chinese relations.

Kazakhstan values highly China's experience in conducting economic reform: its well-thought-out nature, the consistency and firmness of its execution, the high tempo of economic development it has provided, as well as the secure place it has achieved for China in international trade.

The foreign policy of the PRC is also worthy of respect. It is directed at the establishment of friendly relations with all its neighbors and the integration of China into the world community—a community where all countries, whether large or small, powerful or weak, rich or poor, are equal members and where there should not be a place for hegemony and the politics of force.

Kazakhstan and China are geographic neighbors with rich natural resources, mutually complementary economies, convenient forms of transportation and communication, and great potential for the further development of mutually advantageous relations.

Relations with the United States

Bordering Russia and China, two important partners of the United States in international relations, and having large nuclear arsenals inherited from the former Soviet Union, Kazakhstan could not escape involvement in the orbit of American foreign policy. The development of Kazakh-American relations in the two years after Kazakhstan became an independent state showed very clearly the correctness of this judgment.

Kazakh-American relations have reached, in an extremely short period, a level of large-scale cooperation in various spheres and deep mutual understanding. The two nations have become genuine partners, as reflected in the Charter on Democratic Partnership Between Kazakhstan and the United States, signed on 14 February 1994 in Washington by Presidents Clinton and Nazarbaev.[18] The United States and Kazakhstan agreed to intensify contacts in the spheres of politics, economics, culture, education, ecology, science and technology, health services, and other fields.

The issue of guaranteeing the security, independence, territorial integrity, and democratic development of Kazakhstan has the greatest significance in the context of Kazakh-American relations. Cooperation in this sphere will be carried out bilaterally, as well as within the framework of existing international and regional structures of security: the United Nations, the Conference on Security and Cooperation in Europe, and the North Atlantic Treaty Organization. Kazakhstan has expressed its readiness to participate in the Partnership for Peace program.

Article 3 of the Charter on Domestic Partnership has the most political significance for Kazakhstan. It declares that "the United States of America recognizes the security, independence, sovereignty, territorial integrity, and democratic development of the Republic of Kazakhstan as the highest values."[19]

Visiting Kazakhstan in March 1994, Defense Secretary William J. Perry reassured Kazakhstan's leaders of Washington's support and described an attempt to draw Russia, Kazakhstan's chief security threat, into a regional nonaggression pact with Kazakhstan that would be joined by the United States and perhaps Great Britain. The main purpose of this pact, Perry said, would be "to not use force, to use only peaceful means to resolve problems that emerge between any of these countries."[20] Given the current developing, but not so promising, perspectives of interstate relations within the CIS, the importance of this new American initiative holds special meaning.

It could be said that there is no need for such a security pact, because Kazakhstan and Russia had already signed the Treaty on Friendship, Cooperation, and Mutual Assistance on 25 May 1992 and, shortly before that, on 15 May 1992, Kazakhstan, Uzbekistan, Kyrgyzstan, Tajikistan, and Armenia had signed the Treaty on Collective Security in Tashkent. But the Kazakh-Russian treaty may become merely a piece of paper if the supporters of restoring the Russian empire come to power. As for the Tashkent treaty, it does not work yet. Therefore, the role of the United States in preserving Kazakhstan's sovereignty and territorial integrity, as well as those of other newly independent states, is looking more promising.

Of course, this suggested security pact does not mean that the United States will send its armed forces to defend Kazakhstan. As Perry clarified in Almaty, "It is not a guarantee that we would go to war on any issue that arose with Kazakhstan."[21] But the United States has direct influence with Russia and may even exert pressure on Russia through such international organizations as the United Nations, NATO, and the International Monetary Fund.

Relations with the Central Asian States

Already in 1990, at the initiative of Kazakhstan, the leaders of Kazakhstan, Uzbekistan, Kyrgyzstan, Tajikistan, and Turkmenistan gathered in Almaty and signed the Agreement on Economic, Scientific-Technical and Cultural Cooperation.[22] At the January 1993 meeting of the heads of the Central Asian countries in Tashkent, decisions were made to deepen the level of mutual cooperation, and the contours of a possible Association of Regional States were outlined.

As was stated in the meeting in Tashkent, it is possible to create a regional market, with an open economic zone, free movement of labor and capital, a single tax system, coordinated prices, and possibly a single currency. The importance of economic interrelations of the countries of the region and the decision on the creation of a permanent control mechanism for carrying out intergovernmental treaties and agreements were stressed in a joint communiqué. An established commission on oil, energy, cotton, and other economic and social activity is the aim of the integration plans.

Attention at the Tashkent meeting focused on supplying the region's states with energy power and alternate transport communications. Agreement was reached on the processing of Caspian oil at Uzbek and Turkmen plants. The proposal to build a railway line through Iran to the Persian Gulf and Turkey and to begin using the Druzhba oil pipeline, which will provide a way to the Pacific Ocean, was adopted.

In order to establish a unified informational zone, it was decided to organize a common television center in Tashkent and a newspaper in Almaty. In this way, the region hopes to overcome informational dependence on the Russian mass media.[23]

The realization of the integration potential of the region is aided by the conclusion of bilateral treaties and agreements among the governments of the Central Asian region. Mutual relations between the two leading Central Asian countries, for example, are being built and developed on the basis of the Agreement on Friendship, Cooperation and Mutual Assistance Between the Republic of Uzbekistan and the Republic of Kazakhstan, signed on 24 June 1992.

Kazakhstan is not a counterweight to Uzbekistan, or a competitor to the claim for regional power. Rather, it sees itself as a political and economic partner. During the visit of President Nazarbaev to the Republic of Uzbekistan on 10–12 January 1994, both sides agreed on strengthening the developing relations between the two countries. One example is the treaty signed by Nazarbaev and Uzbekistan President Islam Karimov on the creation of a single economic space to encompass both Uzbekistan and Kazakhstan, including the unhindered transportation of goods, services, capital, and workers and the establishment of common credit accounting, budgetary, tax, price, customs, and hard currency policies.

Of special interest are the areas outlined by both sides for future cooperation, including cooperation in the military sphere. The ministers of defense were given the task of examining all the questions tied to this issue, developing concrete proposals for military cooperation, including the preparation of specialists on the basis of training institutions in both countries, and preparing the appropriate agreements.[24]

The most serious conflict situation in Central Asia is that along the Tajik-Afghan border. Kazakhstan has no common borders with Tajikistan, but it has a common interest in defending the borders of all Central Asian states. The main reason for this is that if these borders should be encroached on by, say, Afghanistan, Iran, or China, Russia would have to respond by building new borders on its southern periphery. And if Russia should focus on its borders with Kazakhstan, particularly where the Russian population is heavily concentrated, heightened tensions in Kazakh-Russian relations would result. It is therefore in Kazakhstan's best interests to maintain the existing external borders of the CIS.

This concern was underlined on 3 September 1992, when the presidents of Kazakhstan, Kyrgyzstan, and Russia issued a warning that the Tajik-Afghan conflict endangered the security of the Commonwealth of Independent States. At a meeting on 7 August 1993 in Moscow, the presidents of Russia, Kazakhstan,

Kyrgyzstan, Tajikistan, and Uzbekistan further underlined this "collective responsibility" to guarantee the inviolability of borders. Each state promised to send at least one battalion to the borders.

Relations with the Middle East and South Asia

Kazakhstan has successfully developed relations with Central Asia's nearest neighbors: Turkey, Iran, Pakistan, and India. The Kazakhs and other Central Asian people have common historical ties with the people of these countries that had been interrupted by the Russian and then the Soviet empires.

Kazakhstan and Turkey share many common roots: geographic (they are both located on the border between Europe and Asia) as well as ethnographic and cultural (their populations are related by origin and language). Responding to the desire of the two peoples, both states have made efforts to broaden and deepen mutually advantageous cooperation on a long-term basis in the political, economic, scientific-technical, cultural, humanitarian, informational, and other spheres. The two countries signed a series of important documents, including a declaration on principles and goals of mutual relations, a memorandum on mutual treaties and agreements in the areas of transportation and telecommunications, trade, and economic and scientific-technical cooperation.

Furthermore, an agreement called for Turkish specialists to help restore the mausoleum-mosque Khodz Ahmed Yesevi. The minister of culture of Turkey, Naud Kemal Zeibek, declared that Ahmed Yesevi is the father of culture of all Turkish people, and thus the restoration of the mausoleum was the holy duty of each Muslim.

As for Kazakhstan's relations with Iran, there are good prospects for the development of multifaceted commercial ties between the two countries that can now be exploited thanks to a well-developed transportation system, including rail, air, and sea communications. The goal is to develop the infrastructure for shipping large quantities of oil, grain, animal products, industrial products, and equipment on the Caspian Sea between Kazakhstan and Iran.

Currently, relations between Kazakhstan and Iran are regulated by almost twenty-five different agreements that form a strong foundation for the development of multifaceted cooperation. Naturally, one must keep in mind that Iran, when it discusses its relations with the countries of Central Asia, stresses its leading role in the rejuvenation of political Islam in this region. The other Central Asian countries, looking after their own interests, consider above all else Iran's favorable geopolitical position in the Middle East and the possibility of its serving as an exit to the sea trade routes and markets.

The Republic of Kazakhstan has also established ties with India and Pakistan, the leading countries of South Asia. President Nazarbaev visited both these countries in February 1992, at which time the Declaration on the Principles of Mutual Relations Between Kazakhstan and India and agreements on the establishment of diplomatic and consular relations, scientific, cultural, and sports ties, and economic cooperation were signed. The State Bank of India and the Bank of Foreign Economic Activity of Kazakhstan have concluded an agreement securing financial support for trade and economic ties between the two countries.

A series of agreements was also signed with Pakistan by which mutual trade and financial cooperation would be expanded and a reliable system of communication established. The significance of these improved relations for Kazakhstan is the planned diversification of transport and communication systems in the southern direction. Iran, for one, has offered to build a corridor in its territory from the border with Turkmenistan to the Iranian port of Bandar-e 'Abbās. This port lies on the bank of the Strait of Hormuz, which connects the Indian Ocean with the Persian Gulf.

The implementation of this project presents Central Asian states with the opportunity to broaden their trade and economic relations with India. To this day, goods from India coming to Central Asia are delivered by a long, circuitous route: by sea through the Suez Canal to Odessa or Ilichivs'k, and from there by railway through Ukraine and Russia. However, to Bandar-e 'Abbās from Indian harbors is, as they say, a stone's throw away.

Concerning the suggestion by Pakistan to lead Central Asian states to the banks of the Arabian Sea, uniting them by railway to the port of Karachi, there is one essential flaw—laying a railway line through the unstable Afghan provinces.

In the course of talks with Nazarbaev in January 1994, the minister of foreign affairs of Pakistan, Sardar Asif Akhmed Ali, expressed the hope of the Pakistanis to broaden the system of transport lines. The completion of highways by the middle of 1994 will permit the first convoy of Kazakh trucks to go to Pakistan. A Pakistani diplomat has even suggested the joint construction of a railway line and an oil and gas pipeline between the two states, a suggestion Kazakhstan welcomed.

The realization of such promising projects, however, is linked with certain problems. The projects are first of all conditional on political stability in the region, particularly in Afghanistan and Tajikistan. Therefore both governments must make energetic efforts to resolve the existing conflicts there by peaceful means.

Kazakhstan has developed not only bilateral but also multilateral relations in this region. All the Central Asian states have joined the Economic Cooperation Organization (ECO), which was initially established by Iran, Turkey, and Pakistan in 1964, and now also includes Azerbaijan and Afghanistan. The participation in this regional organization of a number of states that are contiguous to the Central Asian countries presents Kazakhstan with great possibilities for development and entry into the world community.

Cooperation within the framework of the ECO has particular strategic significance for the Central Asian states that do not have an exit to a sea. It presents the opportunity of transporting their cargo to the ports of the Indian Ocean and the Persian Gulf.

The Economic Cooperation Organization is considered in Kazakhstan not as an alternative but as a supplement to the CIS. It does not present itself as any sort of new customs union, and certainly not as a bloc of Islamic states. It is an association; its main goal is the fullest promotion possible of the economic and social progress of all its members. Its principal task is to unite partners with roads and trade. In his speeches at the ECO's summits, Nazarbaev has repeatedly emphasized the economic character of this organization and that it is categorically unacceptable to build mutual relations among state partners on an ethnic or religious basis.

Relations with the Far East

While Kazakhstan has established relations with Japan, the Democratic People's Republic of Korea, and the Republic of Korea, the relationship with Japan has been the most important. The former deputy prime minister and minister of foreign affairs of Japan, Michio Watanabe, and the minister of foreign affairs of the Republic of Korea, Li San Ok, have paid official visits to Almaty.

The Japanese government has taken it upon itself to provide Kazakhstan with $220 million in credits in the near future. Of this, $145 million will be provided in conjunction with the International Monetary Fund (IMF) and the other $75 million in conjunction with the International Bank for Reconstruction and Development (IBRD). Not long ago the government of Kazakhstan turned to financial groups in Japan with the request that they provide a loan in the amount of $1 billion. Part of the requested funds will be provided by the IMF ($170 million) and the IBRD ($180 million).

Japan has demonstrated great interest in financing several projects in Kazakhstan. At the Ministry of Economics in Kazakhstan, Japanese experts were presented with five projects: two involved the renovation of steel production at the Karaganda Metallurgical Combine; two others, the exploitation of oil deposits in Atyrau and Magistu; and the last project, the construction of a pipeline for shipping Kazakh oil abroad.

The Japanese experts gave the proposed projects very high marks, having judged them as extremely profitable. Makoto Sunagava, the general director of the credit department of the Export-Import Bank of Japan—the largest of the state institutions in Japan, having a total investment turnover that in some countries is comparable to the financial turnover of the IMF or the World Bank—declared that Japan is ready to finance them "step by step."[25]

Relations with the European States

In the autumn of 1992, Nazarbaev visited Germany. In the course of the visit, a joint declaration concerning the basis of relations between the two states was signed. Representatives of both sides also adopted an Agreement on the Development of Large-Scale Cooperation in the Economic Sphere and the Industry of Science and Technology and the Agreement on the Encouragement and Mutual Protection of Capital Investment. Flights were established between Almaty and Frankfurt am Main and Almaty and Hanover.

Kazakh-French relations are moving forward on the basis of the Treaty on Friendship, Mutual Understanding and Cooperation, signed on 23 September 1992, in Paris by the presidents of Kazakhstan and France. President Mitterrand was the first of the Western leaders to go to Kazakhstan on an official visit. On his return from the United States, Nazarbaev stopped in Paris for a personal meeting with Mitterrand. French businessmen have shown great interest in Kazakhstan. The activity in the republic of many French firms testifies to that fact.

It is a remarkable fact that in January 1994 an international seminar on the topic "Kazakhstan—A Bridge to the Developing Market of Asia" took place in Zurich. The practical result of this exchange of opinions was the decision by the Swiss confederation to open a line of credit to Kazakhstan. With the goal of forming mutually advantageous ties with European states, President Nazarbaev visited Belgium and Austria in February 1993. An agreement on the exchange of representatives between the European Community (EC) and Kazakhstan was signed at a meeting of the EC in Brussels. Kazakhstan's ambassador to Belgium was named the authorized representative of Kazakhstan to the EC.

Austria was one of the first to recognize Kazakhstan's independence and to open a line of credit to Kazakhstan. Since Kazakhstan has at its disposal rich raw material resources and Austria is a producer of technology, cooperation between the two countries is developing successfully.

The Republic of Kazakhstan is also developing relations with the countries of Eastern Europe. The prime minister of Kazakhstan, Sergei Tereshchenko, visited Hungary and Bulgaria and signed mutually advantageous agreements in the spheres of industry and agriculture.

In July 1993 the president of Bulgaria, Zheliu Zhelev, came to Almaty on an official visit. This was the first official delegation from an East European country to visit Kazakhstan since the disintegration of the Council for Mutual Economic Assistance. As a result of negotiations, the Treaty on Friendly Relations and Cooperation between Kazakhstan and Bulgaria was signed, as well as agreements on agricultural and commercial-economic cooperation, the creation of joint Kazakh-Bulgarian enterprises, and the establishment of a credit investment bank and holding company.

Kazakhstan's Positive International Image

What are the main results of the realization of Nazarbaev's "Strategy for the Development of Kazakhstan as a Sovereign State" in the area of foreign policy and national security?

In the period following the attainment of state independence, much progress has been made toward the establishment of the Republic of Kazakhstan as an independent actor in international relations and, as an equal partner in the international community. Currently, Kazakhstan has been recognized by 108 countries, and has established diplomatic relations with 70 of them. In Almaty there are over forty functioning embassies and representations from international organizations. The network of Kazakh missions abroad is growing. Embassies have been opened in the United States, China, India, Turkey, Iran, and other countries in the near abroad and the rest of the world. Kazakhstan has become a member of the United Nations and has entered such international and financial organizations as the International Bank for Reconstruction and Development, the International Monetary Fund, the European Bank for Reconstruction and Development, and UNESCO. As one of the legal successors to the USSR, Kazakhstan signed the Final Act of the Conference on Security and Cooperation in Europe as well as the Paris charter and thus has included itself in the sphere of European politics.

Kazakhstan also became a member of the NATO-sponsored North Atlantic Cooperation Council, which is playing an important role in the dialogue and cooperation among the NATO member states, the former members of the dissolved Warsaw Treaty Organization, and the newly independent states that arose after the disintegration of the USSR. Contact with NATO is extremely important for Kazakhstan because it presents the opportunity to make use of the rich experience of this organization in undertaking the difficult tasks of building the armed forces of Kazakhstan and the new system of collective security of the CIS.

As an Asian state, the Republic of Kazakhstan has also naturally made itself known in Asia. For the first time a delegation from Kazakhstan took part in the work of a session of the UN Economic and Social Commission for Asia and the Pacific. Kazakhstan's economic development, as well as its entry into the Asian subcontinent and access to its seas and oceans, will clearly be helped by participation in the Economic Cooperation Organization, founded by Iran, Pakistan, and Turkey and later joined by Afghanistan, Azerbaijan, and the Central Asian states. Ties with the countries of Asia, from the great neighboring People's Republic of China to the Kingdom of Thailand in faraway Southeast Asia, are broadening and becoming more meaningful.

Relations between the Republic of Kazakhstan and the United States, Germany, France, and other European states, with great hopes for investment capital and new technologies for the Kazakh economy, are flourishing.

The integration of the republic into the world economy is being rigorously pursued. In the country there are more than 260 representations of foreign firms and banks, and more than a thousand joint ventures have been registered. Among Kazakhstan's partners are some of the leading oil companies in the world, including Chevron and British Petroleum. Cooperation with these companies as well as with others is an increasingly important factor in Kazakhstan's economic growth.

Kazakhstan, thanks to its reasonable, considered foreign policy and its open economy and society, has developed a positive international image.

Notes

1. *Kazakhstanskaia pravda,* 16 May 1992.
2. See Oumirseric Kasenov and Kariat Abuseitov, "The Future of Nuclear Weapons in the Kazakh Republic's National Security," Potomac Papers, February 1993; Oumirseric Kasenov, "Are Assurances of a Nuclear Club Reliable to the Discussion on the Future of the Nonproliferation Treaty?" *Mysl',* 1993, no. 7.
3. *Kazakhstanskaia pravda,* 1 February 1994.
4. *Kazakhstanskaia pravda,* 9 October 1992.
5. *Kazakhstanskaia pravda,* 23 July 1992.
6. "Basic Provisions of the Military Doctrine of the Russian Federation," *Rossiiskie vesti,* 18 November 1993, in FBIS-SOV–93–222-S, 19 November 1993.
7. *Rossiiskaia gazeta,* 25 February 1994.
8. *Nezavisimaia gazeta,* 18 January 1994.
9. *Izvestiia,* 9 August 1992.
10. *Nezavisimaia gazeta,* 18 January 1994.
11. *New York Times,* 20 March 1994.
12. Aleksei Arbatov, "Russia's Foreign Policy Alternatives," *International Security,* vol. 18, no. 2 (fall 1993), p. 29.
13. Zbigniew Brzezinski, "The Premature Partnership," *Foreign Affairs,* vol. 73, no. 2 (1994), p. 72.
14. *Izvestiia,* 23 February 1994.
15. See Kemal Karpat, "The Sociopolitical Environment Conditioning the Foreign Policy of Central Asian States" (paper presented at the Conference on Foreign Policy Priorities, Decision Making, and Foreign Policy of Central Asia and the Caucasus, Russian Littoral Project, University of Maryland and Johns Hopkins University, 21 March 1994), p. 23.
16. M. Gareev, "Priorities of State Interests of the Russian Federation," *Mezhdunarodnaia zhizn'* (May–June 1993), p. 146.
17. Ross H. Munro, "Central Asia and China," in *Central Asia and the World,* ed. Michael Mandelbaum (New York: Council on Foreign Relations Press, 1993), p. 224.
18. *Kazakhstanskaia pravda,* 24 February 1994.
19. Ibid.
20. *Washington Post,* 20 March 1994.
21. Ibid.
22. *Kazakhstanskaia pravda,* 24 June 1990.
23. *Kazakhstanskaia pravda,* 5 January 1993.
24. *Kazakhstanskaia pravda,* 13 January 1994.
25. *Panorama,* no. 5 (February 1994).

13

The Institutions, Orientations, and Conduct of Foreign Policy in Post-Soviet Azerbaijan

Leila Alieva

The geopolitical situation of Azerbaijan, which is located at the crossroads of the East and the West and is of strategic interest to Russia, Iran, and Turkey, is one of the main determinants of the foreign policy of the Republic of Azerbaijan. Being the focus of the interests of three countries, Azerbaijan has endeavored to maintain its independence by maneuvering among them, and at the same time trying to establish secure and harmonious relationships with both the East and the West. Seventy years of development as part of the Soviet Union enhanced the Western and European orientation of the country, a process that had already started in Azerbaijani society with its rapid industrialization during the second part of the nineteenth century and led to the creation of an "infrastructure, similar to those in Europe."[1] Under the colonial Soviet regime, Azerbaijan's links with both the Turkic and Islamic worlds were severed—its borders were closed, alphabet changed, and historians persecuted. However, the cultural identification of the Azeris with the larger Turkic and Islamic world was never completely eliminated.

The other important factor that determines the foreign policy of Azerbaijan is its considerable natural resources, including oil, gas, and minerals. Experts maintain that just the investigated offshore oil resources are from eight hundred million to one billion tons, and this constitutes at least one of the ten largest oil fields in the world. The discovery of new oil fields in this region continues. This fact has made Azerbaijan very important, not only for its neighboring states, but also for major Western oil companies, and has intensified the competition for Azerbaijan as part of a sphere of influence.

Azerbaijan, the Caucasian gate to the East, was the first democratic republic in the Islamic world (established 1918) and provides an example of modernization. It has had a great impact on social and political processes in neighboring Iran, Turkey, and the Central Asian republics. According to Mammad Amin Rasulzade, the leader of the Azerbaijani Democratic Republic, the ADR was the first state in the Turkic world to be created on the basis of nationalism, since historically all the other states of Turkic origin were created on the basis of religion.[2] Russian colonization and the Russian policy of ethnic discrimination toward Azeri Turks since the beginning of the nineteenth century strengthened the Azeri ethnic identity, contributing to the distinction between the ethnic and religious (Muslim) elements. The religious institutions, having merged with the apparatus of the tsarist regime, were perceived in Azerbaijan to be the instruments of the colonization and discrimination policies of the Russian colonial rule. This fact explains the low popularity of religious political organizations such as Ittihad, which used to be in opposition to the national liberation movement headed by Musavat in the beginning of the century. Rasulzade argued that Pan-Islamism was preventing the development of national self-consciousness of various peoples, therefore blocking their progress and development as independent nations.

The creation of Azerbaijan as the first nation-state in the Turkic world was also the result of its historical development, which was influenced by the processes of rapid industrialization and modernization. Industrialization stimulated the creation of a native working class and a national industrial bourgeoisie. However, the ethnic and political composition of the parliament of the Azerbaijani Democratic Republic had never acquired an ultranationalist character. The legislation of the ADR provided for strict measures against fomenting national hatred. The factions of such political parties as Dashnaktsutiun (Armenian Nationalistic Party), the Russian-Slav Society, and others were legally active in the Azerbaijani parliament, and the parliament included representatives of all the ethnic minorities populating Azerbaijan, thus providing for their participation in the process of governing.[3]

The traditions of modernization and democratization, a central feature of the historical development of Azerbaijan in the nineteenth and twentieth centuries, resurfaced during the period of democratization in the Soviet Union and its subsequent disintegration. In spite of the war with Armenia over Nagorno-Karabagh, which should have radicalized Azeri society, and despite the complete isolation of the country (without any support from the Western democracies) and the persecution of the Popular Front during the invasion of Baku by Soviet troops in 1990, the national democratic forces came to power in May 1992.

The breakup of the Soviet Union brought radical changes in the geopolitical situation of the region. Parts of the former union that had a European-oriented population found themselves with a "new" identity—as parts of the Middle East. As noted earlier, the Caucasian republics strategically lie at the confluence of interests of the three most powerful countries in the region, Russia, Turkey, and Iran. The struggle for influence over the newly created states among those

countries is the main determinant of the political processes in the region. However, the main initial orientation in the foreign policies of the first democratic
governments of all the Caucasian republics was to the West. While Armenia,
striving to gain control over Nagorno-Karabagh from Azerbaijan, rapidly turned
to Russia, its traditional historical ally, Azerbaijan and Georgia took strict centrifugal positions and tried to leave the Russian sphere of influence. However,
although they possessed strong liberation movements equal to those in the Baltic
republics, Azerbaijan and Georgia, unlike those republics, did not gain any support from the West and were left alone in their struggle for independence. This
made the fates of the two republics very similar. Unlike Armenia, which became
the most homogeneous former Soviet republic after the departure of the Azeri
and Kurdish minorities, Georgia and Azerbaijan are multinational republics that
are vulnerable to Russian manipulation. There is some evidence of Russian
involvement in the conflicts in Abkhazia and Nagorno-Karabagh. Both countries
suffered invasion by Soviet troops, whose aim was to oppress their democratic
movements. Both suffered bloody wars with more powerful adversaries, as well
as coups d'état that overthrew democratically elected dissident leaders (Zviad
Gamsakhurdia and Abulfez Elchibey) and brought to power former Soviet-era
communist bosses (Eduard Shevardnadze and Gaider Aliev). Although the internal policies and leadership styles of Elchibey and Gamsakhurdia differed significantly (Elchibey succeeded, unlike Gamsakhurdia, in creating political freedom
and tolerance in Azerbaijani society), both became, to a different degree, the
victims of their foreign policies, whose priorities were to escape from the Russian
sphere of influence. Elchibey also assumed that a course leading toward democratic reforms would be supported by the West and the United States, but the
Western support for democracies and their struggles for independence did not go
farther than the Baltic republics. Thus in the midst of ethnic wars, state weakness,
and the absence of Western support, independence became difficult to achieve.

Although experts argue that there are three countries competing for influence
in the region, only Russia is powerful enough to affect events in the region and,
indeed, continues to be unrestricted in its military, political, and economic pressure on the "near abroad." Events have shown that Russia is using threats of
dismemberment toward multinational Georgia and Azerbaijan in order to continue to play the role of protector of Armenia against its Muslim neighbors. For
Russia, Azerbaijan is an important part of its buffer zone against historical rivals
Iran and Turkey. This makes a military presence in the republic one of the main
Russian strategic objectives. Besides, Russia would like to restore its control
over Azerbaijani natural resources, mainly oil, provide access to its industrial
and defense facilities, and guarantee a market for its products.[4]

These objectives clash with the interests of Turkey, which, by presenting a
model of Westernized society for the Caucasus and Central Asian republics, was
seen by the West as a major actor in the region after the breakup of the Soviet
Union. Turkey's objectives are mainly concerned with economic domination in

these regions and prevention of Russia's military pressure on its borders. In addition to its own interests in dominating the region, Turkey, as a member of NATO, indirectly represents the interests of Western Europe and the United States in the region as a counterbalance against a revival of the Russian empire and Iranian fundamentalism. Its failure to fulfill these functions would, according to some experts, undermine Western interests in the region.[5] Azerbaijan and Turkey do have close linguistic, ethnic, and intellectual ties. However, these factors will not solely determine the closeness of Azerbaijani-Turkish relations. There is also correlation of views on the development of secularism, modernization, and democratization. This very factor, namely, the political character of the regime, makes Azerbaijani-Iranian relations more problematic, in spite of the fact that Azerbaijan has had long historical, cultural, and religious ties to Iran. The other factor affecting the prospects for Iranian influence in Azerbaijan is the large Azerbaijani community in Iran, which represents a potential threat of secessionist nationalism. At the same time, Azerbaijan and Iran are tied together by a wide net of communications and intensive trade relationships (Iran occupies second place among the trade partners of Azerbaijan). However, in the case of war, when security issues are paramount, foreign policy priorities would be dependent on the extent to which any country could contribute to the protection of Azerbaijan.

Since independence, the foreign policy of Azerbaijan has been based on two prevailing threats to the country: (1) the attempt by Russia to retain the Caucasus, including Azerbaijan, in its sphere of influence by using ethnic conflicts as a means of pressure on the "insurgent" republics, and (2) the territorial claims of the Armenian Republic.

The foreign policy of President Elchibey's independent democratic government was dominated by the Turkish model of Westernization and modernization. The traditions and memory of the independent and democratic Azerbaijan of 1918–20 appeared to be the most powerful force in the national movement for independence, creating the main ideological basis during Azerbaijan's transition period. Abulfez Elchibey declared his adherence to the motto of the Azerbaijani nationalistic party Musavat (created at the beginning of the century), which was "Turkization, Modernization, Islamization." This reflected the multifaceted character of Azerbaijanis, who draw on the Turkic, European, and Islamic worlds, the last being a cultural rather than a political entity. Elchibey's government was characterized by the pursuit of a secular, independent, and democratic society with a market economy and a parliamentary political system, as well as by a pro-Western and pro-Turkish foreign policy.

The creation of democracy and of a nation-state in Azerbaijan was complicated by the Armenian-Azerbaijani war, which strengthened the desire of Azerbaijan to become independent of Russia. The idea that the Soviet Union previously, and now Russia, used ethnic minority separatist movements to further its aim of keeping the republics in their spheres of influence has already been expressed by several Western experts, although experts and politicians in Georgia and Azerbaijan had been aware of this much earlier. The leaders of the Popular Front had perceived during their opposition to the communist government in Azerbaijan that Moscow's policy of "divide and rule" had to be undermined by the removal of Soviet/Russian troops from Azeri soil. Otherwise, Moscow would continue to hold a pivotal position between the two republics, able to play one side off the other and keep the two countries dependent and destabilized.

This explains the negative view of the Elchibey government toward membership in the Commonwealth of Independent States (CIS), which itself was regarded by Azerbaijan as a new form of empire. The government therefore insisted on rapid withdrawal of Russian troops from Azerbaijani territory. The anti-Azerbaijani stance of the Russian media since the beginning of the Azerbaijani-Armenian conflict and the invasion of Baku by Soviet troops in the winter of 1990, resulting in more than 150 civilian casualties and the oppression and arrest of the leaders of the national democratic movement, made the prospect of Azerbaijan joining the CIS much less likely, thus further worsening the Azerbaijani-Russian relationship.

The Azerbaijani-Armenian war is one of the main factors that shapes Azerbaijan's foreign policy. The occupation of 25 percent of Azerbaijani territory by Armenian troops has threatened the very existence of the Azerbaijani state, forcing Azeri leaders to look for any support possible to counteract the Russian-Armenian alliance. At the same time, the war determined the fate of every leader in the republic, both directly through performance on the battlefield, and indirectly through the aggravation of the economic situation. The losses at the front—the occupation of Shusha and Lachin and the tragedy of Khojaly— caused the downfall of the communist leader Mutalibov, bringing to power Elchibey; and in the same way, Elchibey's downfall was precipitated by the Armenian occupation of the Agdam region. The rapidly increasing feeling of insecurity among the Azerbaijani population, which was caused, on the one hand, by economic problems, the flow of refugees, and the lack of experience exhibited by the Popular Front government in managing the domestic sphere, and, on the other hand, by the persistent effort to steer an independent course from Russia without support from the West or Turkey to protect the Azerbaijani state and democracy, established the basis for the successful coup d'état in June 1993 that brought to power the former communist boss Gaidar Aliev.

However, Azerbaijan shared the common problems of all the former Soviet republics—weak government, the lack of military forces, and an inability to create an efficient army.[6] This colonial heritage was reinforced by the absence of democratic institutions and a disorder in the state structures in a situation whereby the old mechanisms do not work anymore and the new ones have not yet been formed.

After Azerbaijan acquired its independence, the number of foreign policy decision-making institutions remained the same. Although their tasks and functions radically changed when Azerbaijan became an independent state, their specific roles and interrelationships remained unclear. The legislative organ—the Foreign Relations Commission of the Milli Mejlis (parliament)—is supposed to discuss and ratify important foreign policy decisions and legislation. The Ministry of Foreign Affairs is accountable to the commission. However, the main foreign policy direction is defined by the president, who is also open to the advice of the state secretary and the Department for Foreign Relations of the presidential apparatus, in coordination with the Foreign Ministry. Inter-parliamentary relations are implemented by the Department of Foreign Relations of the Supreme Soviet. The degree of coordination and interdependence of these bodies and their contribution to the decision-making process has varied under different leaders.

Since its independence, Azerbaijan has signed several agreements on diplomatic training with such foreign countries as Turkey, Great Britain, France, Holland, India, Iran, Egypt, and Saudi Arabia. While most of the agreements have a short-term focus, the most systematic partner of Azerbaijan is Turkey.

The important factors in the foreign policy decision-making process are public opinion and the position of the main political parties. Although there are more than forty parties in Azerbaijan, few of them are popular or significant. However, there are parties popular enough to influence the decision-making process. The present leader of Azerbaijan, Gaidar Aliev, is under constant pressure from opposition parties, the most powerful of which is still the Popular Front, and has to maneuver among Russia's strategic interests, public opinion, and the pressure of the opposition. However, as a representative of the old system, Aliev, in turn, tries to use his ideological experience and skills to influence and form public opinion. Proponents of Aliev's foreign policy consider the path of joining the CIS and the attempts to satisfy the interests of Russia as the only realistic means of coping with the present situation. This opinion is based on the experience of the last several years of Azerbaijan's struggle for independence, and an understanding of the fact that the West and the United States prefer to sacrifice support for democracy and independence in the newly created states for the sake of supporting stability in Russia. However, Aliev's critics think that going the CIS way will lead to a complete loss of independence and, consequently, an inability to resolve the most important problems of Azerbaijan, which are building democracy, increasing the well-being of its people, and providing security and integrity to the country.

Azerbaijan and Armenia

Azerbaijani-Armenian relations are dictated by the question of Nagorno-Karabagh. Their relations are influenced by geopolitical, historical, political, and psychological factors. Besides the role of Russia in the conflict, there is also the great burden of past Armenian-Turkish relations, which have created a very complicated interdependent set of relations in the region. The memories of the Armenian people and the socioeconomic problems typical of the whole Soviet authoritarian system in the Nagorno-Karabagh region were used by some political leaders of the nationalistic movements in Armenia and abroad for the realization of their ideas of restoring Greater Armenia at the expense of Azerbaijan.[7]

The Armenian-Azerbaijani conflict emerged in the winter of 1988, when the local authorities of the Nagorno-Karabagh Autonomous Region of Azerbaijan declared the "reunification" of the region with the Republic of Armenia. At that time the Nagorno-Karabagh region had a population of approximately 150,000 Armenians and 50,000 Azeris, and there were 121 Armenian schools, 31 Azeri, and 5 Russian. The university in Stepanakert, the capital of Nagorno-Karabagh, had opened in 1973, and provided classes in the Armenian, Azeri, and Russian languages.

The declaration was accompanied by the mass deportation and ethnic cleansing of the Azerbaijani minority in Armenia (in the Kafan and Megri regions) and by bloodshed in Sumgait (Azerbaijan) and in Gukarg (Armenia).[8] This became an undeclared war between the republics that was waged on the territory of Azerbaijan. At the beginning of the conflict, both republics were constituent parts of the Soviet Union, with puppet communist leaders, Soviet troops located on their territories, and open borders that made intervention easy and conflict resolution impossible. The crisis in both republics engendered by the conflict led to the replacement of their communist leaders. The new leaders faced a controversial choice between, on the one hand, submission to Moscow and, on the other, the objective situation in their republics, which demanded very often the opposite behavior. However, this conflict of interests in the transition period was less painful and acute for the Armenian government. In the very beginning, Moscow had tried to remain neutral, and for a very short period, even had sided with Azerbaijan. But later on, the Soviet central authorities and, after that, Russia obviously favored Armenia.[9] At the end of 1989, both republics were gathering arms, attacks on Soviet military garrisons became more frequent, and, Gorbachev issued a decree concerning the disarmament of all the illegal groups in the republics. However, while the Armenian authorities were allowed to fulfill this operation by themselves, Azerbaijan was deprived of this opportunity, and troops were brought into Baku in 1990 in order to suppress quickly the burgeoning democratic movement (the Popular Front). As one of the results of this operation, no guns were left in Azerbaijani hands. (This action was just the continuation of the old colonial tradition of the Russian empire, which had refused to allow the Muslim population to undertake military service, unlike Christian Armenians. Under Soviet rule, Azeris often discharged their duties in construction battalions.)[10] The active resistance by Moscow to the Azerbaijani democratic movement, which was closely tied with the liberation movement, constantly destabilized the political situation in the republic and resulted in a succession of five leaders in a short period.

The Armenian support (both political and military) for the Karabagh Armenians became one of the most destabilizing factors in the region and radicalized the situation in Turkey, Azerbaijan, and Iran. On 1 December 1989, the parliament of Armenia adopted the Decree on Reunification of Armenia and Nagorno-Karabagh, which has never been annulled. In 1990, elections to the Armenian parliament were held in Nagorno-Karabagh, and Armenia included the region into its budget. The present Armenian parliament has twelve members who were elected from Nagorno-Karabagh. This parliament has also adopted a decree rejecting all juridical acts that recognize Nagorno-Karabagh as part of Azerbaijan. The Defense Committee of Nagorno-Karabagh is headed by a member of the Armenian parliament. The attacks on the Nakhichevan region and fierce battles, along with the later occupation of the town Sadarak, caused a negative reaction in Turkey and created a sense of solidarity among its Turkish people with their neighbors. Despite the Armenian government's denial of participation in the conflict and coordination of the actions between itself and the leadership of Karabagh, the Azerbaijani side produced evidence to the contrary: captured soldiers with orders for occupation of the Kelbajar region signed by the chief of staff of the military forces of Armenia, and the creation of concentration camps near Spitak (Armenia) for prisoners of war.[11]

In 1989, the railway link between the two countries was destroyed. There were two routes that connected Baku to Erevan: a southern route through Nakhichevan and a northern route via Gazakh. At the beginning of 1989, attacks began on trains that traversed forty-six kilometers of Armenia before entering Nakhichevan, so that 10 kilometers of the railway were completely destroyed; victims included train conductors and passengers. This resulted in the blockade of Nakhichevan from the Armenian side. The northern route was blocked by Azerbaijan after it realized that transported goods were being used by the Armenians in the war against them.[12]

Armenian-Azerbaijani relations were sharply aggravated in November 1991 after a helicopter carrying top Azerbaijani officials, including the state secretary and minister of internal affairs, who were going to the Karabagh region for peaceful negotiations initiated by the Russian and Kazakhstani presidents, was shot down. The threat of a declared war became very real, but the Azerbaijani government limited its reaction to liquidating the autonomous status of Nagorno-Karabagh, while allowing it to retain its cultural autonomy. On 25 February, when the peace initiatives began to be implemented, Armenian troops attacked Khojaly, an Azerbaijani-dominated city in Karabagh, and massacred more than eight hundred civilians. This precipitated the resignation of the communist leader Mutalibov, who was blamed for the losses by Azerbaijan, particularly as he was blocking the creation of the national army and could not protect the Azeri population.

The Elchibey government believed that the creation of a true popular army would help liberate the occupied territories and push back the Armenian forces. Armenia, on its part, hurried to create a close military union with Russia. Since previous occupations took place right after peaceful initiatives and agreements, reliance on negotiations diminished. The war effort of the Elchibey government in the summer and fall of 1992 aimed at the return of the occupied lands; however, it brought victory only in the northern part of the front. This was accompanied by air attacks on urban areas of Nagorno-Karabagh, which only aggravated relations between the countries.

Many attempts by the Azerbaijani government to get the United Nations to condemn Armenian aggression were blocked by Russia, France, and the United States, three of the five members of the UN Security Council. Seeing little prospect for a peaceful conclusion within the framework of the UN, the Elchibey government focused on resolution of the conflict within the CSCE.

The leaders of the two republics, Ter-Petrossian of Armenia and Elchibey of Azerbaijan, both having the reputation of moderate leaders, started a long process of negotiations within the framework of the so-called Minsk group of the CSCE. However, a series of agreements were broken by the Armenian side through new offensives. In April 1993, the representatives of five countries met in Geneva for consultations on the conflict, while Armenian troops captured the Kelbajar region. In July 1993, the chairman of the Minsk group of the CSCE, M. Rafaelli, visited the conflict area, where the Agdam region of Azerbaijan was being occupied. According to Ambassador John Maresca, with the occupation of the Kelbajar region, the Armenians could no longer use self-defense as a justification for their military activity.[13] "This war was not any longer in defense of a threatened minority, but a war to destroy Azerbaijan."[14] From August to October 1993, five more regions—Fizuli, Gubadli, Zangelan, Goradiz, and Djabrail—were occupied by Armenian forces. The United Nations Security Council adopted four resolutions—822, 853, 874, and 884—demanding the immediate withdrawal of Armenian troops from the occupied territories. However, these resolutions were ignored and have never been fulfilled. The long process of negotiations seemed to lead to a deadlock. The fact that most of the agreements and truces were broken shows that both governments in fact believe that the outcome of the conflict can be resolved only on the battlefield. For the Armenian side, it is a desire to get a more advantageous position and starting point in bargaining, according to the principle that the more that is occupied, the more can be gained as a result of negotiations.

This shows the absence of any real peacemaking mechanisms at the level of international organizations, unless one of the great powers intervenes. This factor makes it clear that the only power that is interested enough to intervene and can do so, because the world community is unable to restrict its activities, is Russia, which is perceived in Azerbaijan and Armenia as an Armenian ally. The rapid rise in nationalism in Russia has generated a more coercive attitude toward the near abroad, making its unilateral intervention inevitable. Russia's interference under the guise of peacekeeping forces will mean legitimization of its covert participation in the conflicts and the establishment of direct control in the region.

There is also the problem of reciprocity of demand. The Armenian demand that Azerbaijan give more rights to its Armenian minority is dismissed in Azerbaijan because of the way Armenia deported the 200,000-strong Azerbaijan minority. This makes concessions from the Azerbaijani side more difficult. Besides that, Azerbaijan considers it unacceptable to negotiate the problem of the status of Karabagh under the pressure of force, because it creates a precedent for resolution of similar problems, especially if they are used with expansionist aims. Armenia, in its turn, finds the withdrawal of troops unacceptable, because of the lack of guarantee of security for the population of Nagorno-Karabagh, and also because the main purpose of the military pressure is the resolution of the Karabagh question in Armenia's favor. However, the resolution of the conflict will be possible when both sides realize that all the Caucasian countries share common problems and enemies. These are the problems of survival of the former colonies, which are too weak and thus vulnerable to manipulation from the more powerful states.

The Karabagh war is increasingly becoming the dominant factor affecting the fate of any leader in the republic. The slow reaction of the United States and the West to the positive changes in Azerbaijan, and the amendment to the Freedom Support Act adopted by the U.S. Congress in October 1992, which prohibited any humanitarian help to Azerbaijan, amounted to a refusal to support the nascent democracy in Azerbaijan. Naturally, this put the Elchibey government in a very weak position. The systematic losses at the front, the inability to hold onto Azeri territory and protect the country from aggression, the feeling of insecurity of the population, the rapidly increasing flow of refugees from the occupied territories, hyperinflation, and the decrease in living standards caused a fast decline in the popularity of Elchibey after only a year. The coup d'état in June 1993 was also possible because of the low popularity of the Popular Front government.

The foreign policy of the Elchibey government was characterized by an idealistic reliance on the support of the Western countries and Turkey to protect Azerbaijan from the threat of an Armenian-Russian alliance. One of the major steps of the Elchibey government was a refusal to join the CIS Treaty on Collective Security signed on 15 May 1992, unlike Armenia. The next day, as a result of double attacks from the Karabagh and Armenia, the so-called Lachin corridor was opened and the whole region outside the disputed oblast was occupied, which meant the actual unification of Karabagh with Armenia and creation of conditions enabling the direct supply of arms and troops to Azerbaijan from Armenian territory. The joint agreement of Russia and Armenia emphasized the continuing presence of the Russian Seventh Army in the republic and the patrolling of the Armenian-Turkish borders by Russian troops.

The new leader of Azerbaijan, and former member of the old Soviet hierarchy, Gaidar Aliev, being aware of the power of Russia, believed that turning to Russia in foreign policy matters would be rewarded by a change in Russia's attitude on the

Karabagh question. The reaction of the Russian "democratic" mass media was unusual—there were several articles praising the new leader of Azerbaijan, despite his past. Unlike Elchibey, who focused on democracy building at the expense of state building, Aliev concentrated on attempts to preserve the state, whose existence at the time was under threat. Since his first days of coming to power he focused on searching for "internal enemies," trying to centralize power, and restricting the opposition. At the same time, he started to improve relationships with Russia and Iran and began intensive negotiations with the local Karabagh leadership and Armenia. Aware that Russia was the only real power in determining the outcome of the conflict, Aliev came to favor CIS membership for Azerbaijan and subsequently agreed to discuss Russian proposals on the resolution of the Karabagh conflict. However, the proposals concerning a partial withdrawal of Armenian troops and the stationing of Russian "peacekeeping forces" in fact meant for Azerbaijan a double occupation and the persistence of the conflict in conditions detrimental to Azerbaijan. It is likely that if Russia does not "reward" Aliev for "obedience," he will probably follow the path of Shevardnadze, turning away from Russia. But, since he has not gained any support from Turkey or the West, Aliev's options are severely limited.

Azerbaijan and Turkey

The relationship between Azerbaijan and Turkey is conditioned by the ethnic, cultural, and linguistic ties of the two peoples, as well as the history of the national liberation movement in Azerbaijan. Elchibey, who adhered to the traditions of Musavat, intended to establish close relationships with all countries that had Turkic populations, primarily Turkey. For Azerbaijanis, Turkey is an example of successful independence and the realization of all the wishes and aims of the first Azerbaijani Republic, which had built an independent secular democratic society but had failed because of the Bolshevik occupation in 1920. It is necessary to note that, in spite of the close traditional relationship with Turkey before the 1920 Russian occupation, the political leaders of the Azerbaijani Democratic Republic resisted the idea of any kind of "united Turkic state." This is consistent with the attitudes of the leaders of the modern Azerbaijani national democratic movement. The close relationship with Turkey was also conditioned by the fact that some of the political leaders in Turkey supported the Azerbaijani democratic forces in the face of complete isolation and lack of any support from outside, although they appealed constantly to Russia and the West for support and cooperation. Turkey was also the first country to recognize Azerbaijan's independence in November 1991, the first to sign a Treaty of Friendship and Cooperation, and the first to open its embassy (13 January 1992). These steps of the Turkish government corresponded to the strategic interests of Turkey in the Central Asian Turkic republics and the region.[15] After the victory of the Popular Front, the relationship with Turkey became more intense. In 1992, Azerbaijan accounted for about 50 percent of the trade Turkey conducted with the six Turkic republics. In May 1992, direct flights by Turkish airlines to Baku (as well as to Almaty and Tashkent) were established. Close ties were also made in the sphere of telecommunications. In October 1992, the Azerbaijani population was able to watch one of the Turkish television channels. Relationships also developed intensely in the areas of phone systems, the private sector of the economy, and education. A significant aspect of the treaties signed with Azerbaijan can be seen in the pipeline project from the Caspian oil fields to the Black Sea terminal in Turkey.

Although Azerbaijan regarded Turkey as the most reliable neighbor and a possible "protector" in the conflict, there was still a high degree of sensitivity and resistance to the possibility of Turkey becoming a new "elder brother." Besides, Azerbaijan did not want to regard Turkey as the only bridge to the West, but preferred to develop direct relations with Western countries whenever possible. In turn, the Turkish government was in an ambiguous position, trying to protect its strategic interests in the region and maneuvering between Western indifference toward Azerbaijan and the sympathy of the Turkish people toward their Turkic brothers abroad. During the period of communist rule, Turkish leaders had been rather careful in their political support for Azerbaijan. After coming to power, the Elchibey government gained more open and decisive support from Turkey. At meetings of international organizations, and also in the mass media, Turkish representatives condemned Armenian aggression. President Özal actively whipped up international support for Azerbaijan in reaction to the Armenian offensive in Kelbajar in the spring of 1993. The preferences and orientations of the population of Azerbaijan at that period were confirmed by numerous sociological surveys, which showed that more than 70 percent of Azerbaijanis preferred the Turkish model of development, whereas only 5 percent favored the Iranian model.[16] However, the idealistic perception of the role of Turkey as a protector of Azerbaijan against Armenia was gradually replaced by disappointment and the realization of the limits that tied Turkey to its membership in NATO and Europe, and of the country's dependence on the West.

After the downfall of Elchibey in June 1993, relations with Turkey initially became cooler as the priority of the new leader's foreign policy was directed toward its northern neighbor. However, the mutual interests of the countries tended to support a continuing relationship, although not as intense as before. The downfall of Elchibey meant a weakened Turkish position in the region and a Russian victory in the two countries' struggle over this sphere of influence. Relations with Turkey, however, became more intense after the occupation by Armenian forces of vast territories of Azerbaijan at the end of the summer and into the fall of 1993. A series of meetings took place at that time. In September 1993, a group of Turkish parliamentarians, headed by Ayub Ashik, the chief of the Motherland Party faction, and Hikmet Chetin, the minister of foreign affairs of Turkey, visited Baku, where President Aliev noted that Azerbaijani-Turkish relations had passed to a new stage, with Turkey confirming its readiness to offer multilateral assistance and support for Azerbaijan. The visit of Turkish Prime Minister Tansu Ciller to the United States in October 1993 was, at least partly, the result of Ankara's concern over the intensification of Armenian offensives and the threat of unilateral control of the region by Russia. The aggravation of the situation on the front precipitated a visit by Hasan Hasanov, foreign minister of Azerbaijan, to Turkey in November 1993, during which both sides expressed their extreme concern with the continuing occupation of Azerbaijani lands. Hasanov visited Turkey again at the end of December, when both sides confirmed the stability of the Azerbaijani-Turkish borders. The official visit of President Aliev and Foreign Minister Hasanov marked the end of the "cold" period of the relationship with Turkey. More than ten agreements were signed in Turkey, and Aliev assured Turkish leaders that the future pipeline would pass through Turkish territory. The future level of closeness of the Azerbaijani-Turkish relationship will depend on the threat to the Azerbaijani state from Armenia and Russia and the extent to which Turkish strategic interests in the region are affected.

Azerbaijan and Iran

Azerbaijani-Iranian relations are most controversial. Azerbaijan shared a significant part of its history with Iran, until their separation in 1813 and 1828 as a result of Russian-Iranian wars. Since that time, the two parts of Azerbaijan have been developed within separate states—one in Russia (with a population of seven million), the other in Iran (with an Azeri population of nearly twenty million). Two main factors have determined these relations: the threat of the rise of nationalism in Iranian Azerbaijan for Iran and the secularism of the population of northern (independent) Azerbaijan. Although most of Azerbaijan (at least its eastern and southern parts) is historically the home of the Shi'i sect of Islam, religion has had a very weak tradition as a political force in Azerbaijan because of the reasons mentioned earlier. At the beginning of the democratization era, there were only two functioning mosques in Baku, which had a population of two million people. President Elchibey's policy toward Iran was conditioned by two factors: the unacceptability of the Iranian model of society, and the assimilationist policies in Iran toward the Azerbaijani minority. President Elchibey called then for the opening of native-language schools in southern Azerbaijan. The relations of the Elchibey government with Iran were restricted to economic cooperation. The Popular Front government, with its adherence to the Westernization of the society, definitely did not consider relations with Iran a priority. At the outset, the population of Azerbaijan had high expectations for Iranian support during the conflict and thus was quickly disappointed by the official position of Iran, which, having realized the political interests and fears of the country, were ambiguous. The ambivalent position of Iran, which seemed to have more interest in supporting Armenia rather than Azerbaijan, helped create an image of Iranian impartiality in the conflict, which, during a certain period, allowed Iran to mediate, but to no effect.

The new leader, Aliev, adhering to his careful foreign policy position, started to cultivate close relations with Iran. Iranian officials quickly responded in order to gain on their Turkish competitors. At the meeting with Aliev, Ali Asqar Nahavendian, the ambassador of Iran to Azerbaijan, confirmed Iranian condemnation of Armenia's recent offensives and its occupation of Azerbaijani lands and noted that Iran regarded its relationship with Azerbaijan as the most significant one. These activities were also connected with the sharp aggravation of the situation on the Armenian-Azerbaijani front, especially after the occupation by Armenian forces of the Kelbajar region, when nearly sixty thousand refugees fled to Iran.

In October 1993, an agreement was reached on the close cooperation and representation in Baku of one of the biggest Iranian foundations, Bunyadi Mustefezan ve Djanbazan. A series of visits by representatives of the Azerbaijani government, including Speaker of the Parliament R. Guliev and Foreign Minister Hasan Hasanov, to Iran and visits by Iranian representatives, including Deputy of the Iranian Parliament Fatima Gumayun Mugeddemi, to Baku showed how the intensification of Azerbaijani-Iranian relations was directly connected to Armenian offensives on the front. As previously mentioned, facing continual occupation and losses on the front, the leadership of Azerbaijan appealed to any neighboring country that showed a readiness to support Azerbaijan. In exchange for this political support, Azerbaijan decreased its resistance to the spread of the religious institutions widely financed by Iran. However, Iranian efforts to disseminate religious materials among the secular Azeris have fallen flat. In conclusion, Azerbaijani relations with Iran as established by the Aliev government showed his attempt to adhere to a balanced approach in Azerbaijan's foreign relations. However, he has continued to make Azerbaijan's relations with Russia the country's foreign policy priority.

Azerbaijan, Russia, and the CIS

As previously mentioned, the Azerbaijani-Russian relationship is determined and mediated by two factors: the anticolonial movement of Azerbaijan and the Karabagh conflict. Concerning both factors, the interests of the two countries conflict. For Russia, Azerbaijan is a strategically important country because of its natural resources and its defense industry. Azerbaijan has the largest radar station in the former Soviet Union on its territory, a powerful industrial complex, and, more importantly, is a buffer zone between Russia and its historical rivals, Iran and Turkey. The strategic importance of Azerbaijan is increasing with the development of nationalism and great-power ambitions in Russia, which is trying to retain Azerbaijan in its sphere of influence. Trying to justify the pressure on Azerbaijan, Russia explains its policy as being necessary to protect the Russian minority in Azerbaijan, to stem the threat of Islamic fundamentalism, and simply to continue Russia's missionary role in its former colonies. The latest justification is to posit Russia as the traditional "stabilizer" and "peacekeeper" in the region.

The Popular Front of Azerbaijan (PFA) from the very beginning of its existence has closely tied its activities to minorities living in Azerbaijan, primarily the Russians. The organizational committee of the Popular Front included representatives of the Russian minority. This fact reflected the historical traditions of the Azerbaijani national liberation and democratic movements. No meeting of the PFA at the Square of Freedom passed without speeches from representatives of Russian, Jewish, Tatar, and other communities. In the headquarters of the PFA, there was a Department on the Protection of Minority Rights, which worked very actively during the conflict. The Russian community organization Sodruzhestvo actively supported and cooperated with the PFA, especially in breaking the informational blockade of Azerbaijan. The activists of Sodruzhestvo regularly visited Moscow, appealing to Gorbachev and then to Yeltsin, arranging vigils in front of the Russian White House, and demanding an end to the anti-Azerbaijani propaganda in the Russian mass media. From the very beginning, the Azerbaijani Popular Front anticipated the important distinction between relations with the Soviet power holders and with the democratic forces of Russia and the Russian people. In every speech at the Square of Freedom, the leaders of the PFA expressed their firm solidarity with and support for the Russian democratic forces. Moscow, however, seemed to respond by sending troops to Azerbaijan in January 1990, which resulted in many casualties among civilians, including Russians.

The tragedy brought the peoples of the republic even closer: at the funerals, where more than one million people participated, grief, condemnation, and political appraisal of the event were expressed by the leaders of the Russian Orthodox Church, the organization Sodruzhestvo, the leaders of the Jewish Synagogue and the Jewish community, and others. Some Russians, frightened by the disturbances and bloody events (Armenian pogroms and massacres of civilians by Soviet troops in January 1990), as well as by anti-Azerbaijani propaganda in the central mass media, decided to leave the country, but most of them soon returned. The Jewish community in Azerbaijan tried to publish its official condemnation of the latest and previous events, explaining them as aggression against Azerbaijan. However, it was taken out of print by the occupying military censors. Despite expectations, no official condemnation or apology from Moscow followed the January tragedy. This had a significant impact on the future of the Azerbaijani-Russian relationship and relations with the CIS. On 7 October 1992, the Azerbaijani parliament overwhelmingly opposed the ratification of the CIS agreements, which had been provisionally signed by former President A. Mutalibov in December 1991.

The course of independence from Moscow realized by Elchibey's government was firm, and consequently covered political, economic, and military spheres.

After coming to power, Elchibey announced plans to introduce a new currency, the *manat*, to hedge against a possible flood of rubles. On 12 October 1992, in Moscow, Elchibey signed the Treaty on Mutual Security and Friendly Relations with Russia, which promised only limited cooperation. Russia's rapidly waning influence in the economic sphere during the Elchibey regime finally expressed itself in a $10 billion oil contract that was prepared to be signed by SOCAR (State Oil Company of the Azerbaijani Republic) and a consortium of big Western companies, including Amoco, Unocal, BP, and Pennzoil. In addition, Elchibey's government preferred to conduct the negotiating process within the framework of the CSCE, endeavoring to build a close economic relationship with all the former Soviet republics, but on the basis of bilateral treaties and agreements, without joining any union.

Political relations with the other Turkic republics were not very cordial because of different domestic and foreign policy orientations. The orientations of the Central Asian republics were less centrifugal, more dependent on the center, and most of them still had authoritarian communist leaders (relations with Uzbekistan were spoiled, for example, when Elchibey noted that the country suffered from a lack of democracy and gave shelter to the persecuted leaders of the Uzbek democratic movement). At the same time, Elchibey initiated the idea of economic cooperation between Azerbaijan and Georgia and Ukraine as a balance to the Russian attempts to integrate those countries into the CIS. However, because of fear of provoking Russia, the idea was not put into practice. As a result of the independent course of the Popular Front government, Azerbaijan suffered both economic and military pressure from Russia. In the spring of 1993, Russia established the highest trade tariffs of all the former Soviet republics, including the Baltic republics, with Azerbaijan.

In June 1993 the Elchibey government collapsed after eight months of unsuccessful attempts to resist the Armenian offensives. The collapse was precipitated by the coup led by the renegade military commander Suret Guseinov with, according to many sources, direct Russian military support.[17] By that time, Azerbaijan had become the only republic among the former Soviet republics that had succeeded in getting Russian troops to leave its territory. The coup took place after Elchibey's refusal to accept Moscow's demands that Russian forces be allowed to return to Azerbaijan under the guise of peacekeeping forces. Before the June coup, Azerbaijan and Armenia were close to signing an agreement on resolving the conflict over Karabagh on the basis of the trilateral plan initiated by Russia, Turkey, and the United States in early May 1993, which involved the withdrawal of Armenian forces from the occupied territories. On 27 May the three countries declared themselves in favor of a settlement between Armenia and Azerbaijan; however, the Karabagh Armenians refused to sign the agreement, insisting on the unilateral intervention of Russian peacekeeping forces, which was unacceptable to Azerbaijan. Having refused to sign the proposal, the Karabagh Armenians did so after the downfall of Elchibey. These facts gave credence to the opinion that, in addition to giving assistance to the insurgents, Russia had deliberately undermined an international peace initiative, of which it was a cosponsor, to further its own objectives.

As a matter of fact, the coup took place several days before the oil contract was due to be signed with the Western consortium, according to which the pipeline would go through Iran to Turkey and the Mediterranean. The new president suspended the signing of the contract, and, later in September, it was announced that one of the oil fields would be developed by the Russian oil firm Lukoil. After a long process of bargaining, with Russia insisting on a 20 percent share in the consortium, the sides agreed on 10 percent. The share given to Russia was deducted from Azerbaijan's share of 30 percent. According to experts, this 10 percent means the deduction of $5 billion in income, which is forty times more than the national budget of Azerbaijan in 1993.[18] Moreover, Lukoil has in common with all the former Soviet oil companies the problems of backward technology, considerable debt, and imperfect equipment, which makes the benefit of this cooperation for Azerbaijan questionable. On 22 August, the Armenian terrorist organization ASALA made it clear that it would disrupt any pipeline going through the territories of the two republics to Turkey.[19]

Very soon it became obvious that Russia would be the major priority in the foreign policy of the new government. During his working visit to Moscow on 5 September, Aliev said, in a conversation with Yeltsin, that the Azerbaijani-Russian relationship should be raised to a new level, and he expressed his dissatisfaction with its previous state. As his first goodwill gesture, Aliev informed the speaker of the Russian parliament of his decision to hand over to the Russian court six Russian mercenaries captured in Azerbaijan who had been sentenced to death a year earlier. Aliev also expressed his hope of Russia's role in the regulation of the conflict and assured Yeltsin of his firm adherence to democratic reforms in the republic. "New Azerbaijan and new Aliev," he declared, and both leaders came to an agreement on increasing the level of interstate relationships and strengthening the traditional friendly relations and multilateral cooperation. The president of Azerbaijan made it clear that Azerbaijan would like to join the CIS. At the meeting with the Azerbaijani president, Russian Premier Viktor Chernomyrdin noted that Russia would help Azerbaijan in its efforts to stabilize the economic and political situation in the republic.[20]

On 20 September 1993 the parliament of Azerbaijan, in a vote of thirty to thirteen, adopted the resolution to join the CIS. However, an independent sociological survey showed that among nineteen political parties in the republic, only six positively approved of Azerbaijan joining the CIS, while the rest expressed negative attitudes to it.[21] During his next visit to Moscow on 24 September, Aliev signed the entire package of agreements related to membership in the CIS, including the Agreement on Collective Security and Economic Cooperation. However, it is unclear how it will be implemented when two members of the commonwealth are in a state of war with each other. The discussion on the implementation of the agreements reveals many contradictions in the positions of Russia and Azerbaijan. First of all, in the matter of the border troops, Azerbaijan expressed its willingness to accommodate the troops on the borders with Armenia, which represented the main threat to the republic, while Russia insisted instead on their accommodation on the Azerbaijani-Iranian borders. Interestingly, the Russian position was accepted by Iran, since the protection of Iranian borders from Azerbaijani nationalism reflects the strategic interests of Iran as well. The other contradiction lies in bringing Russian troops into Azerbaijan under the guise of peacekeeping forces. But despite the assurance of the Russian representatives at the CSCE meeting of the foreign ministers on 30 November 1993 that there were no contradictions in the interests of Russia and its neighbors, they could not get the mandate of a peacekeeping status for the Russian troops from the CSCE. While the ambassador of Russia to Azerbaijan, Valter Shonia, assured the Azerbaijani people that the question of bringing Russian troops back had never been raised and was not being raised then,[22] the Russian representative in the Caucasus, Vladimir Kazimirov, visited Baku on 4 February with a proposal to begin an immediate cease-fire and bring Russian troops into Azerbaijan. President Aliev repeatedly declared, locally and internationally, his unwillingness to bring Russian troops back to the republic, and he said this in particular during his visit to France on 22 December 1993. Meanwhile, on 2 February 1994, the Russian television channel Ostankino said there were plans for Russia to locate five military bases in the Caucasus: three in Georgia, one in Azerbaijan, and one in Armenia.

The other source of pressure and point of discord for the interests of the two countries is the debated status of the Caspian Sea, which would decide the fate of the Azerbaijani oil fields. The discussion over the status of the Caspian Sea, whether it is a sea or a lake, is of crucial importance for Azerbaijan and was the focus of attention at the meeting of the leaders of the Caspian littoral countries in October 1993. The definition of the Caspian basin (which geographically is a lake) as a sea will mean for Azerbaijan the loss of all major offshore oil fields, since all the waters beyond the twelve-mile coastal zone will be declared neutral, and will allow the Caspian Sea to fall into the range of Russian submarines. In his interview with the correspondent of the informational agency Khabar Service, Azerbaijani Vice Premier Guliev said that some countries of the Caspian littoral zone want to change the status of the Caspian Sea, "but they will never succeed."[23] According to some sources (e.g., Turan agency), during the meeting of Russian and Azerbaijani officials in November 1993, Russian representatives made it clear that in exchange for an Azerbaijan reversal of its position on the twelve-mile zone in the Caspian basin, Russia will put pressure on Armenia to withdraw its troops from the occupied territories. In summary, the demands of Russia on Azerbaijan are as follows: accommodating Russian peacekeeping forces in Karabagh and military bases in Giandja; accommodating Russian troops on the Azerbaijani-Iranian borders; allowing Russian participation in the oil contract with the Western consortium; routing the pipeline through Russian territory; and accepting the Russian proposal about the status of the Caspian Sea.

The aforementioned supports the idea that the Azerbaijani-Russian relationship is determined by, on the one hand, the geostrategic interests of Russia in the region and, on the other hand, Azerbaijani interests of security and protection from Armenian aggression in a situation where Russia is using the conflict as means of pressure on Azerbaijan.

Azerbaijan and the Western Countries

The pro-Western orientation of the Elchibey government, conditioned by the domestic course of building a democratic secular society, did not find an adequate response from the Western countries. The two main reasons for this were the informational blockade of Azerbaijan and the misperception in the West that the country was headed toward an Islamic fundamentalist revival, a misperception created by Gorbachev and the Russian media. Besides that, the West was not inclined to interfere in the historically traditional sphere of Russian strategic interests, especially since Russian control of the Caucasian region was preferable to the prospect of dealing with several unstable republics. However, Elchibey's government was rather firm in its pro-Western foreign policy orientation. The relations with the West were made through the prism of the Armenian-Azerbaijani war. Therefore, relations were closer with those countries that did not take an openly anti-Azerbaijani position, for example, Great Britain and Italy, and were colder and more distant with the countries where the influence of the Armenian community was strong, like France. The Western countries' relations with Azerbaijan were determined mainly by their economic interests with the republic. The leading oil companies of the United States, Great Britain, Norway, and Turkey opened offices in Baku and started wide cultural and humanitarian activities. Elchibey declared that Azerbaijan was open for foreign investment and encouraged multilateral economic relations with Western countries. The Elchibey government was preparing for the signing of the $10 billion contract between SOCAR and the Western consortium, including such companies as Amoco, BP/Statoil, Pennzoil/Remco, Unocal, McDermott, and Turkish Petroleum Corporation. However, relations between Azerbaijan and various countries were different, so that for example, Azerbaijani-British relations developed better than those with the United States, where there is a traditionally powerful Armenian lobby.

Meanwhile, the activities of the U.S. embassy in Azerbaijan gradually penetrated the wall of misperception between the two countries, and in May 1993, a delegation of Azerbaijani parliamentarians headed by the speaker of the parliament, Isa Gambar, visited the United States, where they had meetings in Congress and at the State Department and attended the opening of the Azerbaijani embassy. The visit appeared to be the beginning of a shift in the relations of the two countries and marked a positive change in the attitudes of American politicians toward the new Azerbaijani government. At the same time, another delegation of Azerbaijani officials visited Great Britain.

The June coup, however, interrupted the improvement in the Azerbaijani-American relationship and the signing of the contracts with the consortium. While Russia and Iran welcomed the downfall of Elchibey, Turkey and the United States affirmed their support for the democratically elected Elchibey and put pressure on the new government to release the imprisoned former speaker of the parliament, Isa Gambar. London's reaction to the coup was more indifferent, and British representatives were the first to meet with the new president after the presidential elections in October 1993. Moreover, at the meeting with the British foreign minister, the president received an official invitation to visit Great Britain.

It is clear that, in spite of changing priorities in his foreign policy (from Turkey and the West to Russia and Iran), Aliev was undoubtedly hoping to retain ties with the West. However, he suspended the signing of the contract, supposedly under pressure from Russia, although officially the blame was laid on disagreements between oil experts concerning the contract. During his period in power, Aliev regularly met with the representatives of the oil companies, assuring them the contract would be signed soon. The other goal of the new president's foreign policy was improving relations with France. The visit of Foreign Minister Hasan Hasanov to France, where he met with the French foreign minister and President Mitterrand, prepared the way for the 22 December 1993 visit of the Azerbaijani president to Paris, which was his first visit to the West. France and Azerbaijan signed an agreement on friendship and cooperation, including the inviolability of borders and respect for the territorial integrity and sovereignty of both states. Also, British parliamentarians were accepted by the Azerbaijani president in November 1993, and the head of the British delegation declared the intention of creating an Azerbaijani-British interparliamentary group in the coming month. In September 1993, a delegation of the U.S. State Department, headed by the secretary of state's advisor on the NIS, Strobe Talbott, visited Baku. During his meeting with President Aliev, he said that the major aims of his visit were to assist in the peace process in the region and to support the independence of Azerbaijan.[24] Aliev, in his turn, assured Talbott of his adherence to the main principles of democratic development, independence, a market economy, and peaceful relations. On 17 December, Aliev met the Bundestag Deputy Willie Wimmer, whom he informed about the situation on the Azerbaijani-Armenian front and the conditions of the refugees. The Bundestag deputy promised to put forward a proposal at the next CSCE meeting for returning the refugees to their lands.[25] Azerbaijani relations with Israel remained stable and close since the presidency of Elchibey broadened ties with Israel in cultural, political, and economic spheres. Under Aliev, relations continued to improve, particularly in the agricultural and business spheres. In summary, one might say that the countries of the West apparently have rather contradictory interests in the region. In the Azerbaijani-Armenian war, their interests are conditioned by Christian solidarity and by the powerful

Armenian lobby in the largest European states and the United States. Moreover, regarding Russia as a partner, they allow the strengthening of Russian influence in the region through the Russian-Armenian alliance. That, however, leads to the weakening of the Turkish position in the region, and therefore, indirectly, to the weakening of the Western and American strategic position. Furthermore, the war and the ambiguous position of the West in the region can cause the radicalization of countries with Muslim populations (e.g., Turkey) in the region, as well as the possible loss of Azerbaijan as a state, which has been building a democratic society in the Islamic world and could be a political and strategic ally of the West in the region. The main objectives of the foreign policy of Azerbaijan are determined by state security issues and the goals of building an independent, secular, democratic society. The tactics employed in achieving these ends differ for the different leaders. The foreign policy priorities of Elchibey's government were based on a political and ideological principle, one oriented toward the West and Turkey, as a model of Westernized society. Under increasing threats to the country's security created by the war, Aliev preferred to find a balance among the competing aspirations of the most important powers in the region. He tried to achieve this by satisfying their economic and strategic interests.

War and further occupation of Azerbaijani territories are becoming dominant factors in the country's foreign policy, which then determines its domestic policy. The continuing conflict also radicalizes and destabilizes the situation in the republic, blocking the development of democracy. The June coup, which changed the leaders, is the best example and proof of this. The unilateral intervention of Russian troops in Azerbaijan, accompanied only by a partial withdrawal of Armenian troops, will be perceived in the republic as a double occupation, a violation of the sovereignty of the republic, and Russian assistance to Armenia to annex part of Azerbaijani lands. Thus, the presence of Russian troops in Azerbaijan would be possible only under the condition of a repressive regime in the republic. The continuing occupation of Azerbaijan will also cause the radicalization of neighboring countries like Turkey and the polarization of the region by creating new blocs. The lack of Western support to democratic governments in the Caucasus, the "double standard" approach in responding to the conflicts, will push Azerbaijan to find any allies in the region. It will also block the development of democracy in the country and cause disappointment in democratic ideas among the population, creating the basis for fundamentalism. The fate of stability and democracy in the region depends not on unilateral intervention, but rather on the creation of a balance of power and collective efforts by the world community to establish peace in the region.

Notes

1. On Azerbaijan in the nineteenth and twentieth centuries and the formation of social classes, see Audrey Altstadt, *The Azerbaijani Turks: Power and Identity Under Russian Rule* (Stanford, CA: Hoover Institution Press, 1992), p. 20.

2. On the history of the national liberation movement in Azerbaijan and the views of its leaders on the political, religious, and ethnic issues in Azerbaijan, see Aydin Balaev, *Azerbaidzhanskoe natsional'noe dvizhenie: Ot Musavata do Narodnogo Fronta.* (Baku: Elm, 1992), pp. 3–11.

3. On the issue of the ethnic and political composition of the first Azerbaijani parliament, see ibid., p. 8.

4. On the Russian strategic interests and manipulation of the ethnic conflicts, see Fiona Hill and Pamela Jewett, *"Back in the USSR": Russia's Intervention in the Internal Affairs of the Former Soviet Republics and the Implications for United States Policy Toward Russia* (Cambridge: Harvard University Press, 1994); and also Thomas Goltz, "Letter from Eurasia: The Hidden Russian Hand," *Foreign Policy* (fall 1993), p. 96.

5. On the strategic objectives and interests of Turkey in the region, see Stephen Blank, Stephen Pelletiere, and William Johnsen, *Turkey's Strategic Position at the Crossroads of World Affairs* (Carlisle, PA: Strategic Studies Institute, U.S. Army War College, 1993).

6. On this issue, see *Current Situation in Georgia and Implications for U.S. Foreign Policy: Briefing of the CSCE* (Washington, DC, 1993). Witnesses: Charles Fairbanks, Thomas Goltz.

7. On different views on the Azerbaijani-Armenian conflict, see L. Alieva, "Razrushit' stereotipy," *Bakinskii rabochii*, 15 October 1989; T. Swietochowski, *The Problem of Nagorno-Karabagh: Geography Versus Demography Under Colonialism and in Decolonization in Central Asia* (New York: St. Martin's Press, 1993); Charles J. Walker, *Armenia and Karabagh: The Struggle for Unity* (London: Minority Rights Publication, 1991).

8. On the issue of ethnic cleansing and violence in Azerbaijan and Armenia, see Arif Iunusov, "Pogromi v Armenii v 1988–1989 gg.," *Express-Khronika*, 26 February 1990; and idem, "Pogromi v Azerbaidzhane v 1988–1990 gg.," *Russkaia mysl'*, 7 June 1991.

9. The position of the Soviet and then Russian governments in the Nagorno-Karabagh conflict is analyzed in Hill and Jewett, *"Back in the USSR"*; and Goltz, "Letter from Eurasia."

10. The reasons for the weakness of the Azerbaijani army are discussed in Swietochowski, *Problem of Nagorno-Karabagh*, p. 153.

11. These facts were represented in the letter of H. Hasanov, the foreign minister of Azerbaijan, to the president of the Security Council of the United Nations on 4 February 1994.

12. On the issue of blockades, see Ramiz Abutalibov, "The Nakhichevan Connection," *Azerbaijan International* (winter 1994), p. 36.

13. On the process of the Armenian-Azerbaijani negotiations within the framework of the CSCE and Kelbajar offensives, see Ambassador John Maresca's presentation at the Nagorno-Karabagh Conference, Washington, DC, CSIS, 6 May 1993.

14. This is a quotation from Blank, Pelletiere, and Johnsen, *Turkey's Strategic Position*, p. 97.

15. Turkish relations with the newly independent Turkic states and Turkey's interests in the region are analyzed in Philip Robins, "Between Sentiment and Self-Interest: Turkey's Policy Toward Azerbaijan and the Central Asian States," *Middle East Journal*, vol. 47, no. 4 (fall 1993), pp. 593–610.

16. One of the surveys was conducted in Azerbaijan by the Independent Center for Strategic and International Studies (Baku) on the refugees from Armenia and Karabagh in September 1992.

17. Evidence of the close connection between Commander Suret Guseinov and Russian military forces is analyzed in Hill and Jewett, *"Back in the USSR"*; and Goltz, "Letter from Eurasia."

18. The data on Russia's share in the contract are given in the article by A. Tutushkin in *Kommersant Daily*, 19 March 1994, and also in A. Kerimov (former state secretary of Azerbaijan), interview, *Azadlyg*, 17 March 1994. Detailed analysis of the situation in the oil industry and of the contract with the Western consortium is also given by S. Bagirov, the former president of SOCAR, in a series of interviews with *Azadlyg* (November 1993).

19. On the issue of the pipeline, see Hill and Jewett, "*Back in the USSR*," p. 13; and S. Bagirov, interview by Turan agency correspondent, *Zerkalo*, 26 August 1993.

20. On the results of President Aliev's visit to Russia, see the information in *Molodezh Azerbaidzhana*, 11 September 1993.

21. The survey was conducted by Khabar Service informational agency; the results were published in *Zerkalo*, 23 September 1993.

22. Valter Shonia, interview, *Azadlyg*, 19 February 1994.

23. On the issue of the status of the Caspian Sea, see S. Bagirov, "Khazarin statusu barede gerari parliament gebul etmelidir" (the decision on the Caspian Sea status must be ratified by the parliament), *Azadlyg*, 26 October 1993.

24. On the visit of the delegation of the U.S. State Department to Azerbaijan, see the information by F. Askeroglu in *Azadlyg*, 14 September 1993.

25. On the visit of Willie Wimmer, Bundestag deputy, to Azerbaijan, see the information in *Azerbaidzhan*, 17 December 1993.

14

Armenia's Foreign Policy
Defining Priorities and
Coping with Conflict

Rouben Paul Adalian

The foreign policy of countries as small and remote as Armenia generally do not register on the international relations screen. At best they are studied within regional frameworks. Developments in the historically strategic region of the Caucasus, however, have not gone unnoticed for at least six reasons. First, the breakup of the Soviet Union has destroyed the old order and opened a chaotic transitional period, resulting in the emergence of three independent states that need to adopt new political and economic systems, as well as define their place in the world community. Second, the ethnic complexity of the region, the weakness of the Transcaucasian states, and the rise of nationalism have become sources of instability and causes of violent local conflicts threatening to involve other countries. Third, the exploitation and transportation of and access to valuable natural resources have been hampered by warfare along borders. Fourth, the collapse of the economy of the area has brought populations to the brink of famine, and the flight of hundreds of thousands of refugees from the conflict zones has compounded the problem. An ongoing international humanitarian aid crisis has been created. Fifth, as an area classified as the "near abroad" by Russia, the region's problems, difficulties, and conflicts have exposed it to intervention and made it a testing ground for new Russian policies. And sixth, other regional powers, principally Turkey and Iran, are also competing for influence in Transcaucasia, while Western states are vying for a role also.

When it was part of the Soviet Union, in the inventory of statistics once relied upon to study the comparative development of the constituent republics, three facts were routinely cited to highlight Armenia. One, Armenia was the smallest Soviet republic. Two, with over 90 percent of its population Armenians, the country was ethnically the most homogeneous Soviet republic.[1] Three, despite this concentration, the total Armenian population of the Soviet Union was the most widely disbursed of the nationalities.[2] Armenian enclaves dotted Georgia, Azerbaijan, Russia, and Ukraine.[3] One of these enclaves, Nagorno-Karabagh, had been awarded administrative status as an autonomous district. In the final years of the Soviet era, it became the spark that lit a fire still burning across the mountains of Armenia and Azerbaijan. Armenian statehood came into existence against this background.

The Geographical Imperatives

There are two imperatives of geography that govern all of Armenia's foreign policy. The first is the small size of the country—29,800 square kilometers. The second is its position on the map. Armenia is landlocked. These two facts automatically make the security of the state the primary challenge of Armenia's foreign policy formulators. That challenge is made all the greater in view of the kind of neighbors Armenia has on its borders. Azerbaijan is hostile, Turkey is unfriendly, Georgia is in anarchy, and Iran is an international outcast.

Armenia's exposure is therefore considerable. Georgia and Azerbaijan may not be much bigger than Armenia, but Turkey and Iran, in sharp contrast, are sizable states that conduct very active foreign policies in the region, and in certain instances, very aggressive policies vis-à-vis some of their neighbors. Those policies, in and of themselves, may not necessarily confront Armenia. They nonetheless directly impinge upon Armenia's security concerns, because in the international arena, Turkey and Iran stand at opposite poles and defend conflicting interests and values. This places Armenia in harm's way, whether Armenia is involved or not in the contest for regional influence between Turkey and Iran.[4]

This reality locates Armenia's security and foreign policy concerns within a Middle Eastern framework.[5] In many respects, the present-day separation of Transcaucasia from Russia has returned the region to its older historical context. However, Russia remains the main player in the politics of the three former Soviet Transcaucasian republics. While many of the broader interests and objectives of the theocratic regime in Iran and of the secular government of Turkey appear clear and constant, Russia's interests and objectives in the last three years have been evolving. Coping with Russian policies, therefore, has remained a priority for Armenia. That bilateral relationship continues to dominate, and at times dictate, the choices that Armenian policy makers must make in order to guarantee their country a modicum of security.

Armenia's distance from Russia and the absence of contiguity complicate this relationship. The serious interference of Azerbaijan and Georgia in the communication and transportation routes connecting Armenia and Russia has been a constant factor destabilizing the entire region. Armenia's vulnerability to blockade, now a permanent reality on the Azeri and Turkish borders, and an occurrence of some regularity, intentional or not, on the Georgian border, is a determining factor of strategy and policy. Both friends and enemies exploit it.[6]

The Behavioral Determinants

There are other determinants of Armenia's foreign policy. These, too, highlight the question of security for Armenia. In a world where governments are increasingly formulating policy on the basis of ethnicity, the national identity of a population has become a powerful determinant of political orientation. In the case of the Armenians, ethnicity, however, is a factor contributing to isolation rather than integration. They share ethnic kinship with no one else. Despite the strong sense of national identity motivating Armenian political behavior, and certainly driving the animus of the hostilities against Azerbaijan, mainstream Armenian political rhetoric takes pains to describe Armenia's objectives in terms that avoid casting Armenian policy as ethnically motivated. Rather, it prefers to characterize its problems in political terms. Even so, the perception from a distance that an ethnic conflict is being waged over Karabagh has been little influenced by official Armenian explanations.[7] Furthermore, the inevitable territorial dimension, despite denials of territorial claims to the contrary by the Armenian government, has only strengthened the perception that Armenians and Azeris are fighting over a piece of land. The aspect of ethnicity as a determinant of political behavior is therefore a major element in Armenian thinking.

As for religion, while the divide between Christendom and Islam runs deep, in the case of Armenia a common faith with most Europeans has proven too superficial a reason for regional orientation. Rather, Islam provides Armenia a source of disorientation in the sense that it deprives Armenia of a greater level of association with many of its closer neighbors. Religion, then, has imposed a restriction on Armenia's integration into its immediate neighborhood. For instance, Islam is seen ostensibly as a point of commonality among the Central Asian states. In the secular West, Christianity does not provide a similar basis for political conduct. Prejudices may still govern policy, but pragmatic goals continue to dominate Western thinking and as such deprive a country like Armenia of any moral lift it might derive from membership in a larger club. If anything, the West is averse to openly framing policy with religious overtones and prefers to distance itself from conflicts that have a bearing on religion, as the Bosnian situation has shown.

Even so, the fact that Armenia lies along the dividing line of two world religions cannot be minimized. In this particular case the line even straddles the divide between Europe and Asia. An area once depicted as a crossroad is more frequently described now as a fault line between civilizations. Nor has it helped at all that the once-communist world and a region governed by authoritarian regimes converged here also. By some postulations, the cultural gulf between societies on opposite sides of these typologies of defining attributes is the very source of the tension sustaining the current conflicts.[8]

Finally, for the last one hundred years Armenia's economy has been entirely dependent on Russia. The level of industrialization, which was comparatively high in the late Soviet era, and the employment it provided a densely urbanized population, made Armenia a wholly captive economy. While a free enterprise system and open relations with neighboring states might have enhanced economic opportunity, in the short term it was going to do little to alter the colonized economy of Armenia. With no energy resources to power its industrial base or easy access to many of the raw materials used by its factories, the notion of a quick conversion to other modes of production or to products marketable in the global commercial arena was beyond the realm of the possible. Also, because Armenia was so completely integrated into the Soviet production, monetary, transportation, and trading systems, and lacks readily marketable natural resources, it has to maintain close economic relations with Russia. In retrospect, as development funds did not materialize from Western financial institutions, the social consequences of the delay rapidly diminished what options a newly independent state as strapped as Armenia might have gained in seeing its political freedom restored in the wake of the Soviet collapse.[9]

The Two Policy Objectives

When Armenia gained independence, its leaders hoped for a more balanced power relationship than the one currently observed in the region. That may have been a hope that required greater skill and resources than were available to Armenia's leaders. Even so, the desire to avoid making decisions in the shadow of an overwhelming regional power rested at the core of the key foreign policy objectives formulated by Armenian leaders.[10] This same consideration motivated leaders of other former Soviet republics.

To overcome the risk of isolation and to gain guarantees for its national security, Armenia's primary foreign policy objective was defined as rapid integration into the world community. The implementation of this policy was to be carried out on two levels: through the establishment of active bilateral relations with as many countries as feasible, and multilaterally, through participation in international organizations. Both of those approaches were expected to earn Armenia a measure of respectability as a nation wanting to cooperate with the forces governing the international system.

A second objective, however, seriously hindered Armenia's first goal. Before the responsibility of formulating foreign policy had even been thrust upon the Armenian government by independence, the question of Nagorno-Karabagh had redefined the Armenian political landscape. It had even redefined much of the Transcaucasian landscape, and its repercussions were registered as far away as Moscow. Any question with reverberations across such a wide area was bound to interfere in any rationally devised foreign policy. In view of the insistence of the Armenians of Nagorno-Karabagh upon a set of political demands that in the final analysis meant the transfer of sovereignty over the district from the Azeris to the Armenians, Armenian foreign policy was to remain captive to powerful national sentiments. Nationalism swept the country as the Karabagh struggle quickly acquired in the Armenian frame of mind existential dimensions evocative of the catastrophic collision of the early part of the twentieth century when Armenians nearly everywhere in the region were overrun. While the destruction caused during World War I could not be undone, Armenian foreign policy strived to undo the damage of the Stalin era and the errors of the Gorbachev years. Armenia thereby assumed the obligation to defend a threatened population that had resorted to armed resistance based on its understanding of the consequences of those past events.[11]

The reaction in Azerbaijan to the initial stages of the Karabagh movement left a lasting legacy also. The pogrom in Sumgait in February 1988 and the forcible population exchange ignited in November of that year were the evidence in Armenian popular conception of depopulation policies with which Armenians were all too familiar.[12] Any new political leadership rising from the national movement would be held responsible for a favorable resolution of the Karabagh struggle. The alternative appeared unacceptable, for in the aftermath of the expulsion of the Armenians from the rest of Azerbaijan, it became inevitable that lines were going to be drawn in the sand. In many respects that is precisely what the Karabagh conflict has become, a fight to determine the lines that will permanently separate the Armenians and the Azeris.

Reform and Foreign Policy

The Armenian National Movement (ANM), whose leaders now head the government in Armenia, advocated democracy, political pluralism, and a market economy as part of its general program. With few fringe exceptions, these goals represented a national consensus. For Levon Ter-Petrossian, the president of Armenia, espousal of these domestic goals had as much to do with Armenia's foreign policy objectives as it did with the effort to reform post-Soviet society. Hrant Bagratian, the fourth and longest-serving prime minister, in office since February 1993, is a trained economist who has been spearheading the reform programs and conducting the negotiations with international financial institutions.[13] Prior to his appointment, Bagratian had been the deputy prime minister since independence. The strong espousal of a systemic transformation was based on the conviction that adherence to the principles of a free market economy and a liberal democracy would expedite integration into the international community, especially the West.[14] The first major piece of legislation adopted by the new government in Armenia was the privatization of land, which immediately secured the right of private ownership.[15]

Free speech flourishes in Armenia, as the country adopted the UN Covenant on Civil and Political Rights on the same day as its Declaration on Independence and applies the covenant as its supreme domestic law.[16] Critics exist, and can speak, publish, assemble, organize, demonstrate, and openly oppose the government. There has been a surprising consistency in the government's adherence to the reform program on the broader issues defining a civil society. Despite the problems of reform, and the limited degree of economic benefit so far derived by only a very small segment of the populace, the forms and the legal basis of a civil society continue to be introduced and nurtured by the government. In an interesting demonstration of his determination to undo socialism and to proceed with reforms, the president persuaded parliament in January 1994 to reverse a decision adopted in the beginning of the winter season to delay further privatization until the economic situation in the country improved.[17] The desire to reform society is therefore genuine. From the standpoint of Armenia's international priorities, the introduction of those reforms is promoted by the government as evidence of its serious commitment to liberalization. This policy should have earned Armenia an improved status in the world community.

Armenia's policy makers have discovered, however, that this is not necessarily the case. They have observed that Western policy toward the newly independent states is frequently driven by strategic and economic interests irrespective of the type of regime that has taken hold of the country. Armenia's experiment in democracy has earned it less credit than was estimated earlier. That is not to say that the process of democratization is now in jeopardy. What the delayed Western reaction has done, however, is weaken the government, which has failed to demonstrate so far that, by staying the course of liberalization, political benefits could be derived from the international system. On the other hand, if the Armenian government had not pursued political and economic reform, it might have been in worse shape with regard to its international standing.

Even so, opposition parties have raised serious questions about the government's foreign policy. The opposition parties have also been vehemently critical of the government's economic policies. Yet they have not been able to capitalize on mass discontent with the state of affairs because none has formulated persuasive alternatives. On the matter of foreign policy, the opposition has been on the whole the voice of ardent nationalism and militancy on the question of Nagorno-Karabagh. Many of the opposition groups, whether on the right or on the left, also endorse even closer relations with Russia and are proponents of a foreign policy that selects protagonists on the basis of their position on Nagorno-Karabagh. The opposition forces have yet to find leadership capable of galvanizing a sufficient segment of the constituency to be taken seriously by the government. But debate on foreign policy is not muted, because the government itself at times has become divided over some issues. Two figures, among others, who played prominent roles in these debates are no longer in the government because their views challenged the comparative moderation reflecting the president's position. Erstwhile Prime Minister Vazgen Manukian, an early and articulate leader of the ANM, openly endorsed direct intervention in Azerbaijan over Nagorno-Karabagh.[18] Once regarded as a potential presidential candidate, he settled for the premiership. He resigned from the government in 1992, to return briefly in 1993 as defense minister. The resignation of the first foreign minister, the American-born Raffi Hovannisian, also occurred over policy and personality differences with the president, who has preferred a low-key foreign policy conducted on the basis of private diplomacy.[19]

If communism in Armenia has been successfully abolished and authoritarianism so far has been avoided, why has Armenia not yet obtained results that meet its international priorities? The answer is an evident one. The conflict with Azerbaijan over Nagorno-Karabagh has come to dominate all concerns and has overtaken most other considerations in Armenia's foreign policy.

Foreign Relations

Before going into the international implications of the conflict, a measure of Armenia's foreign policy goals and achievements should be taken lest they be obscured by the intractability of the Karabagh problem.

There were four categories of states with which Armenia hoped to establish working bilateral relations. These were, first, its immediate neighbors (Georgia, Azerbaijan, Iran, Turkey); second, the member states of the former Soviet Union; third, the Western democracies (principally France, England, Germany, Austria, the United States); and fourth, countries with large Armenian diaspora settlements (Iran, Syria, Lebanon, France, the United States, Argentina).[20]

What degree of success has Armenia registered in accomplishing this objective? And has it derived any benefit?

Armenia has formal diplomatic relations with Iran and Georgia, but none with Turkey and Azerbaijan. That has aligned Armenia on a north-south axis and precluded it from the other directions in its immediate vicinity. This orientation was not made by choice. It was compelled by the process of elimination. Armenian relations with Georgia and Iran are not on a strong footing either. In the absence of balance, the dependence of Armenia on Georgia and Iran has reduced Armenia's bargaining position.

Georgia and the Spillover Effect

The difficulties with Georgia arise from the chaotic domestic conditions in that country. Though no fundamental differences exist between Armenia and Georgia, that relationship has often become abrasive in view of the continued failure of the Georgian government to secure the transportation links to Armenia. The problem is compounded by widespread highway banditry and extortion by governmental and private forces. With all of its supply lines cut off by Azerbaijan

and Turkey, and with limited connections with Iran, Armenia is wholly dependent on Georgia for the transport of vital goods and resources. These include
food and fuel. The fuel arrives, or is supposed to arrive, in the form of natural
gas purchased from Turkmenistan and piped across Russia. The food, and we
might add, all the humanitarian aid sent by ship, arrives through the Georgian
ports of Batumi and Poti.

This forms the basis of a perfectly sensible commercial relationship from
which Georgia stands to benefit economically and politically. That would have
been the case, however, only if Georgia had a stable government. The civil strife
tearing that country apart has served to undo all the benefits that Georgia might
have derived from the transport dependence of Armenia. Instead, the gas piped
to Armenia is misappropriated and the goods destined for Armenia are frequently
plundered. These disruptions have had the effect of creating pressure on the
Armenian government to take action to secure those transport lines, including the
suggestion of sending armed guards. In an admission of his government's inability to guarantee Armenia the security of those lines of transportation, Eduard
Shevardnadze of Georgia even floated the idea of allowing joint Georgian-Arme-
nian patrolling of the pipelines, roads, and rail lines vital to Armenia. Other
Georgian leaders resisted the idea in view of compromises already made with
Russia for securing the rail lines in the west of Georgia. Also, the president of
Armenia opposed any such commitment because of the risks involved in becom-
ing embroiled in Georgian domestic conflict.

What then is the current status of the Georgian transport lines to Armenia?
They have become hostages of the Karabagh conflict. These lines, principally
the gas pipeline, and the rail lines and bridges, are periodically sabotaged in the
Azeri-populated district of Marneuli in Georgia, which is situated between the
northern Armenian border and the city of Tbilisi.[21] Moreover, Georgia is itself
desperately in need of fuel resources. In negotiating with Azerbaijan and Turkey
on these matters, its leaders, no doubt, have been pressured to desist from providing comfort to the Armenians by protecting those transportation lines.

Iran: An Anxious Neutral

While Iran presents a threat to many governments inside and outside the region,
curiously, Armenia does not feel that effect. This is due less to the fact that
Armenia presents no problems to Iran than to the considerable challenge that
Iran faces with Azerbaijan. While the Azeri-Iranian relationship cannot be addressed here, nevertheless it governs in considerable part how Iran reacts to
Armenia. That reaction is manifest in its desire to appear balanced and cautious,
and therefore Armenia's transport deficiencies are not being met by Iran. While
negotiations have been conducted for a gas pipeline from Iran, construction has
not gotten off the ground. Paying for such a project is not within Armenia's
financial capacity, and funds cannot be raised in the West for a project that might

enhance Iran's own economy. One other far smaller project, a bridge across the Araks River, has the potential of alleviating some of Armenia's economic woes. This, too, is proceeding at a pace that can only raise concerns in Armenia. This bridge, between southern Armenia and northern Iran, has taken the better part of two years to construct. It is being assembled one span at a time at a rate so incremental that the object of its lesson cannot be missed. While concerned with developments in Azerbaijan and the pro-Turkish policies of its government, Iran wants to make sure that it is not perceived as being supportive of Armenia, even though it has demonstrated little desire to side with Azerbaijan.

Turkey and the Pall of the Past

The problems of Armenia's relations with Turkey are many, and if a case can be made about Iranian neutrality, the same cannot be said about Turkey. Turkey has repeatedly introduced new hurdles for even extending diplomatic recognition of Armenia, and lately has conditioned its relations with Armenia entirely on the Karabagh conflict.[22] To make the point, Turkey has closed its border with Armenia. In effect it is supporting Azerbaijan's blockade of Armenia. Turkey has refused to heed numerous Armenian appeals to proceed in developing bilateral relations independent of the Karabagh conflict. Prospectively more destabilizing, however, are the charges made by the Turkish government that Armenia is harboring the Kurdistan Workers Party (PKK). In view of the methods applied by the Turkish government to counter the challenge posed by the Kurdish insurgency, including carrying out cross-border operations, the accusations carry an implicit military threat.[23]

Further complicating Armenian-Turkish relations is the vocal involvement of both Turkish and Armenian society in addressing the nature and content of that relationship. Of all Armenia's relations with other states, the one that is bound to engender the greatest internal debate is policy toward Turkey. To a considerable extent the same is true inside Turkish society. Therefore, internal pressures on the two governments in formulating bilateral policies are sufficiently high as to constrain both governments in ways that neither may want. Given the historical background to that relationship, it would seem that these constraints would be stronger in Armenia. The fact of the matter appears just the opposite. Armenia's government has cautiously embarked on a series of initiatives designed to build confidence in Turkish foreign policy circles about Armenia's long-term goals. It has had little effect. On the contrary, in view of the continuing reluctance of Turkey to normalize relations, the effort has only made the Armenian government seem much too conciliatory with a historical antagonist.[24]

That relationship does not appear to be heading in a constructive direction. For instance, Turkey introduced the PKK matter in order to apply pressure on Armenia. It embarked on this campaign after Karabagh forces occupied Azeri territories in the spring of 1993. Despite Armenia's efforts to prove that there is no substance to the charges, Turkey has continued to supply the Turkish media stories about cross-border activities by the PKK. These newspaper accounts regularly identify certain sites in Armenia as Kurdish bases. Some of the sites coincide with the handful of villages in Armenia inhabited by Kurds. Other sites include the dormant nuclear power plant near Erevan, the capital of Armenia, and more interestingly, the Lachin corridor now connecting Nagorno-Karabagh with Armenia.[25]

There may be undisclosed contact between Armenia and the PKK. Yet it would appear to be hardly in Armenia's national interest to aggravate relations with Turkey, when they are not good to begin with. Even if it were argued that this might serve Armenia as a way to pressure Turkey on an issue that the Turkish government regards as a priority concern, it would not have a great deal of credibility. Armenia is in no position to support the PKK. Besides, it does not want to destabilize a stable border.

It is one of the paradoxes of the Armenian-Turkish relationship that the boundary between the two countries is actually the least unstable. After all, this frontier was that stretch of land where NATO forces directly faced the landmass of the Soviet Union. It was a heavily fortified and closely monitored border throughout the Cold War. Turkish allegations that this border is now porous and that terrorists can cross it are not entirely believable. NATO has not been disbanded, and the Turkish armed forces certainly have not let down their guard. But the charges do serve a domestic purpose in Turkey. They satisfy public hostility toward Armenia over the Karabagh conflict. They also provide an explanation for the intransigence of the Kurdish problem.[26] But this creates conditions that can only complicate future efforts to reduce tensions between Armenia and Turkey. For landlocked Armenia, normalization of relations with Turkey has a very practical purpose. Turkey can provide the most direct access to the West.[27]

It needs to be added that contacts between Turkish and Armenian officials are quite regular despite the tensions and the absence of formal recognition. Armenia's interest and membership in organizations promoting multilateral relations have provided a framework for Turkey to meet with Armenian officials and at least discuss issues of mutual interest. The example here is the Black Sea Economic Cooperation Agreement (BSECA). The meetings of the various committees of the BSECA have seen Armenian Foreign Ministry personnel, parliamentarians, and economists traveling to Istanbul and Ankara. In some respects, the environment in which these meetings occur has improved a little. The late president of Turkey, Turgut Özal, personally and very actively sought an expanded role for Turkey in the entire region.[28] The policy of his successor, Suleyman Demirel, appears more modest, and he has avoided extreme rhetoric of the kind made by Özal suggesting that Turkey bare its teeth with Armenia. This remark stuck in some Armenian circles as emblematic of Turkey's true intentions.[29]

Turkish foreign policy is generally institutionally driven. As a departure, the personality of the head of state in Turkey may well be the defining factor in relations with Armenia. The current turmoil in Turkish domestic politics, however, suggests that relations with Armenia might actually worsen. The political rifts between religious and secular forces evidenced by the March 1994 municipal elections in Turkey have only required Prime Minister Tansu Ciller to rely on institutions that have traditionally defended secular statism, thus highlighting the role of the army all the more. The military will hardly be a moderating force in relations with Armenia.[30]

If one of Armenia's chief foreign policy priorities is to stabilize relations with its immediate neighbors, there has been little success. These relations remain difficult and inconstant. They are frequently marred by tension and complications stemming for the greater part from the Karabagh conflict.

Russia the Resurgent Power

The second group of states with whom Armenia hoped to cultivate relations is the former republics of the Soviet Union. With the exception of relations with Russia, this effort has also registered little progress. This lack of progress, however, has little to do with anything Armenia might or might not be doing, and the Karabagh conflict is not a factor here. The absence of solid relations with FSU states has been determined by the same serious economic ills afflicting Armenia. Furthermore, strategic interests connecting Armenia and the Central Asian states or the more distant Baltic countries are almost nonexistent. Where relations do exist, they are derived from purely economic interest, as with Turkmenistan, from which Armenia purchases its natural gas. Relations with Ukraine and Kazakhstan exist, but little is known of the content of those relations.

In the last three years Armenia's relations with Russia have made a 180-degree turn. Where once Armenia's political leaders were in constant conflict with Mikhail Gorbachev, relations with the Yeltsin government have been very different.[31] That is not to say they have been easy. Especially in the area of economic policy, every program to bring about some change in the Russian economy has had immediate repercussions in Armenia, and of course elsewhere across the FSU. For instance, the uncertain policies about the ruble zone in 1993 led to the serious disintegration of the Armenian economy. It finally compelled Armenia to introduce its own national currency at a time when it had no reserves with which to back it.[32] This has placed Armenia in the odd situation of wanting to maintain good relations with Russia while fearing the direction of Moscow's economic policies. The changes sprung on it by Russia's monetarists have been especially disquieting. Those monetary policies have strengthened Russia's hand with FSU states, like Armenia, whose economic dependence on Russia is not easily reduced. It also means that Russia must find ways to subsidize those faltering economies if Moscow does not want to see complete disarray on its periphery.[33]

For Russia, Armenia has proved to be a reliable strategic partner. In this matter the convergence of interests is very real. Russia wants a presence in the Caucasus.[34] Armenia needs that presence in the Caucasus. That need does not earn Armenia very many points with its neighbors, but it clearly informs Armenia's policies. While voices in the West are raised more and more about the return of Russia to the so-called near abroad, the truth of the matter is that Russia never left. Its forces have remained in many places in the near abroad. In the case of Armenia, the Erevan government made arrangements early on to keep the Russian army posted on the Turkish frontier. Armenia's geostrategic disadvantages compelled its government to make a very quick decision in 1991 when President Yeltsin formed the Commonwealth of Independent States (CIS). Armenia joined as an original signatory to the Treaty on Collective Security signed in Tashkent on 15 May 1992.

There was little faith in the CIS at the time. Georgia and Azerbaijan refused to join, and Armenia's alliance with Russia appeared quite improbable. On other hand, the tug-of-war that then ensued between Russia and Georgia and Russia and Azerbaijan provided little incentive for the Russian Federation to contribute to the stability of those countries. Without argument Russia did the opposite.[35] Thus, comparatively speaking, Armenia was spared domestic unrest instigated by Russian interventionist designs. To date the Ter-Petrossian administration remains the only democratic government formed in the region after the first open elections held in the Soviet Union in 1990 still holding the reins of power, undisturbed by recidivist communists or nationalist extremists. Much of this is due to the fact that the government has stayed the course of reform. No doubt it also has to do in good measure with the fact that the Ter-Petrossian administration defines cordial relations with the Russian Federation as a priority in its foreign policy.

The question remains, is Russia a reliable partner for Armenia? In the matrix of relations conducted by Russia, Armenia, after all, is but one small piece of the volatile Caucasian jigsaw puzzle. In the context of the current unrest throughout the region, Armenia's stock with Russia may be up, but what are the prospects of a continuing partnership when Russia exercises such a preponderance of power? The question acquired some urgency with the turnover in the Azeri government in June 1993, when former Communist Party chairman Gaidar Aliev replaced the Azeri Popular Front leader Abulfez Elchibey in a series of political maneuvers that amounted to a coup. Aliev's subsequent decision to bring Azerbaijan into the CIS in September 1993 and mollify Russia had the semblance of a concession that would restore a more favorable attitude from Moscow. Soon after, observers saw the strange incident of the accidental shelling by Armenian border guards of the automobile convoy carrying Vladimir Kazimirov, the Russian president's special envoy to the region, which occurred in late November, and the public outrage expressed by Russian Foreign Minister Andrei Kozyrev, as evidence that Russian-Armenian relations were souring.[36] When less than a month later the Azeri army staged a massive offensive on all fronts around

Karabagh, the tide of battle also appeared to be shifting. Even so, the matter of stationing Russian troops along external CIS borders proved more than the Azeri government was prepared to concede. Russian-Azeri relations stalled again.[37]

The Armenian government conducts its foreign policy on the basis of very pragmatic considerations. With the exception of the Karabagh conflict, it is devoid of ideological and other programmatic objectives. Its relationship with Russia, however, may well be one of the very few objectives that might be described as holding the significance of a foreign policy doctrine.

The United States and the West

The significance of this doctrine can be appreciated in the context of Armenia's relations with the Western democracies. While the Armenian government understood that economic relations will have to be negotiated and conducted in its immediate region, it looked to the West for three things: financial, technological, and security assistance. The matter of security had to be resolved quickly. Because the West was not forthcoming with any security arrangement for Armenia or any of the newly independent states, Russia was Armenia's only option. That became all the more apparent when the United States advanced the notion that Turkey could serve in the region as its proxy security guarantor. There was logic in promoting Turkey as a model for the other Turkic states of the southern tier and in wanting to see Turkey play an expanded role. The vacuum created at the end of 1991 was daunting, and United States strategists felt they had little resources at their disposal to suggest an American or any other Western presence in those areas. Furthermore, there was concern that Iran, a foe whose revolutionary ideology had been cause for considerable grief, would exploit the vacuum in the region. In effect, that policy was driven less by U.S. confidence in Turkey's capabilities than fears of rapidly expanded Iranian influence. But Armenia could derive no benefit from such a U.S. policy. On the contrary, the policy only highlighted Armenia's potential isolation and encirclement at a time when it already faced serious complications with both Azerbaijan and Turkey. In another paradox that emerged in the wake of the breakup of the Soviet Union, Western policy appeared to confirm for Armenia what the Russians had always found convenient to reinforce: Armenian insecurity about Turkey's ambitions and the potential consequences these presented in light of their past experience.

With its other global responsibilities, the United States did not design a policy so fine-tuned as to factor in every nuance arising from the specific conditions of the newly independent states.[38] In addition, Europe on the whole deferred this matter to the United States. The extent to which security concerns weighed on President Ter-Petrossian's mind became evident during his trip to England in February 1994. His visit took place before the 1993–94 winter offensive by Azerbaijan against Nagorno-Karabagh had ended. For a man averse to saying anything in public on matters of foreign policy that might run a risk in any quarter, his pique was all too evident with the British, who had conducted an openly pro-Azeri policy for purely commercial reasons. Ter-Petrossian is quoted as saying that British policy would be different if Armenia had oil to export, and that Armenia would intervene militarily in Azerbaijan if the Karabagh Armenians were threatened with genocide.[39]

To introduce some balance in the security arrangements that have emerged, the Armenian government has vigorously pursued relations with France. France remains the only European country that has shown a special interest in Armenia. This stems as much from historical ties as from contemporary interest. More critically, relations with France also derived from the Armenian government's desire to reactivate the nuclear power plant shut down after the 1988 earthquake out of concern for the safety standards applied in its construction. Armenia entertained hopes that France, with its advanced nuclear technology and long experience in the civilian use of atomic energy, would be helpful in upgrading the safety of the Armenian plant and in advising on, and possibly financing, its operation.

The concern for a security balance also drives Armenia's relations with the United States. To enhance that relationship the Armenian government has stayed its course of demonstrable structural reform. Unlike U.S. relations with the larger FSU states, which are premised on factors besides progress on liberalization and democratization, Armenia bears a greater obligation to demonstrate progress in view of the aid it receives from the United States. If it did otherwise, Armenia would find itself in a far more questionable position when requesting aid. The U.S. assistance extended to Armenia, much of it in the form of emergency aid, has been important in sustaining the democratic government in Armenia.

Aid, however, was not at the top of Levon Ter-Petrossian's agenda when he traveled to the United States the day after he was elected president of Armenia in October 1991. Instead his purpose was to communicate his pro-Western policies in an obvious gesture of breaking with Moscow. While receiving him as a democratic leader, the United States was reticent to go much further than acknowledging the legitimacy of his government. The symbolism of a White House meeting was important, but it did not go far in bolstering Armenia. In the framework of the relations between two superpowers, an assertive foreign policy by a country far down the totem pole presented a puzzlement to the Bush administration. Mikhail Gorbachev still governed in Moscow as president of the Soviet Union. The pace of events soon outdistanced earlier U.S. policy, and Armenia augmented its efforts to develop closer relations with the United States. That goal remains central to Armenian foreign policy in order to sustain the reform effort. It does not appear as crucial at the moment from the standpoint of security.

The Diaspora: Seeking to Reconnect

It is no coincidence that the existence of a large, active Armenian diaspora community in the United States has contributed to strengthening relations between the United States and Armenia. Armenia's policy of establishing good relations with states where Armenian diaspora communities exist is motivated by the desire to create additional channels of integration into the world community. That policy is designed to derive benefits that the diaspora can obtain for or offer Armenia. This was best evidenced by the reaction to the emergency needs created by the 7 December 1988 earthquake. Similarly, assistance delivered at critical junctures in the worst months of the winters of 1993 and 1994, although not sufficient by itself to alleviate all of Armenia's shortages, has helped define a supportive role for the Armenian diaspora. Armenia is therefore committed to making certain that its policies toward states where these communities exist take this factor into view.

France and the United States remain, however, the only two countries where the Armenian communities also are sufficiently involved in the political process as to exercise some degree of influence. Various groups in these communities, of their own volition, have been working with their governments on the most pressing matter of the day. Their efforts have centered on the delivery of the considerable humanitarian assistance that Armenia has come to depend on in order to feed its population. Yet, despite its stated policy and the benefits its draws, the Armenian government has not exactly figured out how best to connect with the Armenian diaspora. While the Armenian diaspora is not a new phenomenon, working with the Armenian diaspora is a new experience for the Republic of Armenia. It is the subject of considerable frustration all around because of conflicting expectations and general confusion arising from the complexity of the diaspora itself, an organism that is far from being monolithic.[40]

Complicating relations with Armenian diaspora communities has been the role of the émigré political organizations. These were the crucibles of Armenian nationalism during the Soviet era. In the face of the ever-wider dispersion of the descendants of the population exiled from Turkey during World War I and their growing assimilation, these organizations kept the flame of nineteenth-century romantic nationalism alive. The Armenian Democratic Liberal (ADL) Party, despite its conservative political philosophy, had long recognized the Soviet Armenian republic as a legitimate entity. The larger and more ardently nationalistic Armenian Revolutionary Federation (ARF) was the repository of the Armenian irredenta and the advocate of a "free, independent, and united" Armenia. Convinced that the people of Soviet Armenia would turn to its leadership when the time arrived to throw off communist rule, the ARF was surprised and confused when an indigenous liberation movement was organized and attracted a mass following. Sidelined by the ANM, the ARF shifted into an opposition party competing for power in Armenia and withholding the support of its diaspora following for the ANM. Although the wind was taken from its sails, the ARF still has at its disposal multiple organs of the Armenian diaspora press that have become its platforms for criticizing and opposing the ANM. The result in Armenia-diaspora relations has translated into a situation where the Armenian government has not been able to count on the unqualified support of the diaspora, especially those communities where the ARF enjoys political primacy, as in some Middle Eastern countries. The Armenian government has done better in the larger diaspora concentrations of the West, where the size and diversity of the communities meant that organizations outside the control of the ARF would associate freely with the government of Armenia without involving themselves in the domestic competition for power and influence in the country.

The Institutions and Personalities

While in its conception Armenia's foreign policy mapped out reasonable objectives, the implementation of that policy, it has to be said, has been uneven. That is the case for at least two reasons. First, Armenia's options are limited and some of the choices it has made are not necessarily those it would have preferred to make. Its immediate environment requires Armenia to be constantly adjusting to difficult circumstances. While it might have done better, it certainly could have done far worse. Compared to other FSU states, Armenia's record compares favorably. From the standpoint of its critical needs, it has far to go.

The institutions currently involved in the forging of foreign policy in Armenia are three in number. These are the president's office, the Foreign Ministry, and parliament. Independent institutions, such as think tanks, advanced schools, or special interest groups that might exist, still have little influence on the process. Armenia is governed by a presidential system, and the Ministry of Foreign Affairs is a part of the executive branch. That means Armenia's foreign policy is formulated by the president, his close advisors, and key ministers. This concentration was further underlined by the involvement of the State Agency for National Security in foreign policy matters, since the state's security is at the very top of the government's daily problems, given the conflict on its borders. The agency reports directly to the president. Its present role, however, is unclear, since its apparatus is undergoing reorganization.

With little institutional depth, this is a risky way of devising and implementing foreign policy. The political costs of a reversal would be considerable for the government. Until such time when sufficient experience and expertise is acquired by the growing community of individuals in Armenia now involved in foreign policy issues, the likelihood that foreign policy making will acquire a more institutional mode is remote. Parliament is completely absorbed with domestic issues. It is a body functioning with difficulty itself because the government party has only a small plurality of votes. The government has to rely on a large bloc of independent legislators in order to get its programs adopted. Also, parliament is involved in foreign policy making only occasionally. Moreover, there are few foreign policy experts on hand to assist the government or parliament. Virtually all of the staff of the Foreign Ministry and its diplomatic corps is learning on the job. These are serious handicaps for a nation facing mounting difficulties.

An interesting division of labor has emerged to compensate for these deficits and the current shortcomings of the Foreign Ministry. The president, Levon Ter-Petrossian, conducts relations with Russia. His personal appearances with Russian leaders, however, occur frequently within the setting of the CIS Council of Presidents. Economic relations with Russia are handled by the prime minister, Hrant Bagratian, who, for instance, was in charge of the negotiations for the reactivation of the dormant nuclear power plant near Erevan. Russian Prime Minister Viktor Chernomyrdin and Deputy Prime Minister Oleg Soskovets were his counterparts in finalizing the joint venture that was worked out. Bagratian also is the highest-ranking official interacting with international financial institutions. The vice president, Gagik Haroutiunian, holds the portfolio for relations with Iran. The foreign minister, Vahan Papazian, is most active in conducting relations with the Western states as well as organizations like the CSCE and NATO. The most widely traveled official, however, may be the deputy foreign minister, Jirair Libaridian, who, as the president's foreign policy troubleshooter, represents Armenia at the CSCE negotiations for a resolution of the Karabagh conflict. Therefore, he is the Armenian diplomat who meets most frequently with the Azerbaijani Foreign Ministry representatives. He also has a prominent role in conducting relations with Turkey. With Russia promoting its own peace plan since late 1993, the cease-fire negotiations presided over by Russian Defense Minister Pavel Grachev have seen the emergence of the Armenian defense minister, Serge Sarkisian, on the international scene also.

Libaridian and Sarkisian represent the growing sophistication of Armenian diplomacy and the interesting team of people President Ter-Petrossian has slowly gathered about him. The inclusion of diaspora Armenians in the government has been a topic of endless controversy and the source of resentment both in and out of Armenia. Early efforts to be inclusive were reversed as that tended to leave the impression that the Foreign Ministry was rapidly becoming a stronghold of Westerners who would be lacking the skills to deal with the countries in Armenia's immediate vicinity, not to mention Russia and Iran, which would be especially suspicious of them. With the baggage of their diaspora background these Westerners would also be likely to harbor views on Turkey that might make it especially difficult for them to develop relations. Indeed, speculation on the resignation of Raffi Hovannisian has centered on his conduct of relations with Turkey, and whether he elevated the question of the Armenian genocide to the annoyance of the Turks to a level that interfered with the task of solving more immediate problems. That is probably only part of the explanation, but a diaspora Armenian entrusted with the business of dealing with Turkey provides opportunity for speculation everywhere. Yet Jirair Libaridian is an individual especially adept at handling the issue, for in his previous career he was a specialist in the topic of Armenian-Turkish relations.[41]

Serge Sarkisian is an equally complex figure who also has joined the Armenian government from the outside. In Sarkisian's case, home is Mountainous

Karabagh, where firsthand military experience in the defense of the region saw him elevated to the post of defense minister of Karabagh before Ter-Petrossian co-opted him. He has come to symbolize the mutual identification of Armenia and Karabagh in defense matters. His new status as a negotiator for the resolution of the war in Karabagh communicates the Armenian government's commitment to supporting the defense of Karabagh. His appointment could only imply a toughening of the Armenian position and a greater reliance on militarization as faith in a negotiated end of the conflict eroded.

A general impression of the state of domestic affairs in Armenia is one of disarray. So complete a structural and economic transformation under conditions of war and blockade may not allow for much better. For all its gaps, Armenia's foreign policy, where coordination among a set of high-level government officials has been achieved, leaves a better impression. It also says that the Foreign Ministry still is far from being equipped to assume greater responsibility. On the other hand, the constant requirement of the Armenian government to manage a wide array of issues that depend on Armenia's foreign relations may mean that many more ministries than just those of foreign affairs and trade will be involved. As another example, because Armenia must import a disproportionate amount of its energy needs, the minister of energy, Sebuh Tashjian, spends as much time outside as inside the country. Here again, more than the health of the country's economy is in question.

The Karabagh Conundrum

Karabagh is the crux of most of Armenia's foreign policy complications. Notwithstanding the official position of the Armenian government, which asserts that it is not directly involved in the Karabagh conflict, the connection between Armenia and Nagorno-Karabagh is self-evident. What began as a very low-intensity ethnic conflict in a remote enclave has escalated into a full-scale war.[42] And every step in the expansion of the conflict has had serious repercussions for Armenia.

The Karabagh war presents a classic example of conflict escalation. All parties concerned seriously underestimated the potential risks involved in perpetuating the conflict. To begin with, Armenia miscalculated the strategies to which Azerbaijan would resort in order to reestablish control over Karabagh. Azerbaijan misunderstood the depth of the resistance and believed a purely military solution was within the reach of its resources. What others could not foresee was the exceptional determination of the Karabagh Armenians, whose numbers and isolation seemed to indicate that the failure of their particular struggle was a foregone conclusion. In the wake of the complete militarization of the situation in Karabagh and the unexpected operations carried out by the Karabagh army, it has been forgotten that the Armenians had nearly lost the fight. From an analytical standpoint, it is vital to understand this turnaround of events in order to appreciate where the errors were committed, why the conflict has expanded, and why a resolution of the conflict has not been attained.[43] What also needs to be explained is how the Karabagh conflict has tested more than the will of Armenians and Azeris. The conflict must also be seen in the context of the schemes of the regional powers vying for influence in the area. The vacuum in Transcaucasia would have become the source of competition among regional players even without the Karabagh war. The fact that sources of direct confrontation already existed in the region meant that all the players would be increasing their stakes depending on how these conflicts played out.

When the Soviet Union was dissolved and Armenia and Azerbaijan emerged as independent states, overnight the Karabagh conflict was redefined. Azerbaijan's territorial integrity and sovereignty over Karabagh acquired greater urgency, and the Karabagh movement went from one that aspired for self-determination to one that, from a juridical standpoint, had become secessionist. That condition seriously hampered Armenia's political efforts to extend diplomatic support to the Karabagh Armenians. The contested status of an autonomous district of the USSR became the subject of dispute between two sovereign states. At a disadvantage in the international arena, the Armenian government dropped all talk of unification to avoid being accused of expansionism. At the same time, during those critical months at the end of 1991 and the beginning of 1992, the sudden isolation of Karabagh confronted its leaders with certain decisions that would determine the fate of their mountain district. The conflict had matured, however, to a stage where a retreat from the political positions already taken would have meant the collapse of the Karabagh struggle for self-determination.

The wide gulf between the national sentiments driving the conflict was underscored when the Azeri government abolished the separate status of Karabagh and declared Azerbaijan an integral state. That unilateral decision left the Karabagh Armenians with little choice but to proceed with their declaration of independence and to seek separate statehood.[44] While the legality of both the Azeri and Karabagh decisions may be debated, either one by itself would have been sufficient as a declaration of hostilities. In the absence of the Soviet framework, and with the emergence of national states, the autonomous districts created on the basis of the ethnic distinction of the inhabitants from the titular nationality of the republics became time bombs in Transcaucasia. While the republics stood to gain their independence, the autonomous districts stood to lose their prerogatives, since nation-states are far less prone to extend special status to subgroups than federal systems. In the case of Nagorno-Karabagh, the fuse was lit long before.

At this initial stage the Armenian Republic would have been content to find a negotiated settlement of the Karabagh problem in order to keep its government's priorities focused on the domestic agenda. Leaders in the area were also inclined to mediate. President Ter-Petrossian met with Presidents Yeltsin of Russia, Nazarbaev of Kazakhstan, and Rafsanjani of Iran in the search for a mediated settlement. Each of those efforts failed, and the area has not seen this level of involvement from leaders of other states since. These were costly failures for Armenia, and the timing of Ter-Petrossian's meeting with Rafsanjani in Iran, where a cease-fire accord was signed, proved particularly embarrassing. While the Armenian president sought peace, the Karabagh Armenians proceeded with their own plans. The opening of the Lachin corridor in April 1992 brought about the collapse of all these efforts. As for Ter-Petrossian, the military developments cast him in either of two roles: one, as a leader who really did not have control of the situation; or two, as a daring manipulator who was negotiating peace with leaders of neighboring states while other Armenians waged successful battles. That kind of Machiavellianism, however, was far from the kind of diplomacy the Armenian government could afford to engage in with one of the two powerful states on its border. Nor was it the kind of embarrassment a new country would want to inflict on a regime that can unleash considerable forces in the Islamic world. As a matter of fact, the opposite is true. Armenia is fully cognizant of the reality that all the states in the vicinity of Transcaucasia have large Muslim populations. There is one other consideration in Armenian policy toward the Islamic states that.is at times overlooked: the presence of large Armenian diaspora communities in nearly all of them, including Iran. The Armenian government was motivated from the very beginning to establish working relations with these countries and wanted by all means to avoid casting the conflict in religious terms. Against this background, a difficult situation reveals itself: the government of Armenia was exercising only limited influence over developments in Karabagh. Accepting this fact, the Armenian government has since avoided walking into a similar bind. Instead it has worked hard to create understanding in the Karabagh government that, as Armenia is the principal negotiator on the world scene on their behalf, the political costs of their actions on Armenia have to be appreciated.

That was a message the Armenian government had difficulty communicating at first because, in the process of forming their own government, the Karabagh population had given the vote to the ARF. Having failed to score any success in the elections in Armenia, the ARF had invested its resources in Karabagh. The prominence of the ARF in the Karabagh parliament was a serious complication for the Ter-Petrossian administration. It soon supported the formation of the Karabagh State Defense Committee because a civilian government proved too optimistic a method of coping with the siege of the area. While united on defense and military questions, the political divisions in the Karabagh government continue to require special attention from the Ter-Petrossian administration. Similarly, maintaining a political dialogue with Azerbaijan while supporting the armed struggle of the Karabagh Armenians has been a delicate undertaking. With Karabagh forces on the offensive, however, the finer distinctions worked out in 1992 began to blur. The safer Karabagh became defensively, the more exposed Armenia became diplomatically.

This overall effort at coordination might have worked better had the Karabagh

Armenians had more confidence in the Armenian Republic and its government, and had they not faced mounting problems on the ground. The military contest continually changed conditions, and sometimes the changes were dramatic. For instance, the opening of the Lachin corridor also sealed the fate of the Mutalibov regime in Azerbaijan. Rallying the nationalist forces, the new president of Azerbaijan, Abulfez Elchibey, came to power on a plank promising to solve the problem quickly and surgically. He almost succeeded, because he was prepared to take the war to Armenia. His forces captured the northern sector of Karabagh, driving out the Armenian population, and effectively partitioning the enclave. Yet even then a negotiated settlement might have been within grasp. With its successful campaign against the Armenian border cities and the transportation lines from Georgia to Armenia sabotaged, Azerbaijan had Armenia surrounded on three sides and lacked motivation to seek a settlement. It had the upper hand, and the option to prosecute the war to its expected conclusion was chosen in Baku.[45]

That was the real turning point in the dispute between the Armenians and the Azeris. Since then a military contest has been waged. To begin with, instead of confining the conflict to Karabagh, the Elchibey program posed a direct challenge to Armenia. Second, it escalated a conflict still fought with light weaponry into a full-scale war. Third, it drove home to Armenia that the struggle waged by Karabagh now had become its own as well. But last, and unforeseen at the time, was the redefinition of Karabagh in its significance to Armenia. By fusing the defense requirements of Armenia and Karabagh, Azerbaijan inadvertently put Karabagh in a new light. Karabagh became a place of tremendous strategic value for Armenia's defense. That was so for two reasons. One, the Karabagh Armenians demonstrated unusual military skills. Strengthening their capacity to resist the Azeris only made sense, because they were fighting the same antagonist. Two, any effort that solidly attached Karabagh to Armenia would yield the net result of making both of their borders secure. Since spring 1993, the Karabagh forces, joined by fighting men from Armenia, have been closing every gap between Karabagh and Armenia, and Karabagh has created for itself a buffer zone of a depth sufficient to keep Azeri artillery from shelling its towns or for Azeri forces to penetrate easily into Karabagh proper.

From a military standpoint, the Karabagh Armenians engineered an unexpected turnaround. The political and diplomatic fallout, on the other hand, has been very different. On that front, there has been little movement, for by 1994 there was all the more reason for Azeri reluctance to negotiate a cease-fire. If two years earlier victory seemed imminent and a negotiated settlement was deemed unnecessary, now defeat serves as the disincentive.[46]

The timing of this conflict has been at the core of the enormous difficulty in finding a solution. Ignited at the moment when Armenia and Azerbaijan achieved statehood, the Karabagh conflict posed a challenge to the very questions that states need to resolve at an early stage. Frequently the differences are cast in terms of the conflicting principles of state sovereignty or territorial integrity and self-determination.[47] However, far deeper lies the question of nationality and how two opposing definitions of nationhood forged through a long and bitter historical experience do not allow for any kind of a middle ground to emerge. Furthermore, the Azeri government is now hamstrung with territorial losses and population displacements that have created conditions furthering instability in the country.

But this conflict is no longer restricted in its implications to Armenia and Azerbaijan alone. Turkey, Russia, and the West now have a stake in it. If the conflict had been limited to Karabagh, the framework in which negotiations for a settlement have been conducted might have worked better. Without getting into the complexity of the set of negotiations held under the auspices of the Conference on Security and Cooperation in Europe (CSCE), the fact that the CSCE delegated responsibility for promoting negotiations to a group of states that could not remain neutral has meant that the process would be cumbersome.[48] Had the United States led the negotiations, rather than just guided them, greater progress toward a settlement might have been registered.

Yet neither the CSCE process nor the role of the United States should be minimized in their salutary effect; nor has the process been exhausted. Though the CSCE has not met its primary objective, the negotiations served a purpose. They compelled the two sides, and the other states involved, to clarify their positions. On occasion it has even allowed for the Karabagh viewpoint to be unofficially represented as well. That an international framework for conducting negotiations existed offered hope that a solution could be found, because it lets the antagonists sit across a table and make their cases. Otherwise, they would only be fighting.

From the standpoint of foreign policy, the Karabagh conflict has distorted Armenia's relations with a whole host of countries.[49] The conflict has thoroughly complicated relations with Turkey, which chose to support Azerbaijan and oppose Armenia. That action became the convenient excuse for Russia to see to it that the conflict was not resolved in anyone's favor. It has done so by supplying arms to both sides. Russia also found in Karabagh the ready-made source of pressure on Azerbaijan. It is a scenario comparable to the Abkhaz conflict in Georgia. But the escalation has gone further with the introduction of a considerable contingent of mercenaries and advisors in Azerbaijan.[50] Irrespective of what the mercenaries and trainers were recruited to do, and apart from the Karabagh situation, Azerbaijan itself has become a testing ground for the interests competing for influence in the area. In the larger scheme of things, Karabagh has always been secondary, and therein lies one reason that the seriousness of the conflict has been underestimated.

The true prize in Azerbaijan is of course oil, an asset of such strategic significance that very powerful forces would inevitably be arrayed to try to obtain access to it. The sharpening of the conflict in Karabagh is, therefore, due to a considerable level of attention to this matter also. The Western oil interests and the promise of profit all around have given the conflict an international dimension. While the oil fields themselves are not in danger or dispute, how to access the oil is hotly debated.[51] Herein Azerbaijan's one geographic disadvantage has hemmed it into making a decision about building a pipeline that itself has become hostage to the Karabagh conflict. As the final irony of the conflict, it has been demonstrated that the most economical, and from the political standpoint of the West, the most convenient route for the pipeline is right through Karabagh, Armenia, and Turkey to the Mediterranean. Here, however, national interest in purely objective terms and nationalism in its most heated form have totally neutralized one another for Azerbaijan. While the blockade of Armenia by Azerbaijan has virtually wrecked the Armenian economy, it has also cut Azerbaijan's own access routes to the West. Thus the one true power in the region, Russia, has been given even greater leverage over all the newly independent states of Transcaucasia.[52] Day by day Russia has recovered its suzerainty over the region, for the deeper the wedges separating the Transcaucasian states were driven, the more Russia stood to profit from the differences.

Some glaring changes were registered in the second half of 1993. The Russian mediation effort virtually displaced the CSCE negotiations for a settlement of the Karabagh conflict.[53] The Russian role was epitomized in the regular shuttling of Vladimir Kazimirov between Moscow, Baku, Erevan, and Stepanakert. Moreover, Kazimirov, though a Foreign Ministry official and principal Russian representative at the CSCE Minsk group meetings, is President Yeltsin's personal envoy. Nor does Russia engage in the pretense at times that it is dealing with independent states when Minister of Defense Pavel Grachev becomes involved in cease-fire negotiations. One particular meeting with Yeltsin carried all the ceremony of the visitation of provincial satraps to the court of the hegemon.[54] All three Transcaucasian leaders, Shevardnadze, Ter-Petrossian, and Aliev, attended a conference just days after the Russian parliament building was blasted by tanks on 3–4 October 1993. The previously scheduled meeting was designed to give Russia's blessings to the three presidents of the Caucasian republics; as the last holdout, Azerbaijan, had just been brought into the CIS, and a condominium over the region was about to be given shape.

Turkey and Iran were not positioned to be as effective in this kind of complicated chess game. The maneuverability of Russian diplomatic and military representatives in the Transcaucasus has simply not been available to them. Even so, this transitional period is far from being over, and there is little reason to believe that the next six years will hold fewer surprises than the last six years.

Conclusion

During his first two years in office, President Levon Ter-Petrossian repeatedly enunciated the foreign policy slogan, "Normal relations with all our neighbors."

From the onset of independence he sought to reassure the governments of neighboring states that Armenia's principal external goal was swift recognition and rapid development of relations in all facets of life. That effort was important in view of the conflict brewing over Nagorno-Karabagh and the potential complications that could arise with the irresolution of the crisis. However, the insistent communiqués that Armenia as a state was not involved in the Karabagh conflict, that rather, the Armenian people of Karabagh were asserting their right to self-determination, found little resonance in the world. With every passing day it became clearer that the international community essentially regarded the right of a people to self-determination as secondary to the right of state sovereignty, irrespective of the way borders had been drawn in the Soviet Union by one of the longest-ruling totalitarian dictators. In effect, the Armenians of Karabagh were on their own, and Azerbaijan's right to quell the uprising was implicitly recognized. The methods selected by the Azeri government to stamp out the Armenian movement only invited escalation, especially the siege of Karabagh and the aerial bombardment of Stepanakert, its capital, in 1991 and 1992, which turned the conflict into a life-and-death struggle for the Armenians.[55]

In view of the calamity once visited upon the Armenians of the Ottoman Empire at the hands of the Young Turk government, Armenia as a state could not stand witness to the eradication of an Armenian enclave so near its border and not be compelled to come to its defense. Seventy years of Soviet manipulation and propaganda had had no effect in erasing the memory of the years when the Turks invaded Russian Armenia in 1914, 1918, and 1920, and it certainly had no effect in erasing the memory of the 1915 genocide of the Armenians in Turkey. Armenia was peopled by the survivors of those events. Their descendants were determined that such a catastrophe would not recur. Ineluctably, the effort to save Karabagh became Armenia's foreign policy concern of first priority.

These developments did not happen in isolation. Soon Turkey was lined up with Azerbaijan. With no major Western effort to prevent further deterioration of Armenia's situation as the two Turkic states closed the vise, Armenia was left to seek Russia as a guarantor of its security. Efforts by the United States to make the Turkish government change its policies remained fruitless. The country that was expected to play the role of a moderate power, in a word, hijacked Western policy toward Armenia, creating additional rifts in the Transcaucasus and compounding the severity of the crisis in the region. In the process, Armenia, a pro-Western democracy, was slowly alienated from the West by the presumed defender of Western interests in the region.

Resolving the Karabagh conflict, bringing about a modification in Turkish policy, attaining better security arrangements, improving relations with hesitant neighbors, and expanding contact with the West now define Armenia's foreign policy objectives. For that smallest republic of the former Soviet Union, independence may have been the easier challenge. Conducting foreign relations will be an ongoing one.

Notes

1. According to the Soviet census, the population of Armenia was 3.0 million in 1979 and 3.3 million in 1989. With population displacements and a large influx of refugees, by 1991 the population was reported at 3.7 million. An estimated 150,000 Azeris left Armenia for Azerbaijan, and 350,000 Armenians entered from Azerbaijan. Further rapid fluctuations in population were reported by late 1993. Anywhere from 300,000 to 700,000 people were estimated to have departed the Republic of Armenia, some from the minority groups, but mostly Armenians fleeing the harsh conditions of winters without heat, diminishing food supplies, inflation, and unemployment. For more on the Armenian population during the Soviet era, see Viktor Kozlov, *The Peoples of the Soviet Union* (London: Hutchinson; Bloomington: Indiana University Press, 1988).

2. On Soviet Armenia, see Mary Kilbourne Matossian, *The Impact of Soviet Policies in Armenia* (Leiden: E.J. Brill, 1962); Ronald Grigor Suny, ed., *Transcaucasia, Nationalism and Social Change: Essays in the History of Armenia, Azerbaijan, and Georgia* (Ann Arbor: University of Michigan, 1983); idem, *Looking Toward Ararat: Armenia in Modern History* (Bloomington: Indiana University Press, 1993); Claire Mouradian, *De Staline a Gorbachev, histoire d'une republique sovietique: l'Armenie* (Paris: Editions Ramsay, 1990).

3. Though not discussed in this paper, in view of the Karabagh conflict and the ethnic tensions throughout the former Soviet Union, the treatment and status of these communities has the potential of adversely affecting Armenia's foreign relations. It is reported that 437,000 Armenians are living in Georgia. They are concentrated in four areas: (1) the capital, Tbilisi, where they once formed the majority of the population in the nineteenth century; (2) the southern districts of Akhalkalaki and Bogdanovska, where they form 90 percent of the population; (3) the region of Akhaltskha; and (4) Abkhazia, where they constitute 15 percent of the population. See Stephen Jones, "The Unbearable Freedom: Georgia on the Precipice," *Armenian International Magazine*, October 1993, pp. 16–21. During the Soviet period 500,000 Armenians lived in Azerbaijan. They were concentrated in five areas: (1) the capital, Baku; (2) the city of Sumgait; (3) the city of Ganja, formerly Kirovabad; (4) the Shahumian region in western Azerbaijan; and (5) Nagorno, or Mountainous, Karabagh, where they constituted 75 percent of the population in 1988. With the exception of Karabagh, the Armenian population of Azerbaijan was forcibly evacuated between 1988 and 1991. Armenians in Russia are concentrated in Moscow (c. 120,000), St. Petersburg (c. 11,000), and southern Russia, where 793,500 Armenians are reported living. One of the oldest communities, dating back to the eighteenth century, is found at Nor Nakhichevan near Rostov-na-Donu. Others live in Krasnodar province (c. 400,000), Stavropol province (c. 200,000), Sochi (c. 120,000), North Ossetia (c. 26,000), Dagestan (c. 10,000), Chechnia (c. 5,000), and Adigeia (c. 2,500). See Society for the Study of Caucasia, *Newsletter*, vol. 7, no. 1 (1994), p. 2. Armenians in Ukraine are concentrated in the western city of Lviv and in the Crimea, both communities dating back to the Middle Ages.

4. Philip Robins, "Between Sentiment and Self-Interest: Turkey's Policy Toward Azerbaijan and the Central Asian States," *Middle East Journal*, vol. 47, no. 4 (autumn 1993), pp. 593–610; Daniel Pipes and Patrick Clawson, "Ambitious Iran, Troubled Neighbors," *Foreign Affairs*, vol. 72, no. 1 (1992/93), pp. 124–41; Graham E. Fuller and Ian O. Lesser, *Turkey's New Geopolitics: From the Balkans to Western China* (Boulder, CO: Westview Press/A Rand Study, 1993), pp. 76–85; Shireen T. Hunter, "The Muslim Republics of the Former Soviet Union: Policy Challenges for the United States," *Washington Quarterly* (summer 1992), pp. 57–71. For an official view on the subject, see Rouben Shugarian (ambassador of the Republic of Armenia to the United States), "The Disinte-

gration of the Soviet Empire: Consequences for Transcaucasia" (speech to the Los Angeles World Affairs Council, 17 May 1993), in *Monthly Digest of News from Armenia* (June 1993), pp. 64–66.

5. William Ward Maggs, "Armenia and Azerbaijan: Looking Toward the Middle East," *Current History*, (January 1993), pp. 6–11; Shireen Hunter, "Transcaucasia and the Middle East: Patterns of Mutual Impact" (paper presented at the Middle East Studies Association Annual Conference, Research Triangle, NC, 31 October 1993); Daniel Pipes, "The Politics of the 'Rip Van Winkle' States: The Southern Tier States of the Ex-Soviet Union Have Moved the Borders of the Middle East North," *Middle East Insight* (November–December 1993), pp. 30–40.

6. Raymond Bonner, "War, Blockade and Poverty 'Strangling' Armenia," *New York Times*, 16 April 1994; Carey Goldberg, "Spring Brings Little Hope to Blockaded Armenians," *Los Angeles Times* (Washington edition), 12 April 1994; "Armenia Looks to Nuclear to Cope with Blockade," *Boston Globe*, 24 March 1994; Raymond Bonner, "Russia Is Holding Up Seed Bought by U.S. for Armenia Relief," *New York Times*, 22 March 1994; "Azeris Tighten Noose in Fuel Blockage of Armenia," *Platt's Oilgram News*, 6 January 1994; Margaret Shapiro, "Armenia's 'Good Life' Lost to Misery, Darkness, Cold: Armenia Freezes Under Embargo," *Washington Post*, 30 January 1993.

7. Jon Auerbach, "In a Corner of Former USSR, an Ethnic Conflict Rages On," *Boston Globe*, 21 April 1994; Serge Schemann, "In the Caucasus, Ancient Blood Feuds Threaten to Engulf Two New Republics," *New York Times*, 3 July 1992; Charles William Maynes, "Containing Ethnic Conflict," *Foreign Policy* (spring 1993), p. 5.

8. Samuel P. Huntington, "The Clash of Civilizations?" *Foreign Affairs*, vol. 72, no. 3 (summer 1993), pp. 22–49.

9. Vadim Myachin, "Outlook for the Transcaucasus," *PlanEcon Review and Outlook: Analysis and Forecasts to 1996 of Economic Developments in the Former Soviet Republics* (November 1992), pp. 111–35.

10. Vartan Oskanian, "Armenia Abroad: After 70 Years Under Moscow, the Republic Must Now Decide Its Own Foreign Policy Priorities," *Armenian International Magazine*, December 1991, pp. 16–17.

11. Tony Halpin, "Precious Burden: How Internal Crisis and the Karabagh Conflict Determine Armenia's Foreign Relations," *Armenian International Magazine*, January 1994, pp. 16–19. For discussion of the historical evolution of the Karabagh crisis, see Gerard J. Libaridian, ed., *The Karabagh File: Documents and Facts on the Question of Mountainous Karabagh, 1918–1988* (Cambridge, MA: Zoryan Institute for Contemporary Armenian Research and Documentation, 1988); Christopher J. Walker, ed., *Armenia and Karabagh: The Struggle for Unity* (London: Minority Rights Publications, 1991); Richard G. Hovannisian, "Nationalist Ferment in Armenia," *Freedom at Issue*, no. 105 (November–December 1988), pp. 29–35; Merujan Karapetian, "The Ethnic Structure of the Population of Mountainous Karabagh in 1921," *Armenian Review*, vol. 44, no. 4 (1991), pp. 69–85.

12. Samvel Shahmuratian, comp. and ed., *The Sumgait Tragedy: Pogroms Against Armenians in Soviet Azerbaijan* (New Rochelle, NY: Aristide D. Caratzas; Cambridge, MA: Zoryan Institute, 1990).

13. "Prime Minister's February 28 Speech to Parliament," *Hayastani Hanrapetutyun* (Republic of Armenia), 1 March 1994, in *Monthly Digest of News from Armenia* (April 1994), pp. 7–8.

14. On the ANM program, see Gerard J. Libaridian, *Armenia at the Crossroads: Democracy and Nationhood in the Post-Soviet Era: Essays, Interviews and Speeches by the Leaders of the National Democratic Movement in Armenia* (Watertown, MA: Blue Crane Books, 1991). For more on the nationalist movement in Armenia, see Claire Mouradian, "Armeniens d'URSS: Le Nationalisme au Service de la Démocratie,"

Politique Internationale, no. 5 (autumn 1989), pp. 323–43; Ronald Grigor Suny, "Transcaucasia: Cultural Cohesion and Ethnic Revival in a Multinational Society," in *The Nationalities Factor in Soviet Politics and Society*, ed. Lubomyr Hajda and Mark Bessinger (Boulder, CO: Westview Press, 1990), pp. 228–52; "A Region in Turmoil: Armenia," *Soviet Anthropology and Archeology* (fall 1990).

15. For a discussion of the legalization of private enterprise in Armenia and the 1992 Business Law, see Van Z. Krikorian, "Armenian Law Creates Favorable Climate for Business Operations," *CIS Law Notes* (June, August, October 1993), pp. 1–4, 14–16, 12–14, respectively.

16. 23 August 1990. The referendum on independence was held on 21 September 1991.

17. "Privatization Postponed," *Azg* [Nation], 17 November 1993, in *Monthly Digest of News from Armenia* (December 1993), p. 4; Van Z. Krikorian, "New Wave of Privatization to Hit Armenia," *CIS Law Notes* (June 1994), pp. 1–5.

18. Vartan Oskanian and Gayane Hambartzoumian, " 'War Is Inevitable': Vazgen Manoukian on the Dangers Facing the Republic," *Armenian International Magazine*, December 1991, pp. 18–20.

19. Tony Halpin, "The Face of Discord," *Armenian International Magazine*, November 1992, pp. 8–14. A widely held view attributes Raffi Hovannisian's departure from office to pressure from Turkey, as his resignation occurred subsequent to a speech given by the foreign minister at a CSCE conference in Istanbul, where he highlighted the question of Turkey's position on the matter of the Armenian genocide.

20. To date the Republic of Armenia has opened embassies in the United States, the United Kingdom, France, Austria, Greece, Ukraine, Russia, Kazakhstan, Georgia, Iran, Syria, Lebanon, Egypt, and Argentina. The following countries have opened embassies in Armenia: the United States, France, Russia, Iran, Greece, and China.

21. The natural gas pipeline to Armenia was blown up the first time on 23 January 1993, at the height of the winter season. In the winter of 1993–94, the pipeline was blown up on 18 December 1993, the day Azeri forces staged a large-scale offensive on all fronts around Nagorno-Karabagh.

22. Other conditions imposed by Turkey for formal recognition of Armenia have included the reaffirmation of the 1921 Treaty of Kars, drawn up by Moscow and Ankara and imposed on Armenia after partition and Sovietization; the renunciation of any land claims, despite the absence of such by the Armenian government; and the abandonment of the effort to obtain international recognition of the Armenian genocide, despite the fact that the matter has been all along a cause championed by diaspora Armenians.

23. "Army to Pursue PKK Militants into Armenia," *Tercuman*, 17 November 1993, in *FBIS Daily Report: West Europe*, 26 November 1993, p. 52; Hugh Pope, "Turkey Warns Neighbors to Rein In Kurdish Rebels," *Los Angeles Times* (Washington edition), 5 November 1993.

24. Elizabeth Fuller, "The Thorny Path to an Armenian-Turkish Rapprochement," *RFE/RL Research Report*, 19 March 1993, pp. 47–51.

25. For a sampling of Turkish reports on the allegations that Armenia is harboring and sponsoring the PKK, see Sezai Sengun, "Syria Flies PKK Militants to Armenia," *Hurriyet*, 10 November 1993, in *FBIS Daily Report: West Europe*, 15 November 1993, p. 72; Gorsel Polat, "PKK Will Attach with ASALA in the Spring," *Cumhuriyet*, 27 December 1993, in *FBIS Daily Report: West Europe*, 5 January 1994, p. 29; Sinan Onus, "Intelligence Report Details Armenia-PKK Ties," *Aydinlik*, 29 January 1994, in *FBIS Daily Report: West Europe*, 3 February 1994, p. 36; "PKK Reportedly Moving to Iran, Armenia," *Turkish Daily News*, 1 February 1994, in *FBIS Daily Report: West Europe*, 7 February 1994, p. 44; "PKK, Armenian 'Terrorist' Base Reportedly in Cyprus," *Yeni Demokrat*, 30 March 1994, in *FBIS Daily Report: West Europe*, 31 March 1994, p. 52.

26. For an explanation by a Turkish critic of the Turkish government's fabrication of a linkage between Armenia and the PKK and the purposes thereto applied, see M. Can Yuce, "The Essence of the Current Enmity Toward Armenians," *Ozgur Gunden*, 20 December 1993, in *FBIS Daily Report: West Europe*, 27 December 1993, pp. 9–41.

27. Viken Berberian, "Sea of Diplomacy: American Officials in the State Department and Abroad Support the Project: But Can a Turkish Port Provide Armenia with a New Trade Outlet?" *Armenian International Magazine*, February 1992, pp. 26–28.

28. Eric Rouleau, "The Challenges to Turkey," *Foreign Affairs*, vol. 72, no. 5 (November/December 1993), pp. 110–26; Sabri Sayari, "Turkey: The Changing European Security Environment and the Gulf Crisis," *Middle East Journal*, vol. 46, no. 1 (1992), pp. 9–21.

29. Huntington, "Clash of Civilizations?" p. 36; Morton L. Abramowitz, "Dateline Ankara: Turkey After Özal," *Foreign Policy* (summer 1993), pp. 164–81.

30. Paul Quinn-Judge, "Turkey Warns of War Over Armenian Advances," *Boston Globe*, 5 September 1993; "Turkey Moves Troops to Armenian Border," *New York Times*, 4 September 1993; "Turkey, Iran Reportedly Step Up Military Pressure on Armenia," *Boston Globe*, 4 September 1993.

31. For relations between Gorbachev and Armenia, see Thomas J. Samuelian, "Cultural Ecology and Gorbachev's Restructured Union," *Harvard International Law Journal*, vol. 32, no. 1 (1991), pp. 159–200. For a discussion of Gorbachev's overall nationality policy, see Paul Goble, "Imperial Endgame: Nationality Problems and the Soviet Future," in *Five Years That Shook the World: Gorbachev's Unfinished Revolution*, ed. Harley D. Balzer (Boulder, CO: Westview Press, 1991), pp. 91–104.

32. Daniel Sneider, "Snow Falls, Prices Rise in Armenia," *Christian Science Monitor*, 23 November 1993.

33. Daniel Sneider, "Russia and the Caucasus: Empire in Transition," *Christian Science Monitor*, 13 December 1993; Vladimir Stupishin (Russian ambassador to Armenia), "Does the Armenian Audience Need the Russian Theater of Horrors," interview by Andrei Lipovskii and Elena Movchan, *Obshchaia gazeta*, 3 December 1993, in *FBIS Daily Report: Central Eurasia*, FBIS-USR–94–009, 24 December 1993, pp. 4–6.

34. Daniel Williams, "Russia Asserts Role in Ex-Soviet Republics," *Washington Post*, 29 September 1993; Thomas L. Friedman, "Not Red, but Still a Bear," *New York Times*, 28 February 1994; Jon Auerbach, "Russia Tightening Its Grip on Former Republics," *Boston Globe*, 6 December 1993; "Russia Reaches Out," *Economist*, 26 February 1994; Andrei Kozyrev, "Russia Plans Leading Role in World Arena," *Washington Times*, 15 March 1994. See also "Basic Provisions of the Concept of the Foreign Policy of the Russian Federation" (text of Russian Federation Ministry of Foreign Affairs Concept Document no. 615/IS, dated 25 January 1993), in *FBIS Daily Report: Central Eurasia*, FBIS-USR–93–037, 25 March 1993, especially the section on "Relations With Commonwealth Countries," pp. 4–6.

35. Fiona Hill and Pamela Jewett, *"Back in the USSR": Russia's Intervention in the Internal Affairs of the Former Soviet Republics and the Implications for United States Policy Toward Russia*, Strengthening Democratic Institutions Project (Cambridge, MA: Harvard University, John F. Kennedy School of Government, January 1994), pp. 10–22; Thomas Goltz, "Letter from Eurasia: The Hidden Russian Hand," *Foreign Policy* (fall 1993), pp. 92–116.

36. Jon Auerbach, "Armenia Gets Warning After Attack on Russian Envoy," *Boston Globe*, 23 November 1993. "Russian Envoy Kazimirov's Car Fired On From Armenia," ITAR-TASS, 20 November 1993, in *FBIS Daily Report: Central Eurasia*, 22 November 1993, p. 69; "Kozyrev Demands Armenia Apologize for Attack," Interfax, 22 November 1993, in *FBIS Daily Report: Central Eurasia*, 23 November 1993, p. 19; "Official:

Kazimirov Incident 'Planned Provocation,'" *Snark*, 22 November 1993, in *FBIS Daily Report: Central Eurasia*, 23 November 1993, p. 64; "Details Provided on Attack," *Radio Yerevan International Service*, 22 November 1993, in *FBIS Daily Report: Central Eurasia*, 23 November 1993, p. 64; "Papazian Reacts to Kozyrev on Incident," *Radio Yerevan International Service*, 22 November 1993, in *FBIS Daily Report: Central Eurasia*, 23 November 1993, p. 64; "Kozyrev: No Armenian Reaction to Kazimirov," *Moscow Russian Television Network*, 23 November 1993, in *FBIS Daily Report: Central Eurasia*, 24 November 1993, p. 13; Leonid Timofeyev, "Kozyrev Demands an Apology: At Present," *Komsomol'skaia pravda*, 24 November 1993, in *FBIS Daily Report: Central Eurasia*, 24 November 1993, p. 13; "Kazimirov Hopes 'Incident' Will Not Affect Peace Moves," *Armenpress*, 13 November 1993, in *FBIS Daily Report: Central Eurasia*, 24 November 1993, p. 62; Armen Khanbabian, "Yerevan Is Convinced That the Incident of the Russian Federation Ambassador Was Provoked by Azerbaijan," *Nezavisimaia gazeta*, 23 November 1993, in *FBIS Daily Report: Central Eurasia*, 24 November 1993, p. 62; "Kozyrev Views Armenian Explanation on Border Incident," Interfax, 24 November 1993, in *FBIS Daily Report: Central Eurasia*, 26 November 1993, p. 18.

37. "A Hero of Our Time: Russia and the Transcaucasus," *Economist*, 12 February 1994.

38. Raffi K. Hovannisian, "Charting a Course for Peace," *Los Angeles Times* (Washington edition), 25 February 1994.

39. "Armenian President in London," *Azg*, 11 February 1994, in *Monthly Digest of News from Armenia* (March 1994), pp. 17–18.

40. Newspapers published in the Armenian community are replete with discussions of this topic. Articles and editorials in any number of them may be consulted, including the *Armenian Weekly* (Boston), published by the Armenian Revolutionary Federation, the *Armenian Mirror-Spectator* (Boston), published by the Armenian Democratic Liberal Party, the *Armenian Reporter* (New York), and the *Armenian Observer* (Los Angeles), both published independently. On this subject, see also Salpi Haroutinian Ghazarian, "A Man and a State: A Conversation with the President," *Armenian International Magazine*, March 1994, pp. 32–35. The problem is also in part due to the shortage of trained personnel in the embassies assigned to these countries. The embassies are so shorthanded as to require them to focus primarily on state-to-state matters.

41. Gerard Libaridian previously headed the Cambridge, Massachusetts-based Zoryan Institute for Contemporary Armenian Research and Documentation, which focused on the problem of the Armenian genocide. Ter-Petrossian, then, has delegated the handling of this sensitive issue to a diplomat whose background makes him less vulnerable to the Turkish attempt to trivialize the subject by turning it into an item of negotiation.

42. Helsinki Watch, *Bloodshed in the Caucasus: Escalation of Armed Conflict in Nagorno-Karabagh* (New York, 1992); Commission on Security and Cooperation in Europe, *Human Rights and Democratization in the Newly Independent States of the Former Soviet Union* (Washington, DC, 1993), pp. 123–37.

43. Joseph Masih, "Military Strategy in Nagorno-Karabagh," *Jane's Intelligence Review* (April 1994), pp. 160–63; Felix Corley, "Nagorno-Karabagh: An Eyewitness Account," *Jane's Intelligence Review* (April 1994), pp. 164–65; idem, "The Forgotten War," *Wall Street Journal*, 3 March 1994; Mark A. Uhlig, "The Karabagh War," *World Policy Journal*, vol. 10, no. 4 (winter 1993), pp. 47–52.

44. The Republic of Mountainous Karabagh was declared independent on 6 January 1992. These decisions were only the last of a series adopted by the Nagorno-Karabagh Supreme Soviet, the Azerbaijan Supreme Soviet, and the Armenian Supreme Soviet beginning in 1988. The decisions adopted by the Karabagh Supreme Soviet sought the legal unification of the autonomous district with the Soviet Republic of Armenia. The

Azerbaijan Supreme Soviet decisions objected to or annulled the Karabagh decisions, while the Armenian Supreme Soviet decisions affirmed them. The Republic of Mountainous Karabagh is no longer seeking unification with Armenia.

45. For discussion on the military in the region, see Patrick Gorman, "The Emerging Army in Azerbaijan," *Central Asia Monitor*, 1993, no. 1, pp. 31–36; Elizabeth Fuller, "Paramilitary Forces Dominate Fighting in Transcaucasus," *RFE/RL Research Report*, 18 June 1993; Roy Allison, "Military Forces in the Soviet Successor States," *Adelphi Paper*, no. 280 (October 1993), pp. 63–76.

46. Armen Khanbabian, "The Formation of the CIS Enabled Us to Avoid the 'Yugoslav Scenario," *Nezavisimaia gazeta*, 12 January 1994, in *FBIS Daily Report: Central Eurasia*–FBIS-USR 94–009, 3 February 1994, pp. 1–3; Rouben Shugarian, "If Azerbaijan Talks Peace Armenia Will Listen," *Christian Science Monitor*, 8 March 1994.

47. "Armenia, Azerbaijan and Nagorno-Karabagh: State Sovereignty vs. Self-Determination," *In Brief* (United States Institute of Peace), September 1992; Nora Dudwick, "The Quest for Identity: The Struggle for Self-Determination in Nagorno-Karabagh Is a Central Issue for Both Armenia and Azerbaijan," *Cultural Survival Quarterly* (winter 1992), pp. 26–29; Claire Mouradian, *Le Caucase des independances: La nouvelle donne*, Problemes politiques et sociaux, no. 718, Serie Russie (Paris: La documentation Francaise, 1993). For a discussion of the United States position on these principles by the U.S. representatives to the CSCE negotiations on Karabagh and their application to the Karabagh situation, see Edmond Y. Azadian, "A Comprehensive Discussion with Ambassador John Maresca," *Armenian Observer*, 16 March 1994.

48. Elizabeth Fuller, "Nagorno-Karabakh: Can Turkey Remain Neutral?" *RFE/RL Research Report*, 3 April 1992, pp. 36–38. The eleven CSCE member states in the group include Armenia, Azerbaijan, Belarus, the Czech Republic, France, Germany, Italy, Russia, Sweden, Turkey, and the United States.

49. Halpin, "Precious Burden."

50. Steve LeVine, "Afghan Fighters Aiding Azerbaijan in Civil War," *Washington Post*, 8 November 1993; Jon Auerbach, "Azerbaijan Hires Afghan Mujahideen to Fight Armenia," *Boston Globe*, 8 November 1993; idem, "Clandestine Russian Forces Back Azeris," *Boston Globe*, 22 November 1993; Daniel Sneider, "Afghan Fighters Join Azeri-Armenian War," *Christian Science Monitor*, 16 November 1993; Alexis Rowell, "U.S. Army Veterans 'Drill' Azeris Under Cover of Oil Firm," *Observer* (London), 28 November 1993; idem, "U.S. Mercenaries Fight in Azerbaijan," *CovertAction* (spring 1994), pp. 23–27; Sezai Sengun, "Conditional Supply of Arms to Azerbaijan, *Hurriyet*, 23 December 1993, in *FBIS Daily Report: West Europe*, 30 December 1993, p. 28; "Army Sends 5,000 Troops to Assist Azerbaijan Army," *Aydinlik*, 13 January 1994, in *FBIS Daily Report: West Europe*, 18 January 1994, p. 53; Semih D. Idiz, "Army Questions Azerbaijani Offensive Effectiveness," *Turkish Daily News*, 28 January 1994, in *FBIS Daily Report: West Europe*, 1 February 1994, pp. 38–39; Sebahattin Onkibar, "Cetin Cited on Bosnia, Armenian-Azeri Conflict," *Turkiye*, 12 February 1994, in *FBIS Daily Report: West Europe*, 17 February 1994, pp. 42–43; " 'Sources' Confirm Iranian Troops Enter Azerbaijan," *Anatolia*, 3 September 1993, in *FBIS Daily Report: West Europe*, 7 September 1993, p. 45.

51. James M. Dorsey, "Oil Pursuit Proves Slippery in Azerbaijan," *Washington Times*, 23 April 1994; Howard Witt, "Oil Firms Find New Wild West, in Azerbaijan," *Chicago Tribune*, 21 June 1992; Michael Specter, "Azerbaijan, Potentially Rich, Is Impoverished by Warfare," *New York Times*, 2 June 1994.

52. Steve LeVine, "Moscow Pressures Its Neighbors to Share Their Oil, Gas Revenues," *Washington Post*, 8 March 1994; idem, "The Great Game Revisited: On How Russia, the West, and Turkey Are Jockeying for Baku's Oil Favours," *Financial Times*, 7

March 1994; Laurent Ruseckas, *The Nagorno-Karabagh Crisis and the Future of Oil Development in Azerbaijan* (Cambridge, MA: Cambridge Energy Research Associates, 1992).

53. Elizabeth Fuller, "Russia's Diplomatic Offensive in the Transcaucasus," *RFE/RL Research Report*, vol. 2, no. 39 (10 October 1993); Margaret Shapiro, "Russian Mediation Urged in Caucasus: Talks Sought to Halt Five-Year-Old Armenian-Azeri Conflict," *Washington Post*, 9 September 1993; Paul Quinn-Judge, "U.S. Is Said to Favor a Russian Sphere: Backing a Role in Ex-Republics," *Boston Globe*, 14 January 1994.

54. For another description of this relationship, see Melor Sturua, "Yeltsin's Newest Proconsul: Moscow's Grip on Georgia," *New York Times*, 27 October 1993.

55. Helsinki Watch, *Bloodshed in the Caucasus: Indiscriminate Bombing and Shelling by Azerbaijani Forces in Nagorno-Karabagh*, vol. 5, issue 10 (New York, 1993).

15

Conclusion

Imperialism, Dependence, and Interdependence in the Eurasian Space

---

Karen Dawisha

What does the evidence presented in this book suggest? Paragraph after paragraph, authors come back to the preeminence of Russia: analyzing its potential strength, assessing the impact of its domestic political divisions, speaking of the Russian impulse to empire, and chronicling the near-total obsession that elites in neighboring countries have with managing the relationship with Moscow. In so doing, many of the authors lament the inability of elites in all the new states, including Russia, to develop a more positive conception of national interest that will allow their foreign policies to extend beyond the new states of the former Soviet Union. But the frailty of new institutions for formulating foreign policy in all the new states reduces the likelihood that any of them will soon be able to move the primary focus of their external politics outside the Eurasian orbit.

The fact that the interrelationships among these fifteen states is likely, for the foreseeable future, to occupy the first rank of their concerns means that the international community will also interact with them through the prism of these relationships. Consequently, the ability of the international community to effect change in these relationships will depend on a clear understanding of their essential nature. This underlines the importance of analyzing them dispassionately, with a yardstick that can be applied more generally and that is rather unchanging over time.

The task can be approached by posing a number of questions:

1. What would Russian imperialism look like? Is there such a pattern of Russian imperial behavior that exists now? Specifically, can a country with low state capacity and no avowed ideology of imperialism nevertheless be an empire? In other words, can a "naked emperor" exist?

2. Will the international system allow Russia to emerge as an imperial power, and can it prevent Russian imperialism from emerging?
3. Can new states break out of the cycle of dependence on Moscow, and what measures would one use to determine their level of independence?
4. Is dependence on Moscow in the objective interest of some of the new states at least some of the time?
5. Do all great powers have rights and responsibilities? What are the rights and responsibilities of Russia as a power in the Eurasian region?

Russian Imperialism

An empire as a polity and imperialism as a system of ideas that guides policy intersect conceptually, in that the first is an outgrowth, a result, of the latter. This apparently trivial and obvious point gets to the heart of the first requirement of empires, namely, that they be established on purpose, with the objective of the elites in the metropole being the gaining of unfair advantage through coercion or threat over countries or territories in the periphery. A policy of imperialism pursued by the center is, of course, unlikely to be advertised as such, but it is important nevertheless to distinguish imperialism as an effort by one country to wrest formal sovereignty from another. It is more than the exercise of influence over the policies of another country.

As such, while it is highly unlikely that any state would openly declare in advance that it was going to create an empire, nevertheless, it would be more than possible to determine whether a state has both the capacity and the will necessary to pursue such a course. The drive to empire has to have a overarching motive, whether economic (as with the British drive to India), messianic (as with the missionary expansionism of Iberian Catholicism), or ideological (as with Bolshevism in the USSR). While the motivation may differ, nevertheless it must be present in order for the foreign policy of a state to be characterized as imperialistic. In this sense, Winston Churchill's statement that "the empires of the future are the empires of the mind" informs the discussion by pointing to the central aspect of intent. Discerning current intent is particularly important in the case of those states that have a heritage of imperial behavior or that are geographically large and economically powerful. Failure to consider the motivation of elites in the metropole, therefore, would lead one to blur the conceptual distinction between, for example, French policies in Algeria before and after independence. Factoring in the change in Algeria's formal status and the changed motivation of French elites allows one to distinguish between an imperial-colonial relationship, on the one hand, and a great power–developing state relationship on the other. Both are relations of inequality, but they are quite different both in their essence and in the level of independent action open to Algeria.

To take the case of Russia, its continuing preeminence in Eurasia as the dominant geographic colossus and economic power gives it an enormous natural advantage. But to conclude, from this alone, that Russia will "naturally" exercise imperial ambitions over the other new states is to overdetermine for geography. Russia's geographic capability did not prevent invasions by much smaller countries in centuries past, nor has it allowed Russia such an overarching advantage as to satiate previous rulers in Moscow and deter them from expansion. Just as Japan invaded the much larger China at the outbreak of World War II, and China has managed to have equitable relations with the much smaller South Korea in recent decades, relative smallness or largeness is not in and of itself a guide to motivation.

Where geography becomes a factor is in enhancing capability. When given the political will to create an empire, the size and extent of natural resources are important inputs into any state machine bent on imperial expansion. It is a common fallacy that states build empires to become rich: states, and/or their leaders, may seek additional enrichment, but in fact, it requires significant state resources to undertake and sustain colonial expansion.

The chapters in this volume recounted the extent of shame and humiliation felt among some circles in Russia about the loss of empire, the rhetorical support among the Russian right wing especially for the restoration of the USSR, and the fears in the new states of a renewal of Russian imperial drive. Yet the overwhelming evidence showed the absence of any coherent Russian articulation of what might be termed "national imperialism" at the state level and a grave lack of state capacity—defined by Checkel as "the administrative and coercive abilities of the state apparatus to implement official goals"—to achieve any renewal of expansionist tendencies outside the country. Indeed, it would appear that much of the state's capacity in the foreseeable future will be focused on preventing the boundaries of Russia from shrinking even further, particularly given the location of so many restless national minorities at the periphery, especially in the North Caucasus and Siberia.

The issue of Russian imperialism remains an important one, however, because so many of the new right-wing leaders and parties in Russia espouse it openly. Historically, individuals and political groups have always acted as the agents for the germination of the imperial idea. Whether one considers Cecil Rhodes (whose own vision of capitalist imperialism in South Africa came to be adopted by the British), or the Pan-Turanists in Ottoman Turkey (who sought unsuccessfully in the dying days of the Ottoman Empire to revive it on the basis of the unity of all Turkish-speaking peoples), or Vladimir Zhirinovsky and his Liberal Democratic Party in contemporary Russia, these individuals and groups become important when and if their ideas become "the ruling ideas." Before Zhirinovsky can recapture the states on Russia's border, he must first capture Russia, and such a result by the electoral procedure now in place is not very likely. What does bear considering, as discussed in Nodari Simonia's chapter, is the extent to which these views can gradually filter into the highest echelons of the political, military, and economic elites, and from there shape a more assertive foreign policy. Whether Zhirinovsky will go the way of Rhodes or the Pan-

Turanists is difficult to gauge, but it is important to monitor the fate of his ideas and his appeal, not least because the impact of the rhetoric of the Russian right on Russia's relations with neighboring countries, particularly Ukraine, is very significant in its own right.

In sum, therefore, the Russian state currently possesses neither the capability nor the will to reassert its imperial persona. That Russia has conflicts on its borders, and that Russian politics is beset by many voices calling for revanche are both undeniable, but it is difficult to see an easy, necessary, or swift transition from the politics of humiliation to an achievable policy of wholesale expansion.

Imperialism and the International Community

While empires have existed in both the modern and ancient worlds, the Age of Empires really lasted for the briefest period, from the mid-1800s to World War I. During this time, virtually all the European powers expanded their power, culture, and economic influence by means of the formal acquisition of territories worldwide. The very essence of the international regime was itself imperialist. The wars between empires (as with the Crimean War and the endless wars in the Balkans) that broke out in this period were not about the unacceptability of empire per se but about contested territory between empires. Consequently, alliances among empires could be established, agreements not to attack one's flank when at war with another empire could be signed, and, all in all, discussions about the rights of nations and peoples to self-determination could be sacrificed to the interests of maintaining a balance of power within Europe.

But now that a century has passed, and the USSR—in some ways an empire—has collapsed, the talk of empire, specifically the possibility of the reemergence of a Russian empire, has resurfaced. The USSR succeeded in the early 1920s, in a weak and divided international community, to establish itself and incorporate by force many of the territories of the former Russian empire. Would the international community allow such a phenomenon to be repeated today?

Several important factors mitigate against such a repetition. First, there is the greater awareness of the elites in the neighboring countries of the nature and potential of Russian power. The chapters by Leila Alieva, Oumirseric Kasenov, Vyacheslau Paznyak, Peeter Vares, and Nikolai Kulinich all display an acute acknowledgement of Russia's potential and a caution about its future orientation that signal the fact that states on Russia's borders are stronger and more self-aware now than they have ever been in the past and, therefore, they provide a significant deterrent in and of themselves to expansion: for example, reabsorbing Kazakhstan today, with its cities, educated elite, developed infrastructure, and communications links to the outside world, would be a far more difficult task than it was in the 1920s, when the indigenous peoples were nomadic, illiterate, and had no history of independent statehood.

Second, the international system has come to more fully accommodate as governing norms the principles of state sovereignty, national self-determination, and the unacceptability of the use of force to change boundaries or legitimate governments. To the extent that force has been sanctioned by the international community through the United Nations, it has been to uphold these norms (as in Kuwait, Haiti, or Bosnia). It is practically inconceivable that the international community would support a wholesale Russian policy either of using force to absorb states that are recognized as sovereign and independent or of systematically undermining by the use or threat of force democratically elected governments within those states. Not only would such a policy bring international censure, but many of the international institutions to which Russia has turned in an effort to restructure its economy would undoubtedly conclude that the upturn in military spending that such a policy shift would necessitate would so weaken Russian economic recovery as to negate the very basis on which the original loans and investments were made. In this way, the international community could both isolate and punish Russia economically for any policy of expansionism. The extent to which that punishment would be effective either in deterring the adoption of the policy in the first place or, failing that, in ensuring that Russia would be economically unable to pursue such a policy would depend not only on the extent to which the policy has domestic support within Russia that could be sustained even with hardships but also on the extent to which the Russian economy first becomes integrated within the international economic system. And as demonstrated in many chapters, including the chapter by Andrew Bouchkin, Russia has moved significantly over the last decade to integrate itself fully into the international political and economic system.

The international system has ceased being ruled exclusively by laissez-faire and realpolitik principles alone. It has become more norm-governed. However, inequalities within the system are still acute, dependence is more often the watchword than interdependence, and great powers still hold tremendous sway. These facts are as apparent in Eurasia as anywhere else, and this is the subject of the last section.

Dependence and Interdependence

While the chapters in this book on balance reject the possibility of a renewed and concerted Russian drive for empire, nevertheless they also underline a uniform concern about the resurgence of Russian great-power chauvinism. As the largest and strongest country of the former USSR, and the one that has benefited the most from the institutional inheritance of the Soviet state, Russia is in a position of enormous comparative advantage.

These chapters have demonstrated that Russian leaders have often exercised this advantage to the detriment of the other new states. Thus, Russia has used its position as the least dependent economy in the former Soviet space to exert economic pressure, particularly through the supply or withholding of energy.

Russian leaders have maintained their interest in all the new states joining the Commonwealth of Independent States, which Russia dominates. And the Russian military, via a network of formal basing agreements, contingents "temporarily" stationed abroad, loan-service personnel, and peacekeeping missions sanctioned by regional treaties, is the only force in the former Soviet space capable of sustained independent action beyond its borders.

Because of the fragility and comparative weakness of most of the new states, Russia is able to exert enormous leverage with relatively little effort. As discussed by Kemal Karpat, foreign policy institutions in the new states are weak and still tied in numerous direct and indirect ways to Russia, which maintains an enormous institutional advantage over these states. The way Russia has been able to shift between the Armenians and the Azerbaijanis, as shown in the chapters by Leila Alieva and Rouben Paul Adalian, by supplying energy to one side and then another, or by withdrawing relatively small numbers of forces here and then employing them there, also shows its ability to alternatively punish and reward without itself suffering significant or proportionate loss.

Russia's military presence in Tajikistan, its legal claims to the Crimea, and the protection accorded in Russia's military doctrine to ethnic Russians living abroad are issues that spring from different situations and political motivations. But, as Jonathan Valdez writes, they nevertheless reflect an overall consensus in Russia that, at a minimum, the former Soviet area constitutes a natural Russophone zone over which Moscow has "always" been able to exercise political, economic, and cultural leadership. Even President Yeltsin and Foreign Minister Kozyrev, long associated with a view of foreign policy that emphasizes international and Western links, have long come to embrace the notion that Russia has rights and responsibilities as both a great power and a civilizational force throughout the region.

The central point in this thesis is that the other new states, however hostile to Russia, being weaker and more fragile, nevertheless need it. Sometimes, as Mark Katz showed in his analysis of Central Asia, that need extends even to the reliance of elites on Russia to maintain their power. And certainly, none of the new states regard Russia as inherently untrustworthy as a partner in all matters. As shown in Vyacheslau Paznyak's chapter, Belarus, with an economy that is even more inflation-ridden than Russia's, has tried to forge an economic union with Moscow, only to be kept at arm's length on certain monetary issues. And virtually no state has failed to continue to rely heavily on Moscow for continued trade, for expertise, or for communications networking with the outside world. This reliance comes about not necessarily because of any nefarious design by the current Russian government but because these countries (with the partial exception of Estonia) have yet to be incorporated into any regional or global network that bypasses Moscow. As Disraeli once said, "Colonies do not cease to be colonies just because they are independent."

The ability of these states to become more independent of Russia will rest not only on their own behavior but also on the extent to which the interests of outside powers become engaged in these new states. As shown by the chapters by Bouchkin, Mesbahi, and Vares, the interests of neighboring powers cannot be denied and will undoubtedly have a role in affecting the direction and content of all the foreign policies of the states of the former Soviet Union, including Russia.

In this context, therefore, it is necessary to distinguish between the fact of Russia's self-perception as the dominant power in the region and the other countries' objective dependence. The legacy of the Soviet empire has left them dependent, but overcoming the consequences of that dependence is primarily the responsibility of these new states themselves. Much the same phenomenon as witnessed following the emergence of postcolonial Africa and the Middle East can be expected in the new states of Eurasia. Many leaders in these states, faced with almost intractable problems, have already chosen to use Moscow as an excuse for their inability to implement a credible development strategy.

Looking at the patterns that have emerged in the decades since decolonization began in the developing world, one can find many reasons to conclude that this process will be no less difficult in Eurasia. The proximity of the former colonial power, in particular, and the harsh economic straits that Russia finds itself in predispose one to conclude that the interrelationship between Russia and its neighbors is likely to be more intense than between most former colonial powers and their newly independent states. Russia will not have the "luxury" of having a debate about casting off "the white man's burden" as the British did when discussing the benefits of withdrawal from India, because twenty-five million Russians found themselves in these new states after the breakup of the USSR, and because Russia's weak economy makes these states a more natural partner than India was for Britain. And as for the other new states in Eurasia, they cannot easily form regional security systems to bolster their independence from their former colonial master, as the newly independent African and Middle Eastern states did in the Organization of African Unity and the Arab League, because whereas Britain, France, and Portugal withdrew over the horizon when these empires collapsed, Russia continues to reside in their midst.

By far the most realistic course, therefore, for the foreign policies of all the new states is to promote interdependence. Such a course will be difficult for the reasons elaborated above: the legacy of *diktat* and distrust, the domestic political climate in many of the new states that fuels mutual antagonism on all sides, and an international climate that alternately promotes Russia as a great power in the region and punishes it for exercising the prerogatives of such a power. Absence of consensus and clear thinking about what constitutes imperial behavior and what needs to be done to promote the independence of Russia's neighbors all contribute to the problem. States that are not truly independent cannot participate in an interdependent world; and until the states bordering Russia make further strides, their full participation will remain only a distant objective.

Appendix: Project Participants

List of Workshop Attendees, March 7, 1994
The Making of Foreign Policy in Russia

Ermias Abebe, University of Maryland
Ibrahim Arafat, Cairo University
Andrei Artamonov, Embassy of Russia
Sally Blair, U.S. Institute of Peace
Stephen Blank, U.S. Army War College
Peter Clement, Central Intelligence Agency
David Coder, National Endowment for the
Richard Dobson, U.S. Information Agency
Marcus Franda, University of Maryland
Robert Freedman, Baltimore Hebrew University
Raymond Garthoff, The Brookings Institution
Philip Gillette, Old Dominion University
Sergei Gretsky, Adviser, Muslim Spiritual Board, Tajikistan
Jon Gundersen, Department of State
Griffin Hathaway, University of Maryland
Nancy Hewett, Department of State
Oumirseric Kasenov, Kazakhstan Institute for Strategic Studies
Catherine Kelleher, The Brookings Institution
Judith Kipper, The Brookings Institution
Israel Kleiner, Voice of America
Amy Knight, Congressional Research Service
Nikolai Kulinich, Ukrainian Institute of International Relations
Erjan Kurbanov, Moscow State University
Irena Lasota, Institute for Democracy in Eastern Europe
George Liska, School of Advanced International Studies
Michael Nandelbaum, School of Advanced International Studies
George Mirsky, Institute of World Economy and Int'l Relations
Tom Navratil, Department of State

Elena Osokina, The Kennan Institute
Soli Ozel, School of Advanced International Studies
Linda Petrou, University of Maryland
George Quester, University of Maryland
Alvin Richman, U.S. Information Agency
Trudy Rubin, The Philadelphia Enquirer
Mourod Sattarov, Tashkent State Economics University
Miraj Siddiqi, Council of Pakistani Organizations
Yuri Sigov, *'Vek'* Moscow Weekly
Aida Simonia, Institute of Oriental Studies, Moscow
Jack Sontag, Department of State
Stephen Szabo, School of Advanced International Studies
Thomas Thornton, Georgetown University
Vladimir Tismaneanu, University of Maryland
Misha Tsypkin, Naval Post-Graduate School, Monterey
Michael Turner, University of Maryland
Joan Barth Urban, Catholic University
Ekaterina Usova, Institute of Oriental Studies, Moscow
Adam Wasserman, Department of State
Vladimir Yanin, Embassy of Russia
Volodymyr Zabihailo, Embassy of Ukraine
Tom Zamostny, Department of State
Volodymyr Zviglyanich, George Washington University

List of Workshop Attendees, March 14, 1994
The Making of Foreign Policy in the Russian NIS

Ibrahim Arafat, Cairo University
Andrei Artamonov, Embassy of Russia
Nicholas Babiak, The Washington Group
Charles Ball, Stanford University
Andrei Bouchkin, Institute of World Economy and Int'l Relations
Patricia Carley, U.S. Institute of Peace
Martha Chomiak, National Endowment for the Humanities
David Coder, National Endowment for the Humanities
Adeed Dawisha, George Mason University
Richard Dobson, U.S. Information Agency
Charles Fairbanks, School of Advanced International Studies
Martina Fox, National Foreign Affairs Training Center
Marcus Franda, University of Maryland
Raymond Garthoff, The Brookings Institution
Philip Gillette, Old Dominion University
Sergei Gretsky, Advisor, Muslim Spiritual Board, Tajikistan

Jon Gunderson, Department of State
Alec Guroff, Center for Strategic and International Studies
Griffin Hathaway, University of Maryland
Irina Isakova, Institute of USA and Canada Studies
Oumirseric Kasenov, Kazakhstan Institute for Strategic Studies
Catherine Kelleher, The Brookings Institution
Israel Kleiner, Voice of America
Erjan Kurbanov, Moscow State University
Irena Lasota, Institute for Democracy in Eastern Europe
George Liska, School of Advanced International Studies
Michael Mandelbaum, School of Advanced International Studies
Piotr Mishchenko, United Nations
Elena Osokina, Kennan Institute
Soli Ozel, School of Advanced International Studies
Phillip Petersen, The Potomac Foundation
Ilya Prizel, School of Advanced International Studies
Marion Recktenwald, University of Maryland
Peter Reddaway, U.S. Institute of Peace
Igor Safonov, International Unity Science Institute
Mourod Sattarov, Tashkent State Economics University
Yuri Sigov, *'Vek'* Moscow Weekly
Nodari Simonia, Institute of World Economy and Int'l Relations
Stephen Szabo, School of Advanced International Studies
Thomas Thornton, Georgetown University
Michael Turner, University of Maryland
Joan Urban, Catholic University
Ekaterina Usova, Institute of Oriental Studies, Moscow
Sheila Ward, School of Advanced International Studies
Sharon Wolchik, George Washington University
Vladimir Yanin, Embassy of Russia
Volodymyr Zabihailo, Embassy of Ukraine
Volodymyr Zviglyanich, George Washington University

List of Workshop Attendees, March 21, 1994
The Making of Foreign Policy in the Southern NIS

Ibrahim Arafat, University of Maryland
Andrei Artamonov, Embassy of Russia
Igor Barsegian, Institute of Philosophy and Law, Erevan
Stephen Blank, U.S. Army War College
Andrei Bouchkin, Institute of World Economy and Int'l Relations
Patricia Carley, U.S. Institute of Peace
Martha Chommiak, National Endowment for the Humanities

David Coder, National Endowment for the Humanities
Heather Conley, Department of State
Catherine Dale, U.S. Institute of Peace
Adeed Dawisha, George Mason University
Richard Dobson, U.S. Information Agency
Nora Dudwick, The Kennan Institute
Martina Fox, National Foreign Affairs Training Center
Marcus Franda, University of Maryland
Robert Freedman, Baltimore Hebrew University
Raymond Garthoff, The Brookings Institution
Philip Gillette, Old Dominion University
Heather Giordanella, Central Connecticut State University
Sergei Gretsky, Advisor, Muslim Spiritual Board, Tajikistan
Alec Guroff, Center for Strategic and International Studies
Griffin Hathaway, University of Maryland
Mahir Ibrahimov, Embassy of Azerbaijan
Irina Isakova, Institute of USA and Canada Studies
Olga Karazhas, American University
Catherine Kelleher, The Brookings Institution
Nikolai Kulinich, Ukrainian Institute of International Relations
Erjan Kurbanov, Moscow State University
George Liska, School of Advanced International Studies
Dan Matuszewski, IREX
David Naile, Central Asia Monitor
Rusi Nasr, Central Asia Associates
Susan Nelson, Department of State
Phillip Petersen, The Potomac Foundation
Igor Safonov, International Unity Science Institute
Mourod Sattarov, Tashkent State Economics University
Cevdet Seyhan, Voice of America
Miraj Siddiqi, Council of Pakistani Organizations
Yuri Sigov, 'Vek' Moscow Weekly
Nodari Simonia, Institute of World Economy and Int'l Relations
Rasim Tajuddin, Khazar University, Baku
Thomas Thornton, Georgetown University
Joan Urban, Catholic University
Ekaterina Usova, Institute of Oriental Studies, Moscow
Carola Weil, University of Maryland
Vladimir Yanin, Embassy of Russia

Index

Abdujabbor, Tohir, 251
Abdulatipov, Ramazan, 109
Abkhazia, 288
Academy of Sciences, 26–27, 34–35
Acid rain, 265
Adamishin, Anatolii, 100–101, 103
Afghanistan, 221, 224, 227–29, 255, 279
Agreement on Economic Cooperation
    Between Latvia, Lithuania, and
    Estonia, 158
Akaev, Askar, 191, 203, 222
Alash Party, 251
Aliev, Gaidar, 12, 290–91, 295–96,
    298–99, 302–03, 305, 320, 331
Ambartsumov, Evgenii, 53, 274
Amu Darya River, 265
Anarchy, 47–48
ANM. *See* Armenian National Movement
Antonov, V., 122
Araks River, 317
Aral Sea, 265
Arbatov, Aleksei, 275
Arbatov, Georgii, 49
ARF. *See* Armenian Revolutionary
    Federation
Armed forces. *See specific geographic
    locations*
Armenia, 11–13, 229, 237–38, 287, 288,
    289, 309–32
  and Azerbaijan, 291–96, 301
  behavioral determinants, 311–12
  diaspora of, 322–24, 333*n.3*
  economy, 312
  foreign policy,
    institutions and personalities, 324–26
    objectives, 312–13
    reform and, 313–15

Armenia *(continued)*
  foreign relations, 315–24
  genocide of, 332
  geographical imperatives, 310–11
  national identity of, 311
  population of, 333*n.1*
  religion in, 311–12
Armenian Democratic Liberal (ADL)
    Party, 323
Armenian National Movement (ANM),
    313, 323
Armenian Revolutionary Federation
    (ARF), 323–24, 328
Arms market, 32–33, 92
  Chinese, 72–73
  and Ukraine, 123
ASALA (terrorist organization), 302
Ashik, Ayub, 297
Ashkhabad summit, 221
Asia-Pacific Economic Cooperation, 39
Association of Ethnic Koreans, 76
Atheism, 179
Atlanticists, 6, 67–71, 100
Austria, 127, 128, 283
Autarky, 128
Aven, Peter Olegovich, 225
Azerbaijan, 11–12, 178, 184, 186, 229,
    237–38, 286–306
  armed forces of, 202, 203–04
  and Armenia, 290, 291–96, 301, 310,
    313, 315, 316, 320–21, 326–31
  and CIS, 199, 272, 320
  decision-making institutions, 291
  defense industry in, 299
  ethnic identity in, 287
  geopolitical situation of, 286
  industrialization in, 287

Tojikstan (newspaper), 251
Trans-Asian Railway, 265
Treaty on Collective Security, 145,
    199–200, 229, 249, 278, 295
Treaty on Economic Union, 21
Treaty on Friendship, Cooperation, and
    Mutual Assistance, 272, 278
Treaty on Mutual Security and Friendly
    Relations, 301
Treaty on the Creation of the Economic
    Union, 272
Treaty on Unity and Cooperation (Baltic
    states), 158
Turkey, 10, 118, 211–12*n.13*
    and Armenia, 310, 315, 317–19, 321,
        325, 330, 335*n.22*
    and Azerbaijan, 12, 287–89, 291, 293,
        296–98, 305
    and Central Asia, 178, 186, 189, 204,
        208, 209, 217–20, 236–37, 256–57
    and Iran, 238–39
    Islamic forces in, 256–57
    and Kazakhstan, 280
    nationalism of, 178
Turkmenistan, 121, 186, 205, 206, 249,
    319
    armed forces of, 203
    and Iran, 218, 222
    opposition party in, 251
    political evolution of, 247–48
    and Turkey, 218
Turlais, Dainas, 172

Uigurs (people), 199, 254–55
Ukraine, 7–8, 20, 21, 89, 113–32, 226,
    319
    aid to, 131–32
    armed forces of, 202
    arms sales, 241–42*n.33*
    atomic power in, 120–21
    and Baltic States, 16
    currency stabilization, 132
    defense conversion in, 122–23
    economic risk in, 136
        external, 138
    energy crisis in, 120–21
    foreign debt of, 134
    foreign investment in, 8, 119–20
    foreign policy,
        economic issues in, 117–21
        goals, 116–17

Ukraine *(continued)*
    military-political issues, 121–25
    geopolitical environment in, 113–17
    and international institutions, 116–17
    national interest priorities, 116
    national security in, 116
        threats to, 117
    and neutrality, 126–28
    nuclear disarmament, 116–17, 123–25
    privatization in, 120
    and Russian military, 31
    socioeconomic reforms, 125
    sociopolitical risk in, 137
    strategic choices of, 126–30
    trade, 118–19
    Western relations, 131
United Nations, 32, 230, 273, 277, 294, 344
    Russian peacekeeping operations, 90–91,
        97, 98–99, 103
    Ukrainian peacekeeping operations, 121
United States, 69, 71, 92, 225–26
    aid to CIS, 134
    and Armenia, 321–23, 330, 332
    and Azerbaijan, 295, 304–05
    and Baltic States, 164
    and Central Asia, 186, 232, 244*nn.57,
        58*, 254
    and Iran, 238
    and Islamic fundamentalism, 223, 254
    and Kazakhstan, 277–78
    and Russia, 38–39, 82
    strategic arms reduction, 124–25
    and Ukraine, 118
Unmet. See Islamic community
Uzbekistan, 186, 189, 198, 224, 228
    armed forces of, 203
    and Azerbaijan, 301
    economic development in, 205, 206
    and Iran, 221–22, 250
    and Kazakhstan, 279
    political evolution of, 247
    and Turkey, 218

Velliste, Trivimi, 168
Via Baltica transit road, 164
Vietnam, 33
Vorontsov, Iulii, 92

Wahhabism, 194
Walesa, Lech, 130, 148–49
Wallace, William, 126